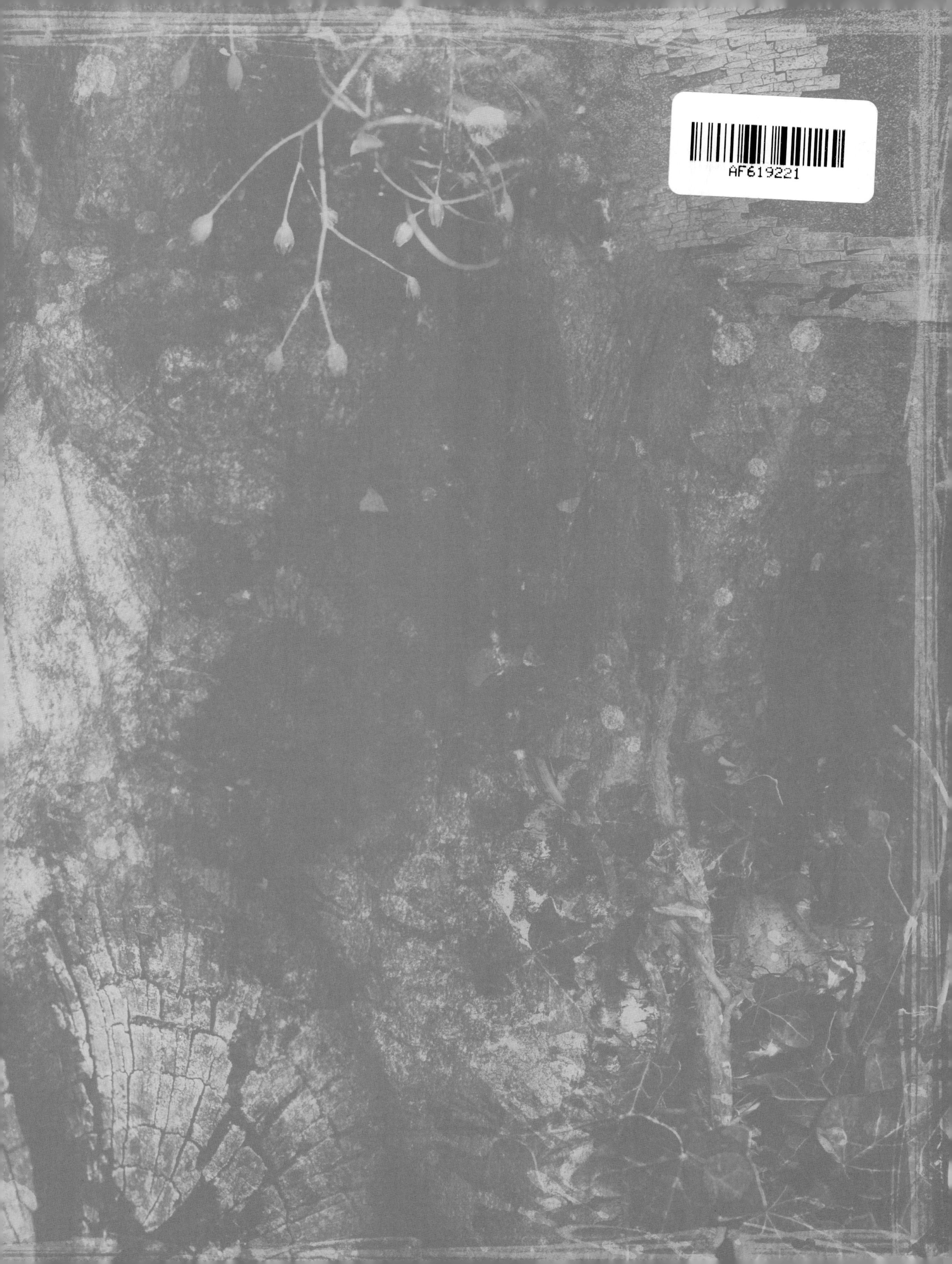

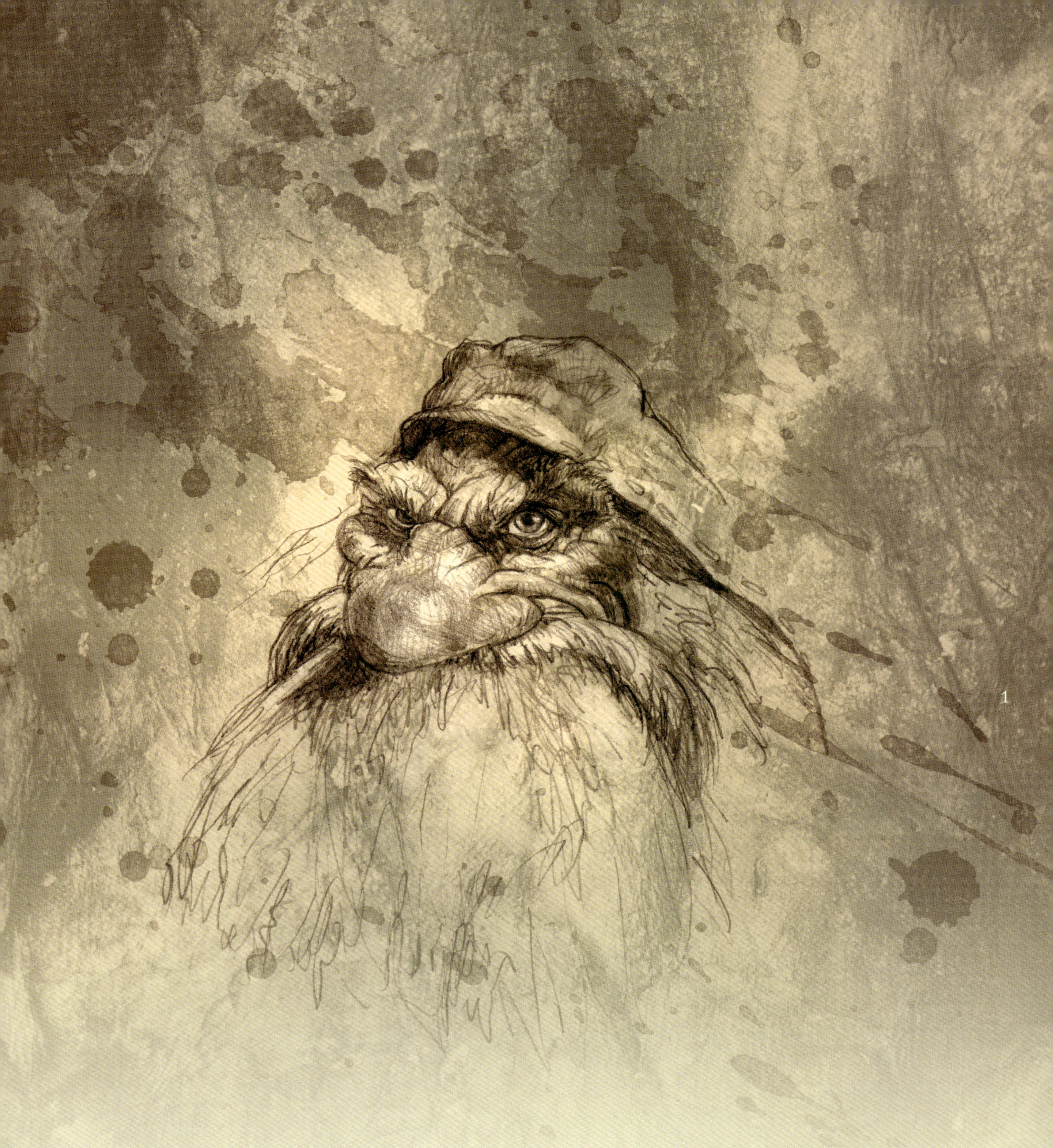

The art of Paul BONNER

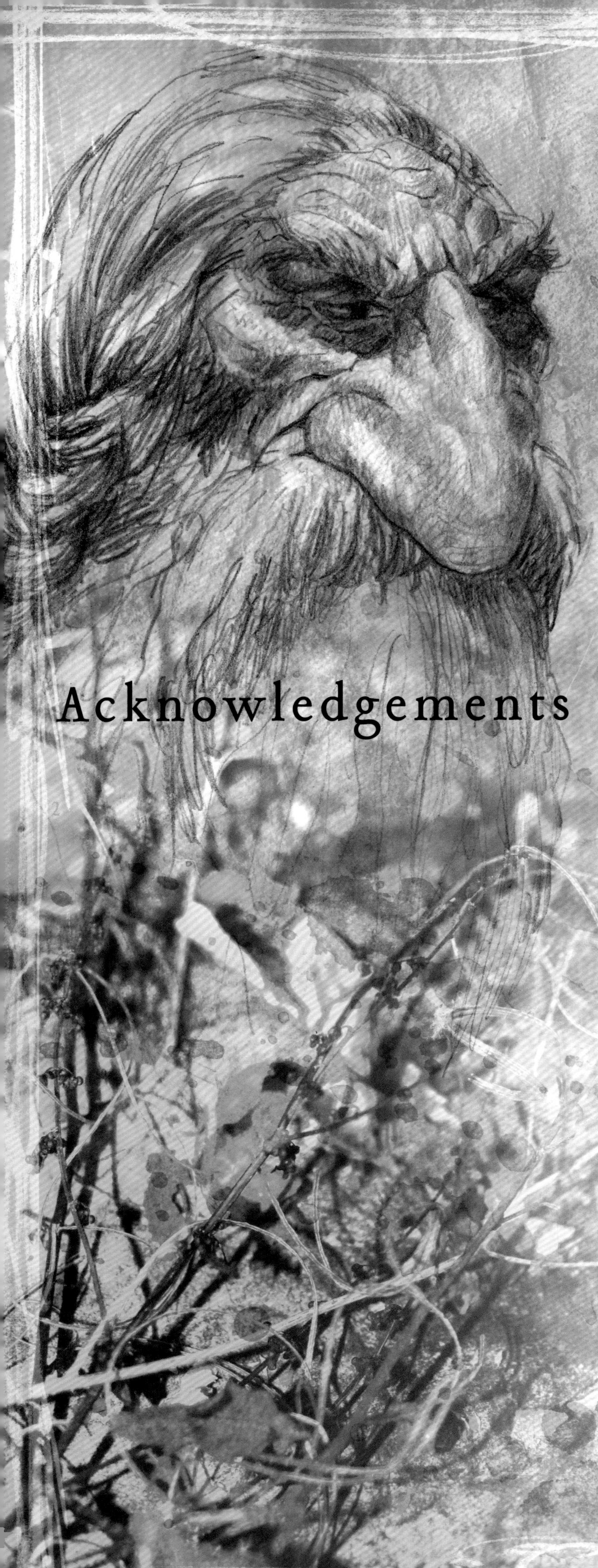

Acknowledgements

For my Dad and Mum, Peter and Connie Bonner, who provided the endless supply of plasticine, crayons, paints, paper and patience that were necessary to accommodate the outpourings inspired by years of wonderful books, and being taken to the mountains and forests of the Lake District.

Charlotte and little Arthur, for being, both, delightful distractions and life affirming inspirations. Happily, they need no promises of sandwiches and views to accompany my continued wanderings.

For making this book possible....

Nick Parry-Jones at Legends for his commendable foresight in suggesting the book to the right person, and providing much good-natured backup during the whole somewhat lengthy process.

Jérôme Martineau at Tournon, for seeing the wisdom of Nick's suggestion, and, with a minimum of fuss, just letting us get on with it, without once imposing himself or making me aware of any restrictions, even when my text *started arriving in his mail box.*

Franck Achard, for his beautiful design and layout work, that always surpassed my expectations. But mostly for his patience in having me at his elbow, with endless tentative variations on trying to suggest that Maybe that little sketch there would look better – just a little bit more over here?

John Howe, for his kind words, belief, and practical insight. Arnie Fenner for his encouragement and much appreciated advice. Sascha Mackic, for his beautiful photography, done at the drop of a hat. Theodore Bergquist, John Blanche, Nils Gullikson, Jim Nelson, Jean Bey for their contributions; Matt Adelsberger, Sharon at WhizKids and Jesper Ejsing for his enthusiasm.

Fellow practitioners Paul and Craig, for many years of convivial company, conversation and, usually, constructive criticism, over the odd *ale or two. Much valued mirth has always accompanied our discussions on a multitude of inspirations, that have had to put up with been dissected, dismantled - and on one memorable occasion, destroyed.*

Many pages could be filled with a list of people, places and things that have contributed to this book being in existence at all. From childhood, through art college and out into the world, there are many who have encouraged, tutored and inspired, or just shown a genuine interest in whatever it was I was trying to do at the time. Some have given me priceless introductions to books, films, music (J.L.L. for being very Live *at the Star Club, Hamburg!), museums, nature and all manner of art. Others have provided glimpses of ideas and flashes of inspiration through convivial conversations in convivial surroundings.*

Heartfelt thanks to anyone, and everyone who feels they ought to be included.

And heartfelt apologies to anyone who still feels forgotten.

Finally, a big hello to John, Peter J, and Katherine; Judith, Nicola and Robin and the rest of the clan. Mathew, Melanie, Carla, Caroline, Harry and Flynn.

Paul Bonner

Preface

Paul Bonner is something of an enigma. Therefore, everything that follows is pure speculation, it may all be wrong. As I said, Paul is something of an enigma.

I had the pleasure of meeting Paul only once. Picture three illustrators (Ciruelo Cabral was there also) sitting at a terrace café in a most extraordinary piazza (built inside the ruin of a Roman coliseum) in Lucca, Italy, discussing plots to illustrate this theme and that, carefully distilling experiences and opinions, trading stories of skirmishes with games companies and publishers. It was a rare kind of encounter, conspiratorial and convivial, with the kind of eager bashfulness that strikes when chance brings you face to face with people whose work you admire.

(Come to think of it, what better place for three wayward illustrators to meet. An Argentinian settled in Spain, an Englishman domiciled in Denmark and a Canadian who calls Helvetia home; three expatriots who spend most of their time abroad anyway, wandering in the worlds built inside their own heads.)

Paul's work is of course exquisite. It is a curious blending of the whimsical and the deadly serious. His mastery of space is, well... masterful in every way. His horizons fade into powder blue or dusk, his shadows are obscure and mysterious. His landscapes are somehow familiar, the kind you see on hikes, or contemplate while sipping from a flask of tea and devouring a well-earned sandwich. The denizens of his landscapes, however, are the kind that you would not like to meet on a narrow trail or in the deep woods...

His compositions are always perfect and often sublime; witness "Eldsjal", with the graphic slash of the (carefully detailed) waterfall. When Paul does night scenes, his firelight is so convincing it makes you look for stray sparks. Paintings like "Drakar och Demoner" or "Eld och sot" are in a narrative and pictorial world class of their own.

Looking at Paul's work, I think of John Bauer, for his love and understanding of dim northwoods walls of vertical tree trunks and horizontal November light. Looking at Paul's work, Richard Dadd comes to mind, for the uncommon ability to indulge in lavish detail without ever losing sight of the whole image. There is something of Brian Froud in the profiles of his trolls, something of the folly of Frank Frazetta in his capacity to capture movement in mid-air, a few steroids from Simon Bisley in the biceps of his axe-toting warrior heroes, a hint of Arthur Rackham in the silhouettes he paints, and atmospheres worthy of Gallen-Kallela or Vasnetzov.

But, to assume that Paul Bonner's work is a conscientious patchwork of the best a century of illustration has to offer is totally wrong. Paul Bonner is entirely his own man, his universe is unique. He is in perfect equilibrium between detail and freedom. His pictures tell stories; they are all balanced on that crucial instant of "but-what-happens-next?" Nevertheless, the imagery is poised and centred; Paul is an arch tight-rope walker, managing the all-too-rare equilibrium between *pictura* and *gnarus*.

There is no contradiction between fantasy and functionality in his work. His costumes are colourful and his weapons and armour outrageous and original, but they work. Paul doesn't just look at landscapes, he knows his history too. All his illustrations are a masterful distillation of anecdote and archetype.

Paul's talent for observation is laser-sharp, with that precious distance that is the gift bestowed by circumstance on the voluntary exile. Every stone, every tree or blade of grass in his work is as though observed for the first time; nothing is taken for granted.

All this combined lets us wander in one of those all-too-rare places: a landscape of the mind, world of an artist, recognizable at a glance, unfathomable when you attempt to look deeper.

So, with all this, you might ask, well what DOESN'T he do well? I suppose there is a dearth of body-builder females clad in chain mail bikinis with a backdrop of dead saurians, suitable for posters and screensavers, but Paul has chosen substance over surface, interest over admiration; you'll have to excuse him if he doesn't cater to fashion, he's busy building a universe.

And what's more, he works in WATERCOLOURS (remember those? In tubes?). He uses a BRUSH (that's a short stick with hairs affixed to the end) and works on PAPER (yes, it's made of linen or cellulose). None of these are available from software companies. They aren't updated regularly, you don't have to buy a new version every 6 months. Didn't I say he was an enigma?

John Howe

Neuchâtel, December 22, 2006

Foreword

Dark rain-filled weekend afternoons, sitting at the kitchen table trying to coax dinosaurs and monsters out of mud coloured lumps of plasticine, or covering page after page of paper with felt-tip and crayon drawings of various armies locked in struggles to the death, which usually involved sky darkening flights of arrows and generous use of red shades. I'd like to think that I sometimes attempted to draw more wholesome subject matter, but I don't think so, and my memory has effectively barred me from re-visiting those early scenes.

Having conscientious parents helped fuel my imagination, as, not just content with supplying vast quantities of plasticine (that always ended up a mud colour), my mum also supplied a steady stream of library books. I remember most collections of folk and fairytales from around the world. With some wonderful illustrations in them, these soon became firm favourites. I can clearly remember a collection of Swedish tales, with illustrations by John Bauer. His were pictures I just wanted to step into, and wander off. His moss covered stones and deep, dark forests inhabited by an assortment of rather shy trolls struck some chord, that resonates just as much now.

My dad was a qualified engineer. Equations, angles and technical drawings and a touch of mathematics hinted at a terrifying world I have never been able to approach without palpitations to this day. He had, however, a remarkable eye for form, and during many family holidays he would fill sketchbook after sketchbook with beautifully simple drawings of us, landscapes and their inhabitants. Dogs, cows, horses. They appeared magically on the clean white paper. It captivated me, seeing him create something out of nothing. That's still the magic. Bringing something into existence on a blank piece of paper. Seeing other manifestations of this strange act of creation helped me begin to cobble together a world of infinite possibilities, as certain experiences stamped themselves indelibly upon my consciousness.

Like many others, I remember cowering in fear, or more probably bursting into tears, when the queen in *Snow White* transformed herself into the murderous witch. Likewise the dragon in *Sleeping Beauty*. In *Fantasia*, the Night on the Bare Mountain was awe inspiring; no-one having thought to tell me that mountains could do that. An East European television production of a folk tale called *The Singing Ringing Tree* produced similar emotions. I still feel a tingle of disgust and fear when I remember the manically laughing, thoroughly evil dwarf, flying above

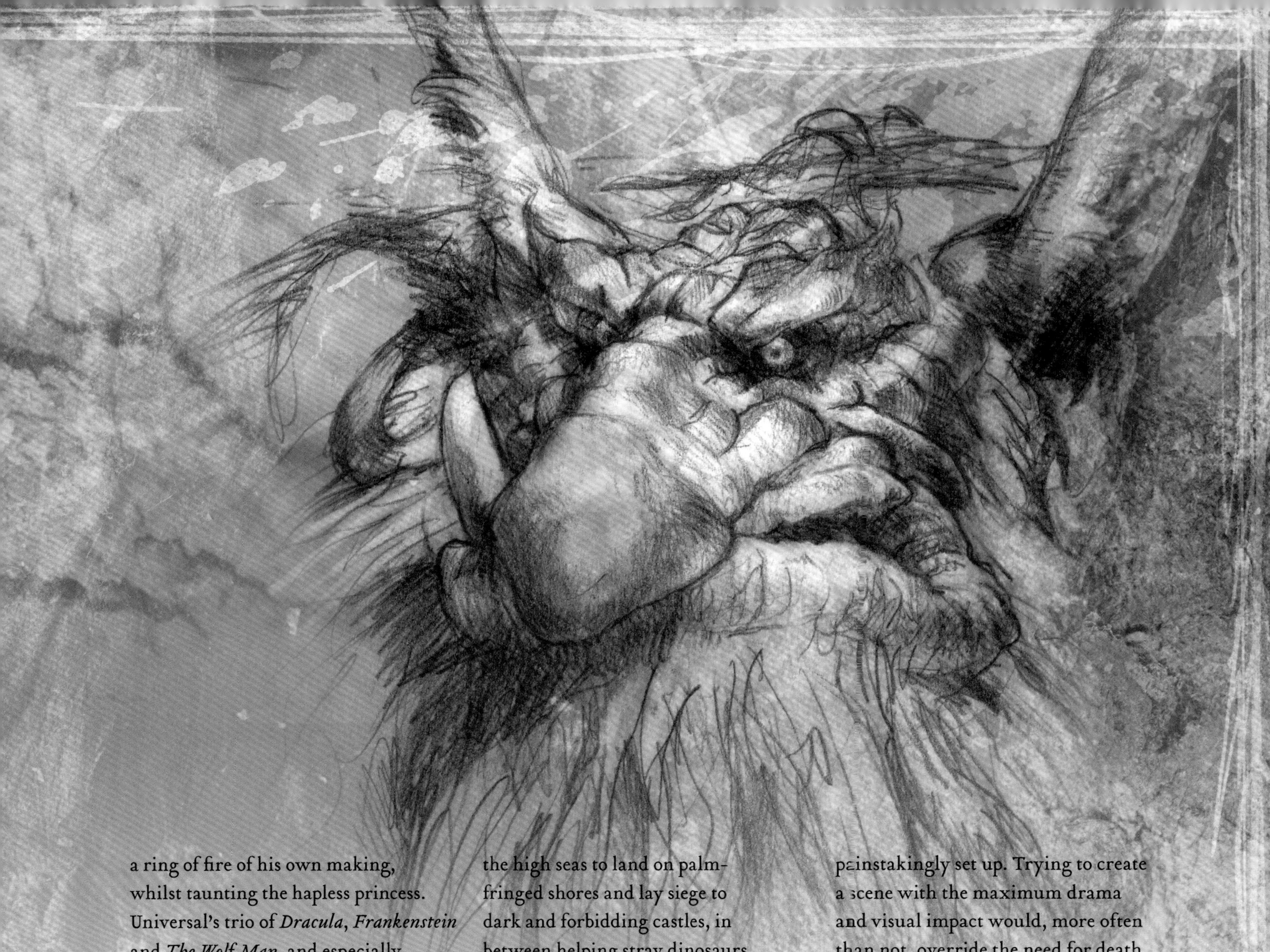

a ring of fire of his own making, whilst taunting the hapless princess. Universal's trio of *Dracula*, *Frankenstein* and *The Wolf Man*, and especially *Creature from the Black Lagoon*, all contributed to a fear of sleeping, and I remember being thrilled and mortified as an assortment of dinosaurs and shuffling, nightmare ape creatures caused all sorts of problems for Raquel Welch in *One Million Years B.C.*. Dinosaurs! A love affair that has persisted to this day, in spite of constant infidelities with dwarves, goblins and trolls. I think *Fantasia* brought them to life for me first, and then Harryhausen's wonderful creatures stomped and roared their way into my dreams, swiftly followed by a full supporting cast of various cyclops, harpies, hydras and of course fighting skeletons. Hollywood epics like *The Vikings*, *El Cid*, and *Spartacus* inspired career possibilities that involved me donning a horned helmet and sailing the high seas to land on palm-fringed shores and lay siege to dark and forbidding castles, in between helping stray dinosaurs on their way to extinction.

Lack of the necessary qualifications caused me to abandon these plans, and I was forced to create my own battles using a huge collection of plastic knights along with a much treasured fort my dad made for me. How I revelled when cutting swathes through their ranks with plasticine balls hurled from catapults and trebuchets. Those individuals on the battlements stupid enough not to take cover, paid with their lives, being skewered with cocktail sticks fired with deadly accuracy from ballistas. Though it appears I had a taste for carnage, I would spend even more time with my head pressed to the carpet, seeking out the best position from which to view the intricate tableaux that I would painstakingly set up. Trying to create a scene with the maximum drama and visual impact would, more often than not, override the need for death and destruction. With my eyes at floor level, long lines of thundering hooves and lowered lances, though plastic, looked wonderfully real to me.

This kind of activity progressed to painting hundreds of miniature Napoleonic soldiers, and on a suitably landscaped table top, they would be marshalled into positions which, again, gave my critical eye, roving the perimeters, the best possible viewpoint. I never made it to the serious mechanics of wargaming. It was always the visuals. Youngsters I have met in conjunction with Games Workshop, the Mutant Chronicles and Rackham often express dismay or even mild disgust at this relevation, and swiftly move on, to seek comfort from a more accommodating artist.

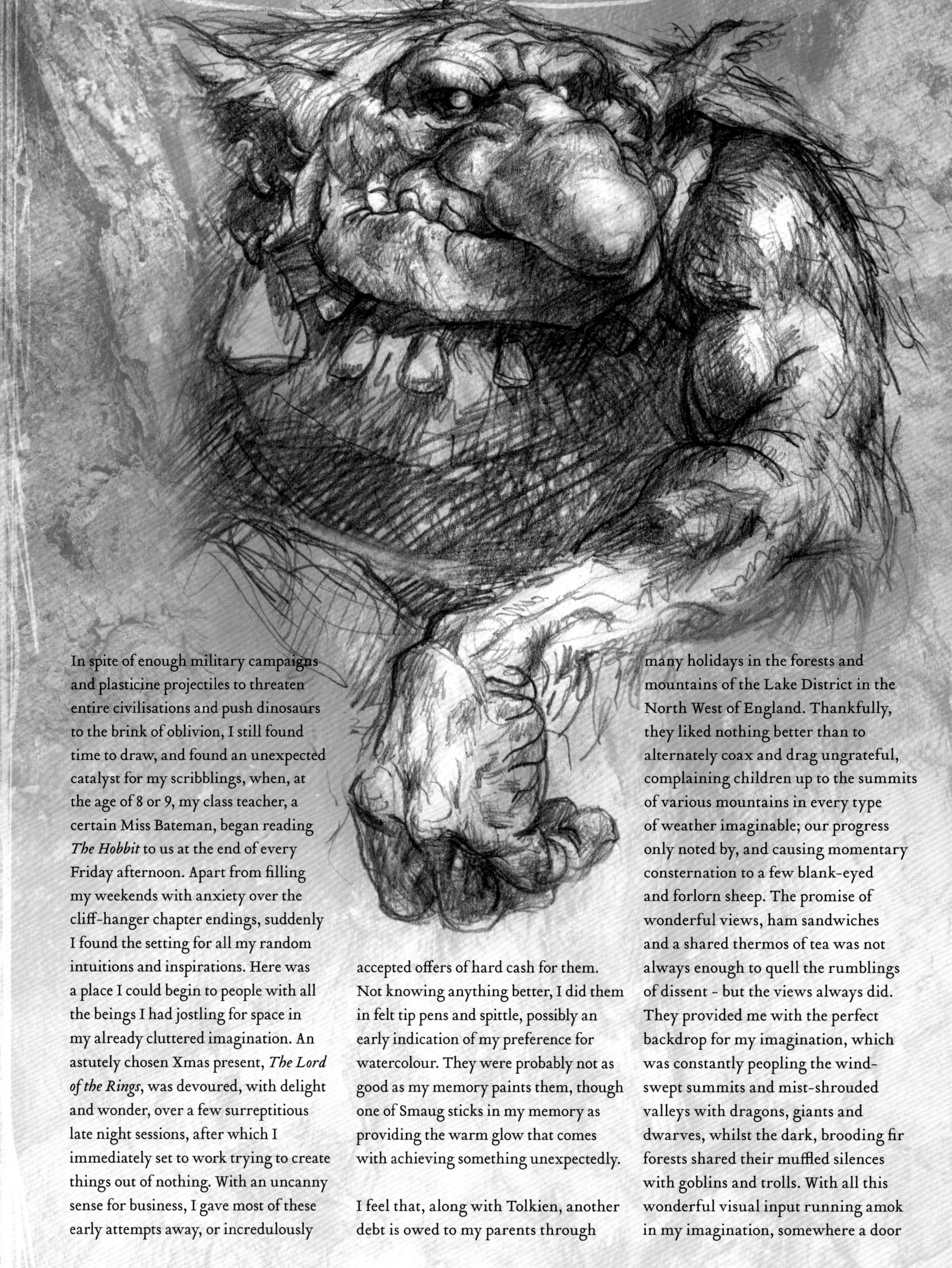

In spite of enough military campaigns and plasticine projectiles to threaten entire civilisations and push dinosaurs to the brink of oblivion, I still found time to draw, and found an unexpected catalyst for my scribblings, when, at the age of 8 or 9, my class teacher, a certain Miss Bateman, began reading *The Hobbit* to us at the end of every Friday afternoon. Apart from filling my weekends with anxiety over the cliff-hanger chapter endings, suddenly I found the setting for all my random intuitions and inspirations. Here was a place I could begin to people with all the beings I had jostling for space in my already cluttered imagination. An astutely chosen Xmas present, *The Lord of the Rings*, was devoured, with delight and wonder, over a few surreptitious late night sessions, after which I immediately set to work trying to create things out of nothing. With an uncanny sense for business, I gave most of these early attempts away, or incredulously accepted offers of hard cash for them. Not knowing anything better, I did them in felt tip pens and spittle, possibly an early indication of my preference for watercolour. They were probably not as good as my memory paints them, though one of Smaug sticks in my memory as providing the warm glow that comes with achieving something unexpectedly.

I feel that, along with Tolkien, another debt is owed to my parents through many holidays in the forests and mountains of the Lake District in the North West of England. Thankfully, they liked nothing better than to alternately coax and drag ungrateful, complaining children up to the summits of various mountains in every type of weather imaginable; our progress only noted by, and causing momentary consternation to a few blank-eyed and forlorn sheep. The promise of wonderful views, ham sandwiches and a shared thermos of tea was not always enough to quell the rumblings of dissent - but the views always did. They provided me with the perfect backdrop for my imagination, which was constantly peopling the wind-swept summits and mist-shrouded valleys with dragons, giants and dwarves, whilst the dark, brooding fir forests shared their muffled silences with goblins and trolls. With all this wonderful visual input running amok in my imagination, somewhere a door

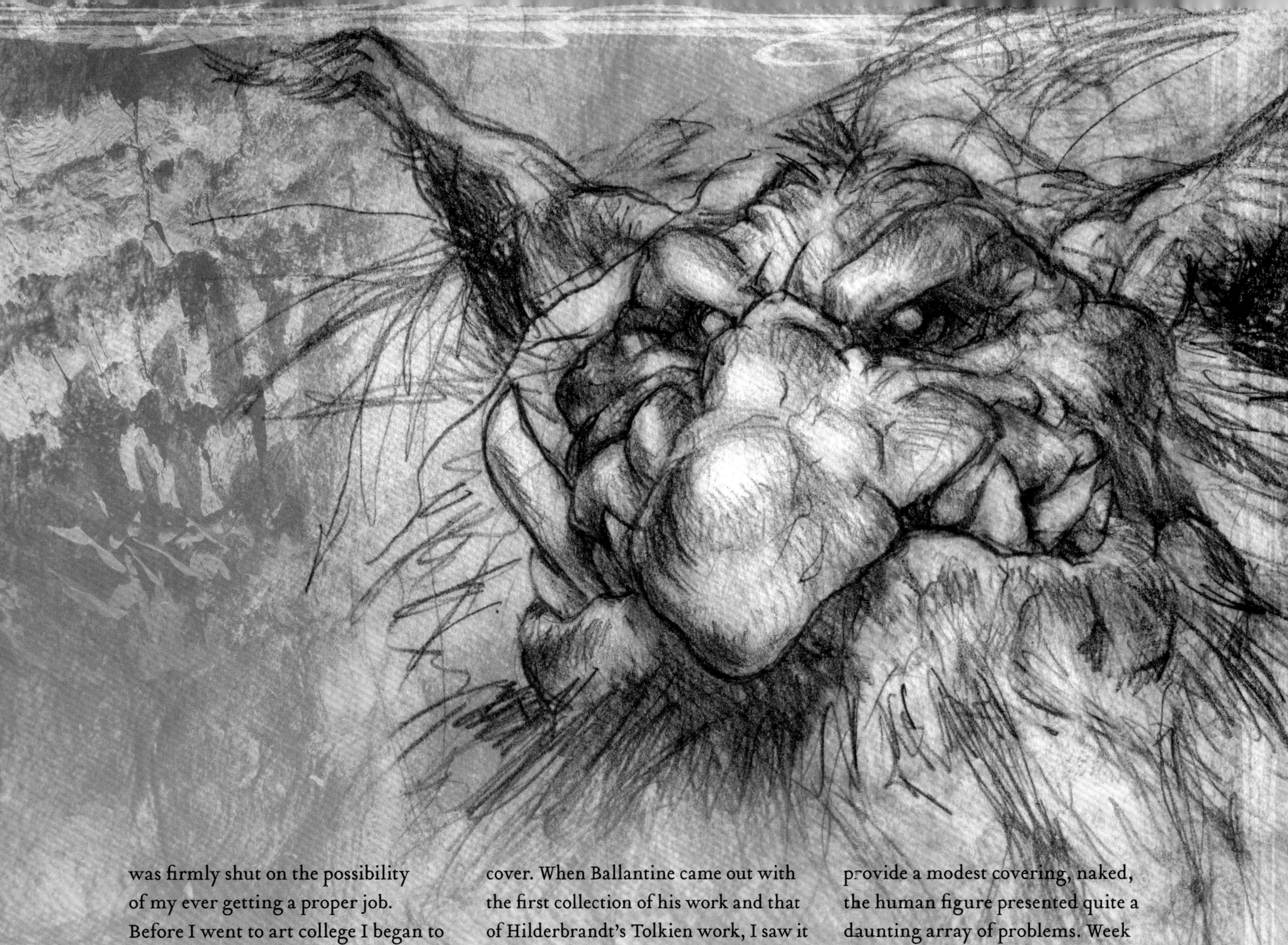

was firmly shut on the possibility of my ever getting a proper job. Before I went to art college I began to be aware of several artists who fuelled my fires and made me aware I wasn't alone in these passions and that maybe there was a path I could follow. It seems these days we are really spoilt for choice, with specialist shops filled with shelves groaning under the weight of books, games, comics and cards bulging with depictions of all things fantastical. The pickings seemed a lot sparser in my own prehistory. A series of books by Pan renewed an aquaintence with Arthur Rackham, and introduced me to Kay Nielsen, Edmund Dulac, Brian Froud and Julius Detmold. Like my contemporaries, discovering Mr Frazetta's Conan paintings caused hot flushes and a barely contained exultation, when upon scouring local market stalls and second hand book shops I would discover a battered book with an as yet unseen painting on the cover. When Ballantine came out with the first collection of his work and that of Hilderbrandt's Tolkien work, I saw it was possible to follow your passion, and maybe even survive. With hindsight, an extremely risky conclusion, but you don't question the logic or reason of things you love to do. You just do them.

Art college placed a much needed emphasis on seeing the world as it was, and learning to portray it through traditional drawing skills. Our tutors were all good in their own field, and thus it was easier to take their sometimes brutal but always constructive criticism. I feel we were quite smug and self satisfied just with being art students - but the first time we were sat in front of a real life naked human being and told to get on with it, more than a few shortcomings were made very quickly apparent. Without studded shoulderpads, spiky helmets and assorted animal skins to provide a modest covering, naked, the human figure presented quite a daunting array of problems. Week long drawing exercises, whether in the ripe atmosphere of London Zoo's elephant house, under the tail plane of a Lancaster bomber at an aircraft museum or the hushed, dusty silence of the Natural History Museum, all helped convince me of the need to be able to portray reality before I could go tramping off to realities of my own choice.

Of course, it's a never-ending process - trying to overcome infinite moments of getting it wrong, before persistence and observation lead the way to little triumphs, which in turn just signpost the way to more problems, waving frantically to get noticed and dealt with. This neatly leads to the rather daunting task of trying to say something deep and meaningful about a process that mostly becomes intuitive.

Paul Bonner

RACKHAM

Meeting Paul in 1999 marked a decisive turn in Rackham's artistic approach. Plunged into fantasy worlds for many years, I admired his evocative works. Paul always knew how to make me dream, and I'm really proud to have him as one of the artist that illustrates the universe of the game *Confrontation*. As a game publisher, Rackham produces a lot of research and character designs that will serve as models for the sculptor to produce the miniatures necessary for the game. Paul is a travelling magician: only he could capture at the same time our universe, our miniatures and our designs to give them life in the universe of *Confrontation*. He was the first to concentrate all the creative directions of Rackham: the universe, the game and an original universe. Paul's paintings are much more than an illustration of our ideas, they are potent and magical visions, as is Paul, a friend, a unique creator and a really great artist.

Jean Bey
Creator of Rackham
Art and editorial director of Confrontation

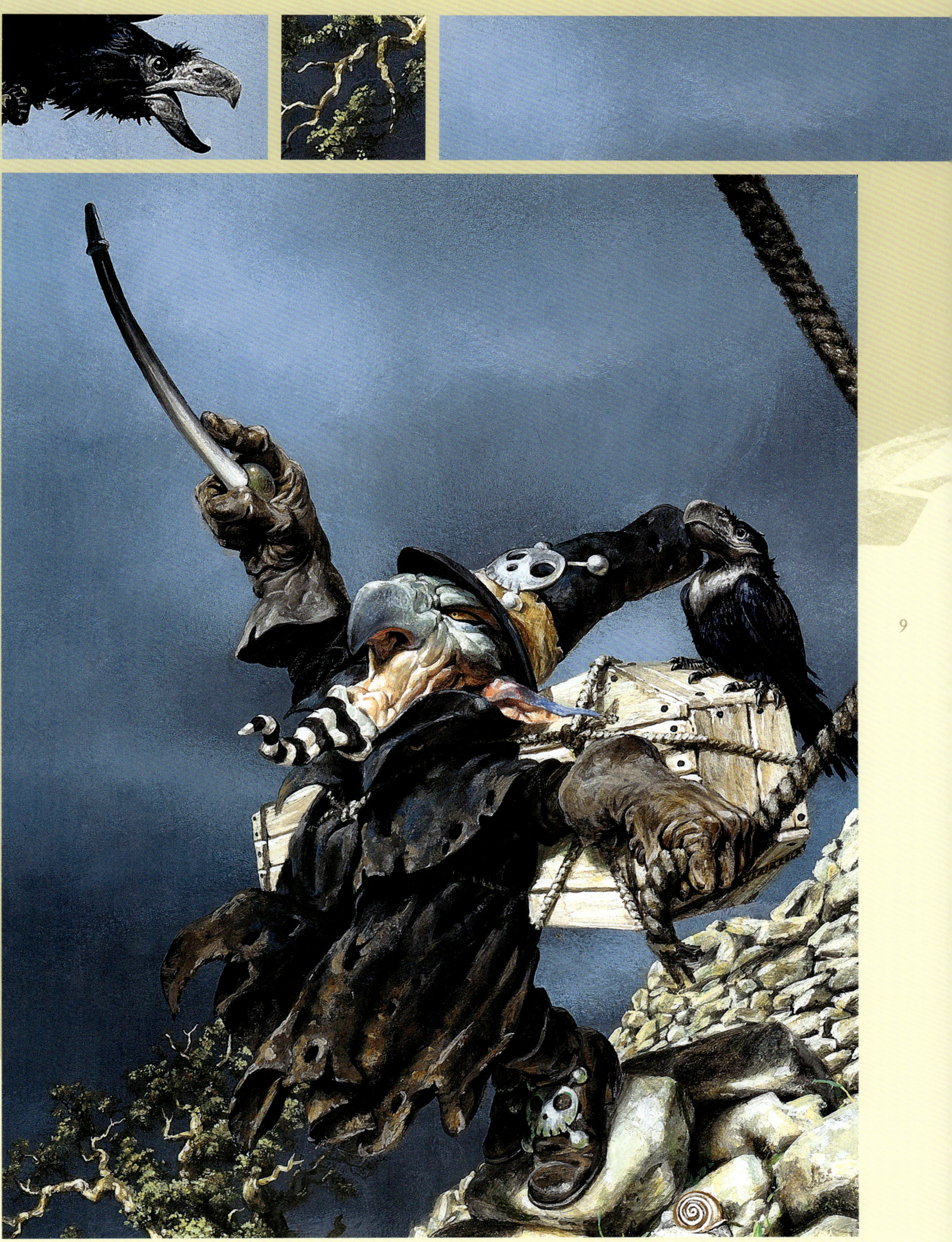

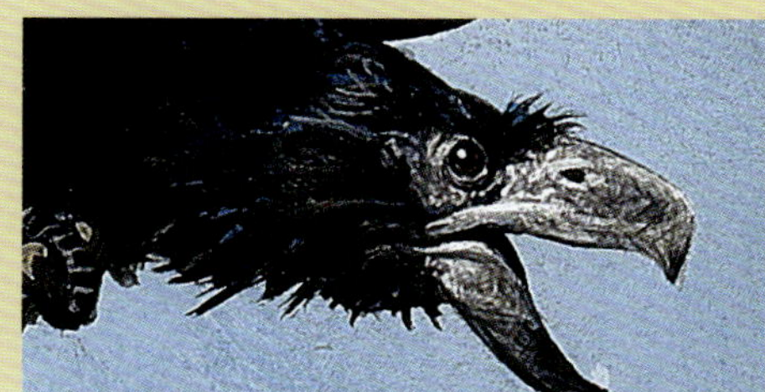
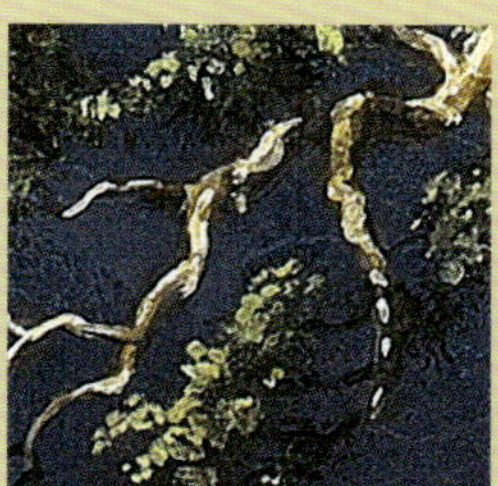

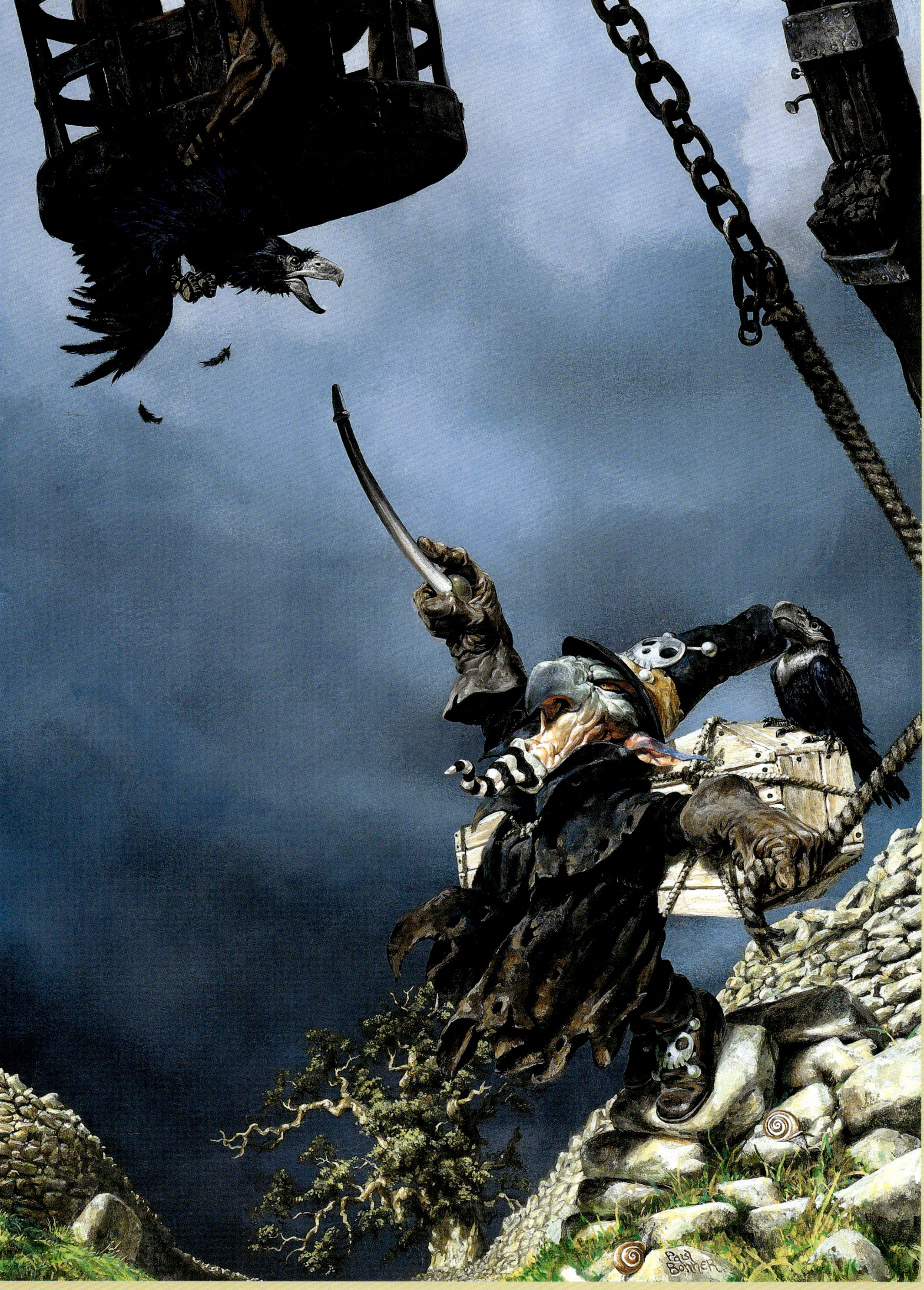
Paul
Bonner

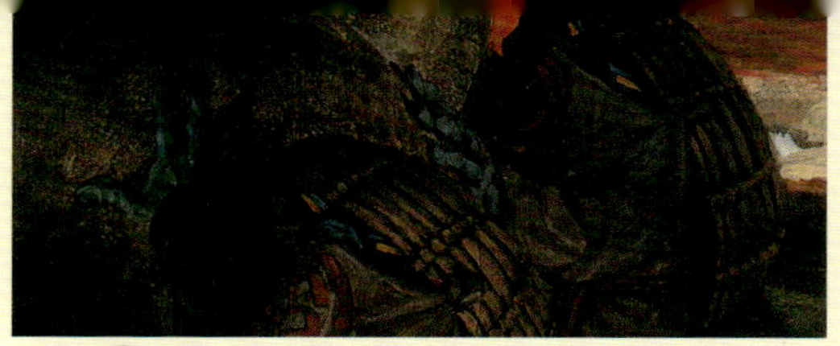

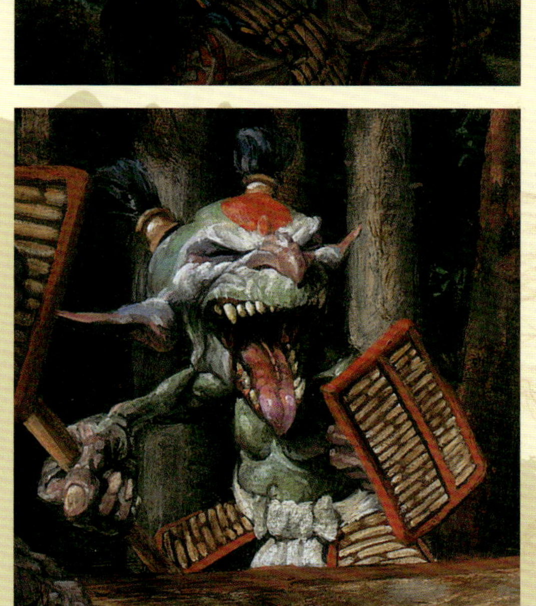

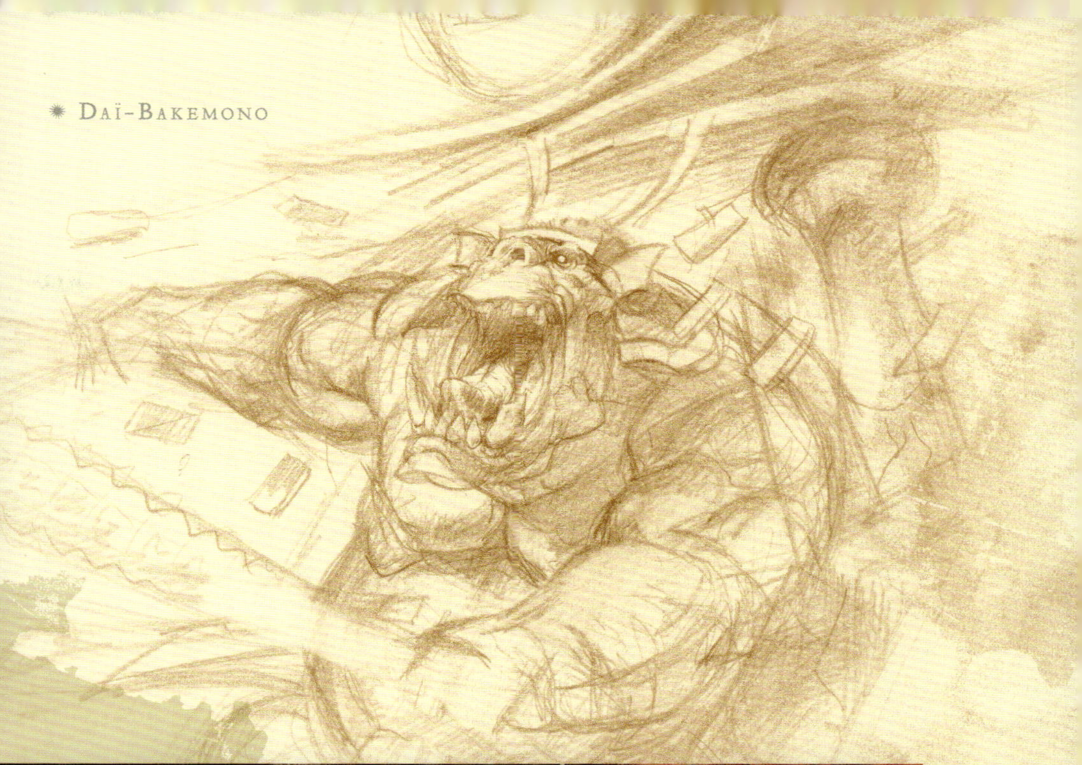

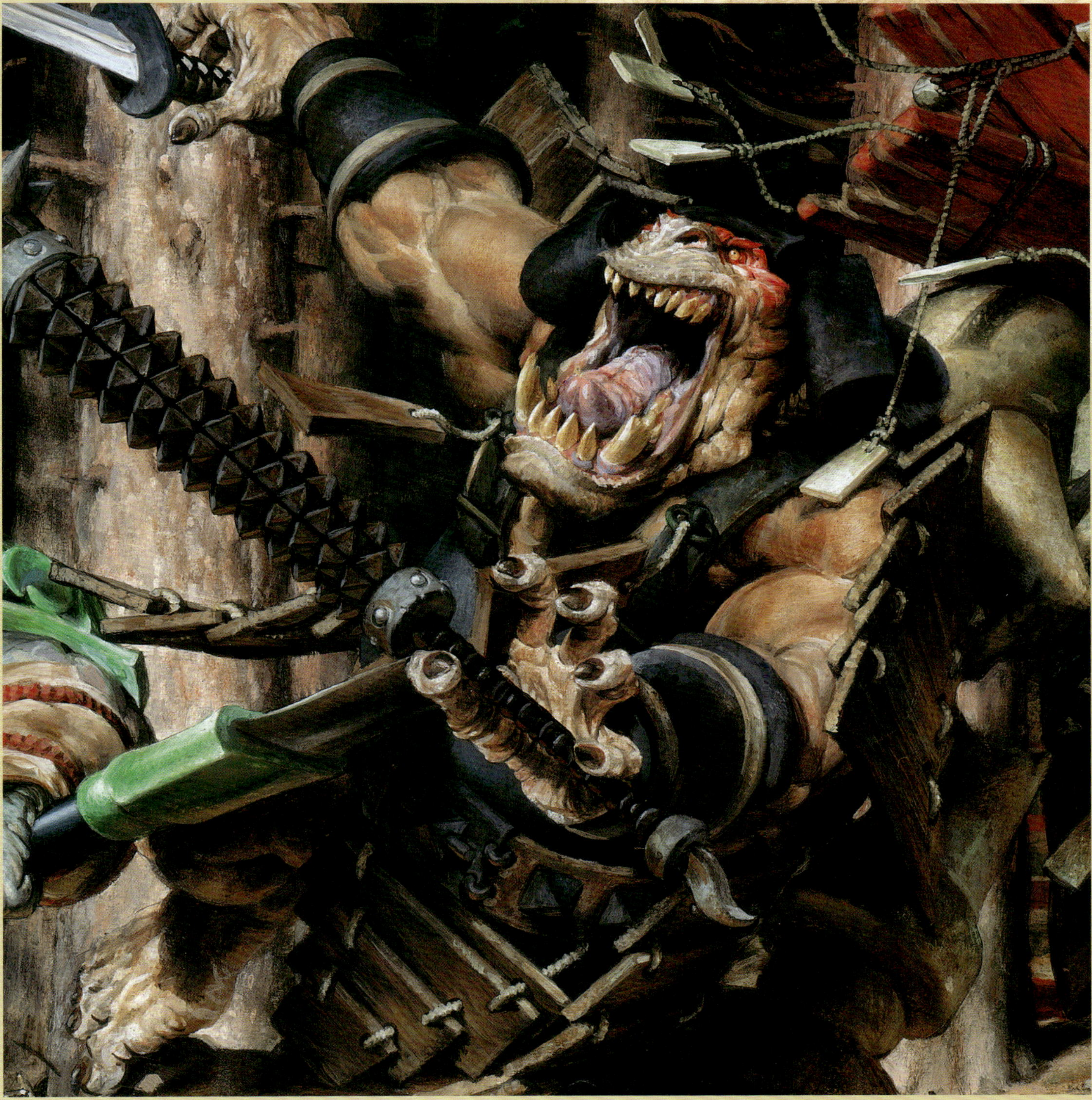

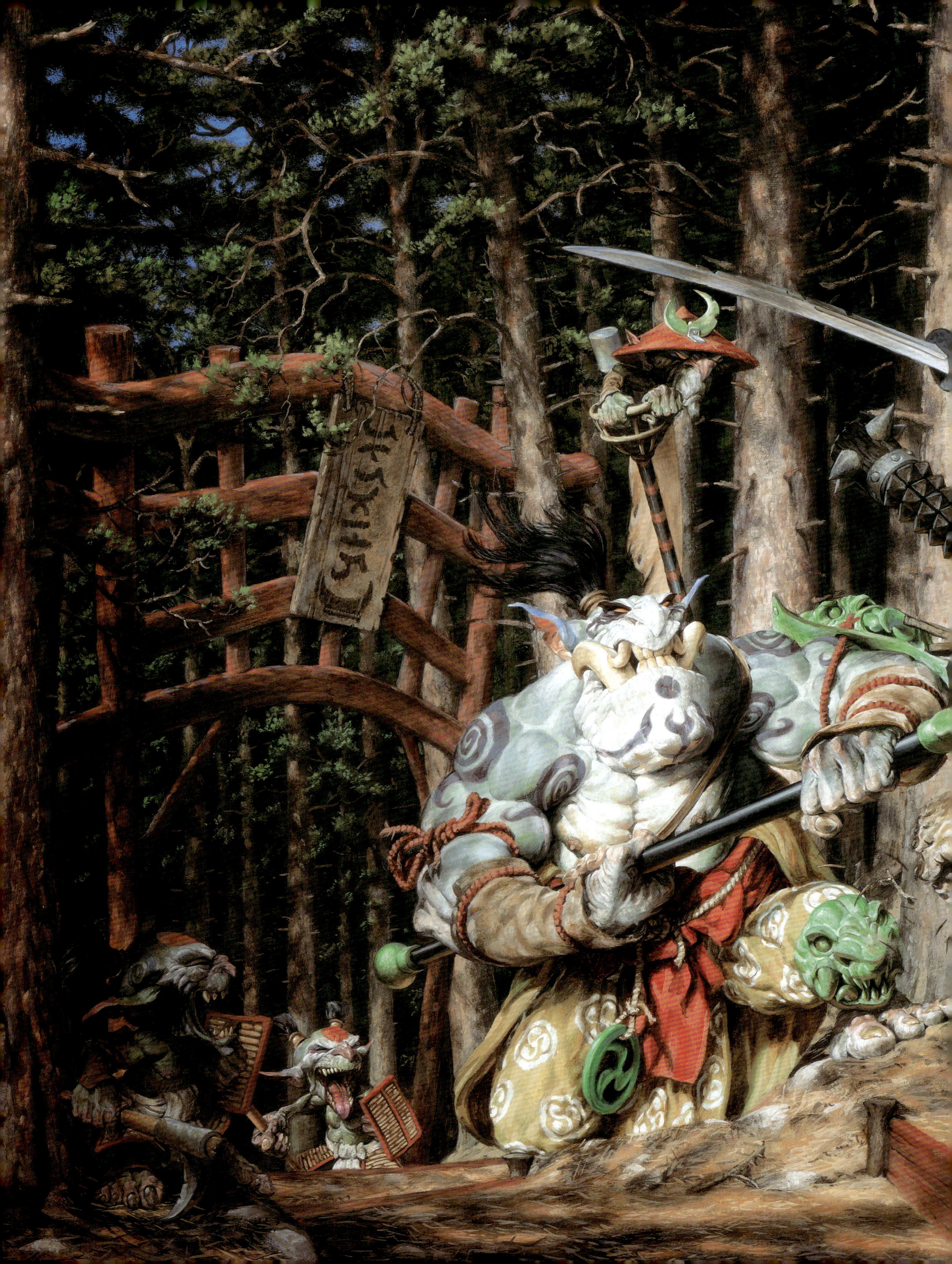

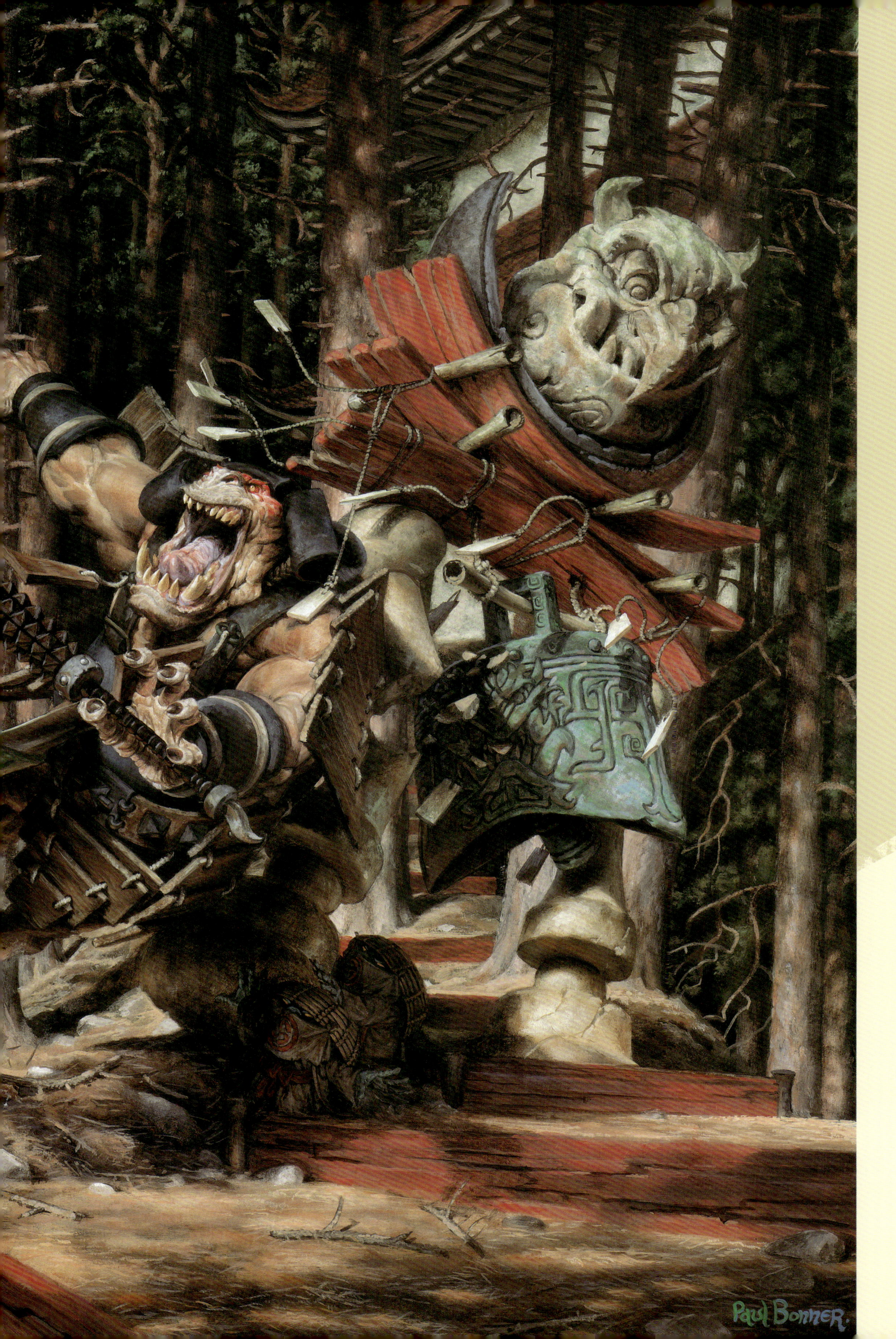
Paul Bonner.

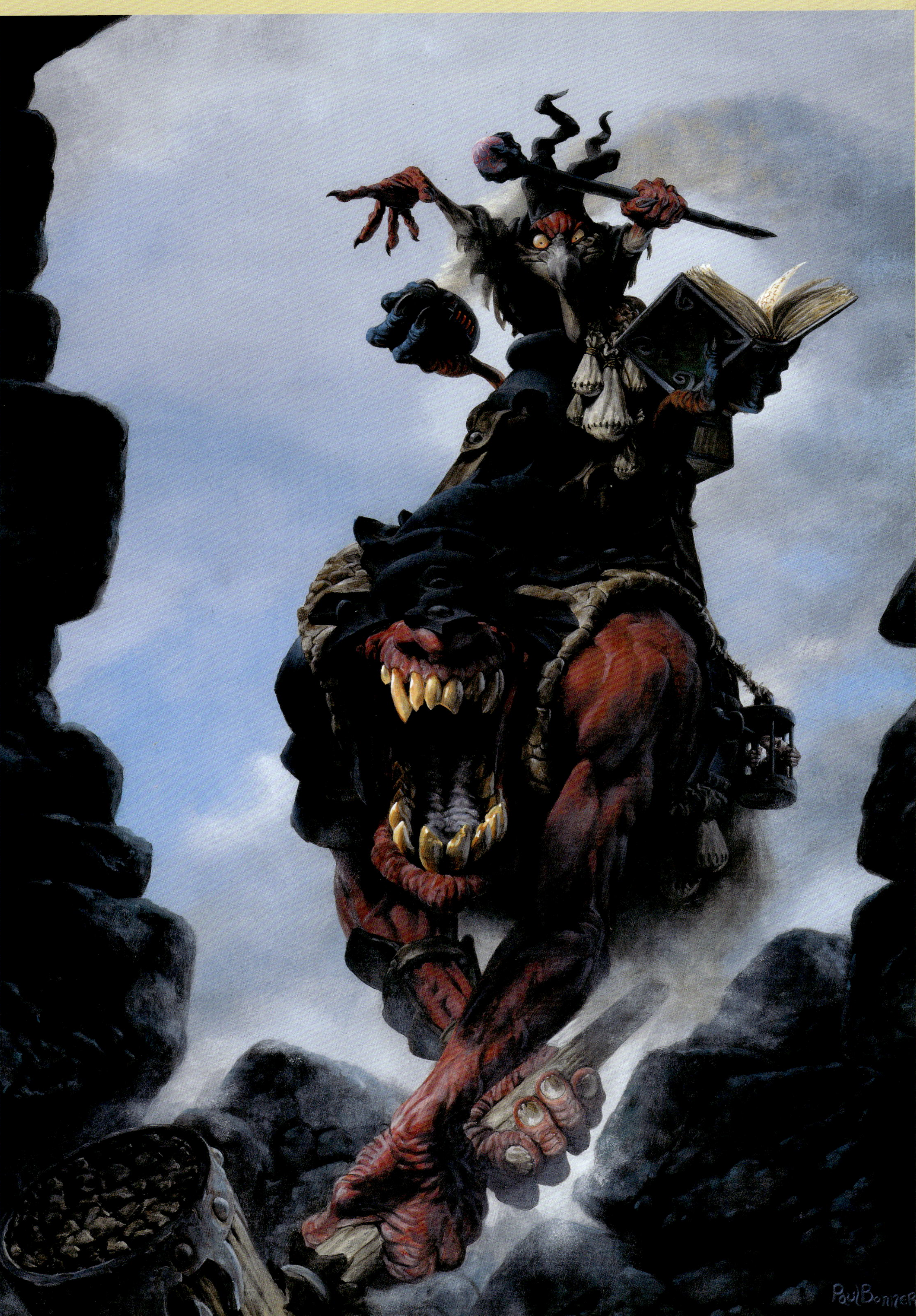
Paul Bonner

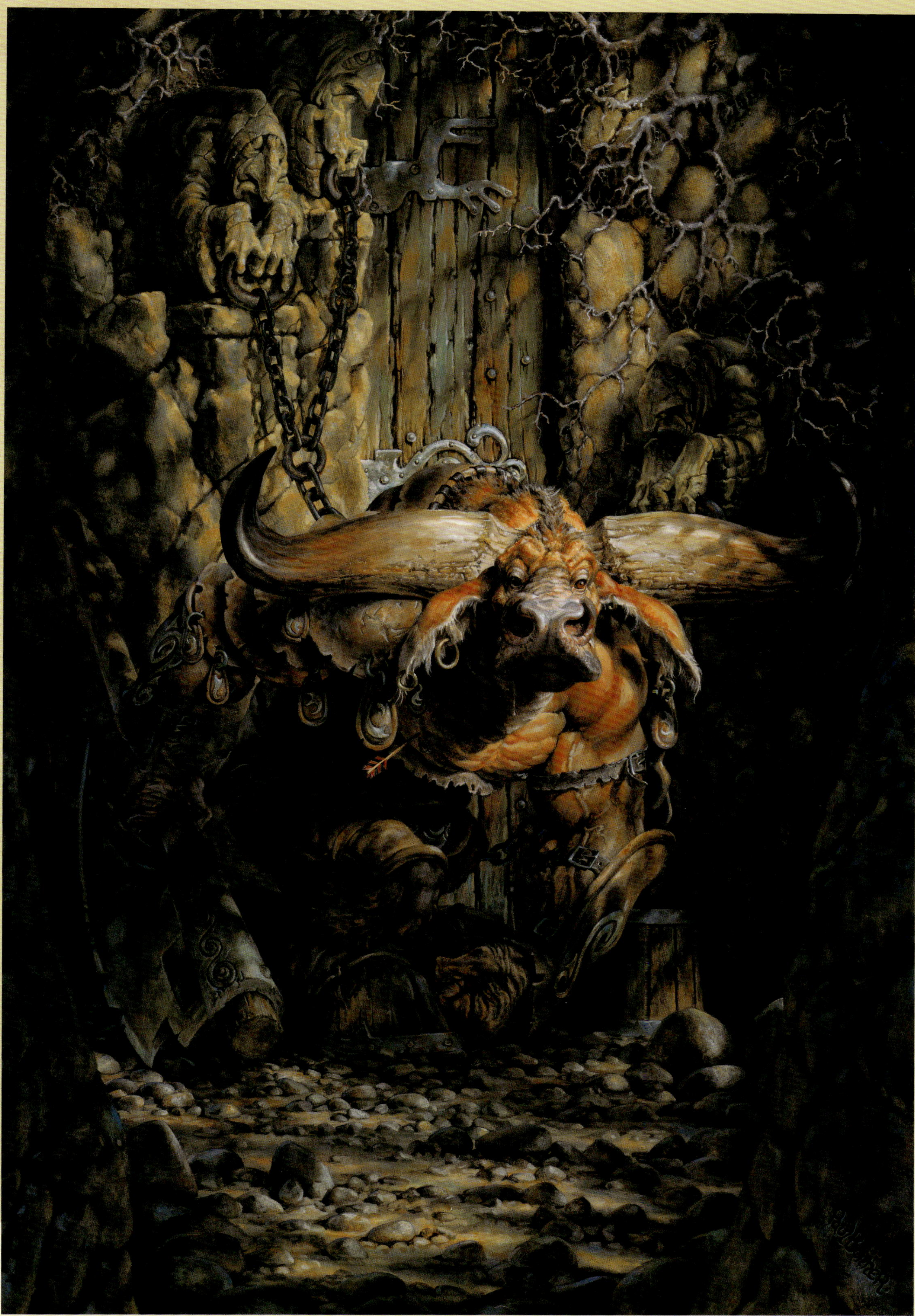

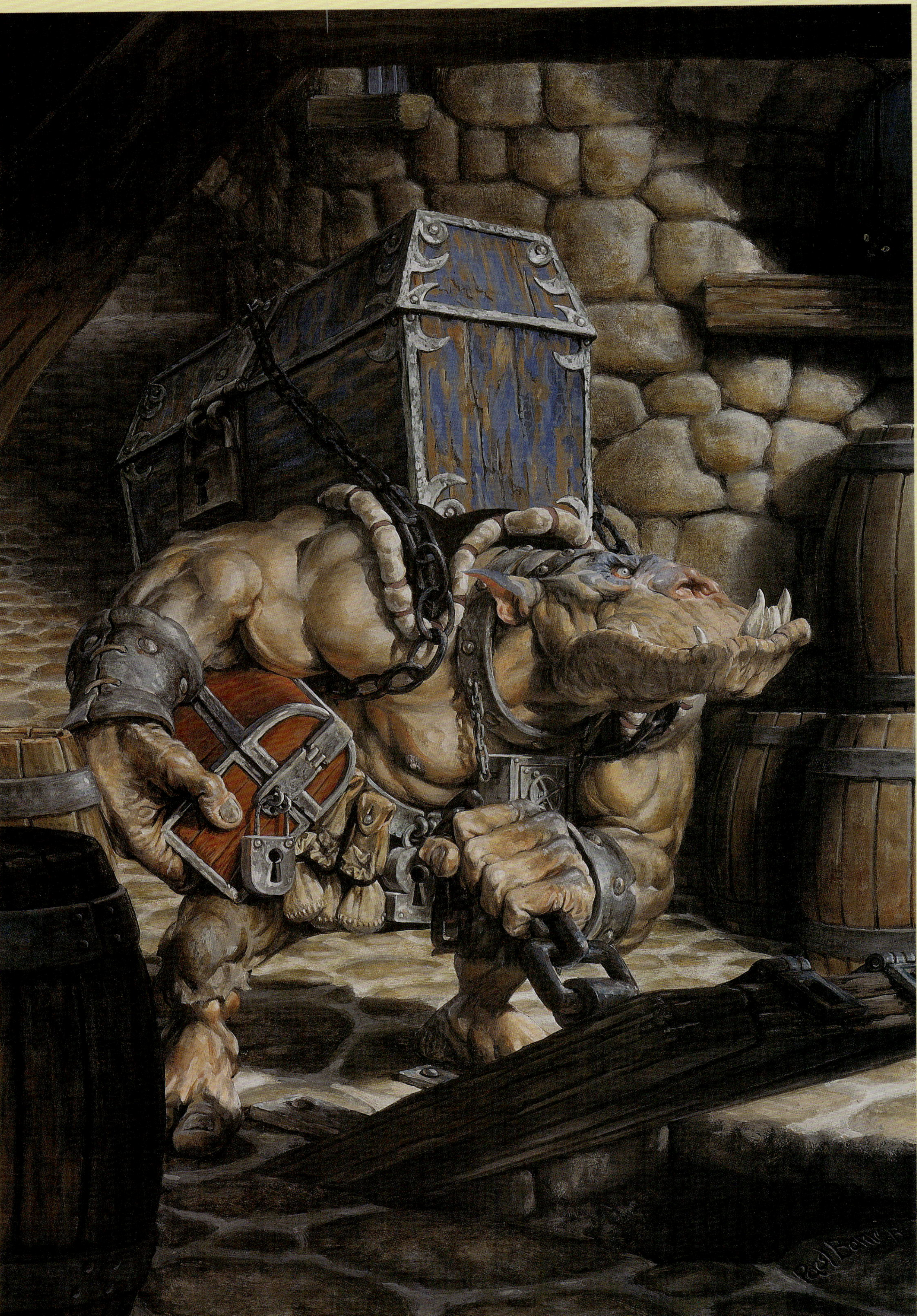

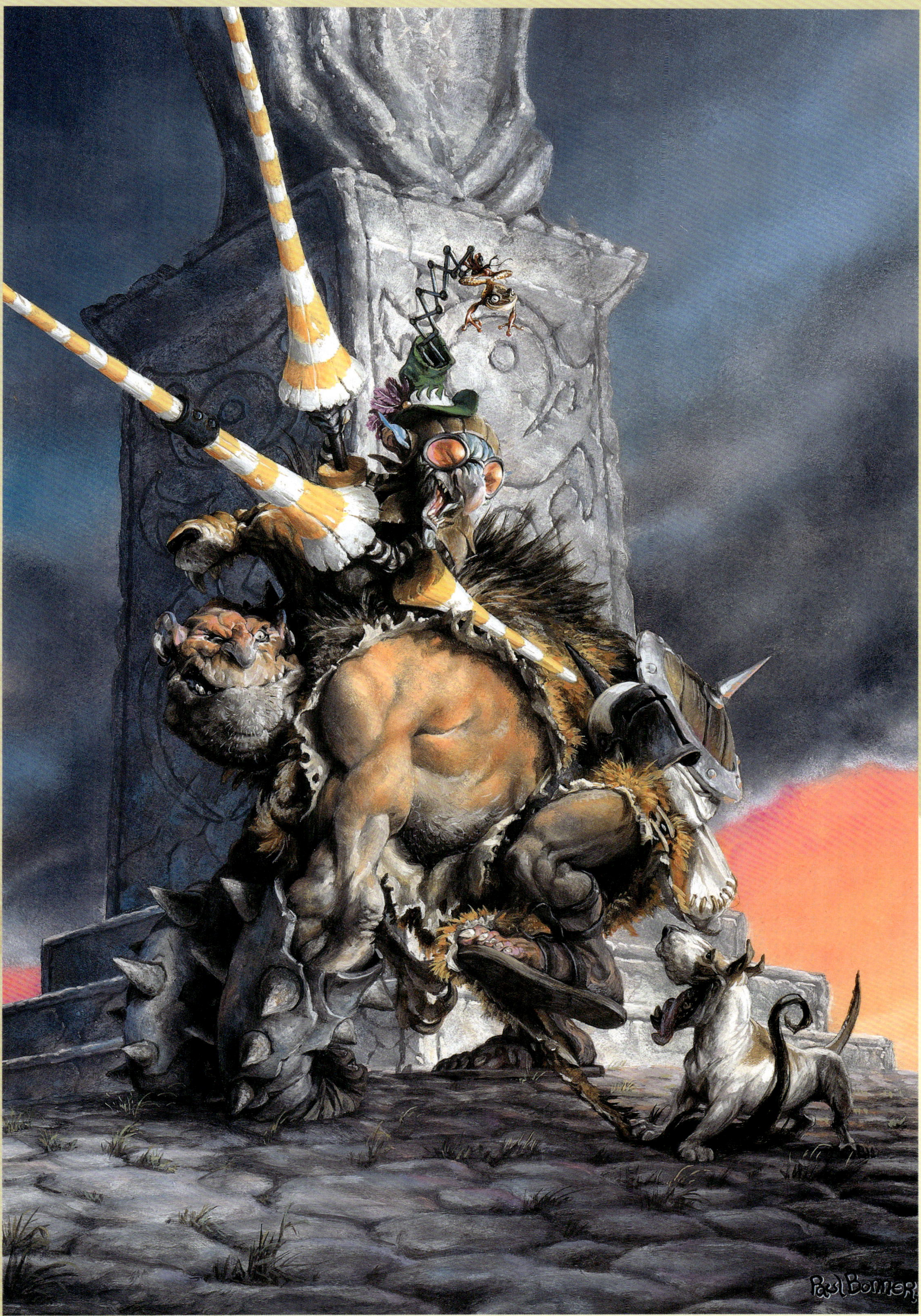
Paul Bonner

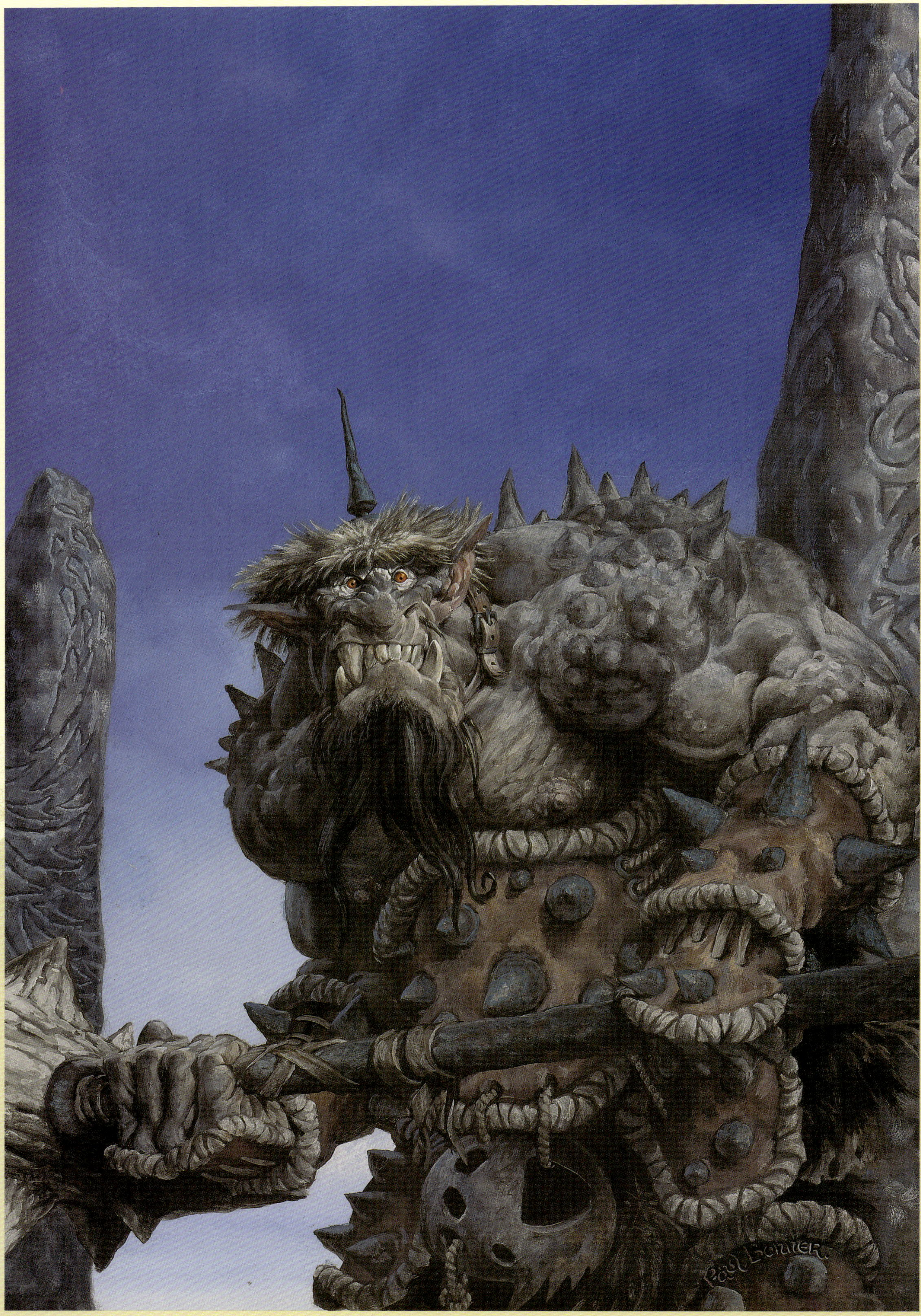

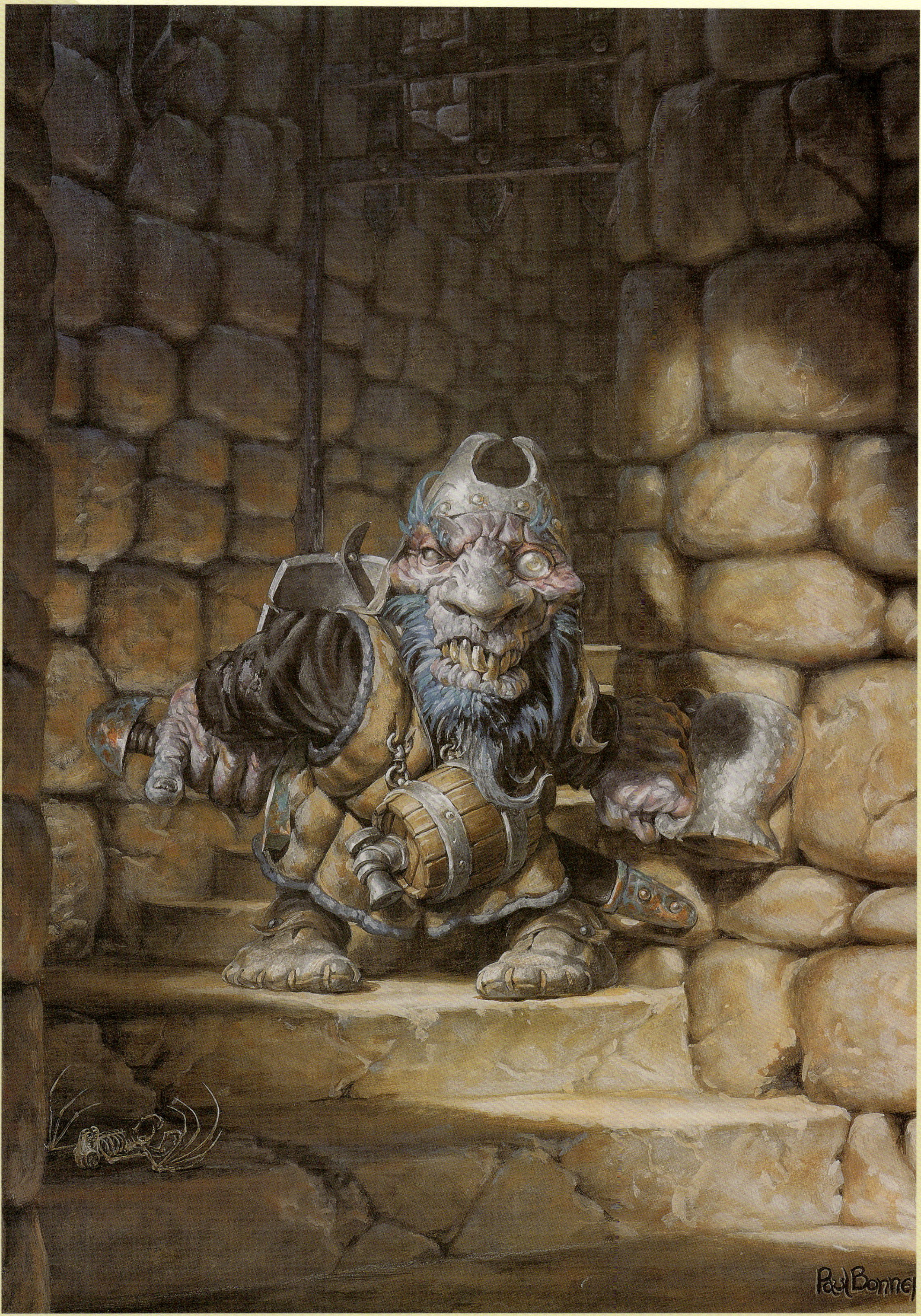
Paul Bonner

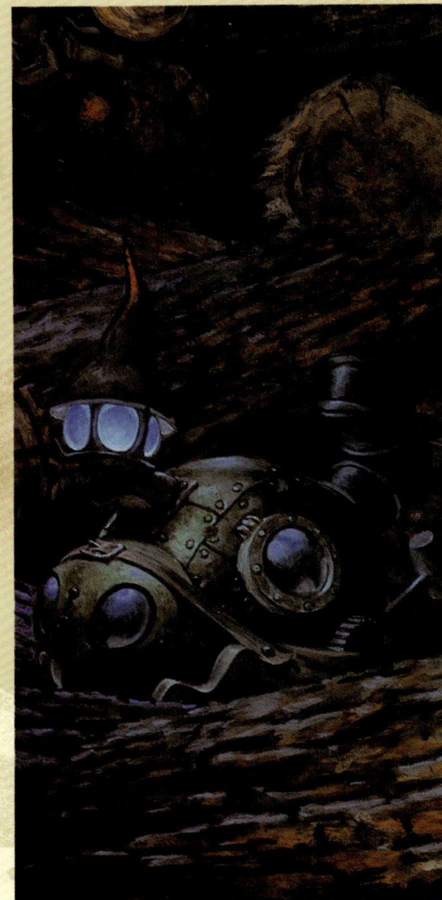

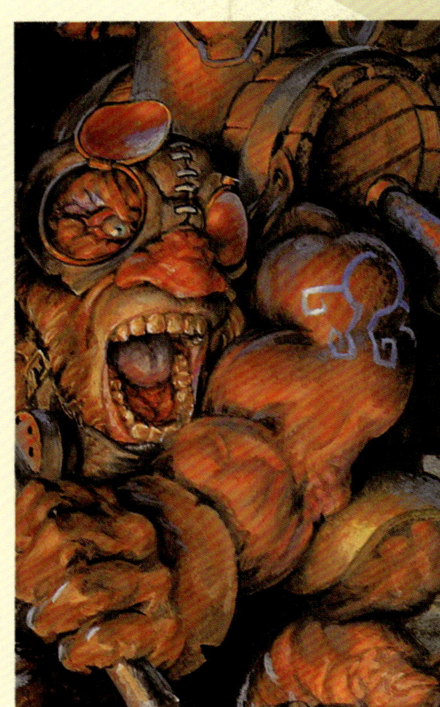

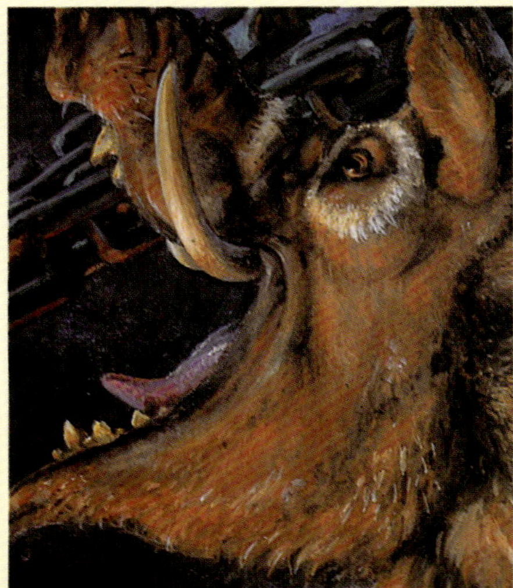

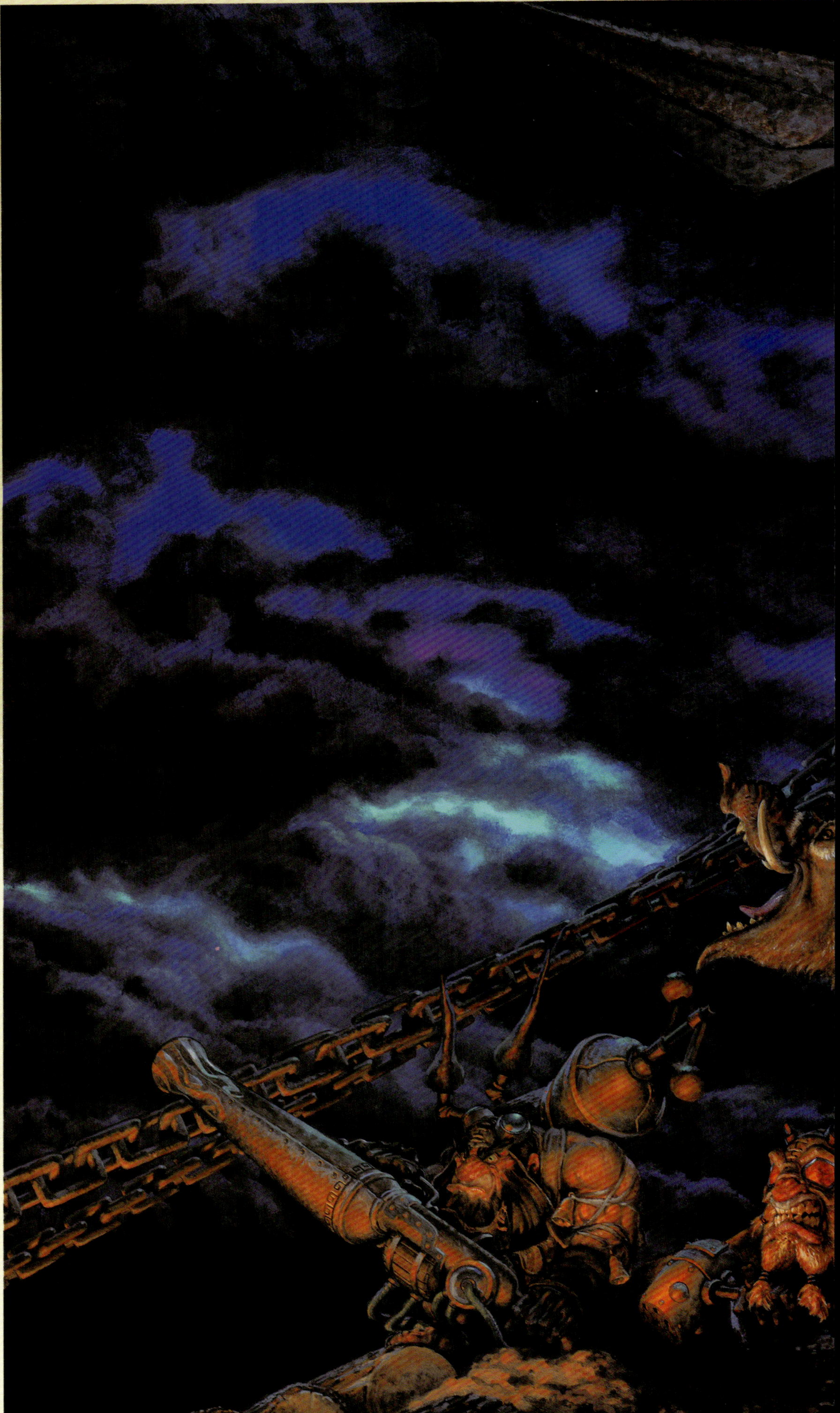

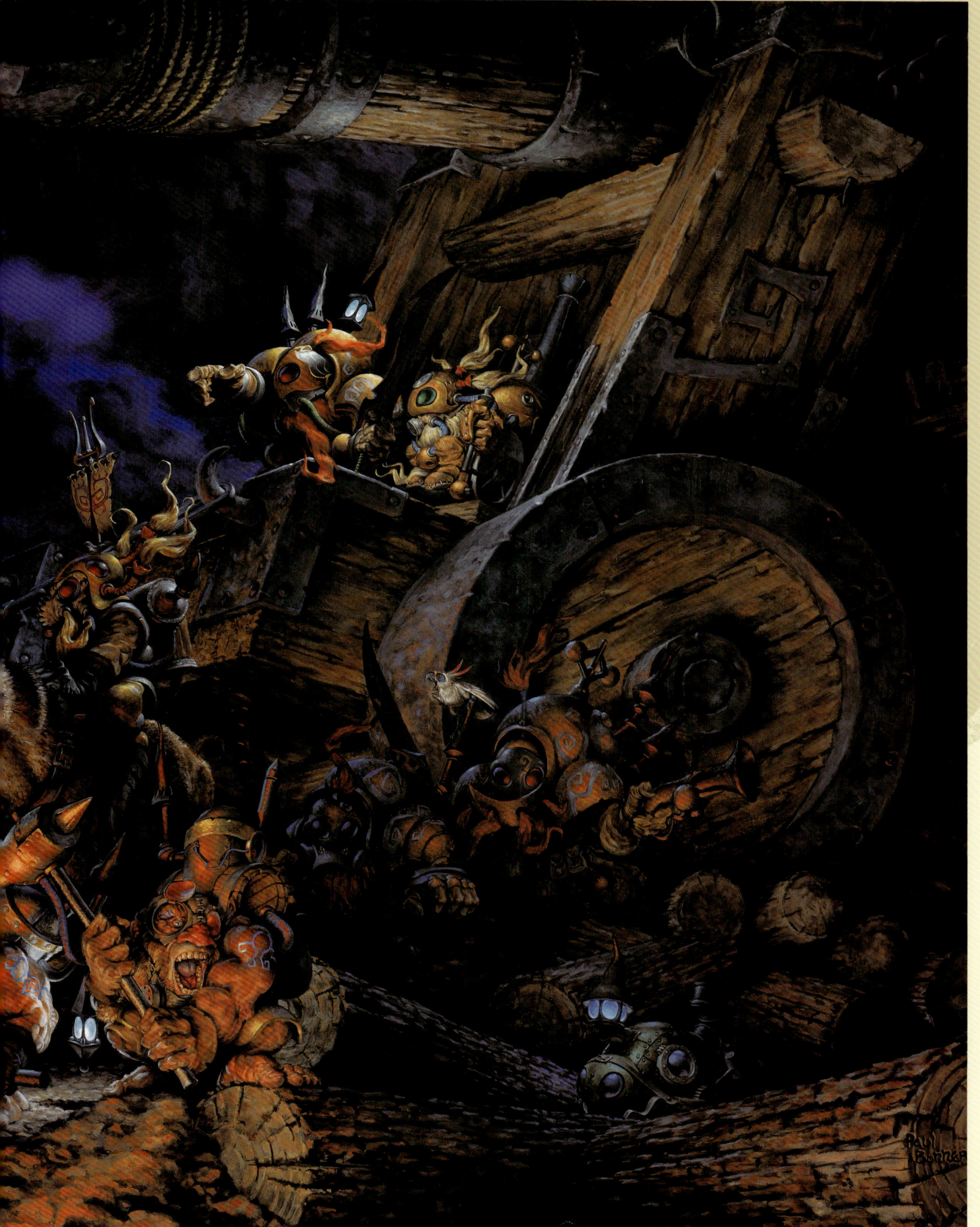
PAUL BONNER

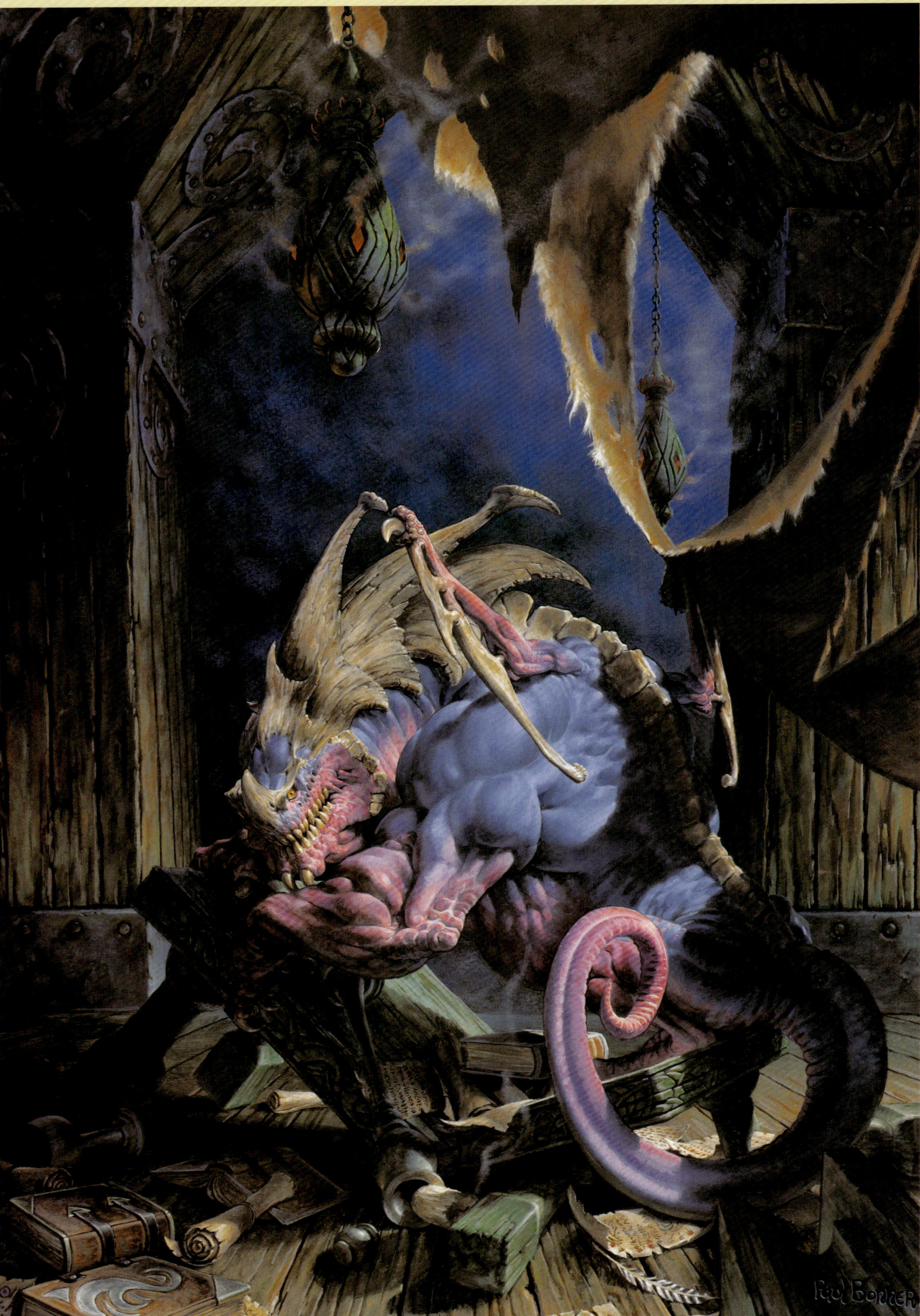
Paul Bonner

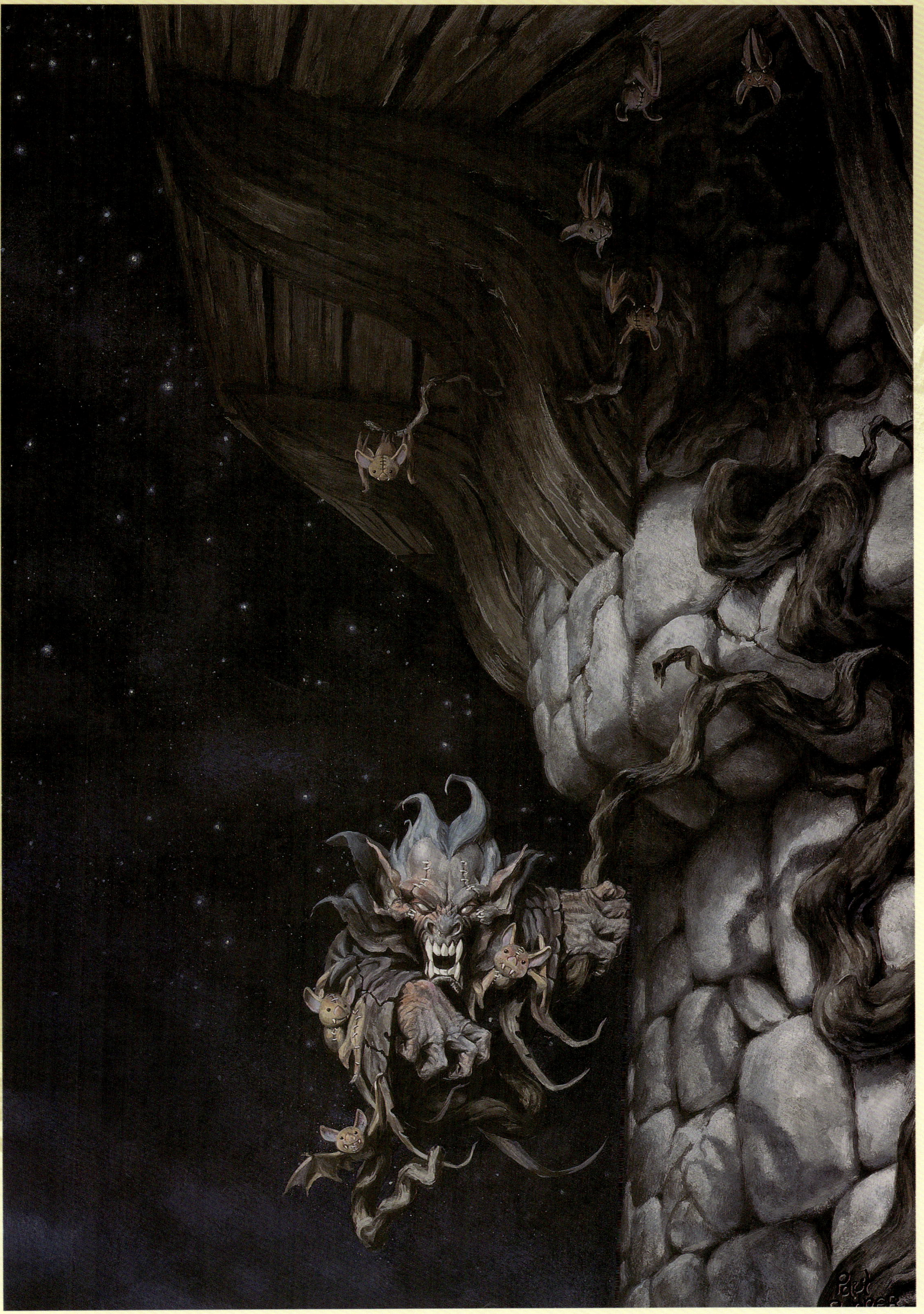

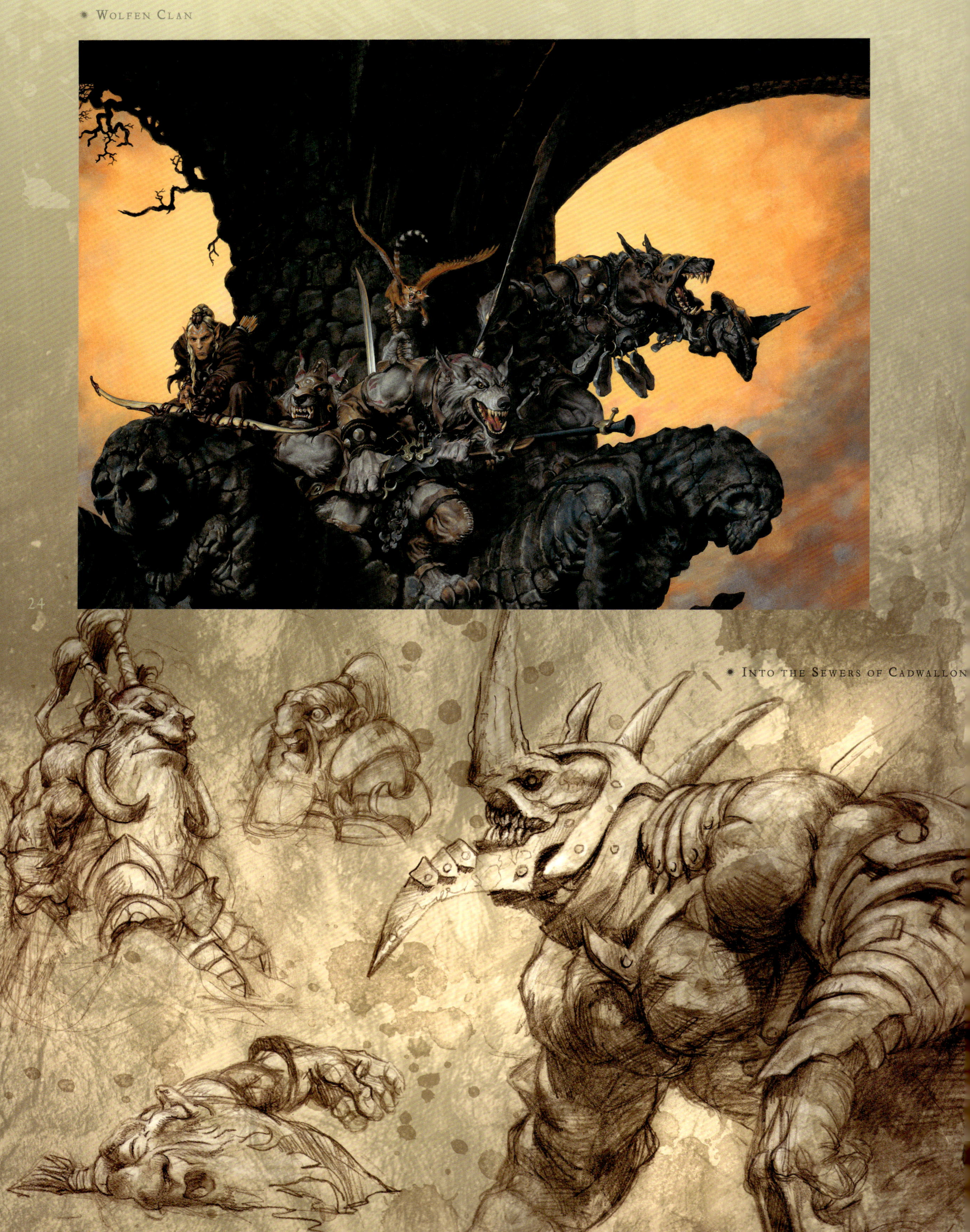

* Into the Sewers of Cadwallon

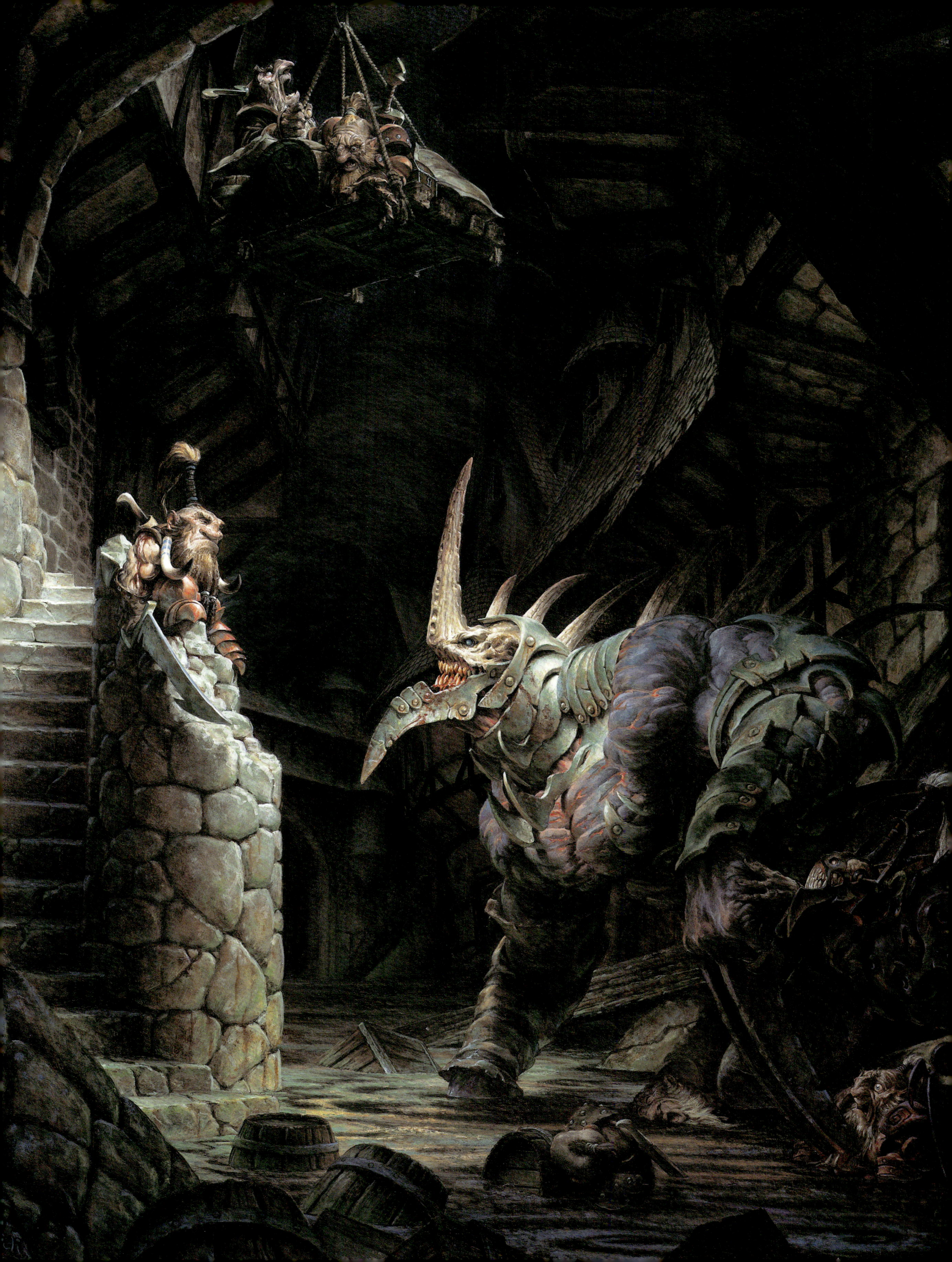

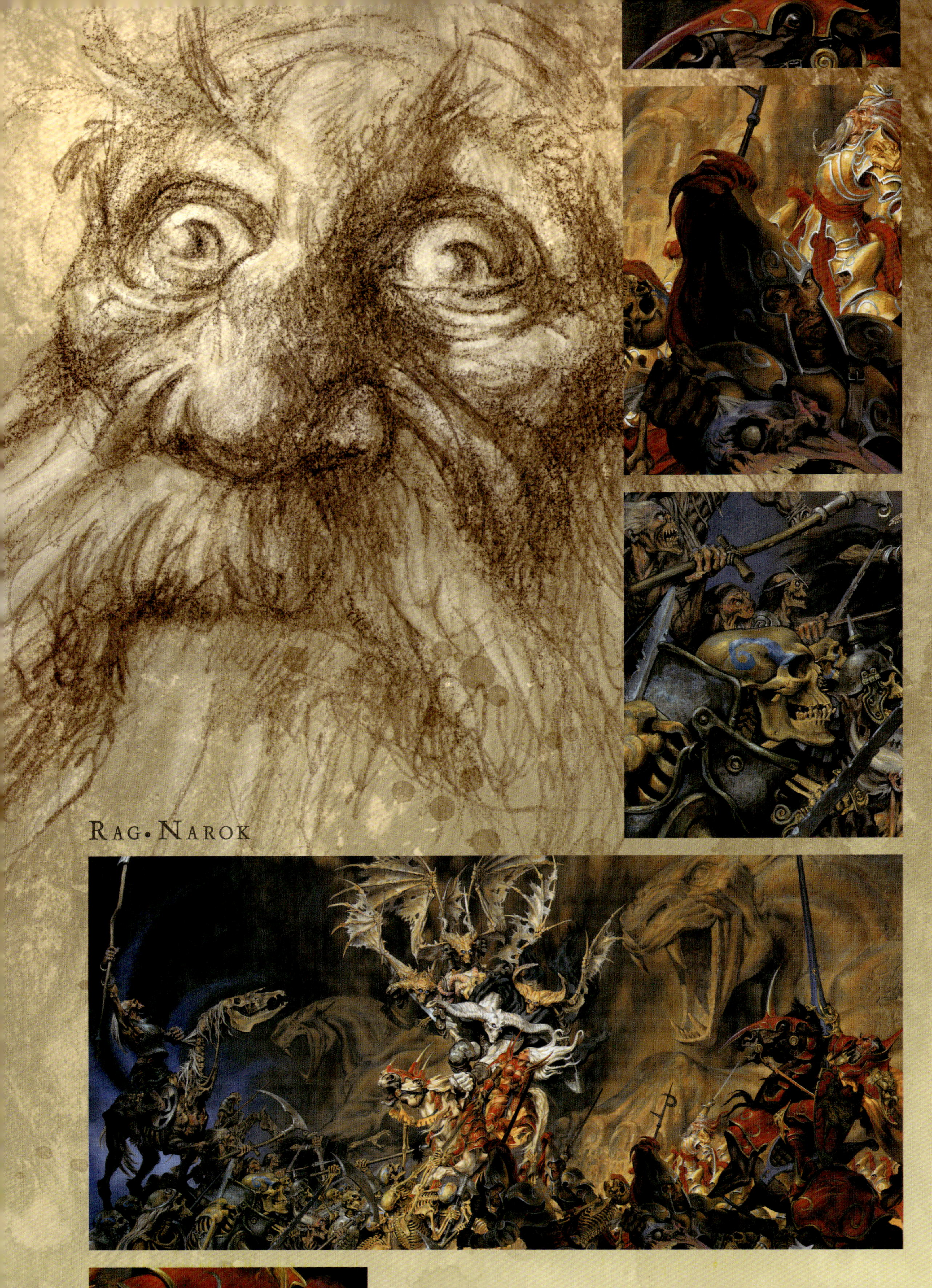
RAG•NAROK

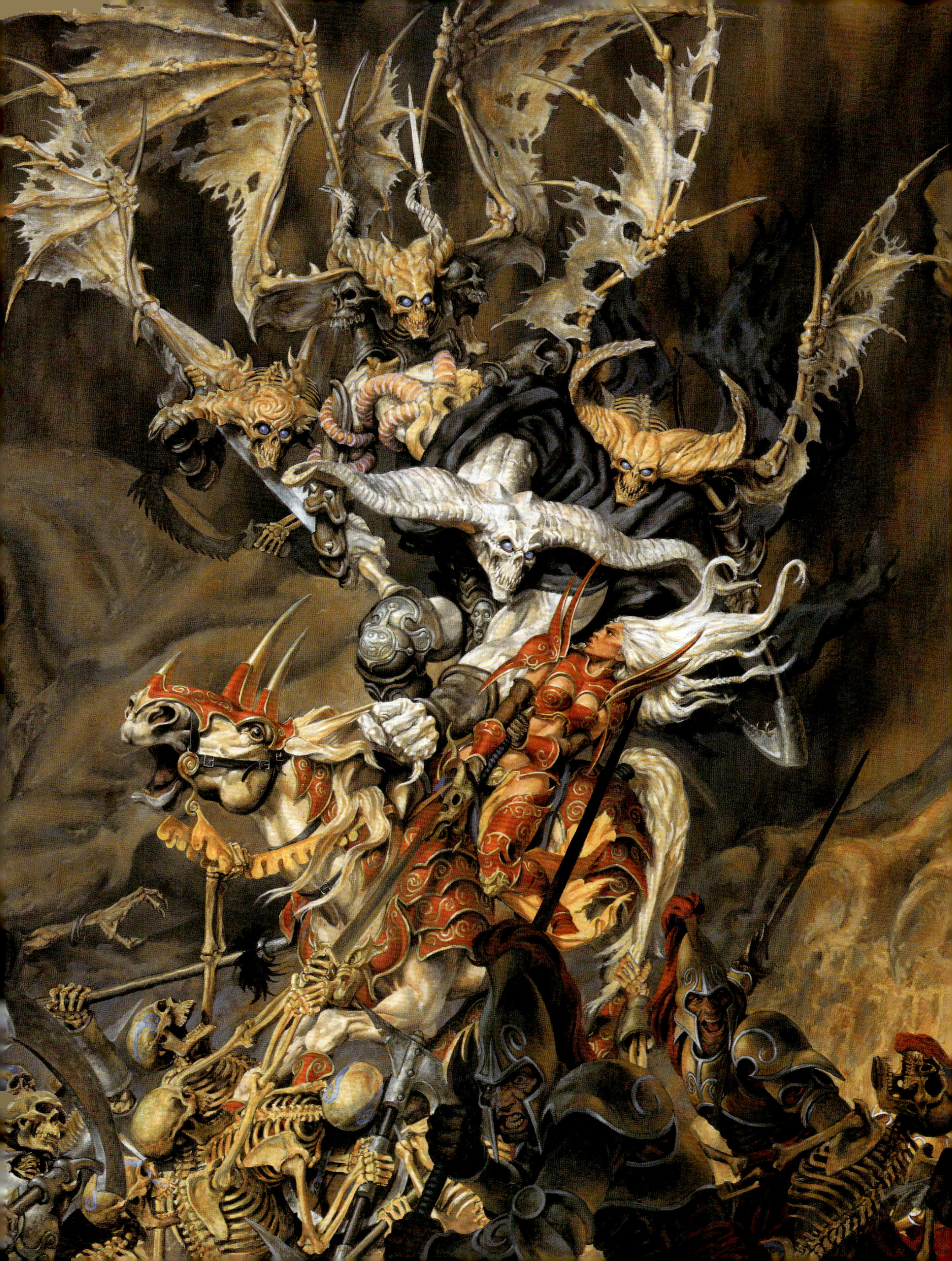

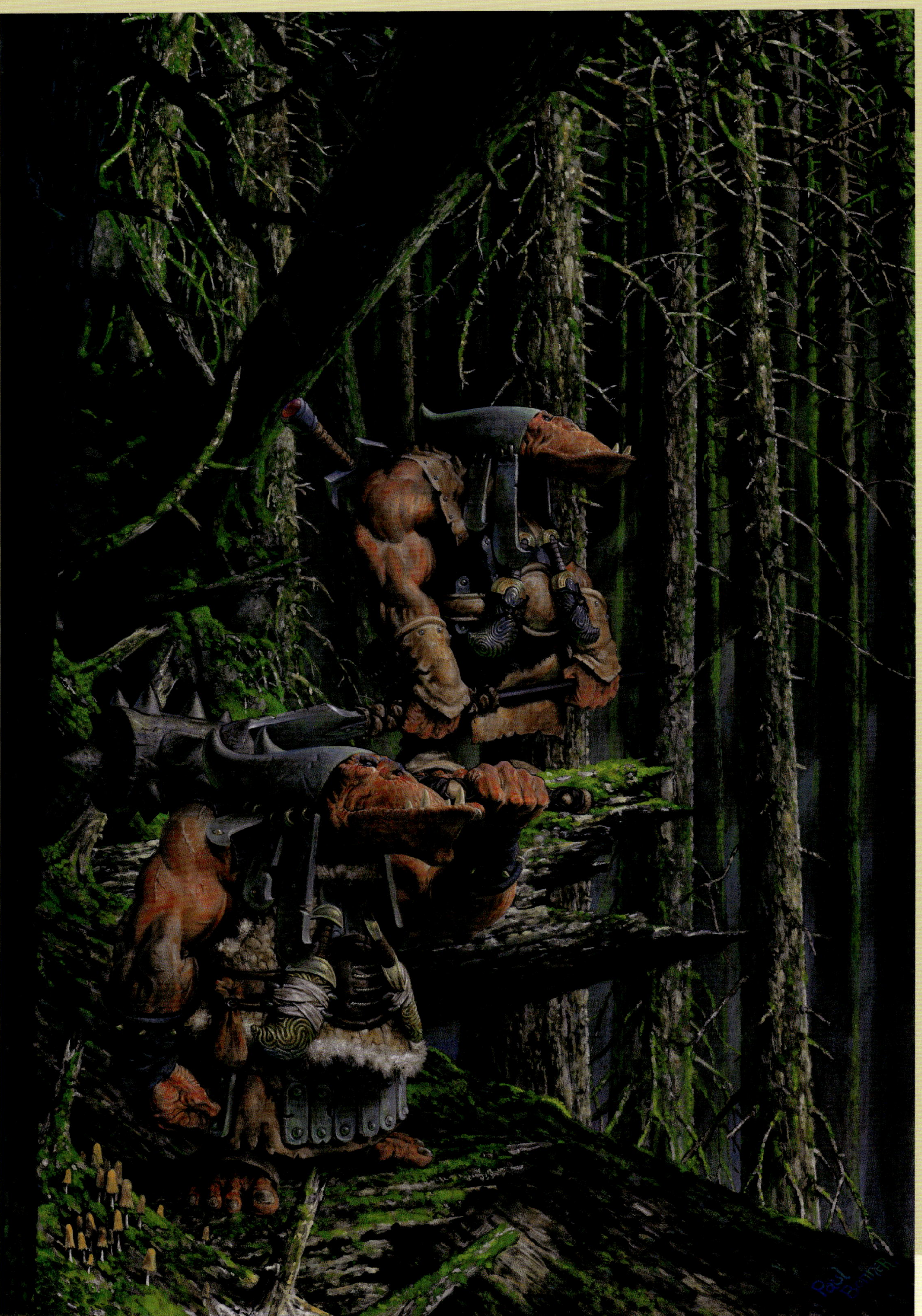

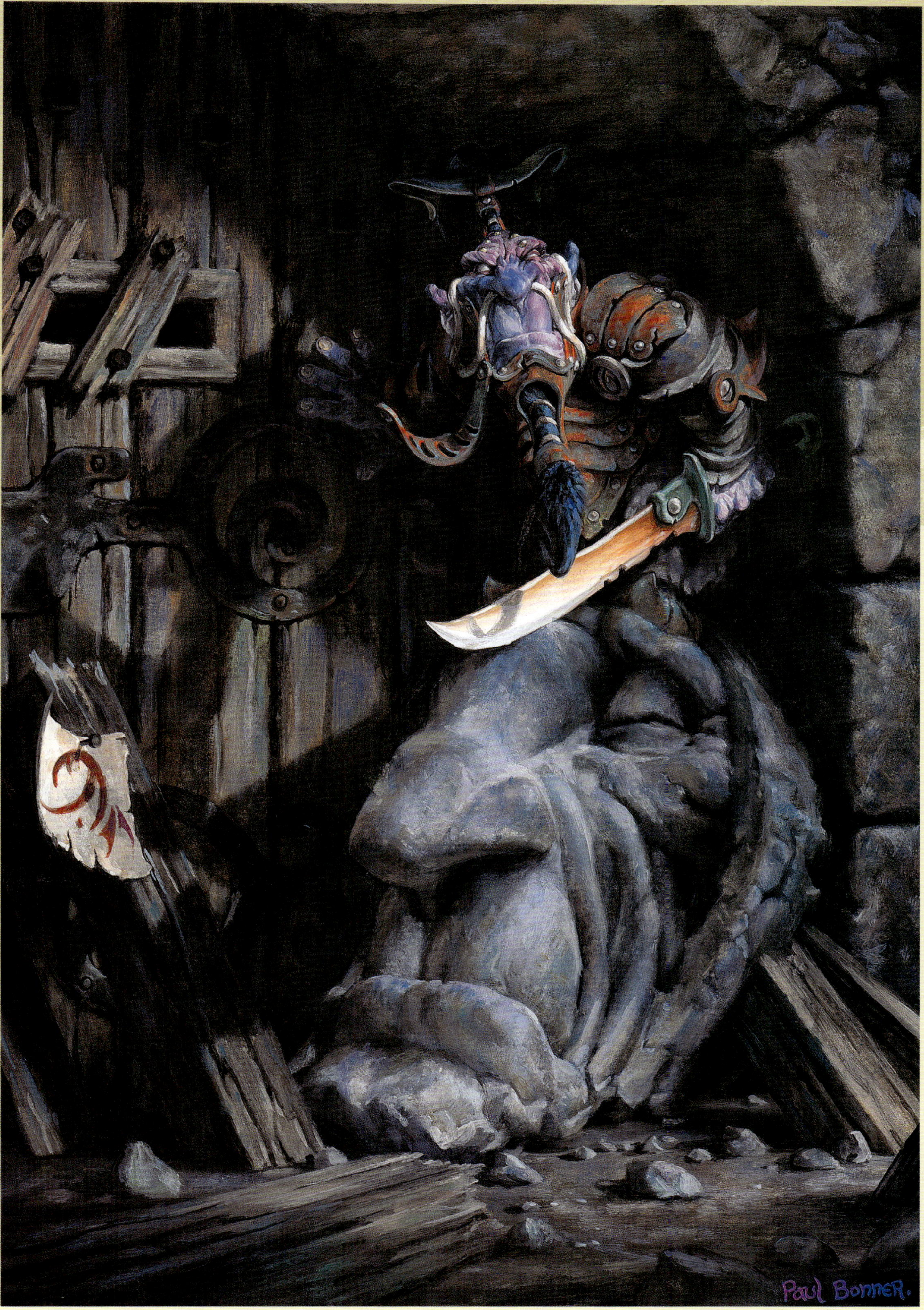

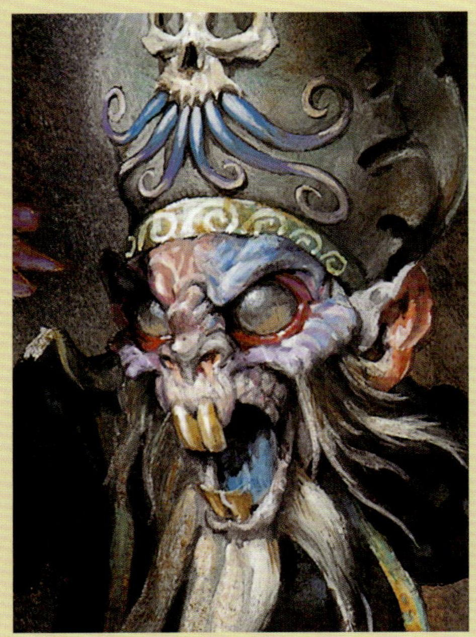

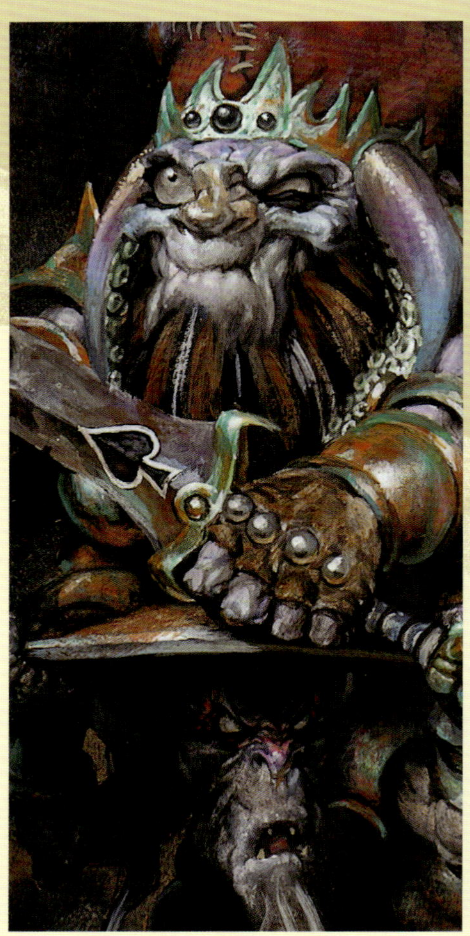

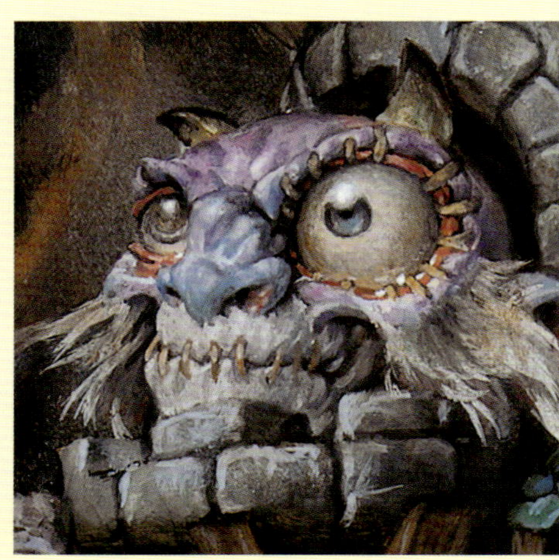

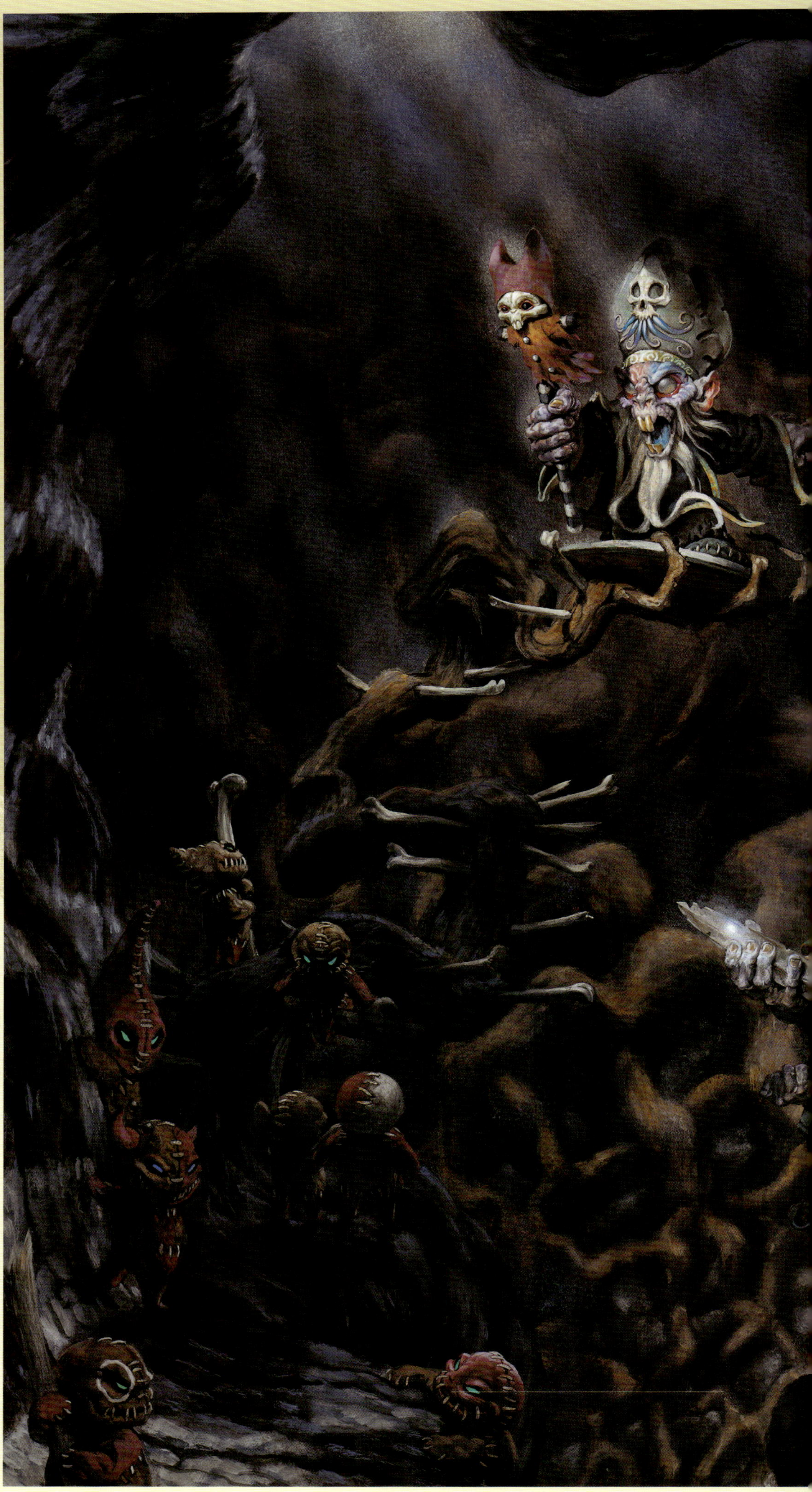

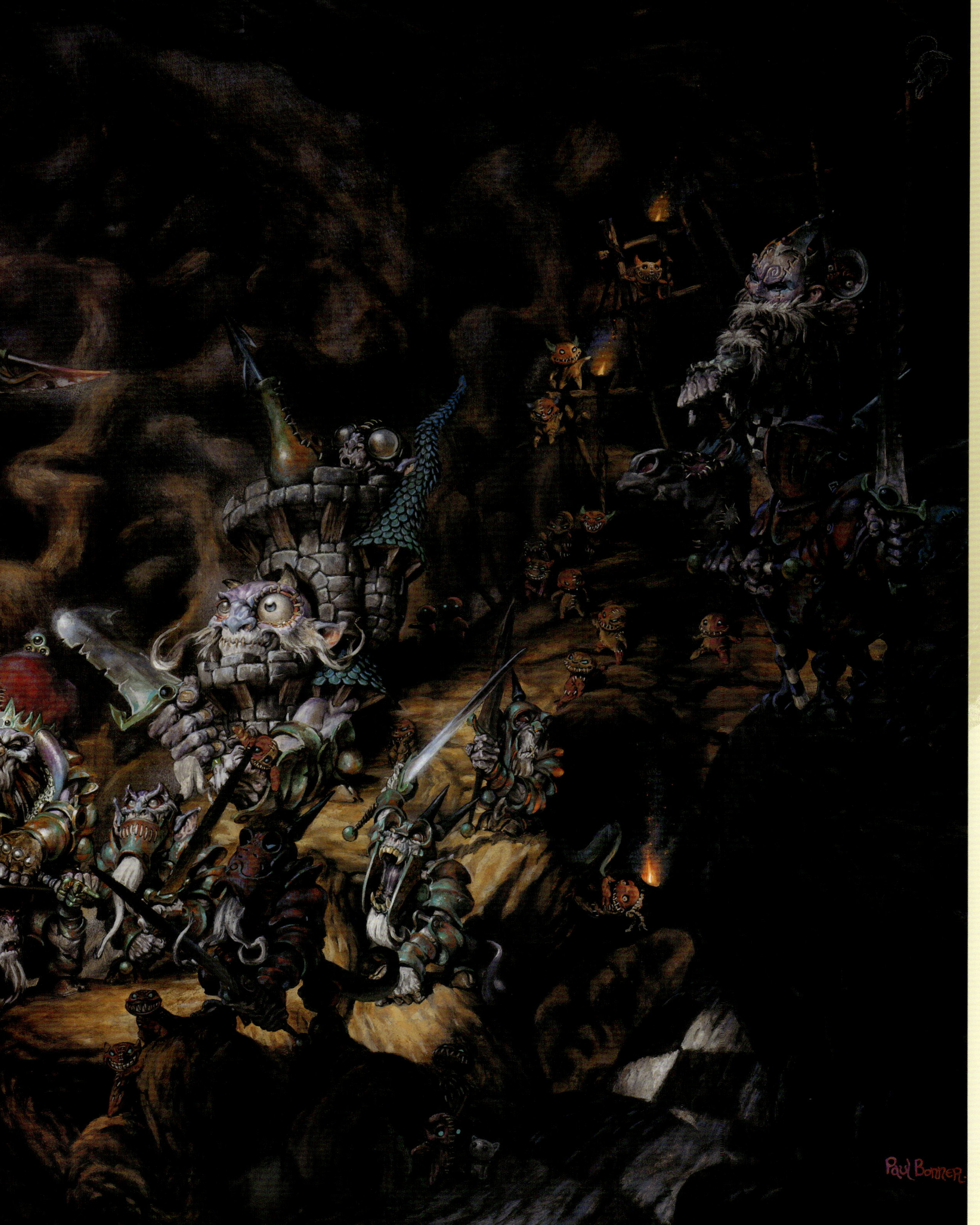
Paul Bonner

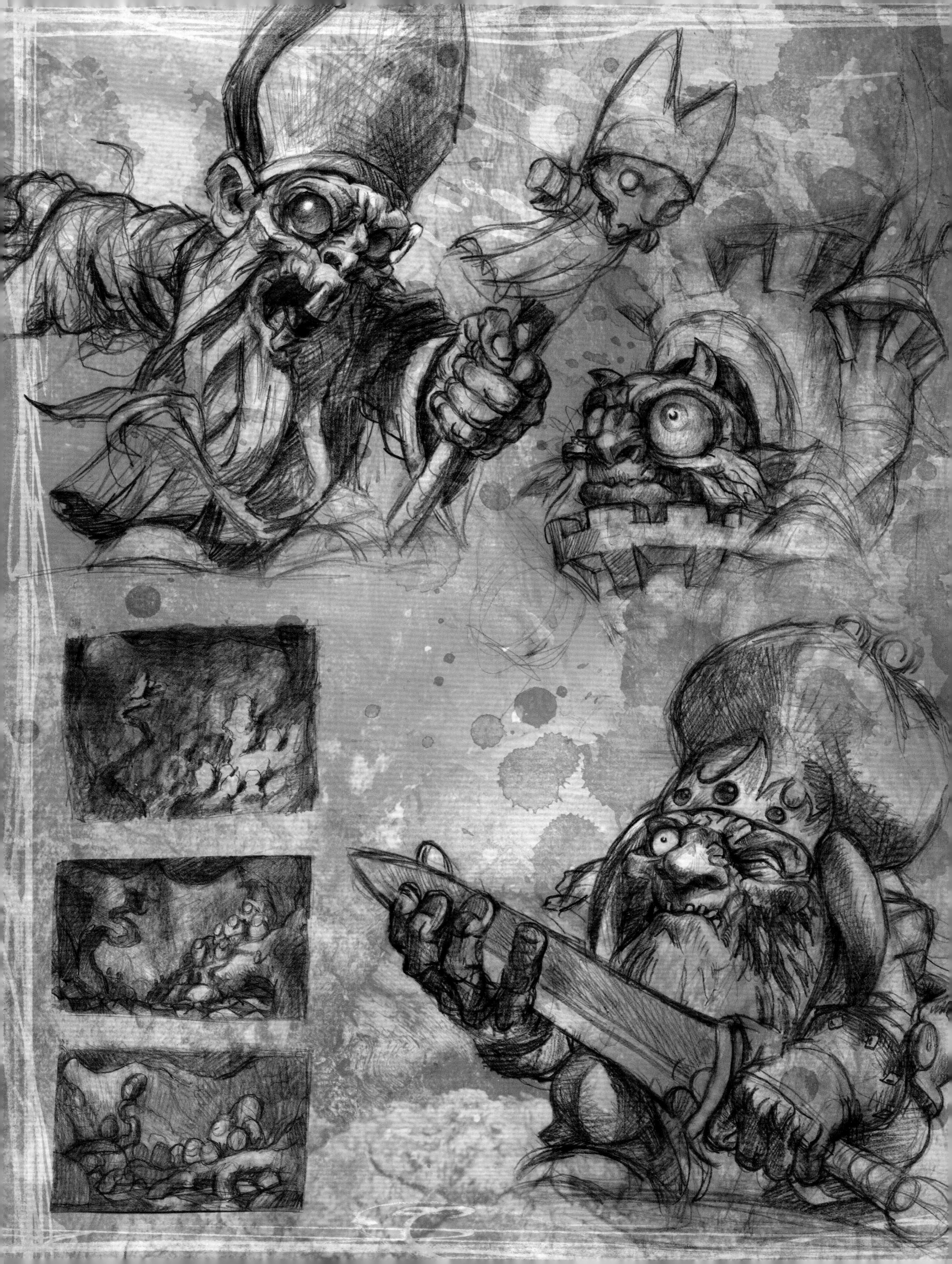

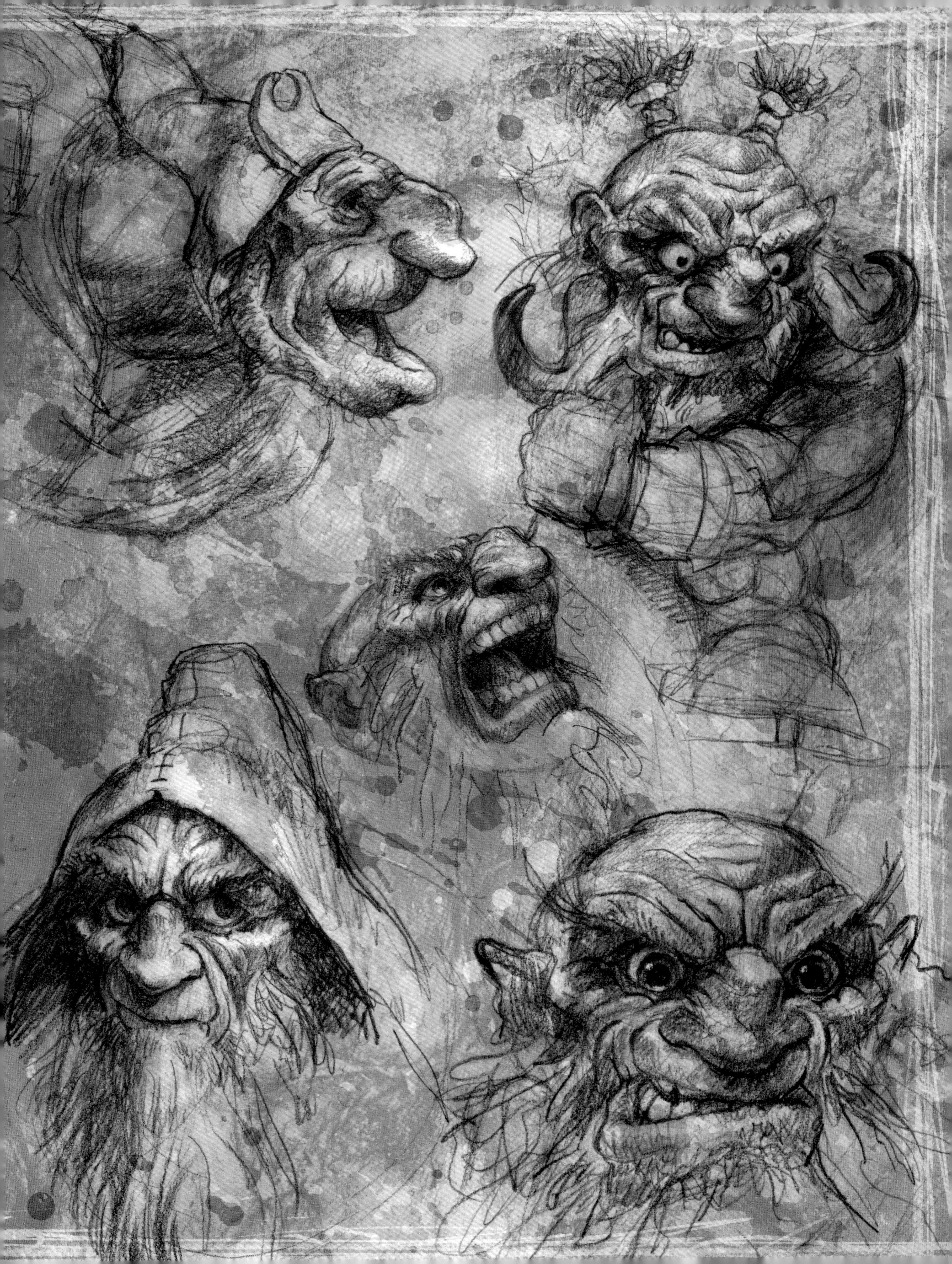

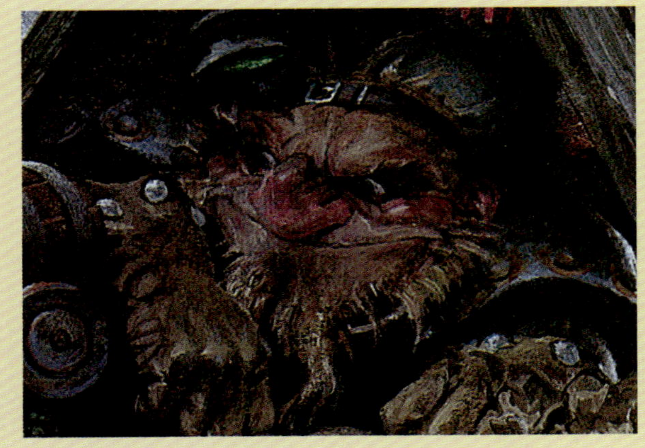

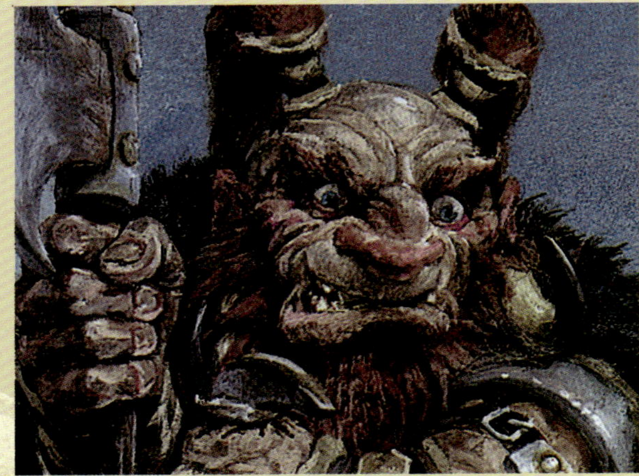

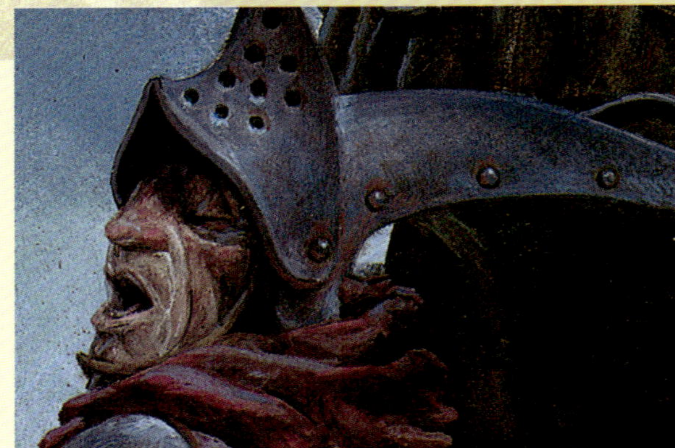

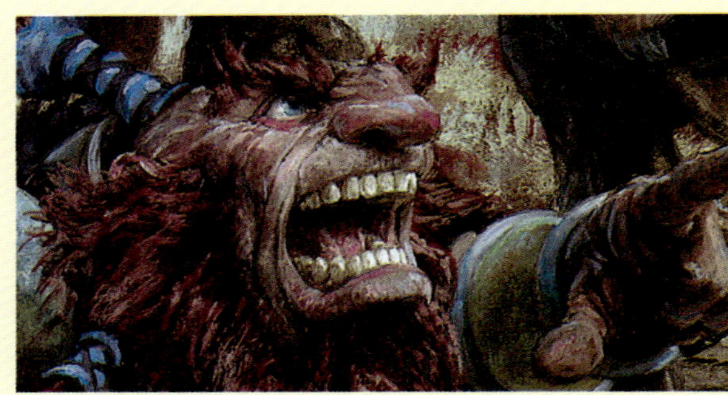

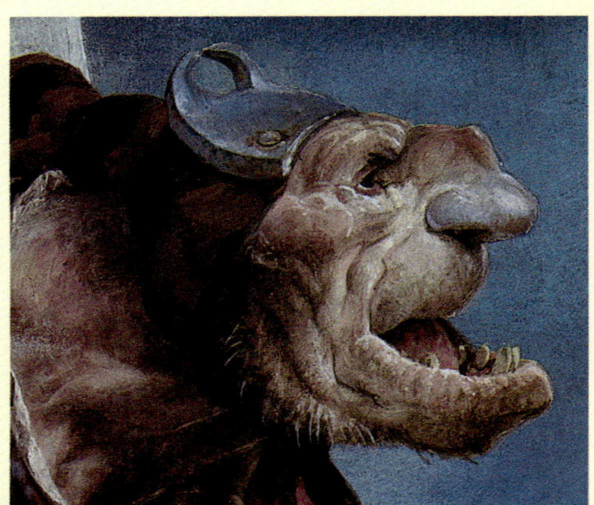

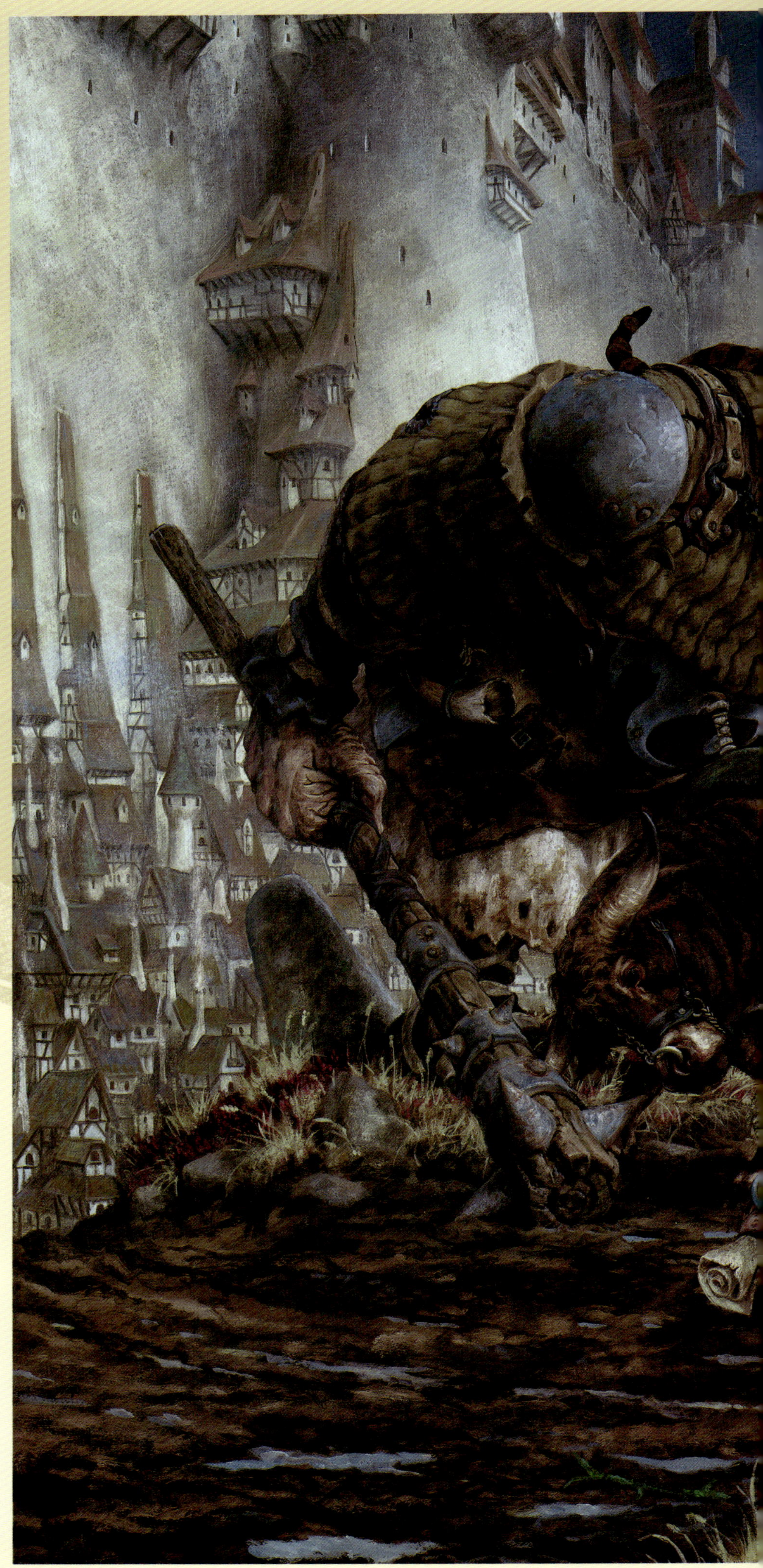

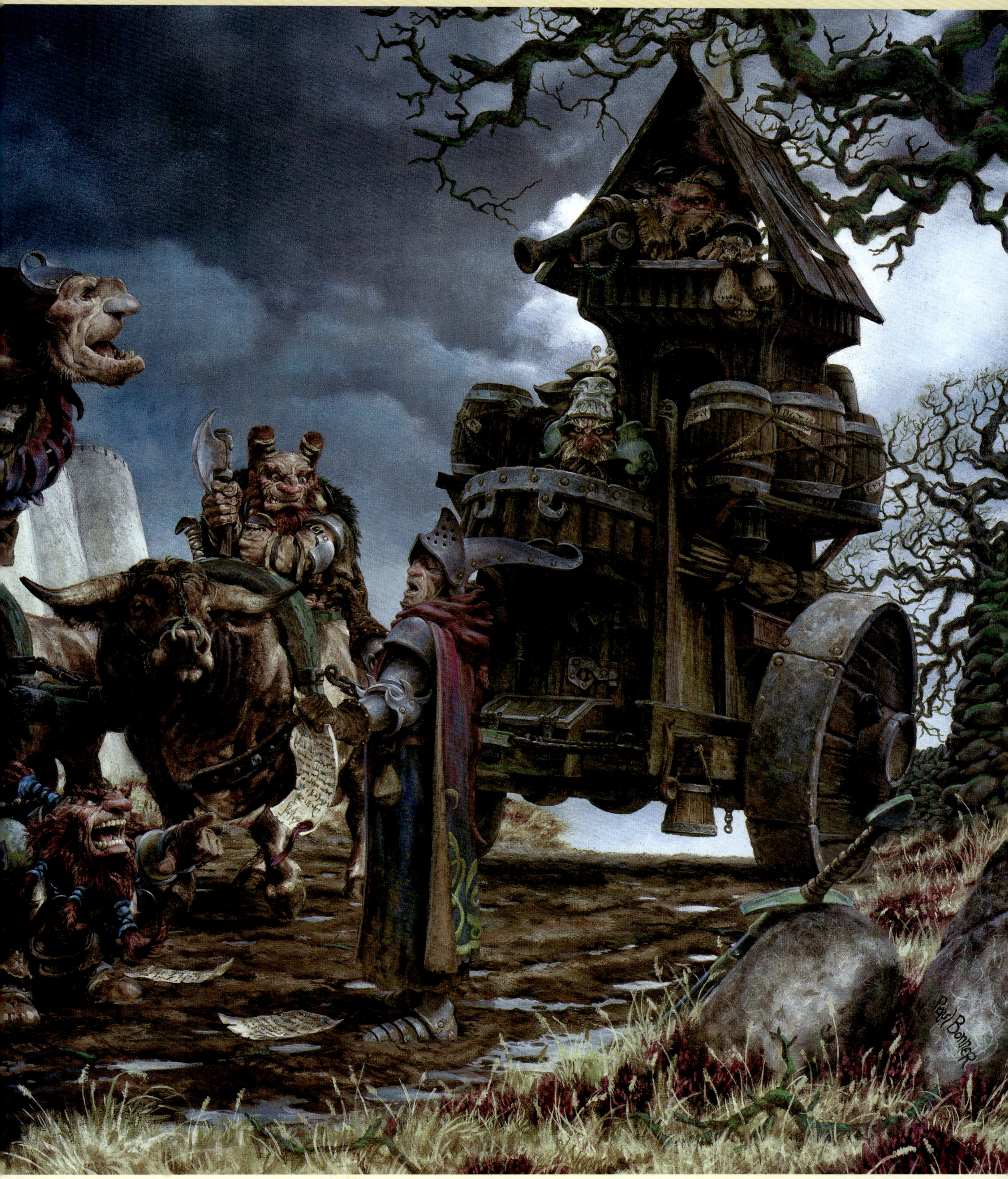
Paul Bonner

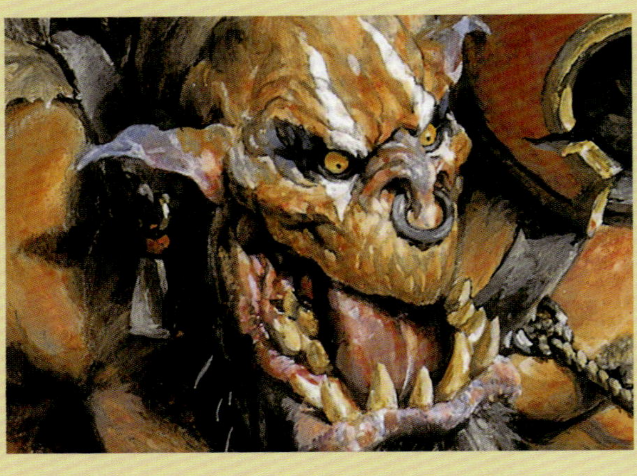

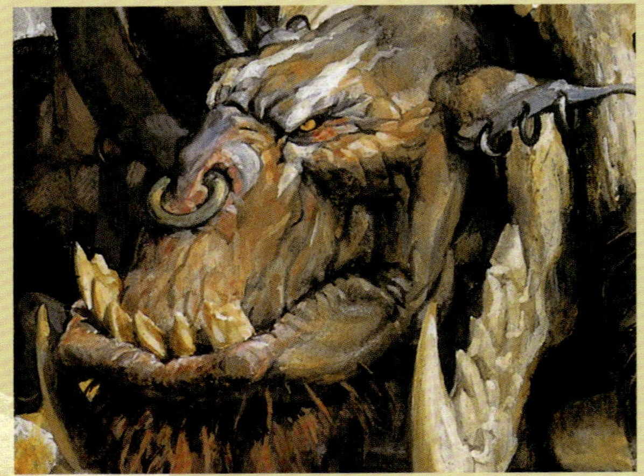

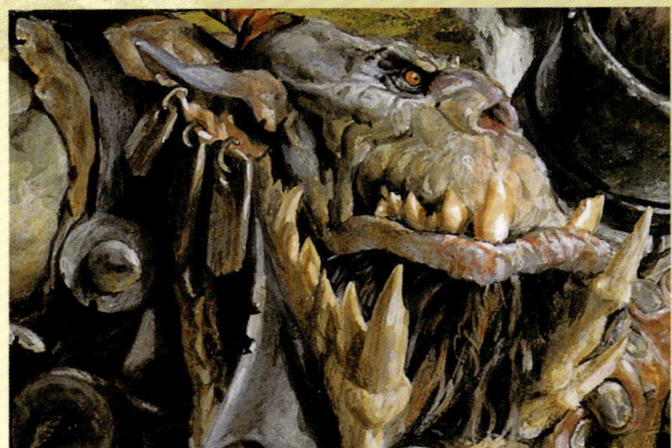

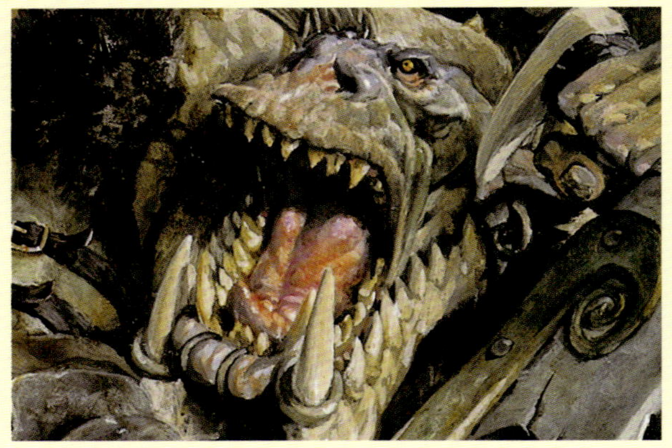

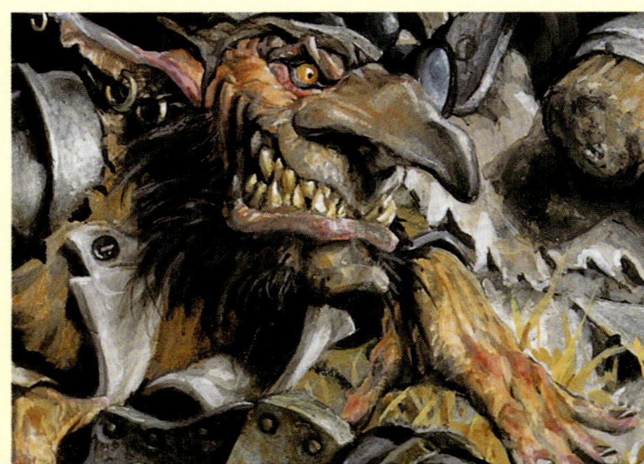

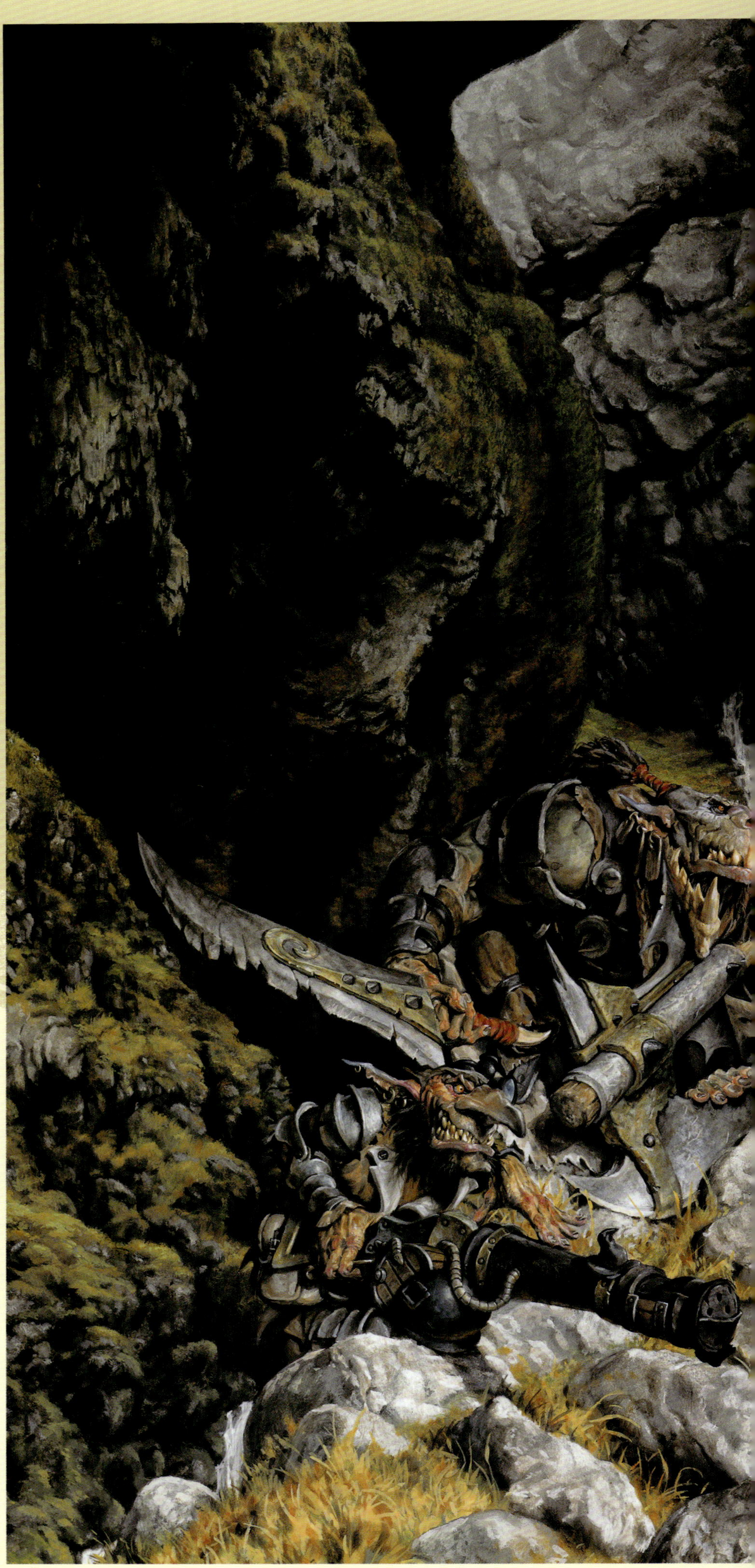

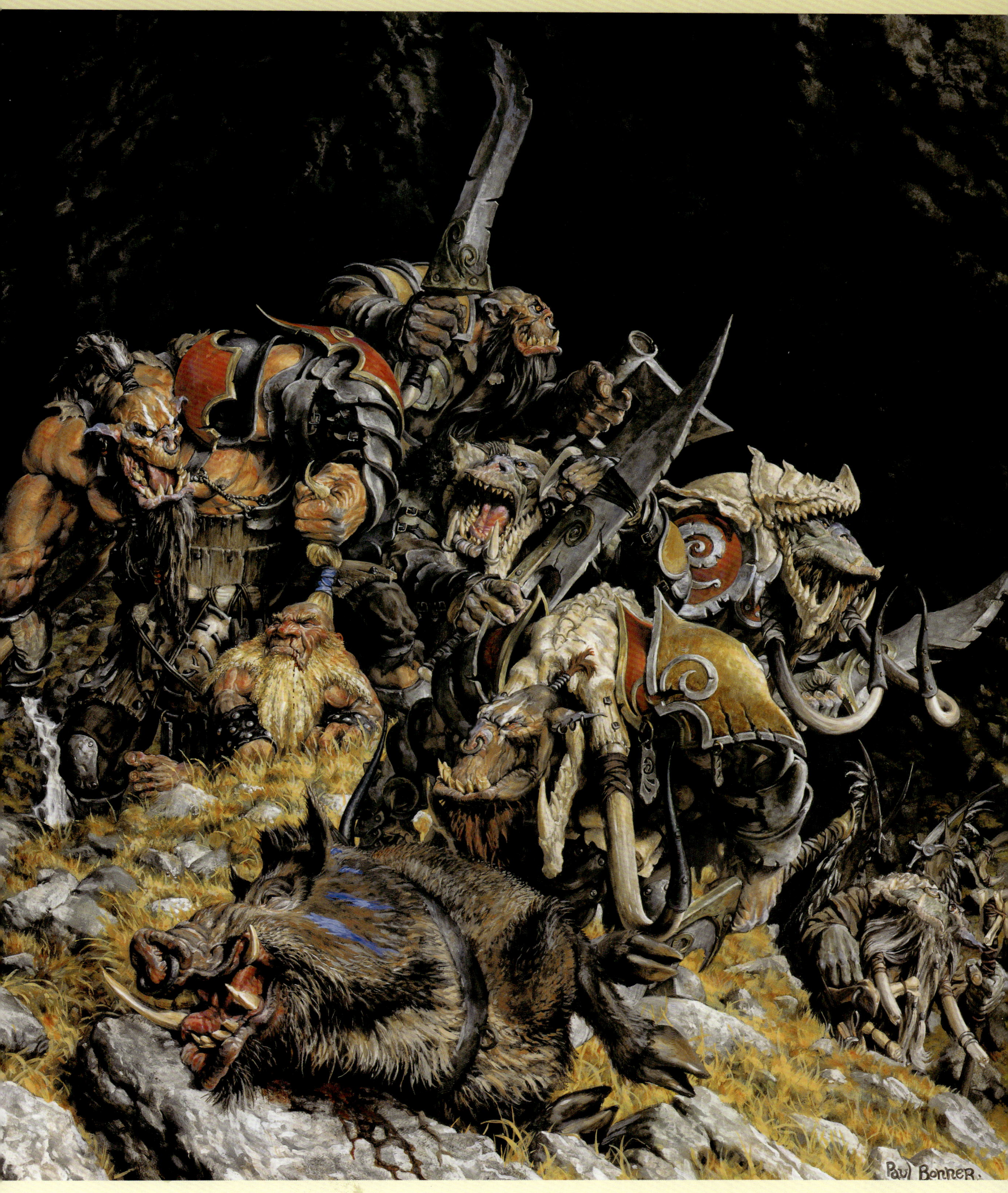
Paul Bonner.

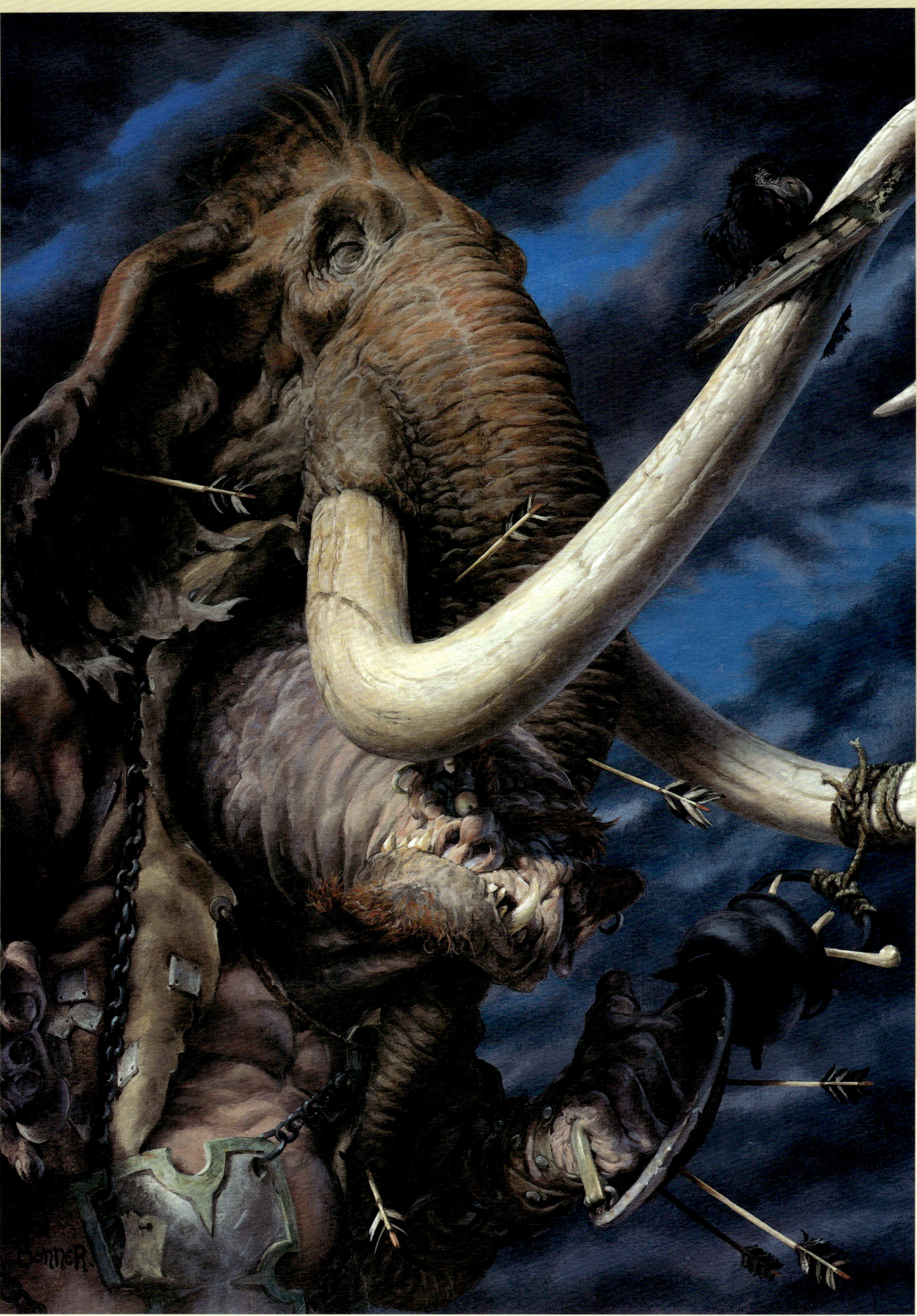
Bonner

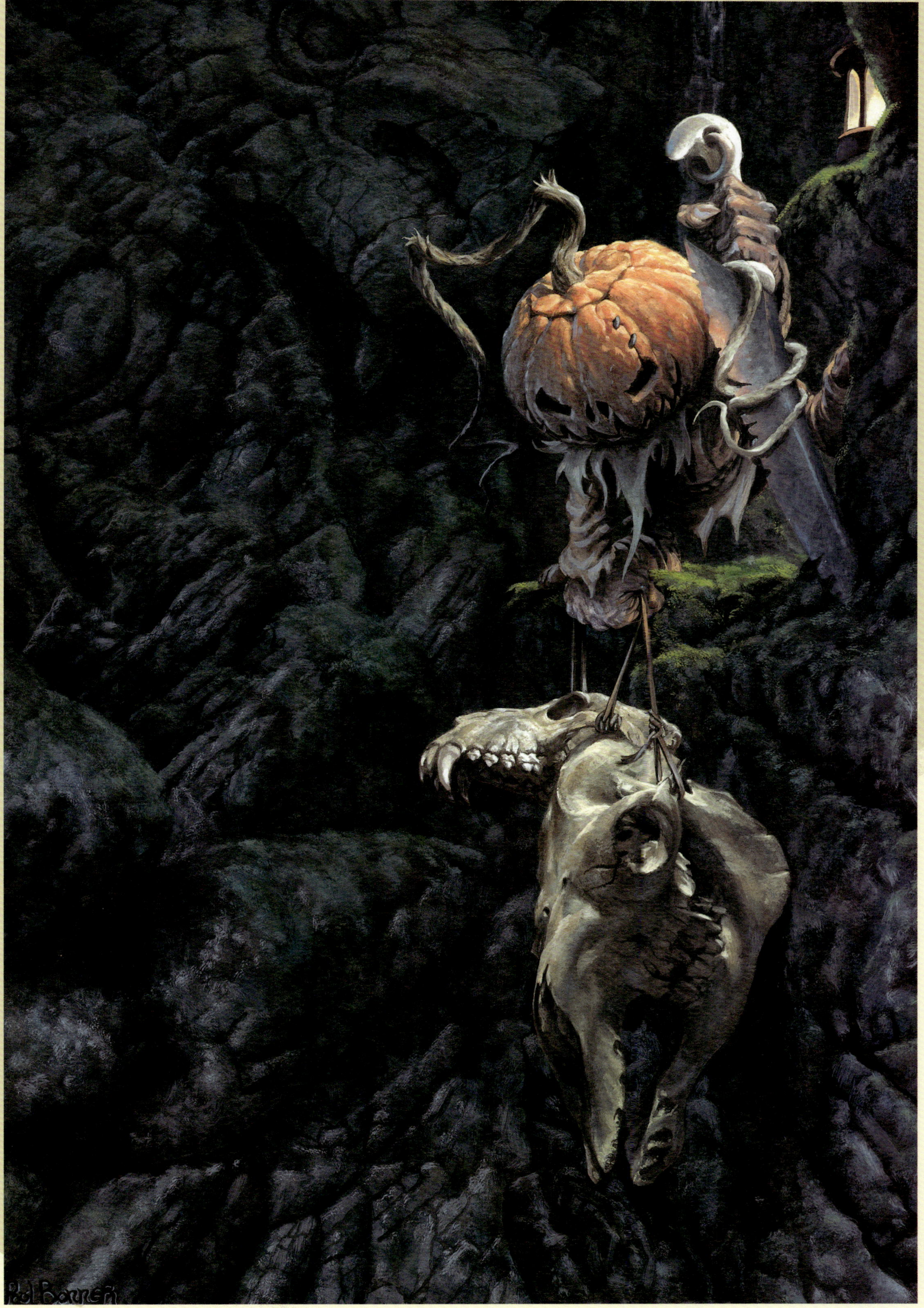

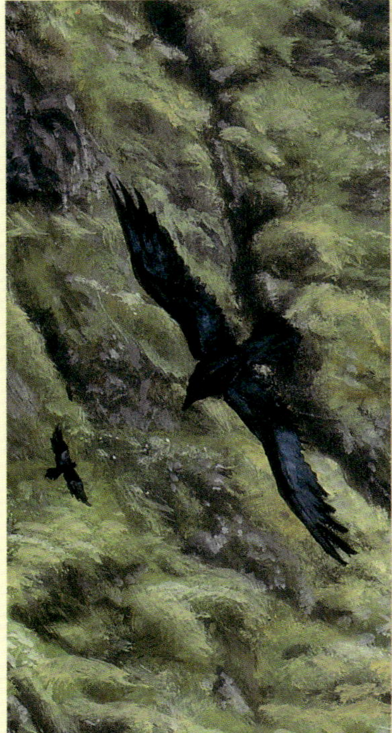

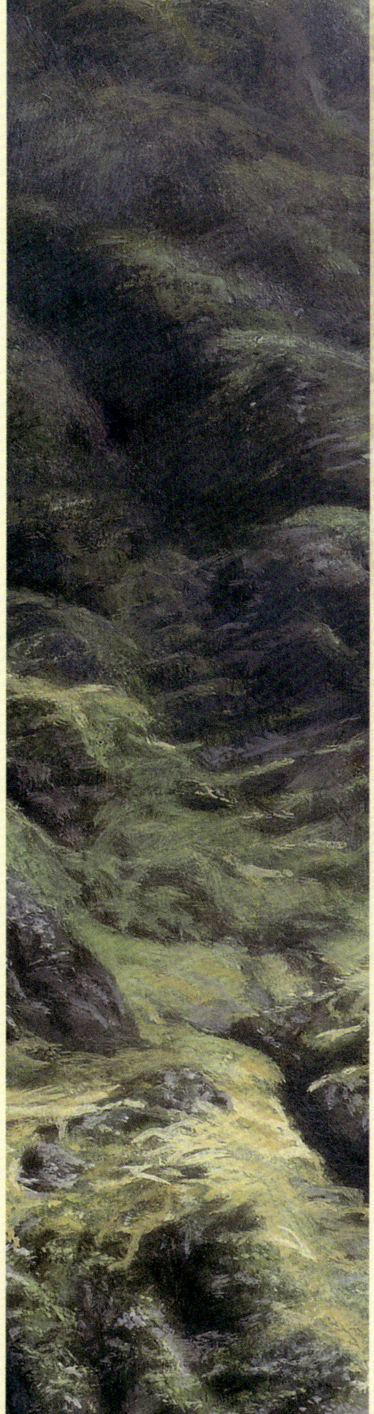

Thanks to Paolo Parente, I was invited to spend a few days in Paris being entranced by the Aladdin's cave that was the Rackham studio. A ramshackle, backstreet building, where around each corner or stairwell I would be captivated by the silent, intense acts of creation that I found taking place there. Being a perfectionist necessitated Jean Bey, one of the company founders, to gather about him a team of only the best artists, sculptors and craftsmen. I've been back many times since (it's tough having customers in Paris), and my reaction has always been the same. A lack of words is replaced with an inner excitement at seeing in others the same passion that ignites and inspires me. They are never content to stand still though and bask in the self-congratulatory knowledge of a job well done. They are always pushing for new levels of creativity. Holding true to an artistic vision by refusing to be limited by the technology available, or by what has already been achieved. Apart from having provided me with some sumptuous, though often, due to their dedication to work, very late, dinners, Jean is the perfect art director... in that he doesn't direct. With just a vague guideline as to the races involved, he leaves me to flounder in my own imagination, trusting me implicitly to come up with the goods. With this amount of faith being put on the table, it doubles the desire to better myself and justify it. Still, it is difficult pulling that one frame out of the movie in my beleaguered imagination, so sometimes a phone call is necessary to try and pin him down to one or two specifics. This invariably draws the response, "Something dramatic. Something atmospheric. Something exciting." That's about as specific as it gets. Some would say that this is not really art directing, but, after the initial panic of figuring out just what exactly I am going to do - the pleasure of being allowed to make my own unhindered decisions kicks in. Jean has always wanted the paintings to be not just a collection of information, illustrating salient points, but thankfully has always placed much more importance on the narrative. Something that draws the viewer in. Like me, he is in the painting watching something unfold.

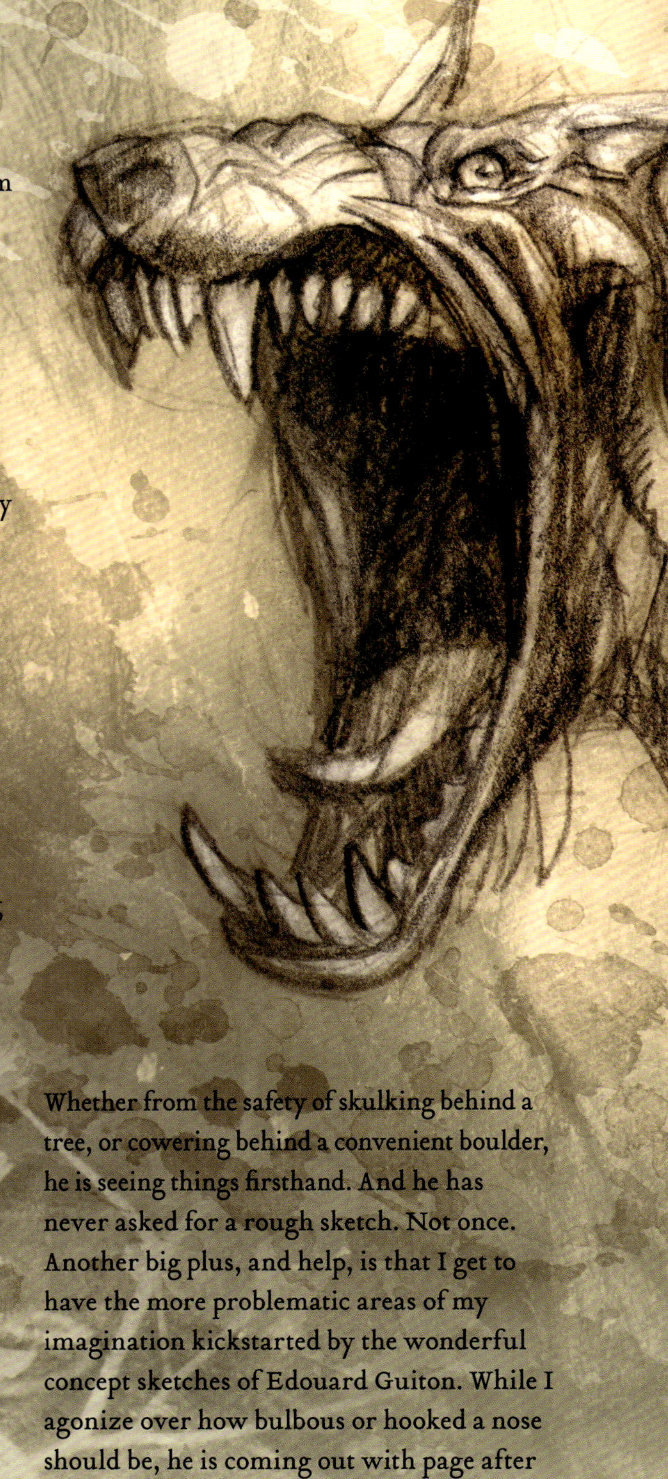

Whether from the safety of skulking behind a tree, or cowering behind a convenient boulder, he is seeing things firsthand. And he has never asked for a rough sketch. Not once. Another big plus, and help, is that I get to have the more problematic areas of my imagination kickstarted by the wonderful concept sketches of Edouard Guiton. While I agonize over how bulbous or hooked a nose should be, he is coming out with page after page of astounding creations. Beings with faces that suggest the bastard offspring of Walt Disney and Pieter Bruegel, kitted out with accoutrements and apparel that echo hints of everything from gothic galleons in full sail, to teetering piles of discarded pots and pans. A fearsome array of lethal yet escethically pleasing weaponry suggest an equally fearsome array of foes. A veritable treasure chest of ideas, with an open invitation for me to plunder. Wonderful stuff, that often provides me with a perfect beginning for my own questing. So, a talented, committed, and hospitable bunch, whose attitude and energy make working with them a pleasure.

Paul Bonner

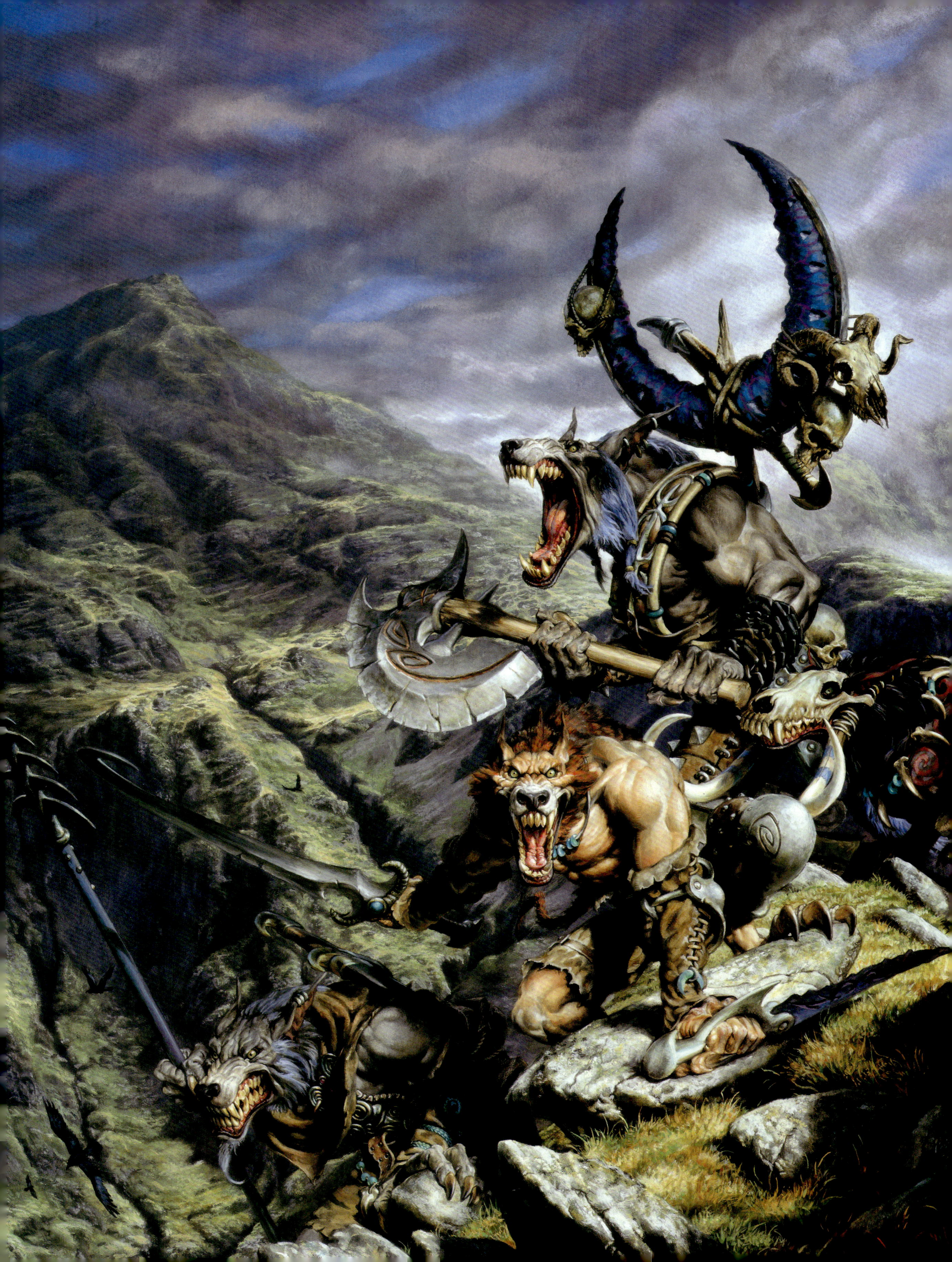

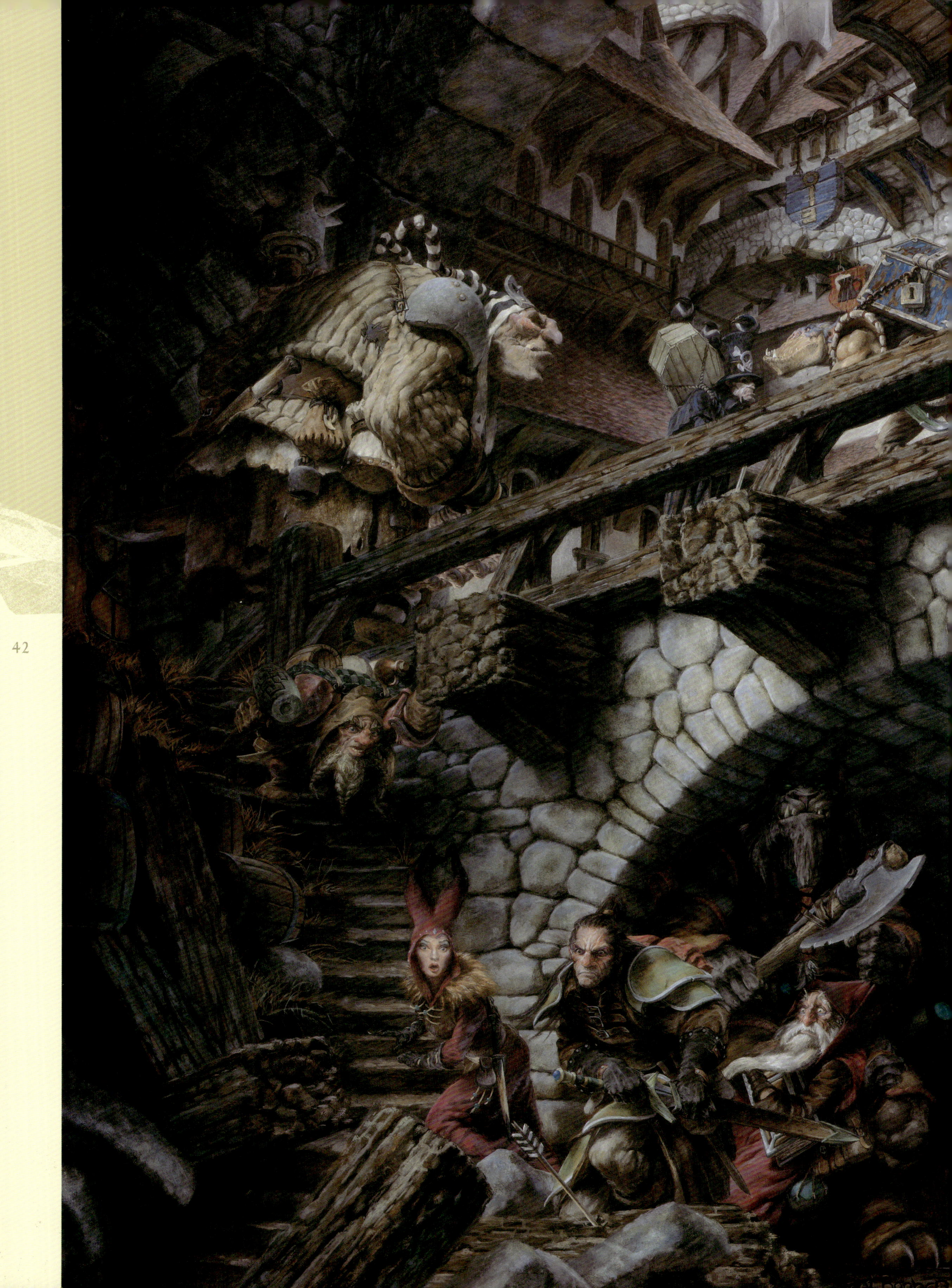

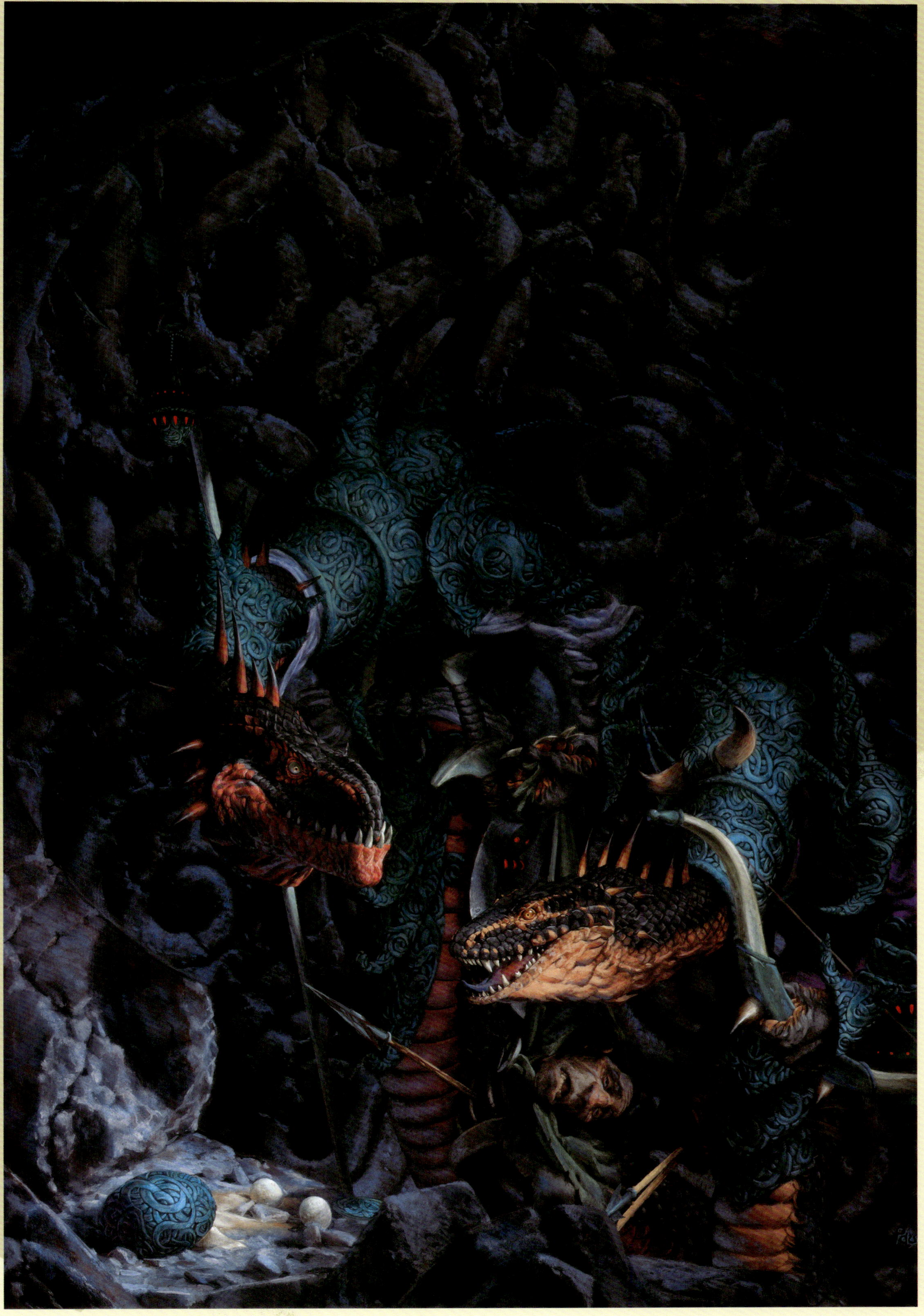

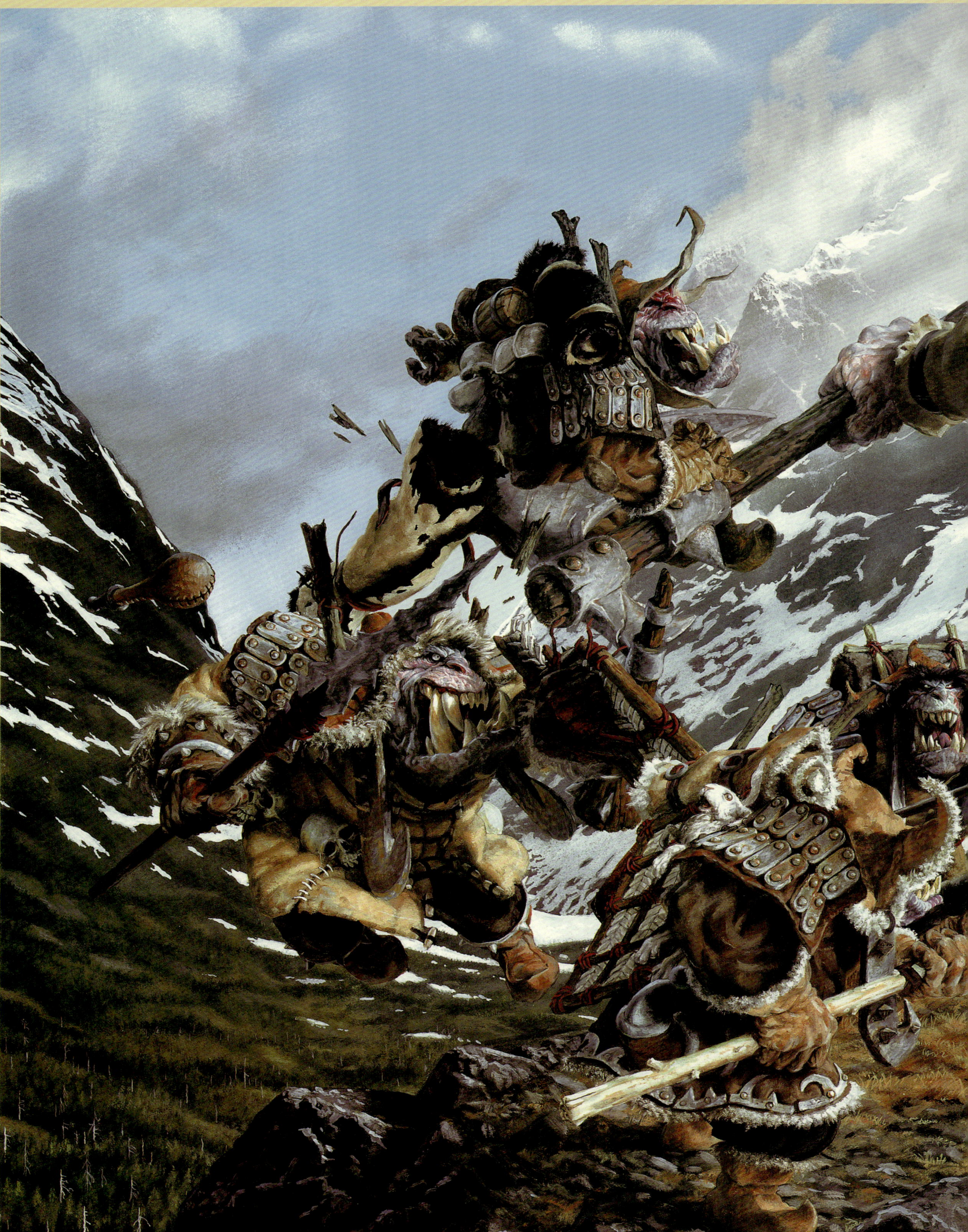

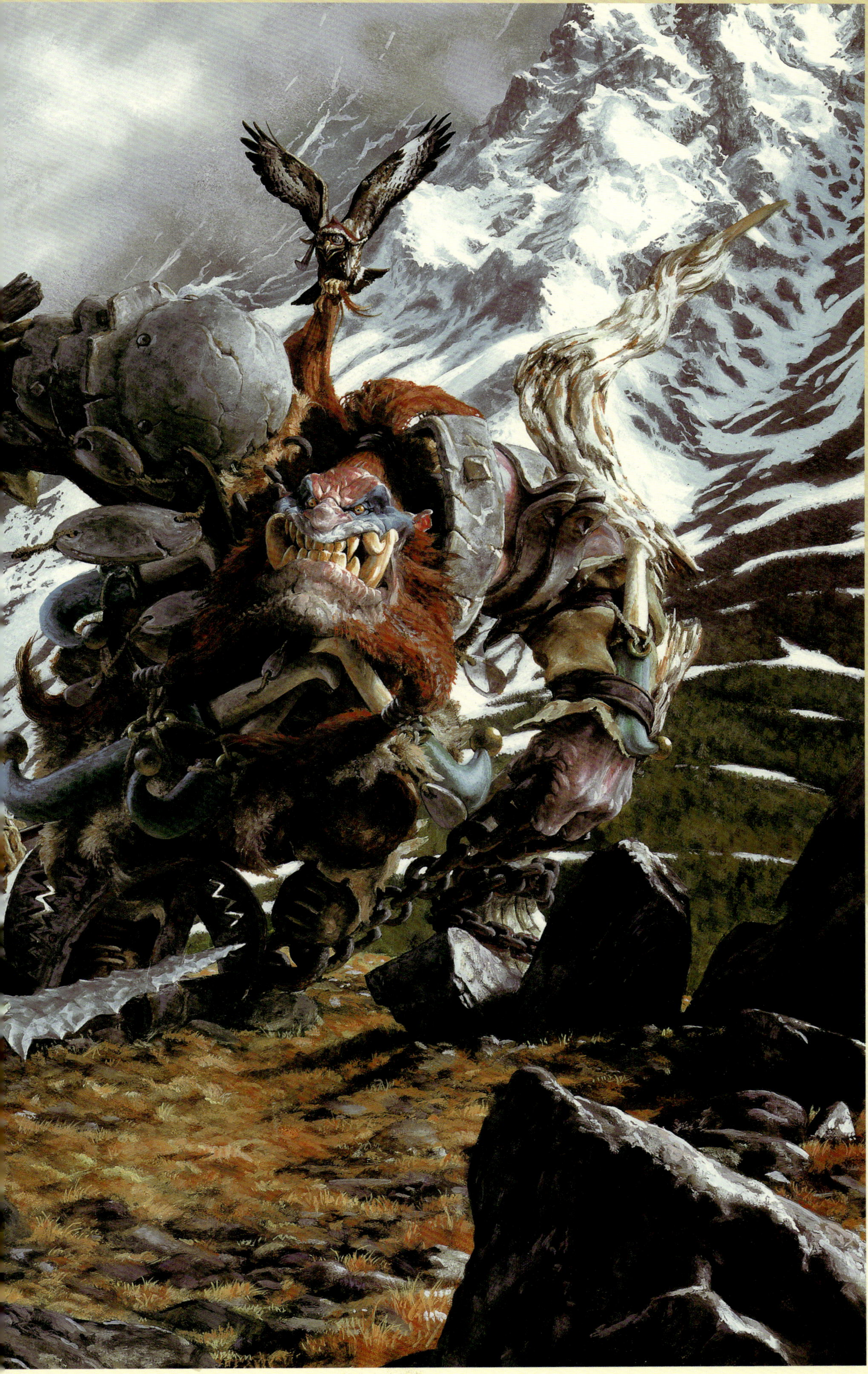

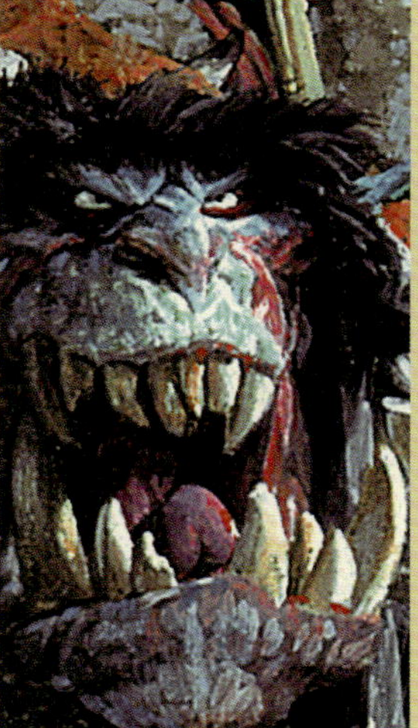

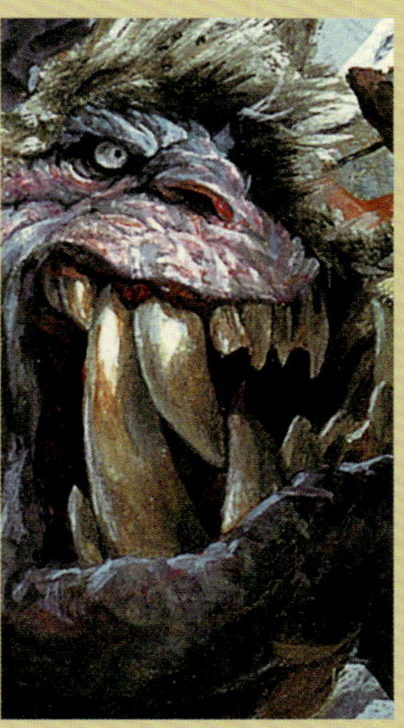

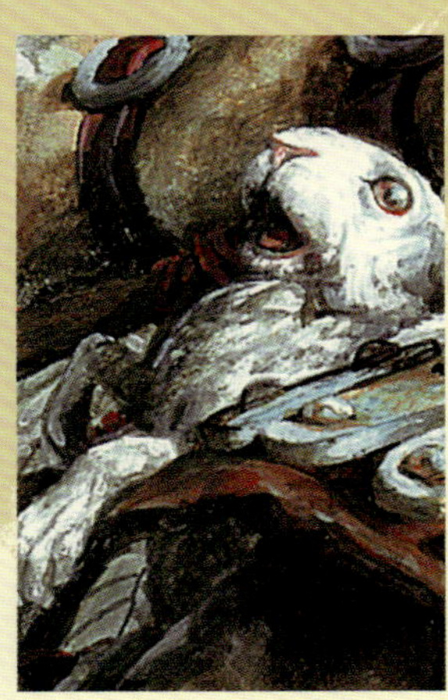

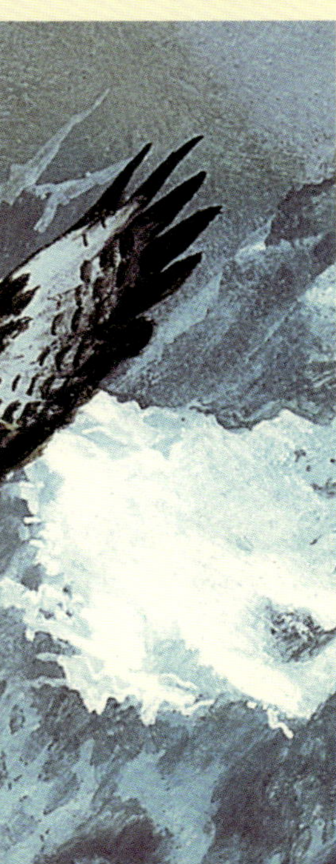

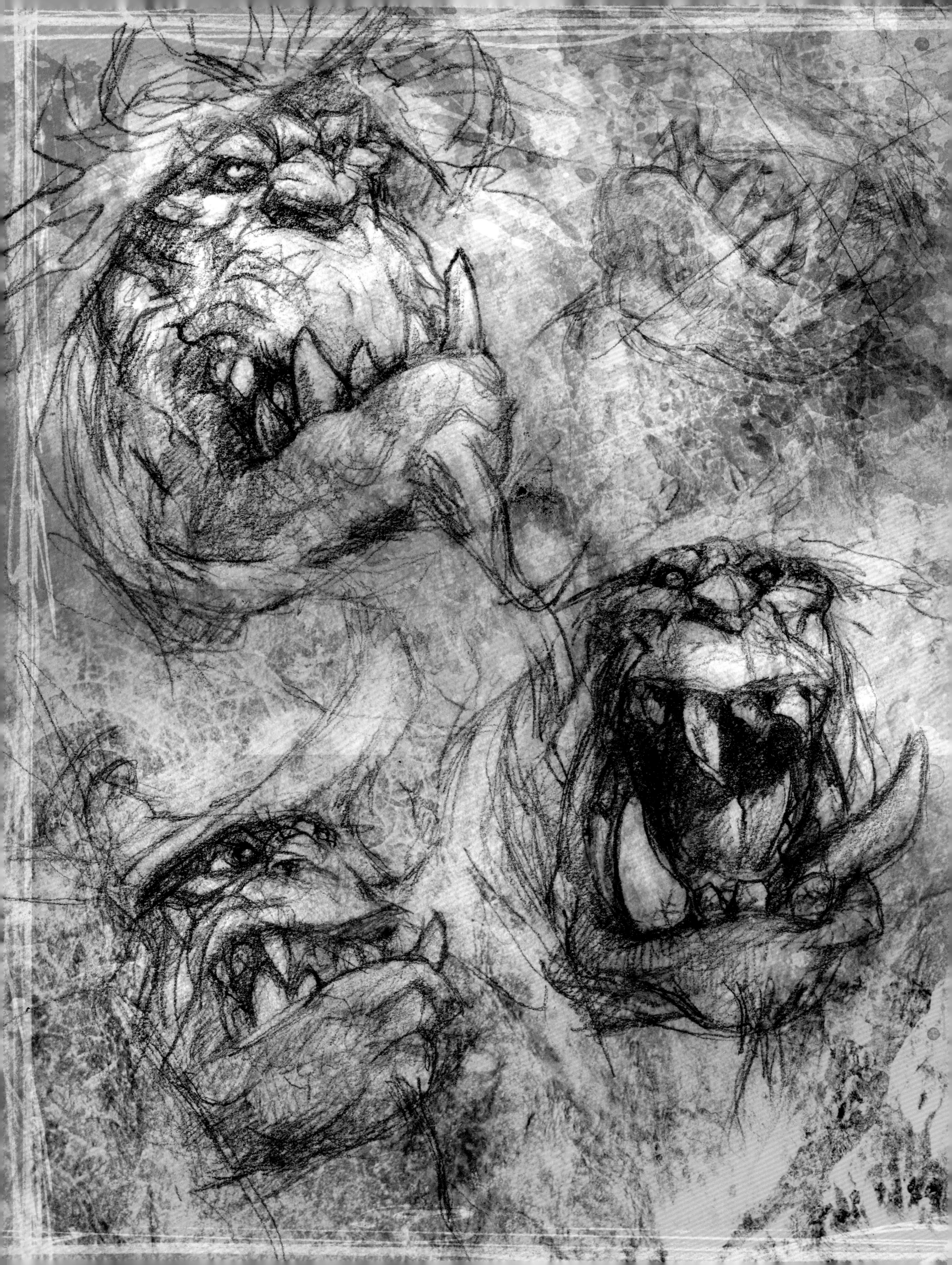

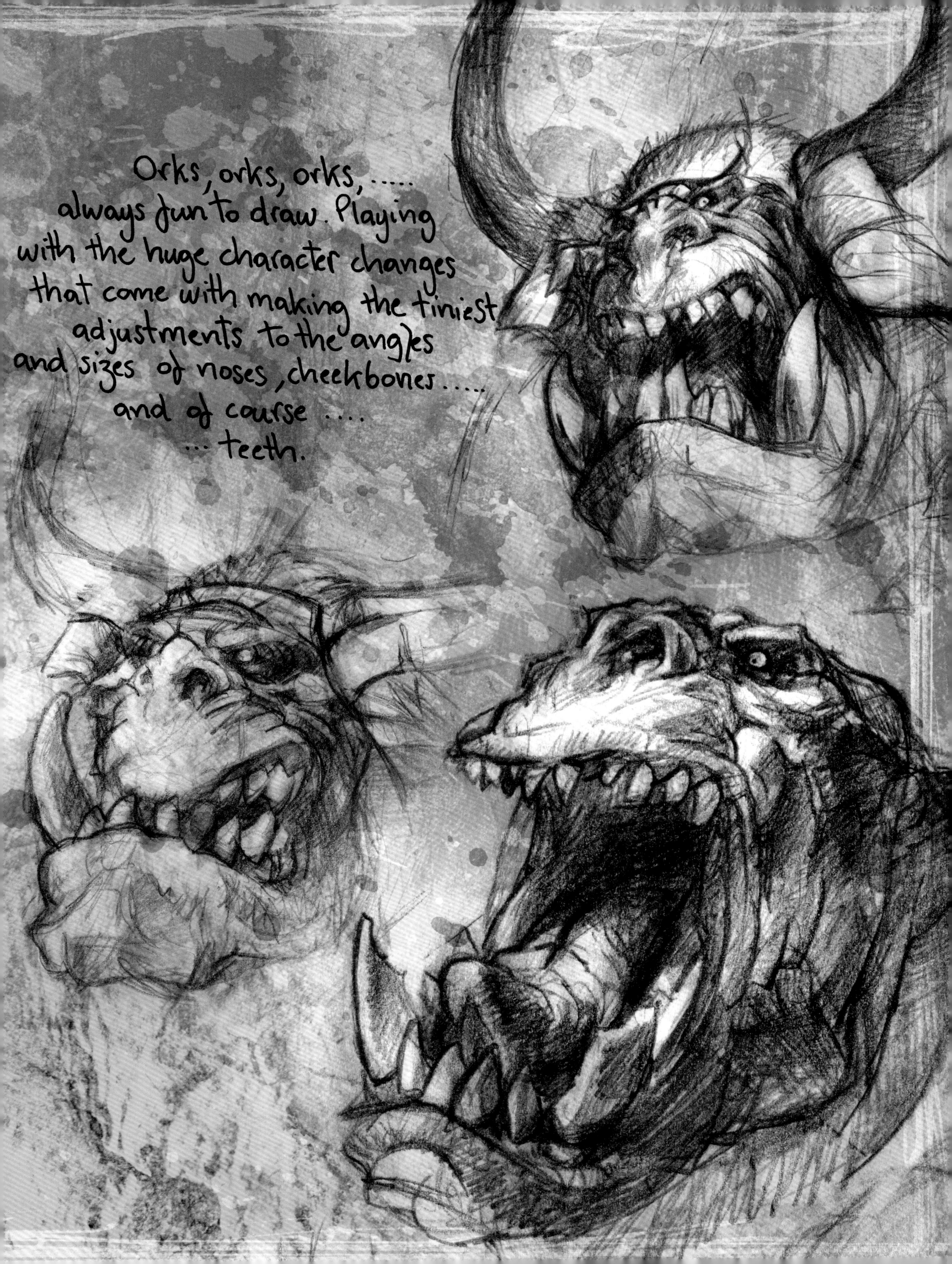
Orks, orks, orks, ...
always fun to draw. Playing
with the huge character changes
that come with making the tiniest
adjustments to the angles
and sizes of noses, cheekbones.....
and of course ....
... teeth.

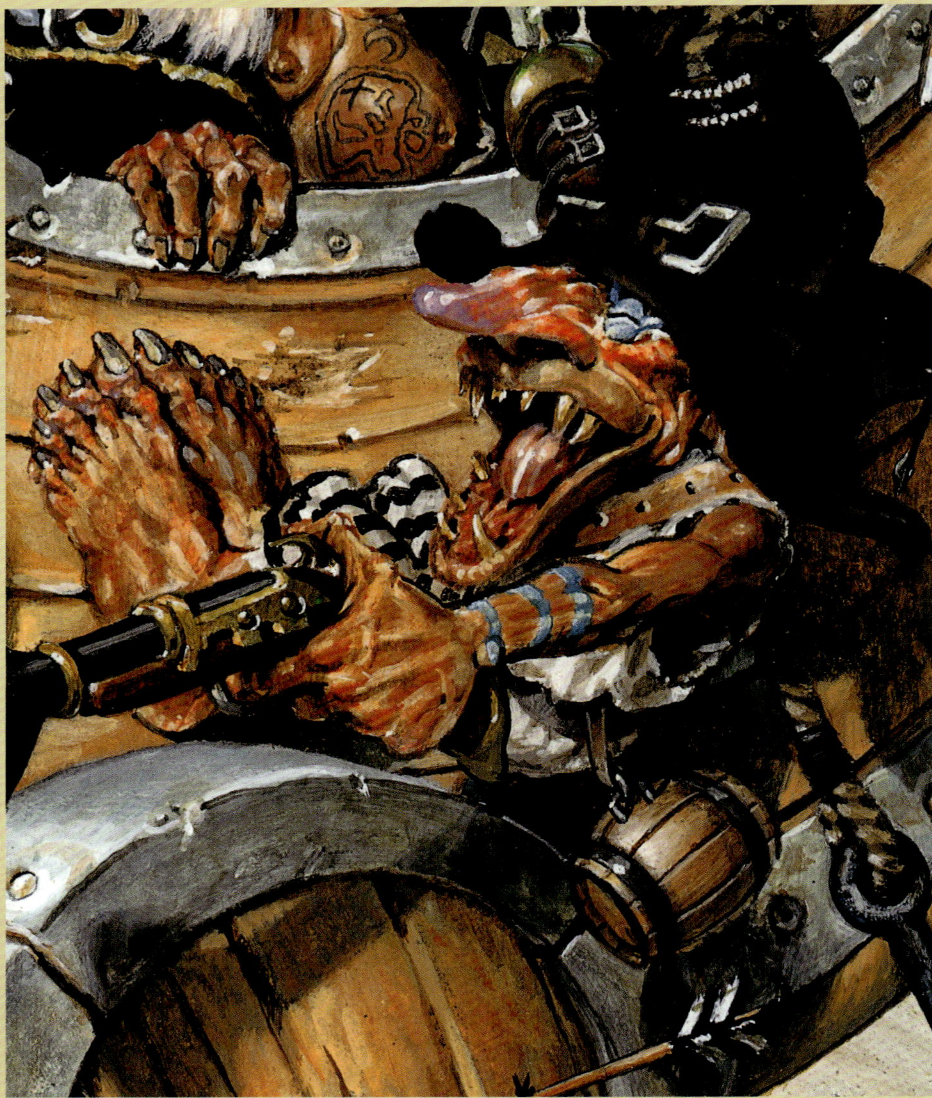

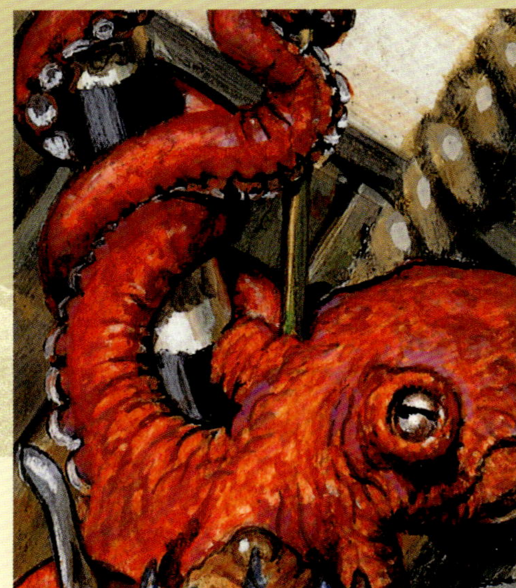

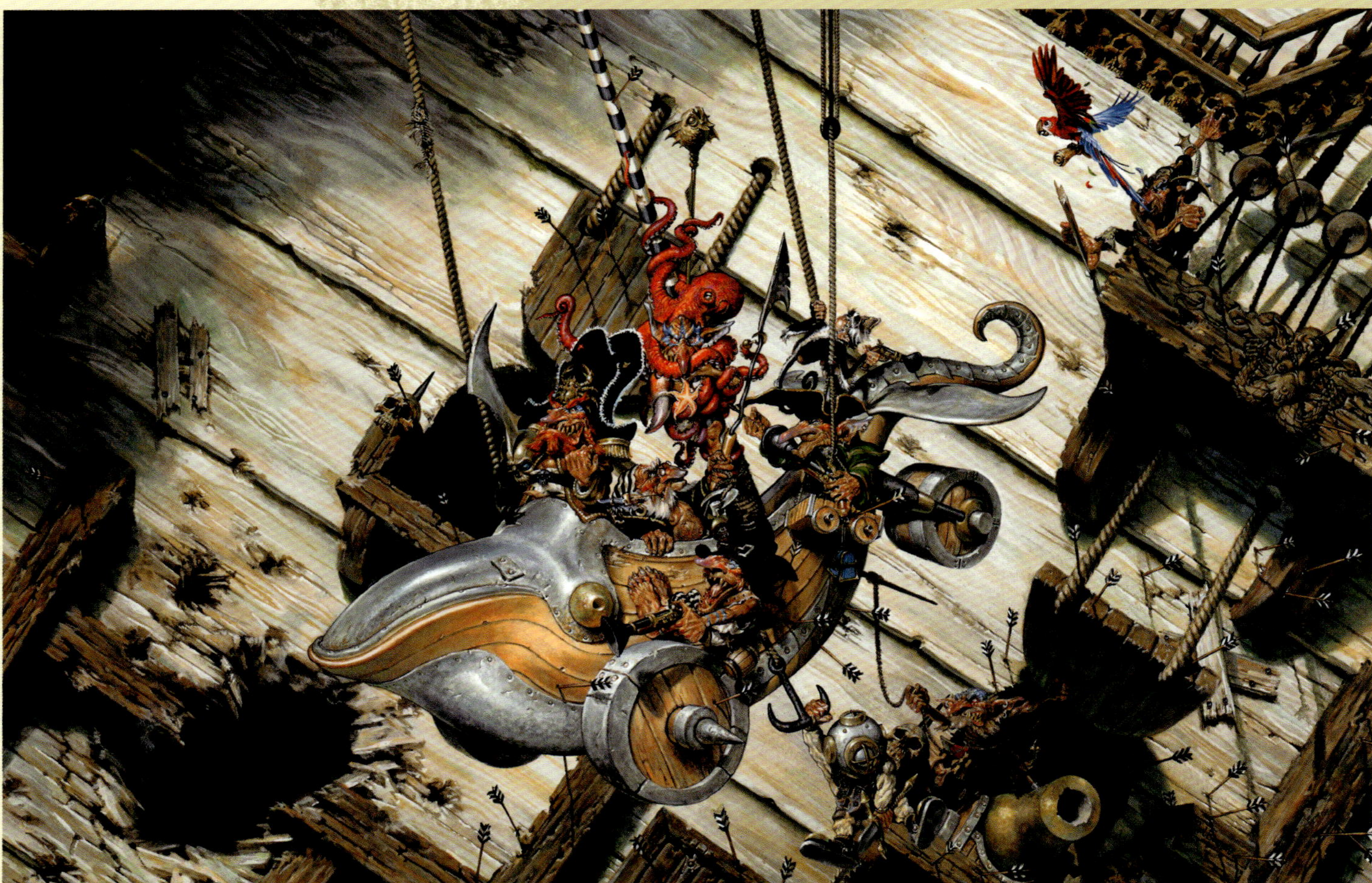

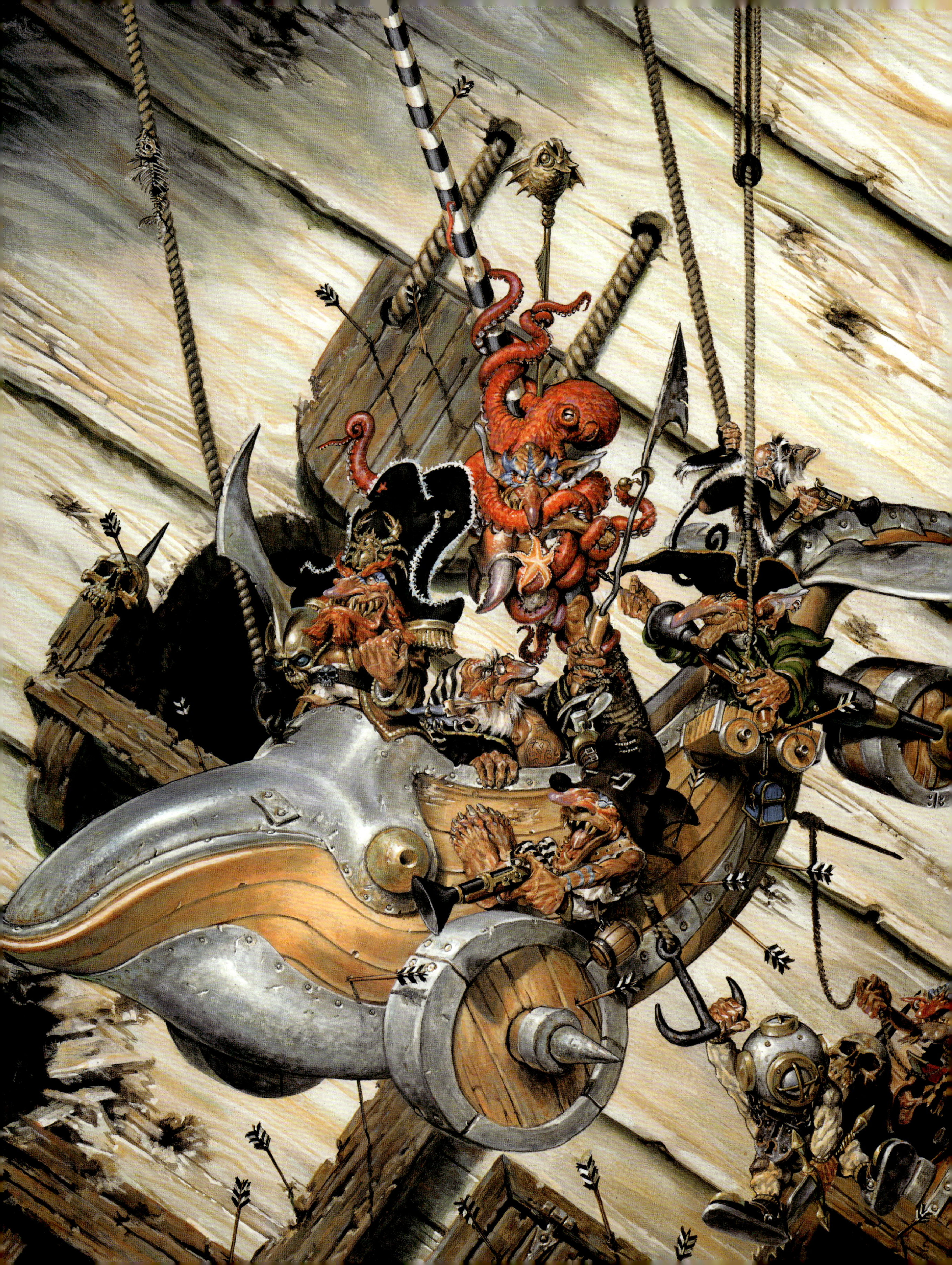

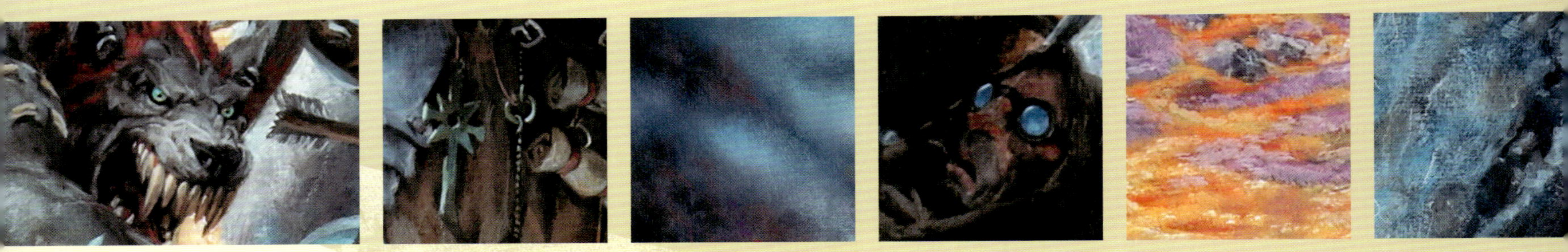

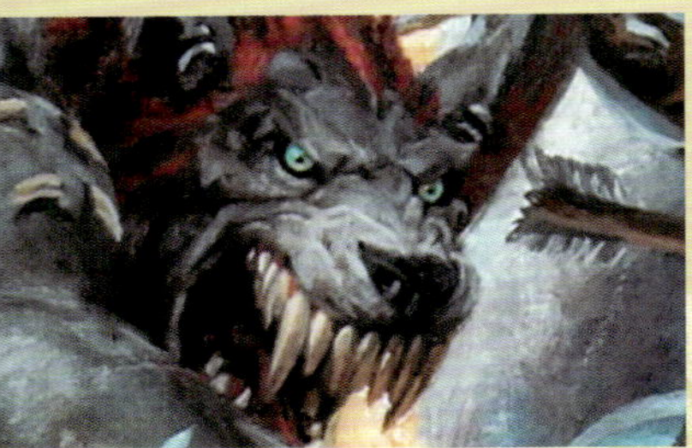
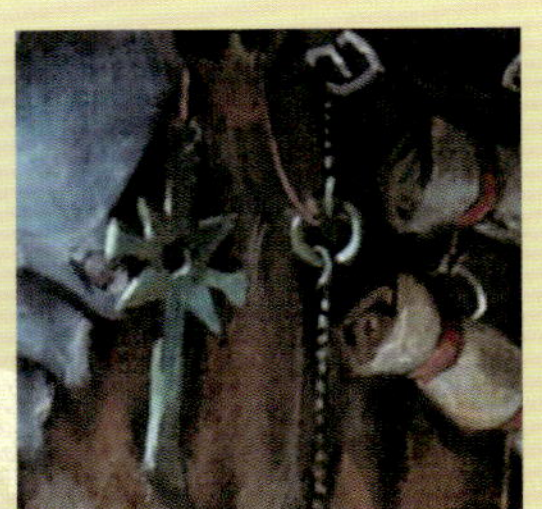

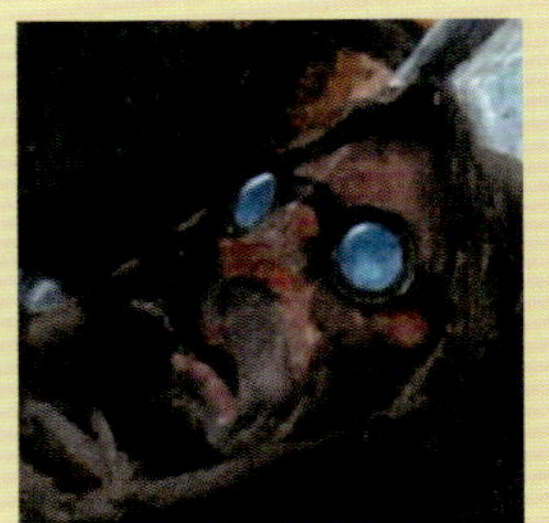
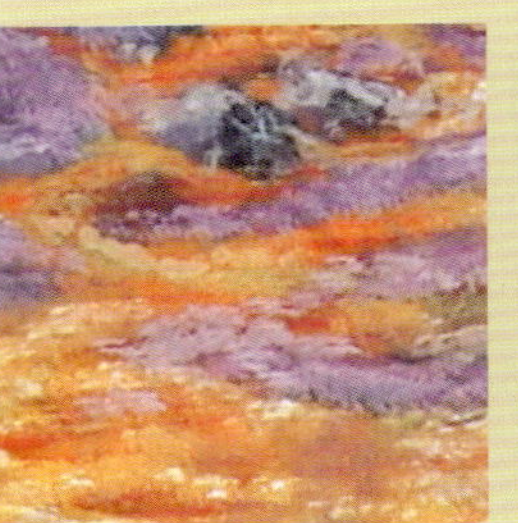
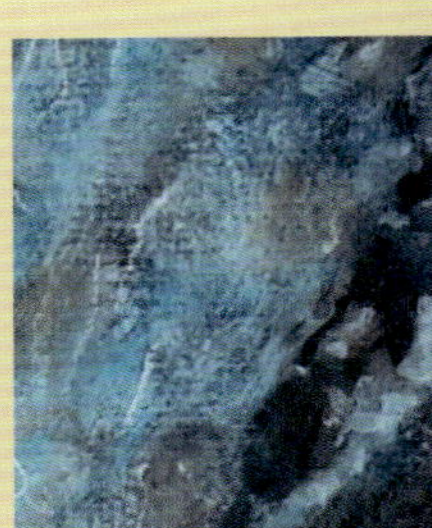

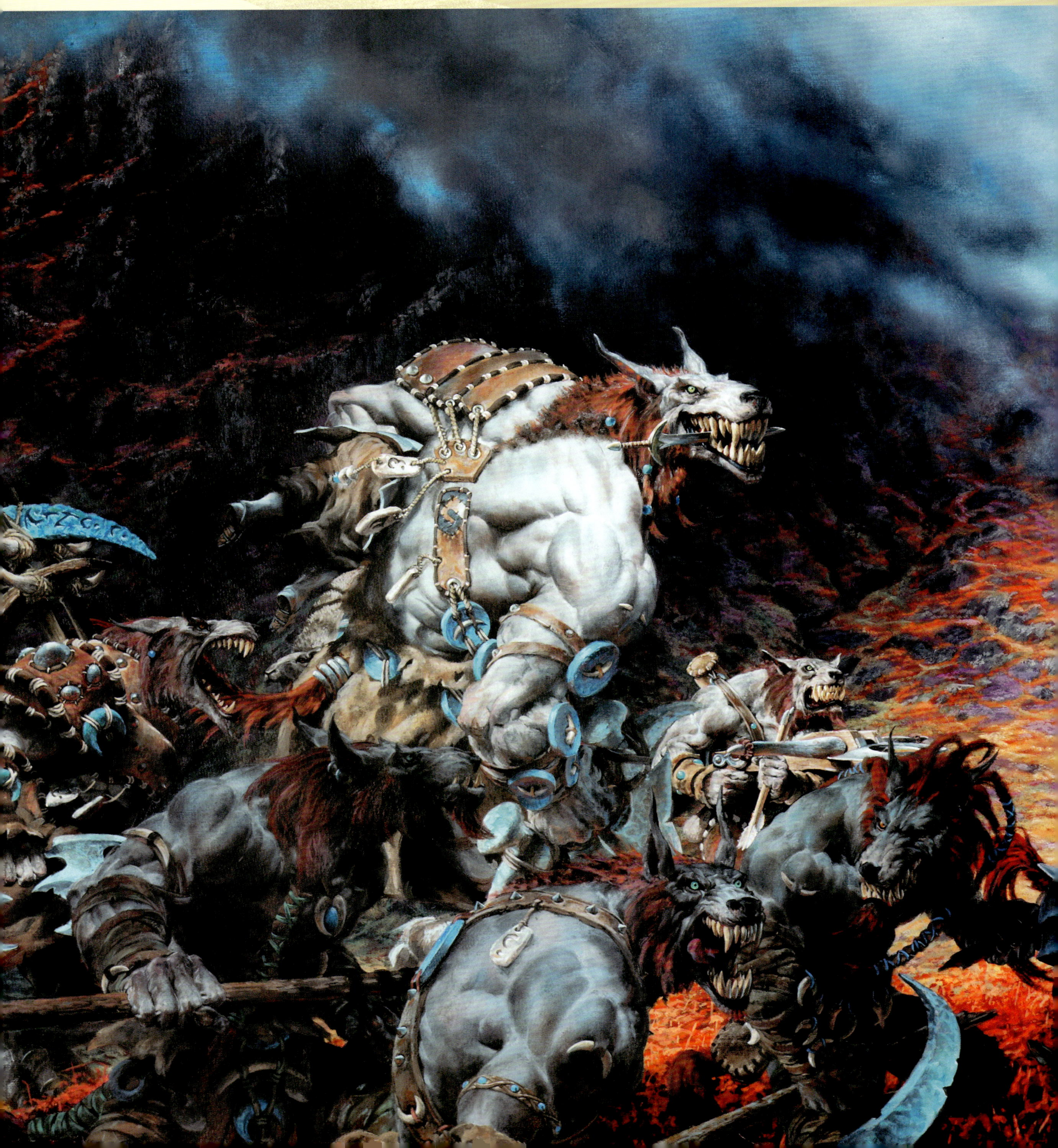

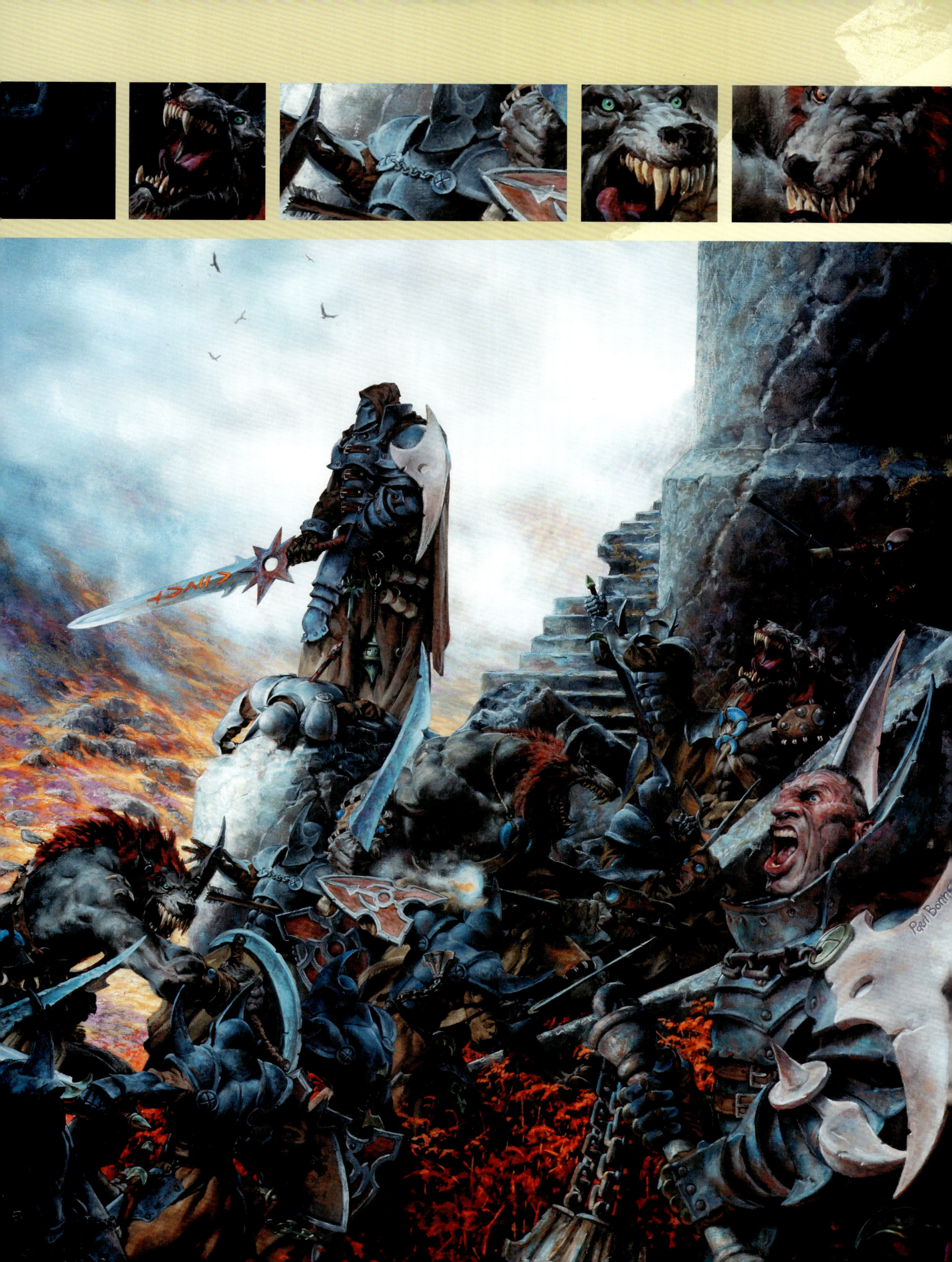

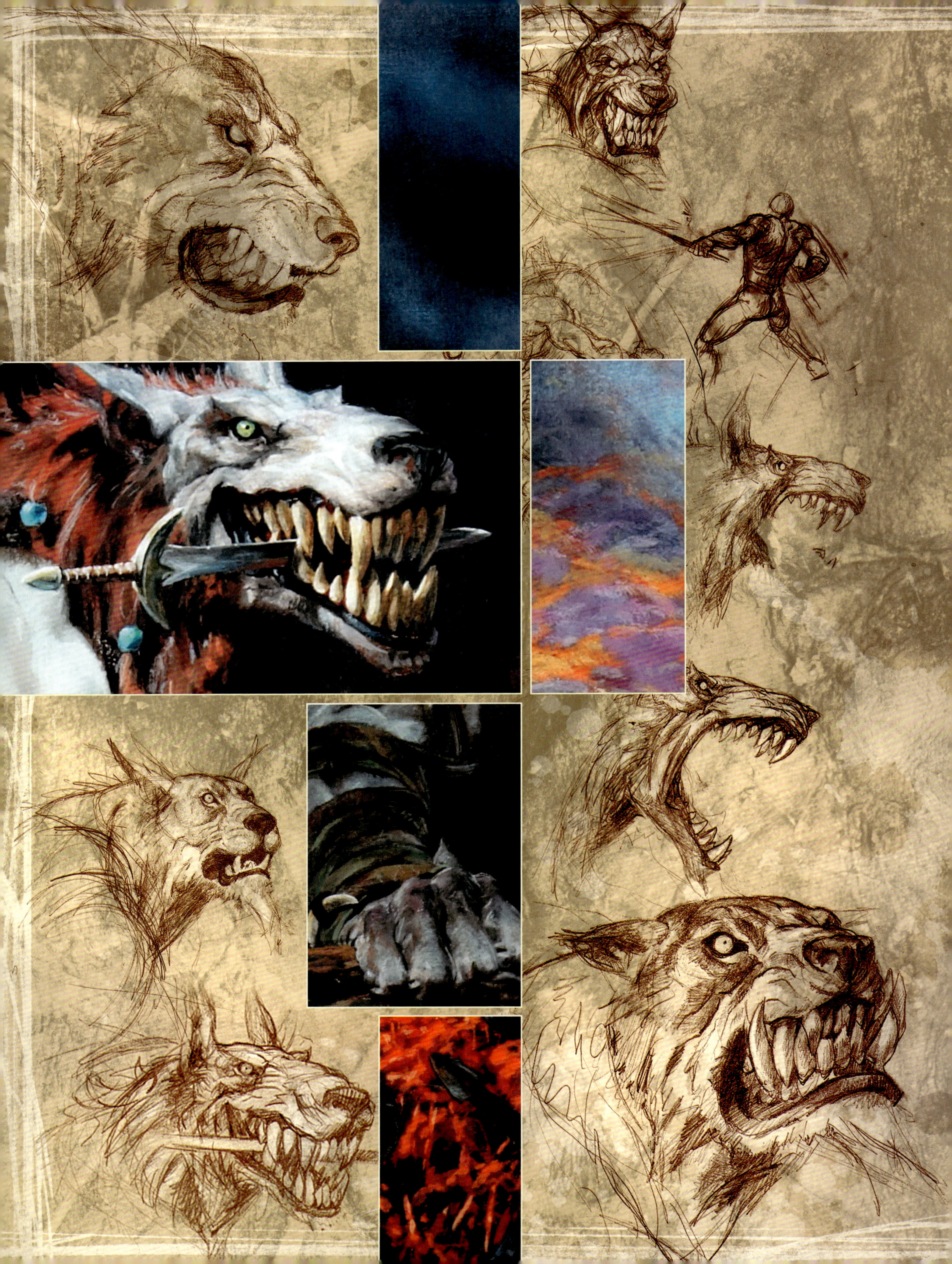

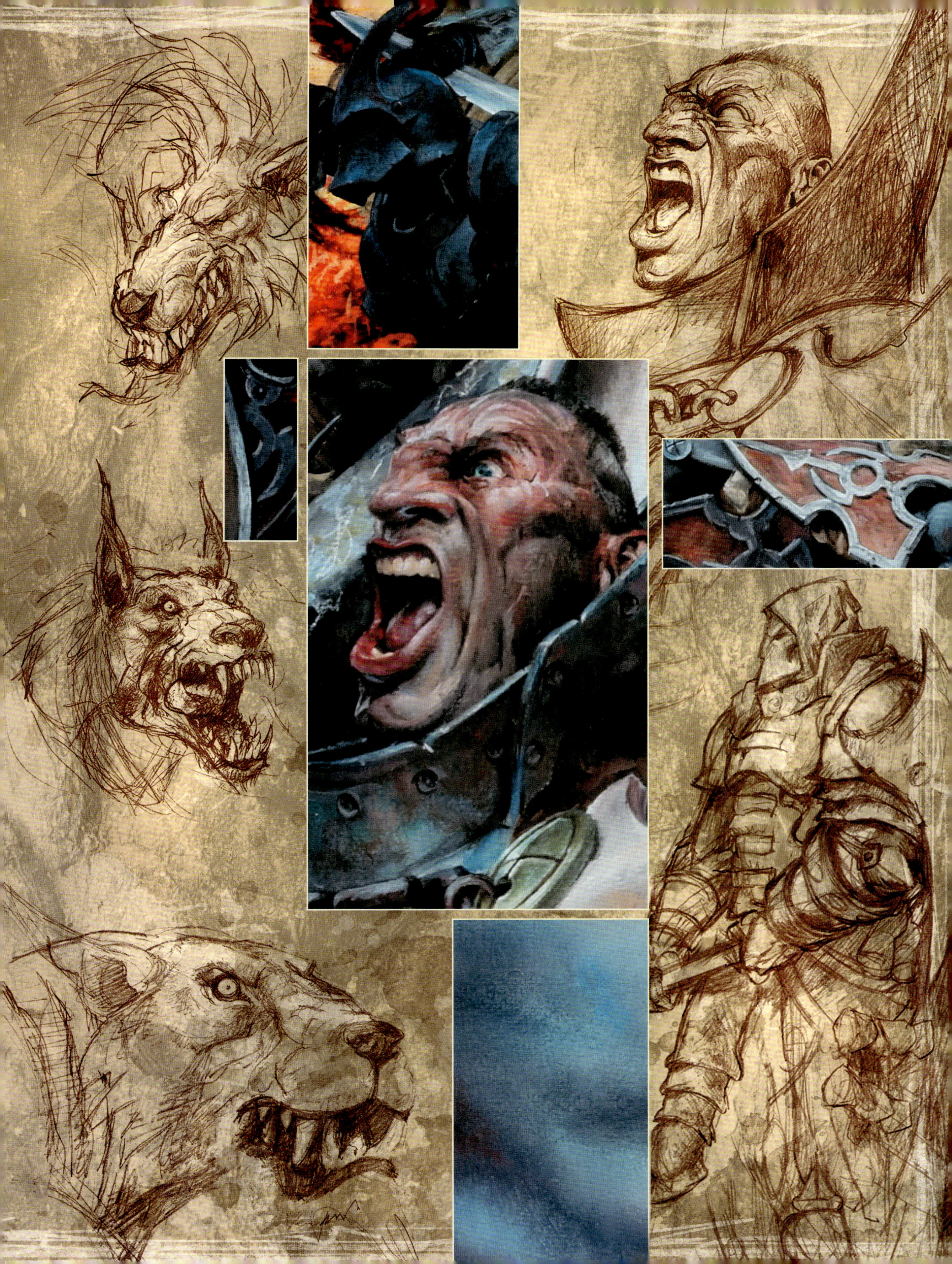

Mutant

I first heard about Paul and his work from a co-worker named Bob Watts. Bob had previously been with Games Workshop and one day when we met he started to talk enthusiastically about this artist named Paul Bonner who like himself had a previous career at Workshop. I heard about this guy who was a genius but had only really done black and white stuff and then had moved to Copenhagen because he loved John Bauer and Scandinavia. I looked at some of the drawings he had done, and then finally Bob said that Paul had done some color pieces in his spare time and that one of the paintings had ended up on the back of *White Dwarf* magazine. This was a dramatic piece with a bunch of space orcs looking really cool. The artwork eventually ended up on a book called *Freebooters*, but what really struck me was that there was a huge portion of humor and personality in the characters and you just loved them.

At this time, which was the beginning of the nineties, the company I was working at, Target Games, was developing a science-fiction universe called Mutant Chronicles and we were looking for talent that would take our ideas and texts into something with a very clear visual style. It felt a little like fate, we looking for a very distinct artist, Paul obviously looking to do cover pieces, and both of us in Scandinavia, so we went forward and the proper contacts were made. The first thing we did together was a piece that really only was used in Sweden and it was the embryo of what really became Mutant Chronicles. The premises of the universe were a little all over the place if you just looked at it – it was military sci-fi mixed with retro design "Batman style" enviroments and a good portion of demonic "Clive Barker-like" enemies. Yet a few of us knew that the vision would work if someone could tie it together, and I sent off a huge pack of drawings and sketches, mostly my own work that was crude and, at best, showed a direction rather than style.

When the first painting was about to arrive it was almost Christmas for us, and I remember being a little sceptical when I saw the size of the package that was maybe slightly bigger that A4 (bear in mind that this was a time when digital images and scanning were only available to a very limited number of people in the world). And, looking back, this first picture was probably the only one we had to rework – the image is that of two heroes standing on a pile of zombie mutants, blasting away in all directions in front of a blood red sky, and in the clouds above a demonic commander's face appears, looking generally just evil. However, after one turn of retouching it turned out great. But the next job was probably a punishment for Paul, because it was a series of standalone figures from the universe, some heroes, some grunts and some villains, in color on a plain white background, instead of the bombastic, detailed coverpieces with dinosaur-like creatures that I suspect Paul really wanted to do.

From a universe-building perspective the character work was some of the most important, because I think it gave Paul time to get into the world and make it more his own. We gradually saw all of these guys coming to life, and even though Paul was very truthful to the original concepts, he added little things, changed color schemes into really bold and intricate patterns, and sometimes he simply misunderstood some of the rough details on the uniforms and gadgets with a fantastic and unique result. When Paul did the big piece for the first roleplaying game I think I went mad and became greedy because I envisioned a wraparound cover that would be like an 80s movie poster, basically showing all the elements involved in the universe. It ended up in an art direction sketch, with a ton of references for what should go where, featuring gothic cities, shady businessmen, demons, techno highlanders and a thousand other things, and Paul just went right at it, whereas most people would have argued for simplifying it or making some compromise, if for no other reason than it would be visually stronger if it was plainer. The end result was a turning point for me, because I realized that Paul could do virtually anything, and he would constantly add things in the background, in the characters' expressions and in the overall atmosphere, that made him constantly exceed our expectations. The artwork that Paul produced for us became in many ways more important than the written material because it inspired the writers, it gave ideas for spinoffs and it created unique characters that you liked and were fascinated by. In the end, the work of Paul Bonner not only became bigger in size but also the very spirit of Mutant Chronicles, and several times when we presented the universe it was praised largely because of the artwork. I had the privilege to work with Paul for several years and on a large number of paintings focusing on the Mutant Chronicles, but on one occasion I asked him to do a cover for a game based on Swedish history – again a very detailed job with ships, horses and historically accurate references to faces and designs. Again it turned out way better than my wildest dreams, and if anyone at this stage had thought of Paul Bonner as merely a talented genre artist they were obviously mistaken. Paul Bonner is one of the most talented artists today, period.

I'm really proud to have been involved in Paul's work for Mutant Chronicles and, combined with him being one of the most likeable and gentle people in the world, it's also a very pleasant memory.

Nils Gulliksson

Creative Director 1985 – 1999 Target Games AB

Chronicles

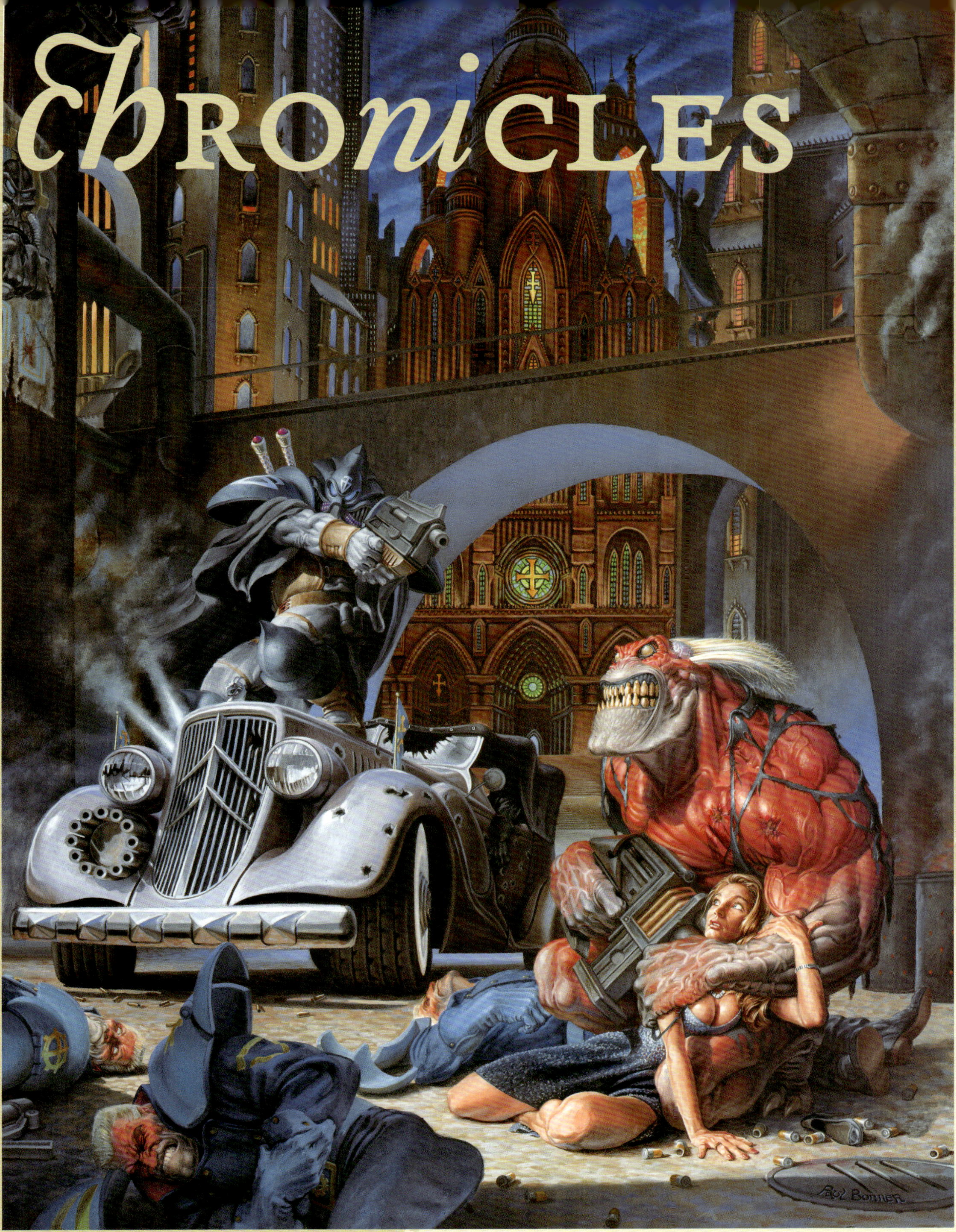

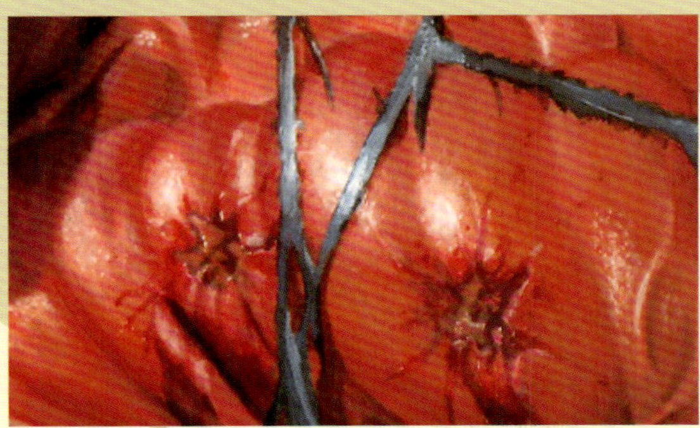

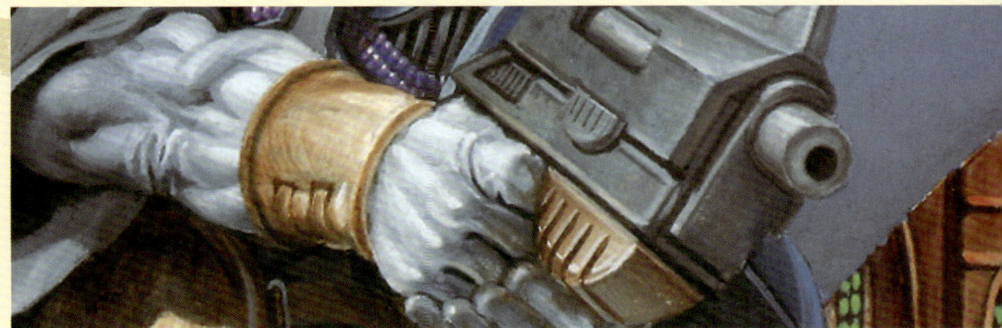

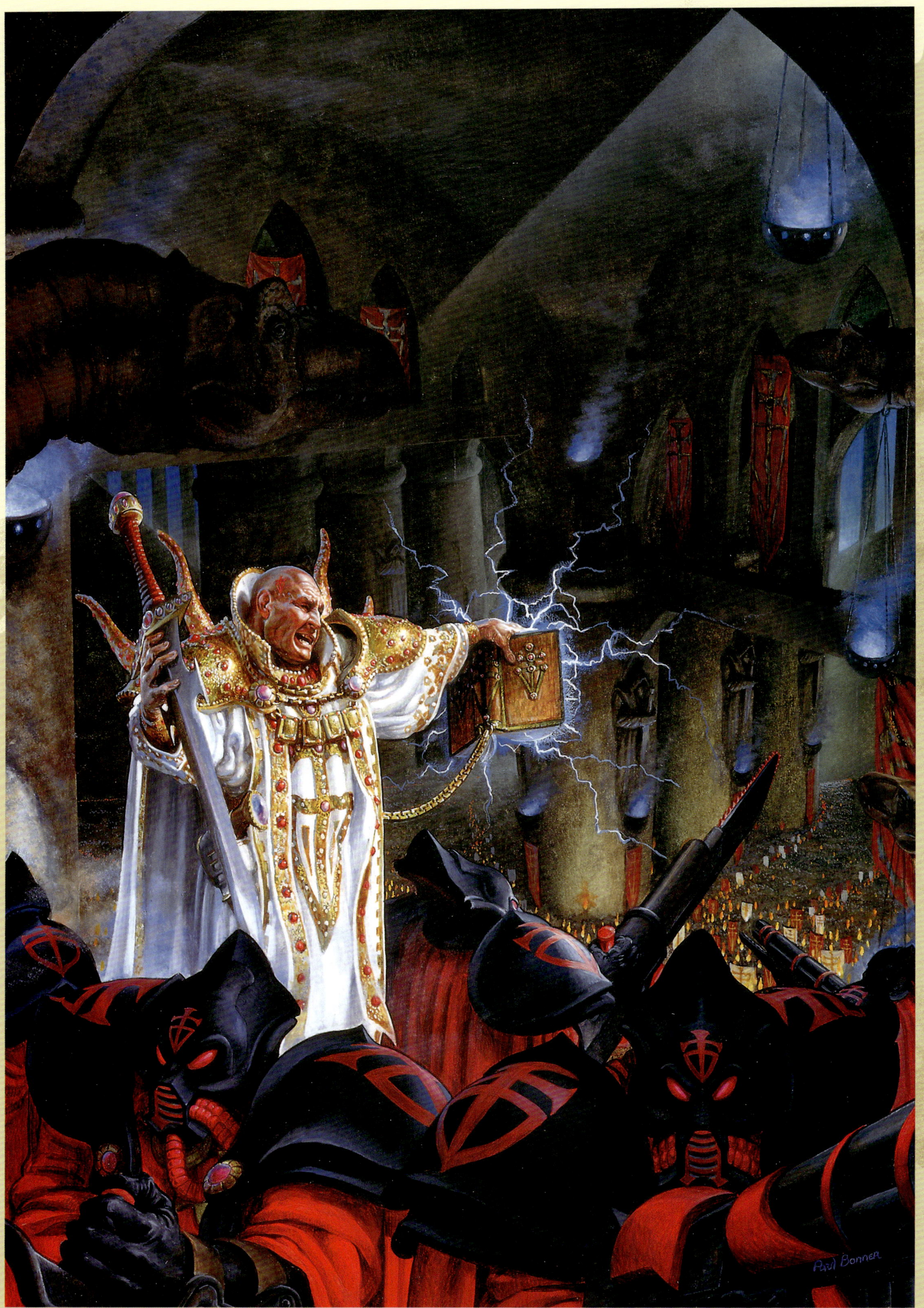
Paul Bonner

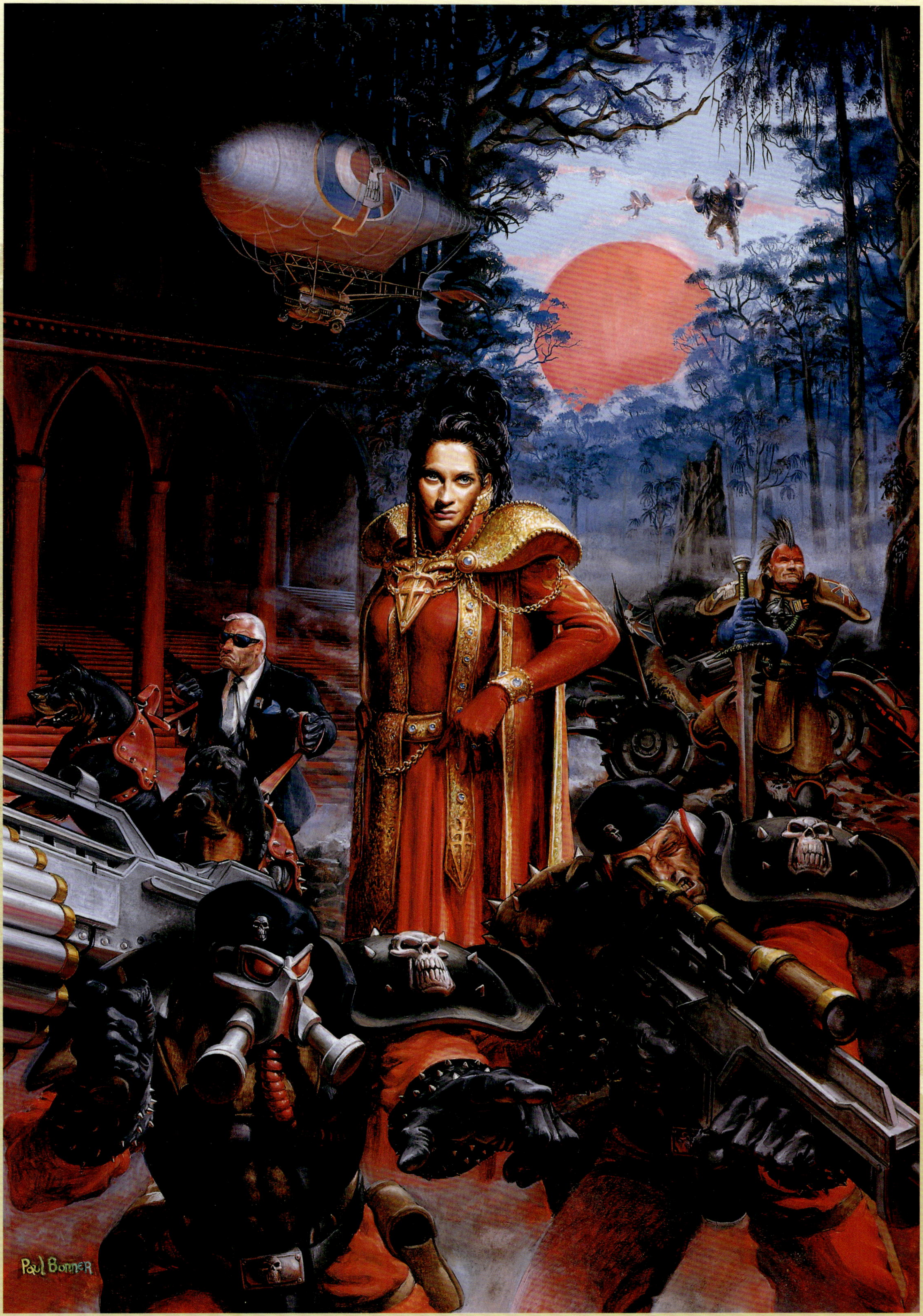

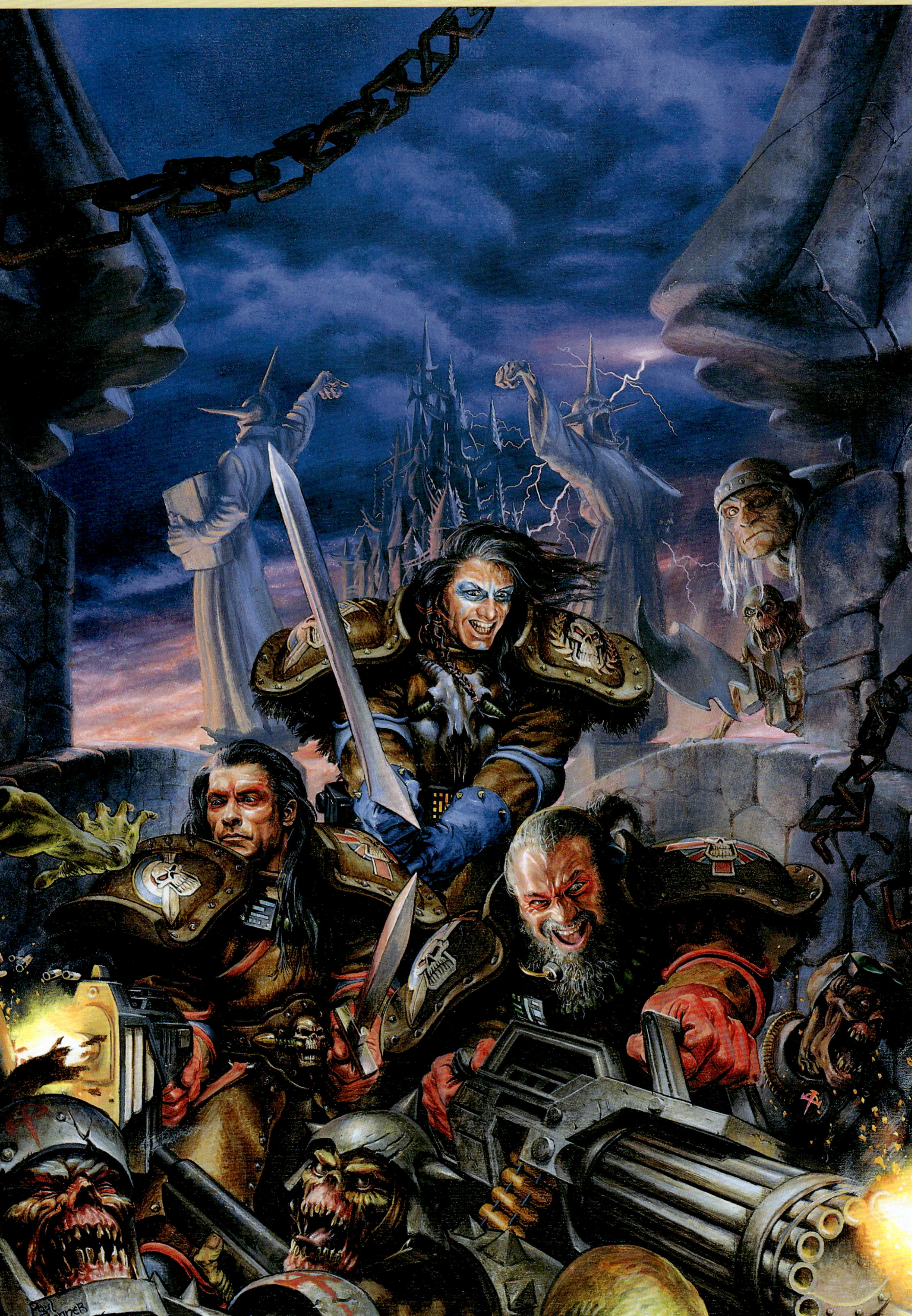

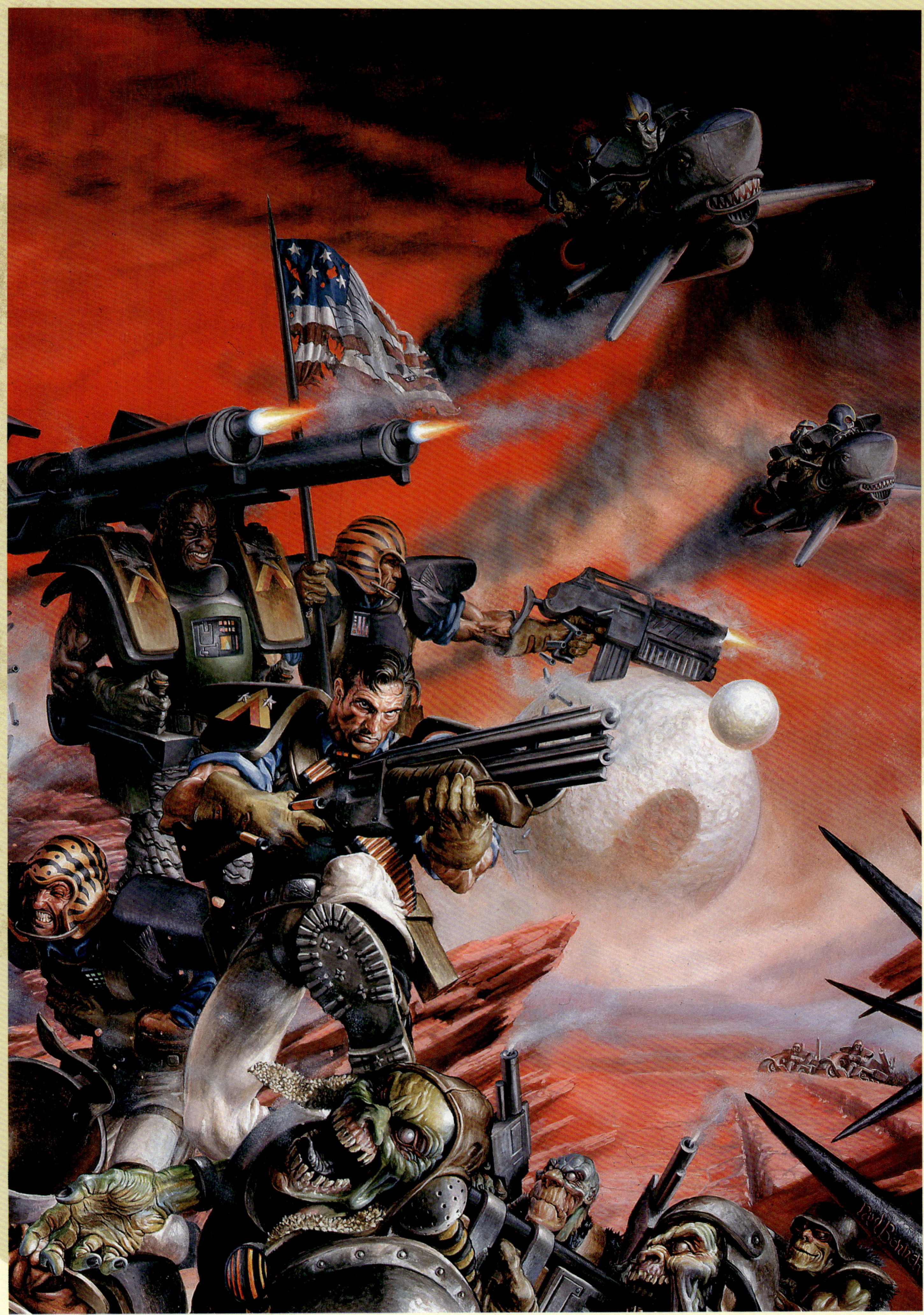

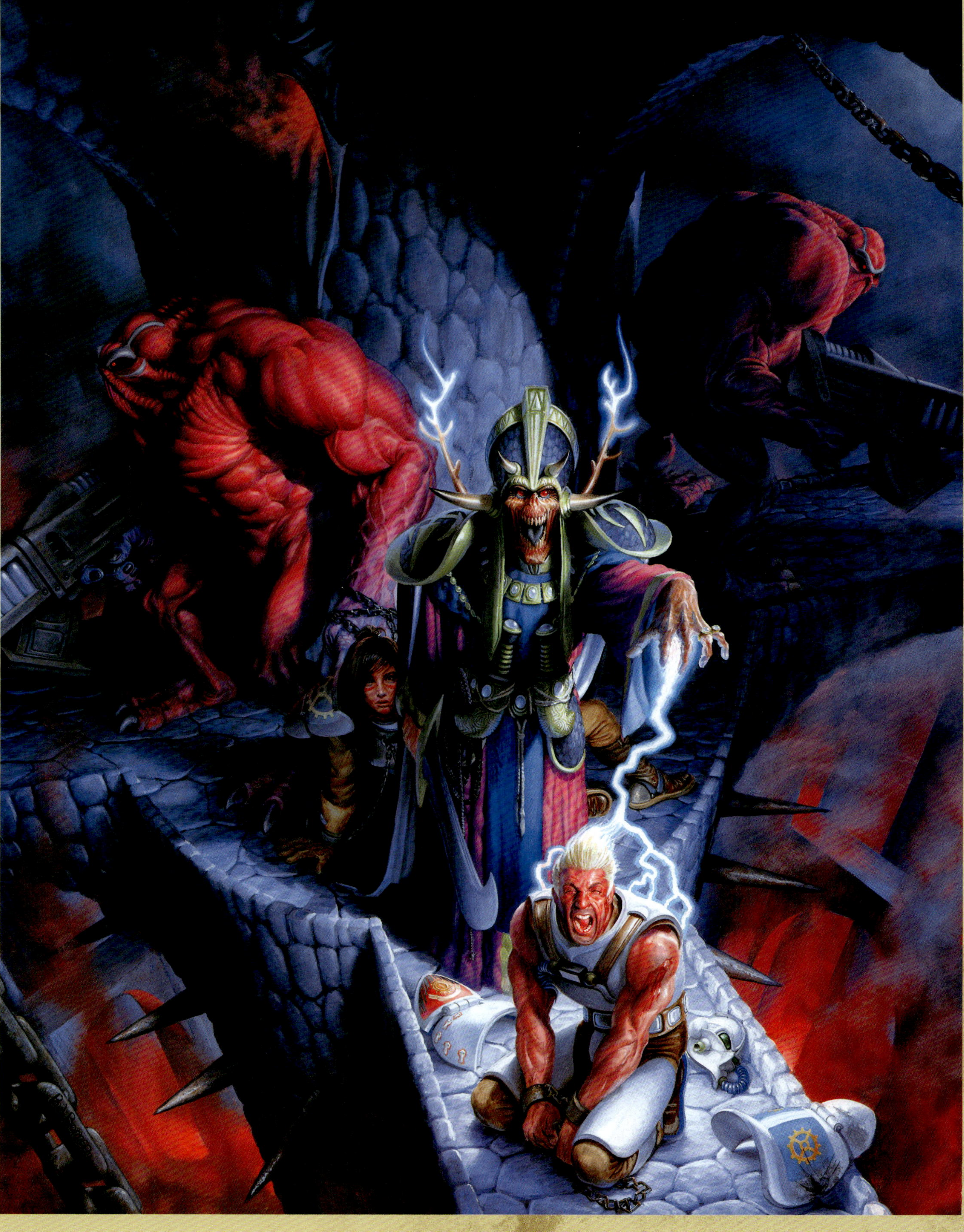

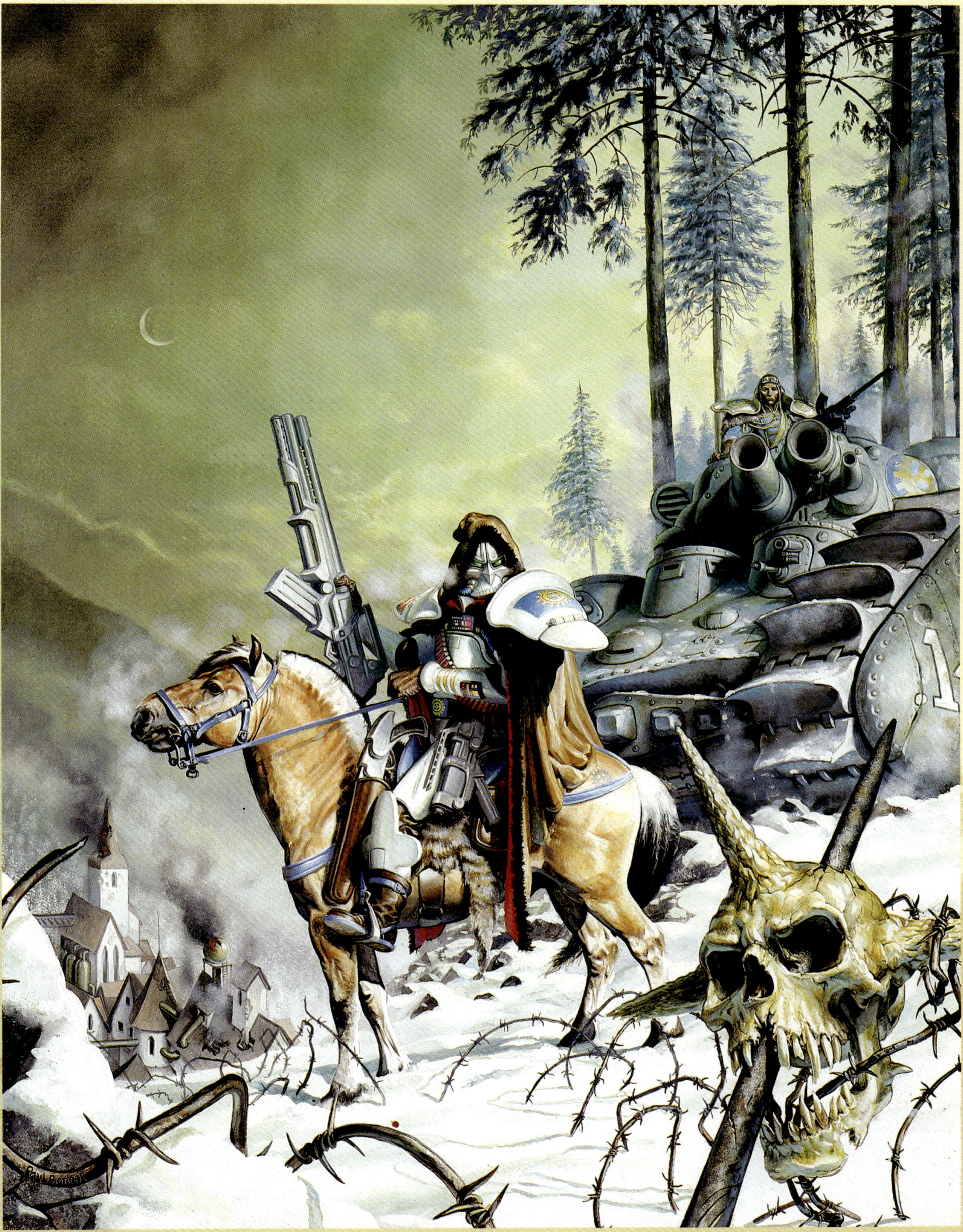

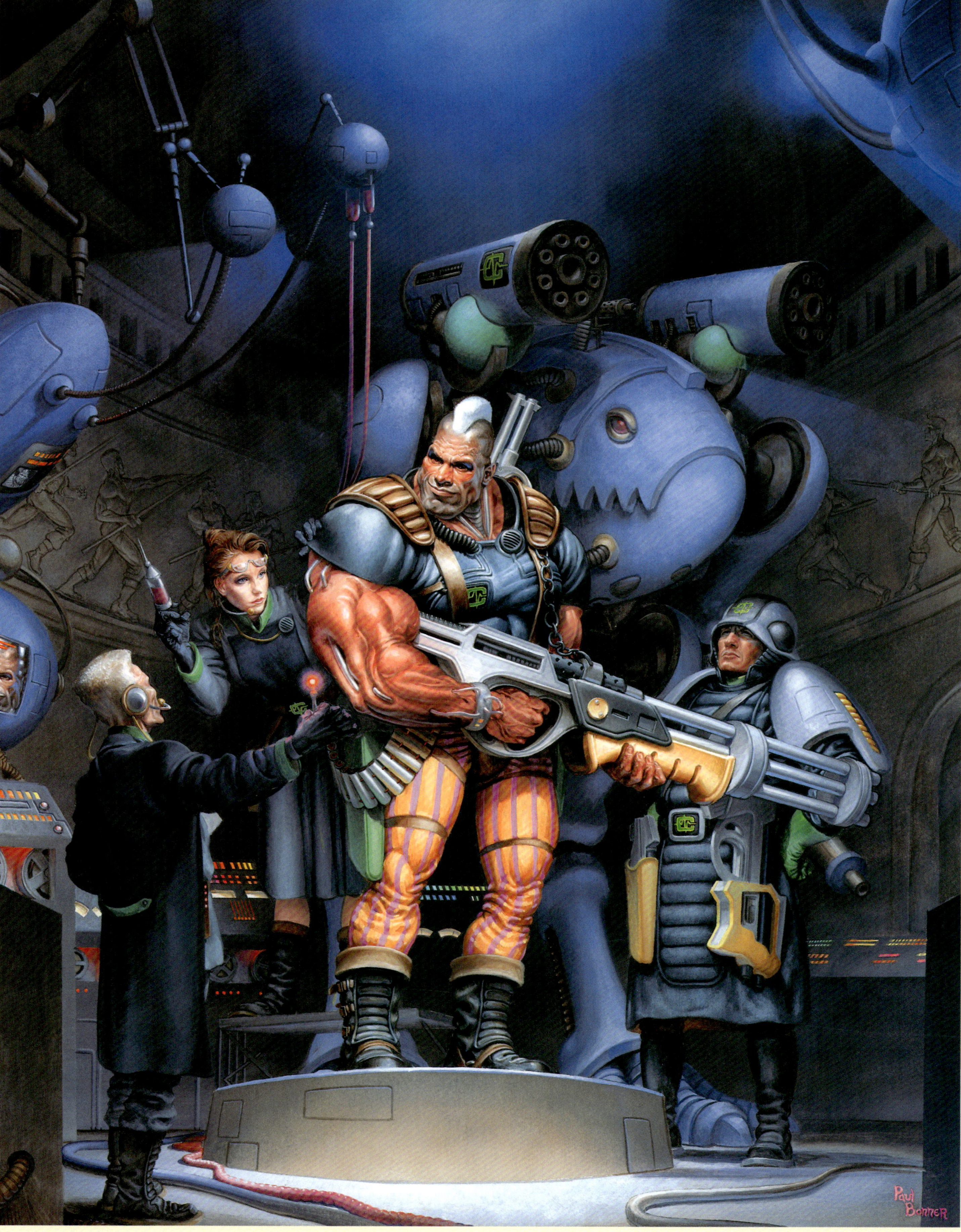
Paul Bonner

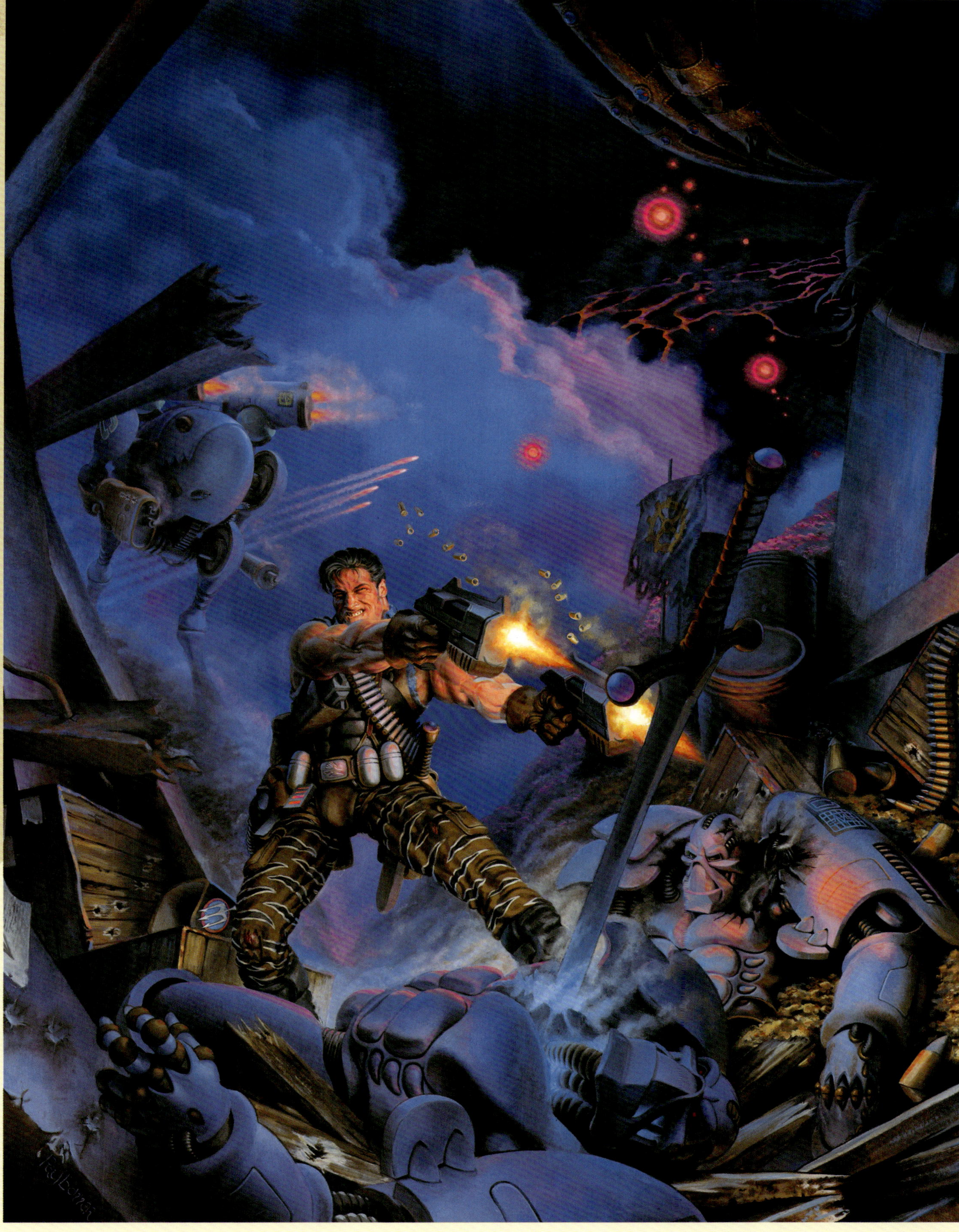

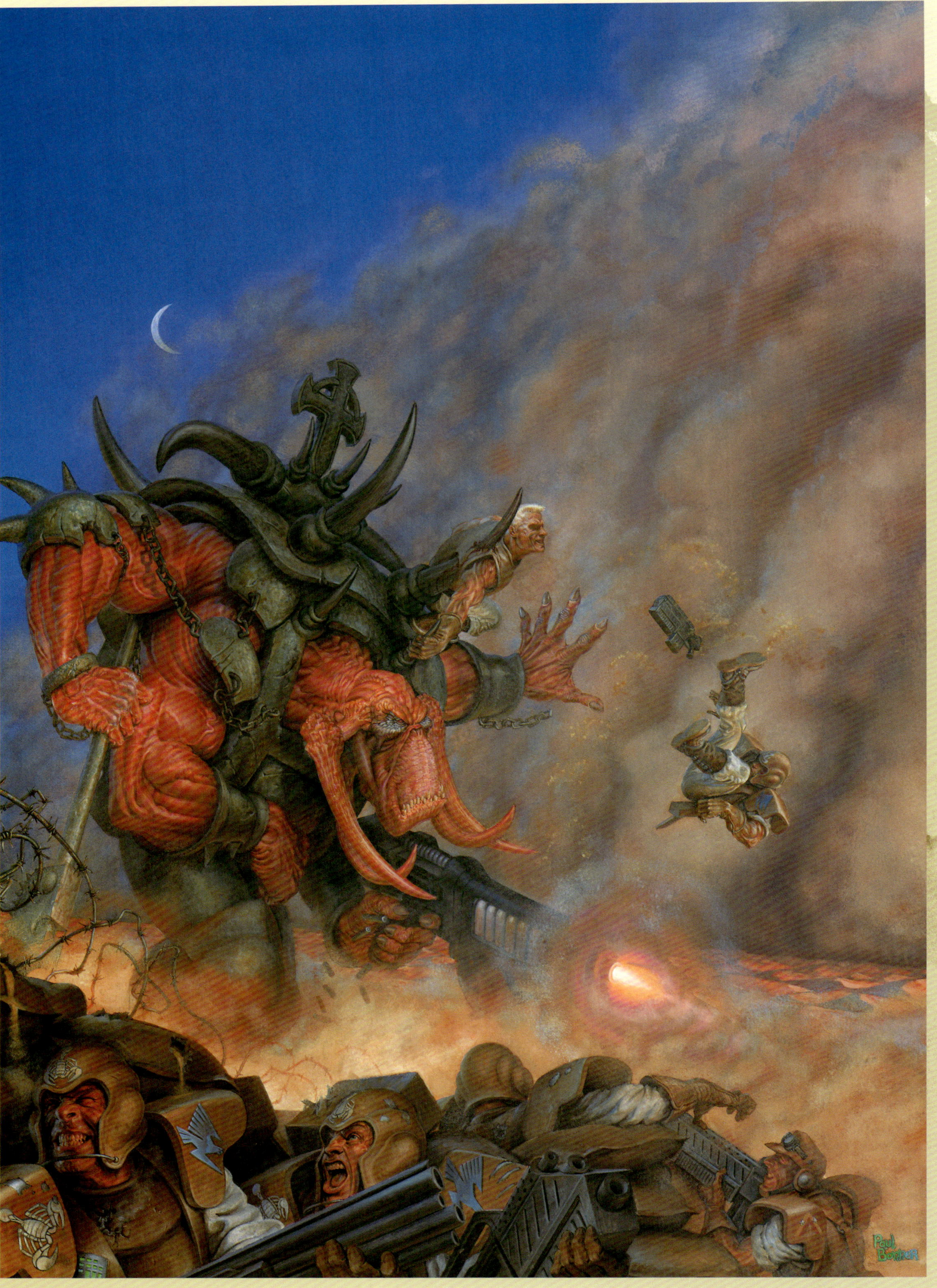
Paul Bonner

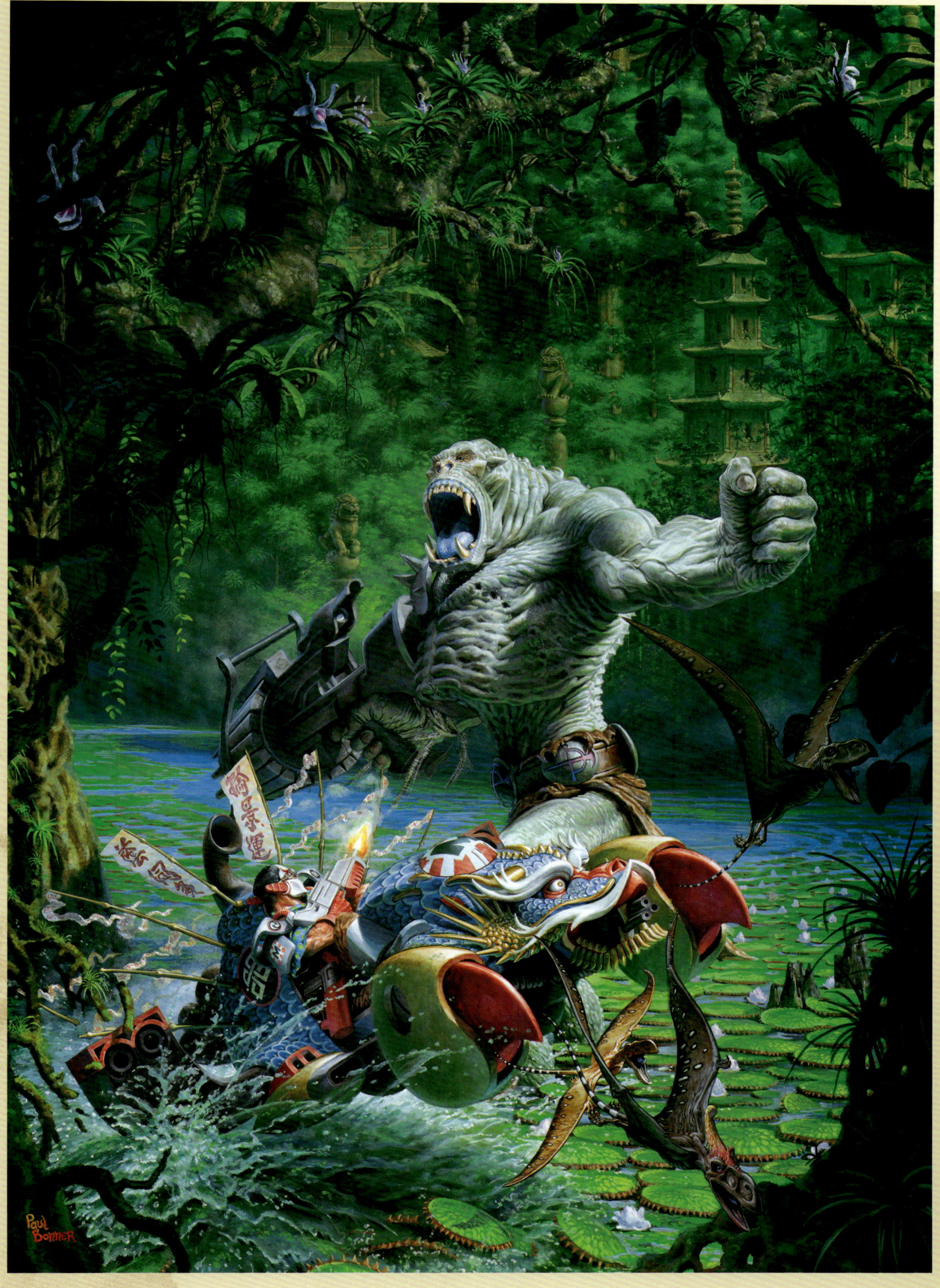
Paul
Bonner

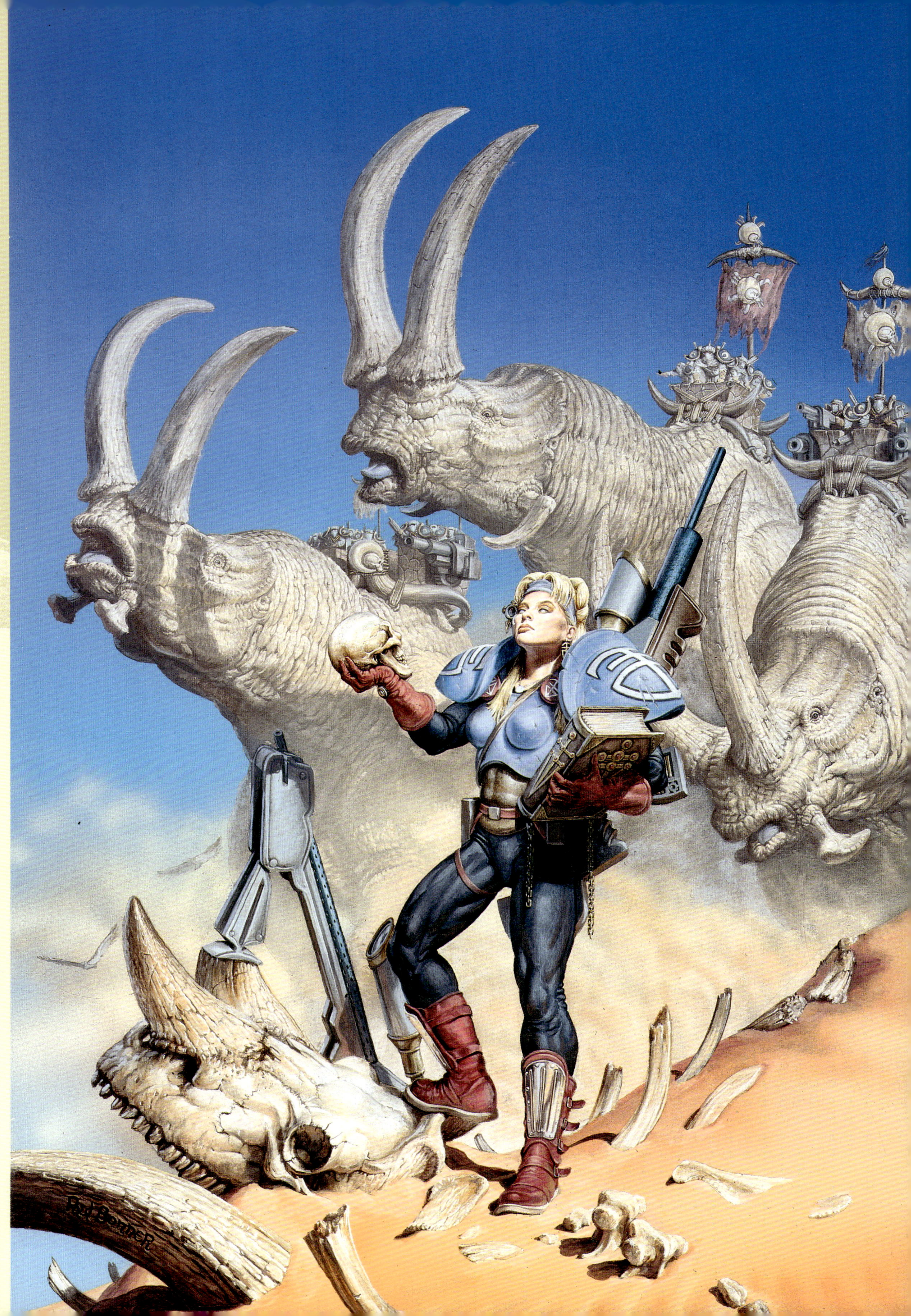

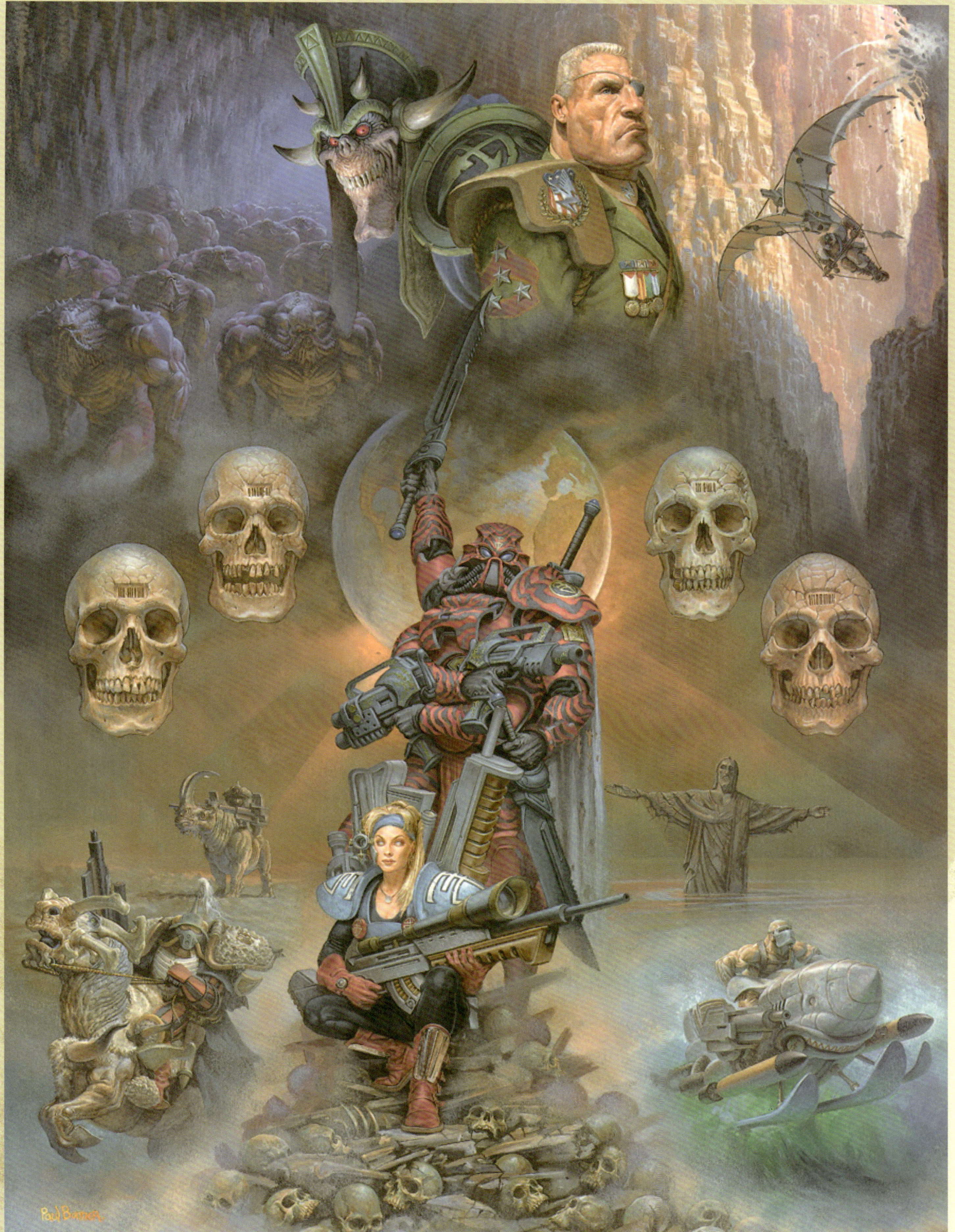

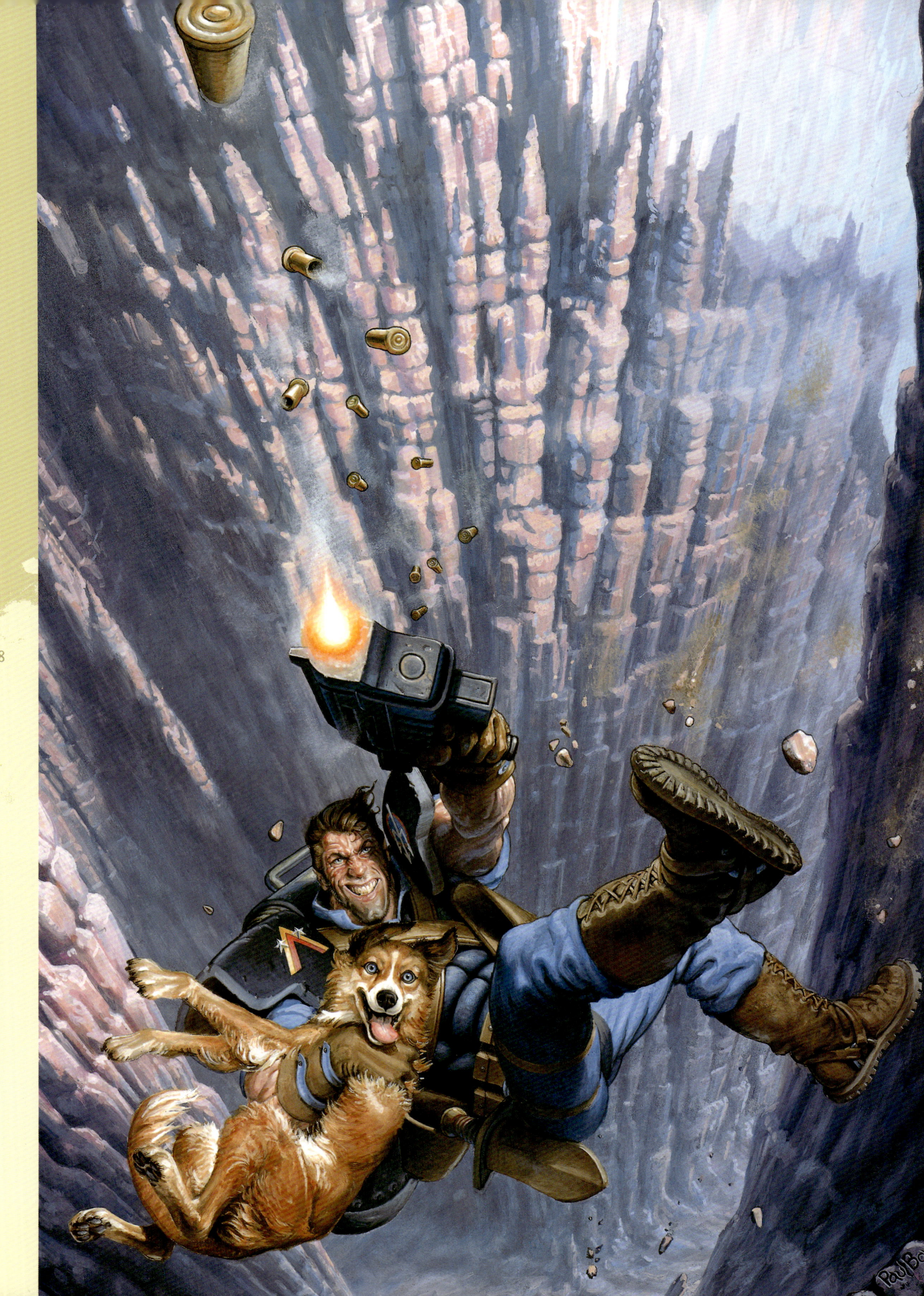

◂ Mitch Hunter with Friend

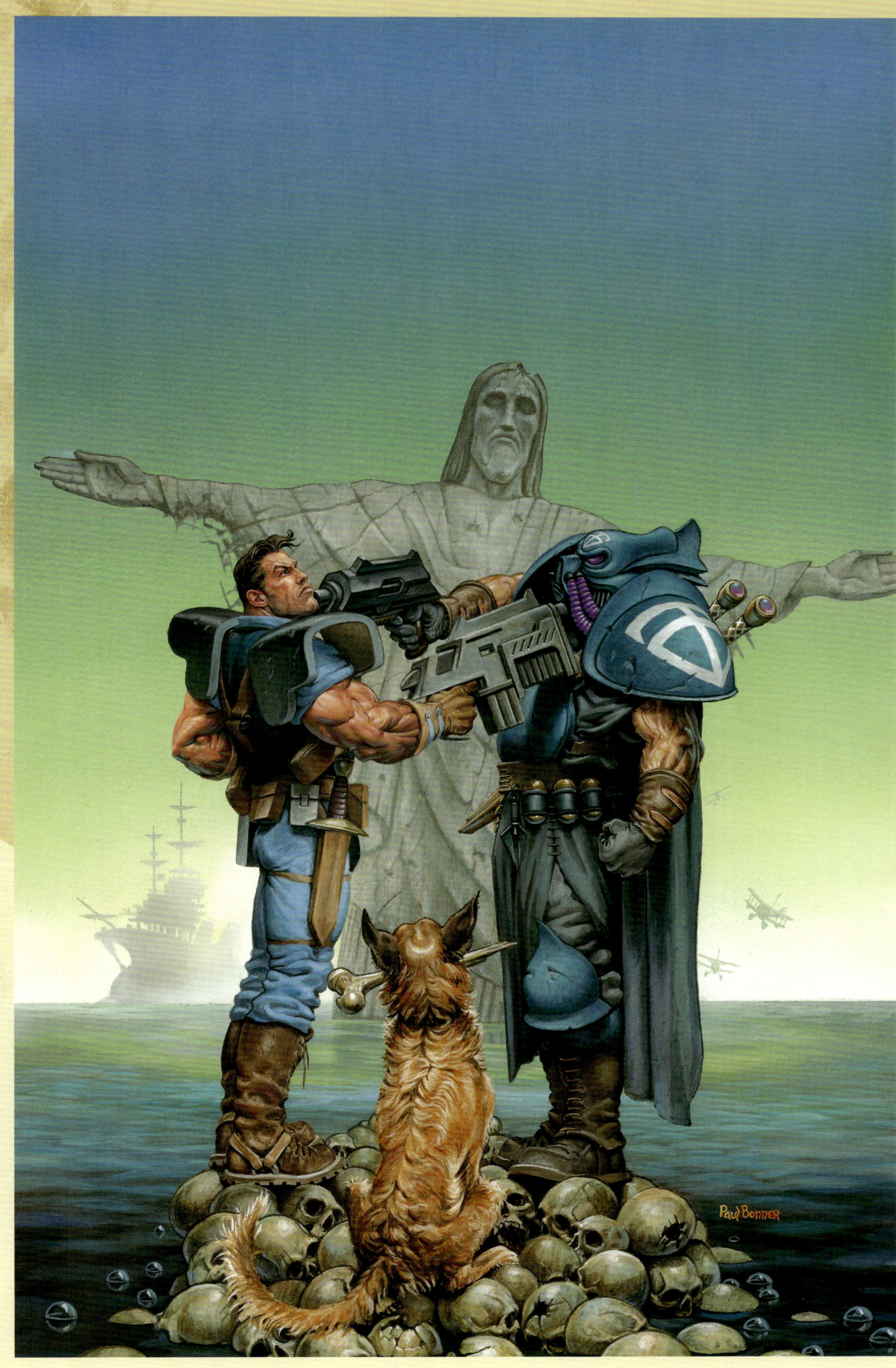

• Mitch Hunter with Enemy (and Friend)

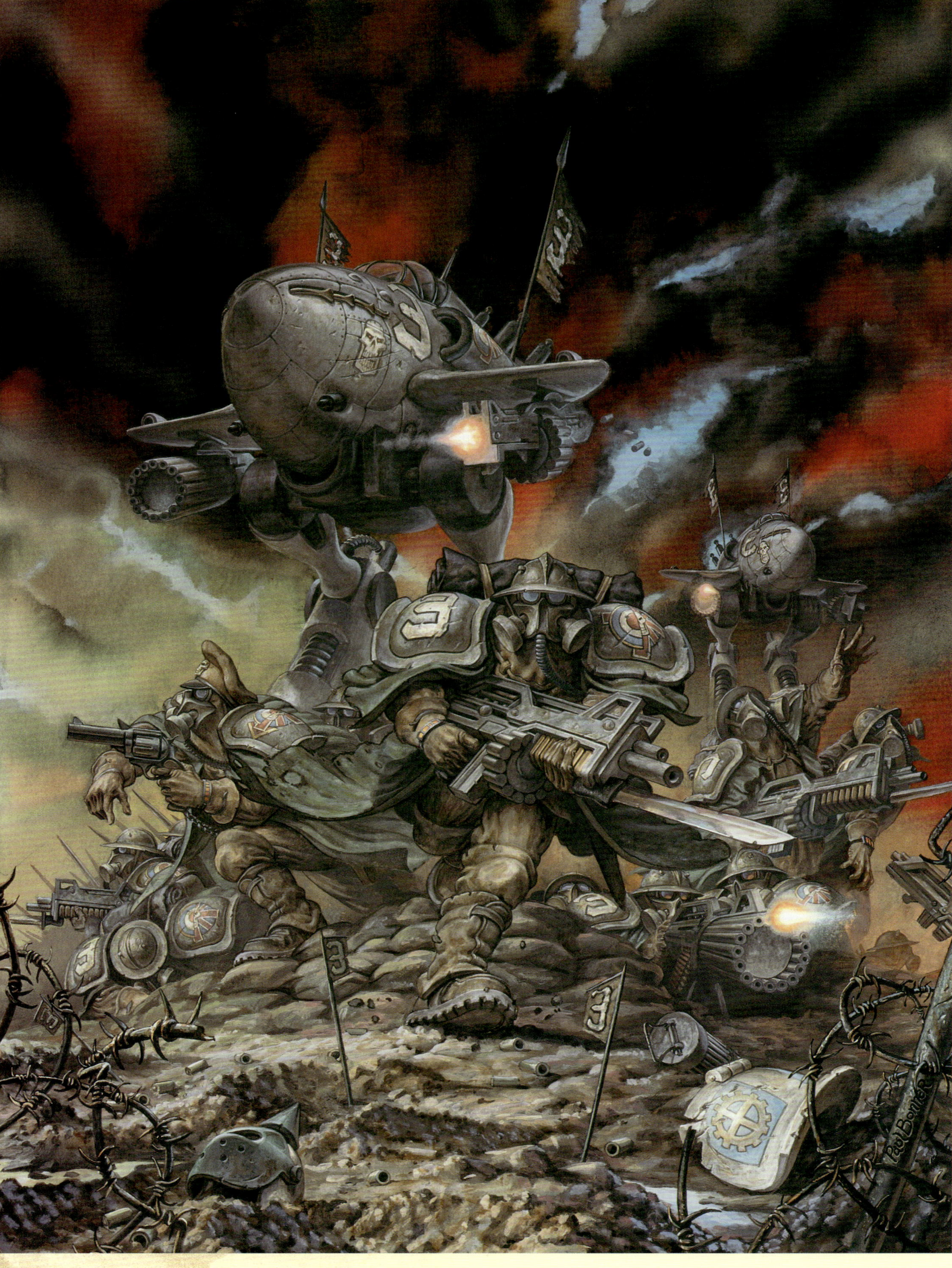

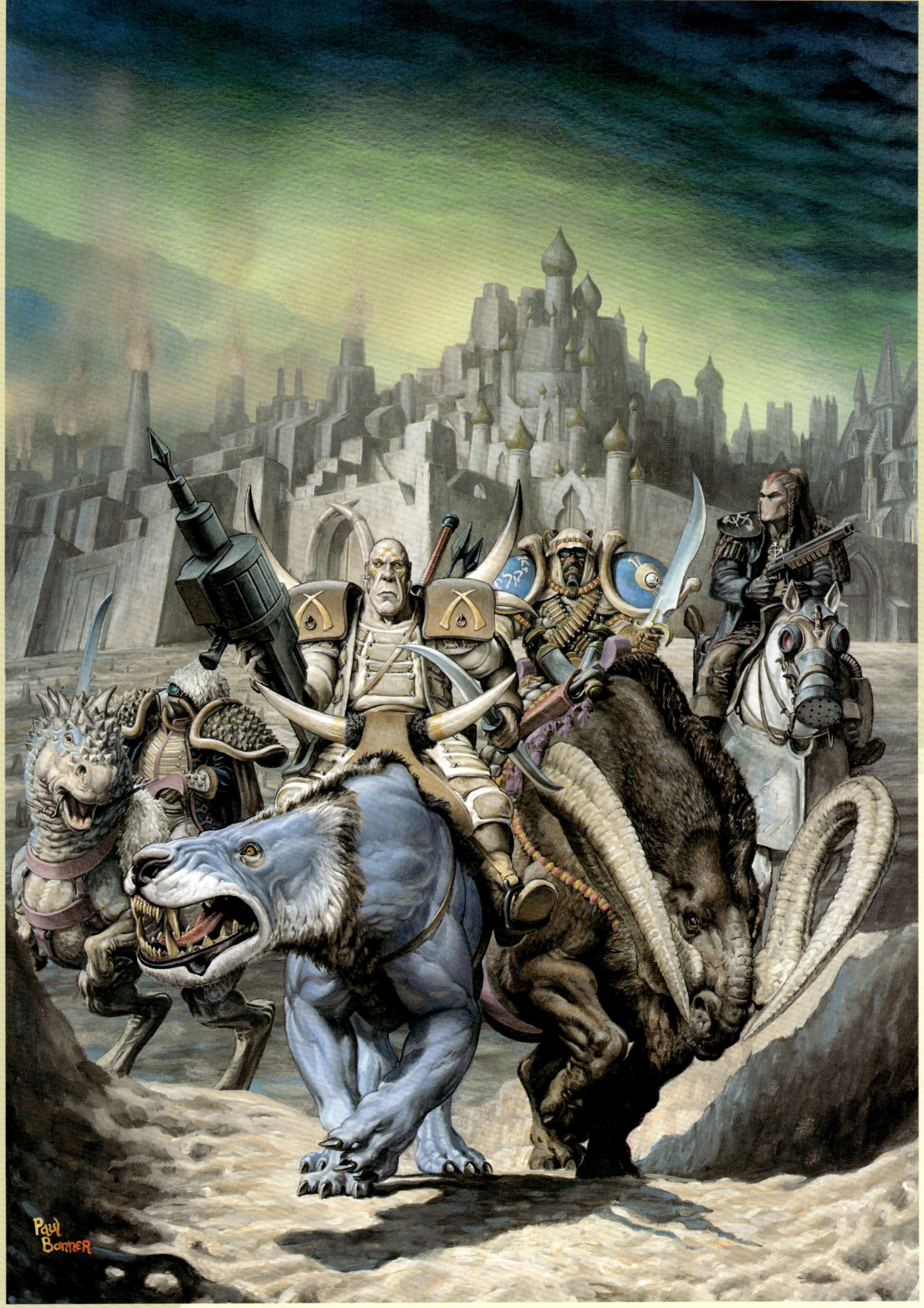
Paul
Bonner

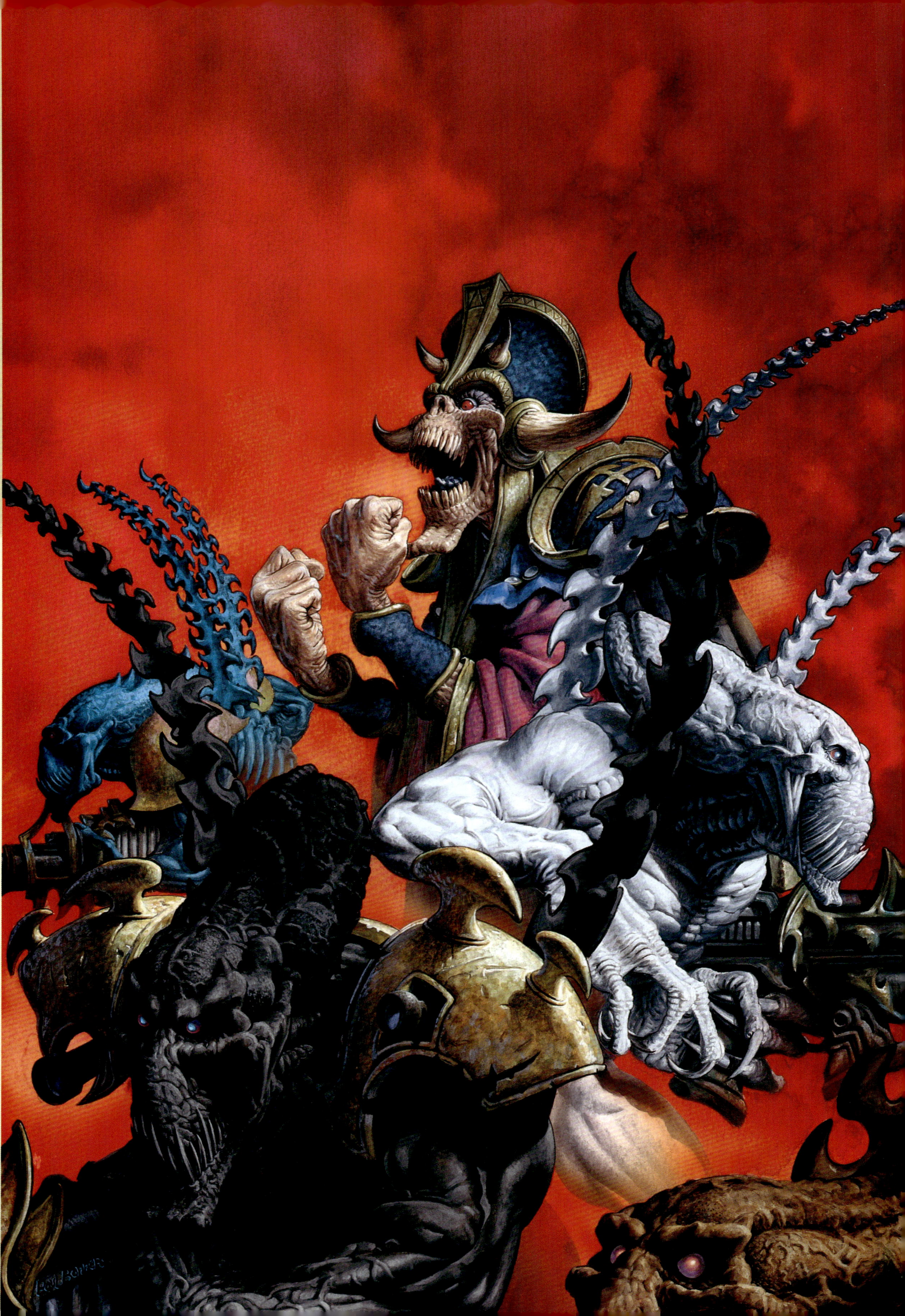

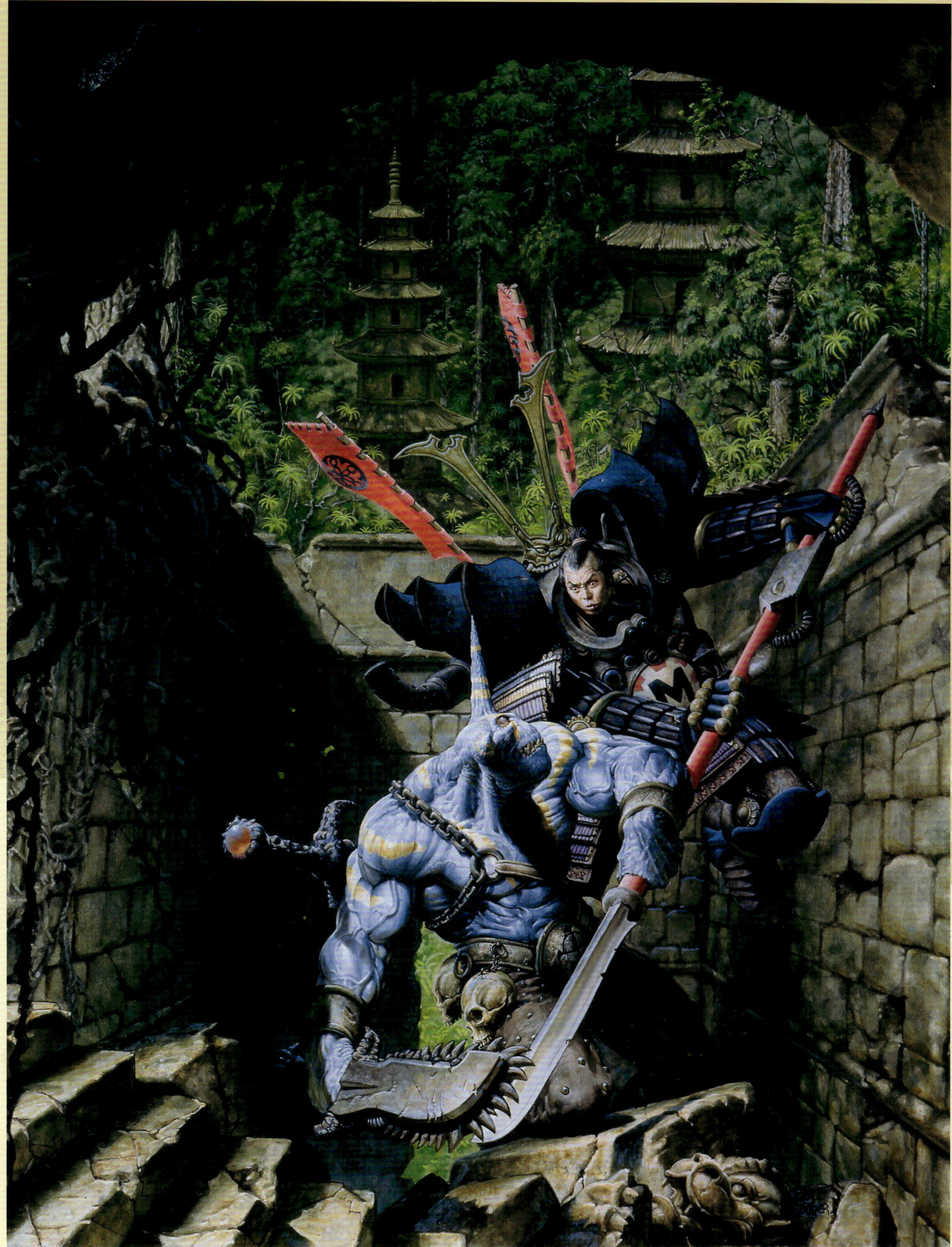

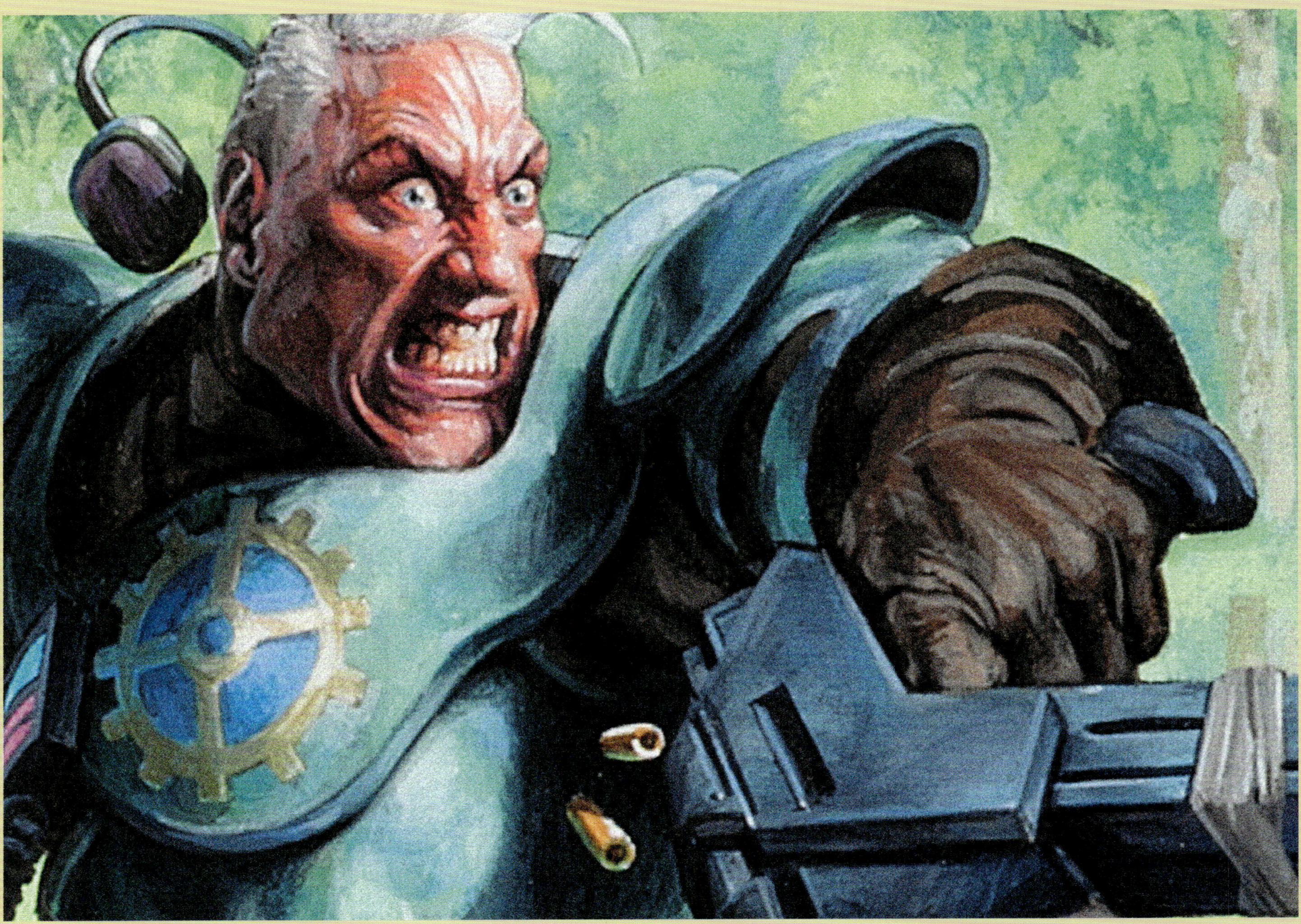

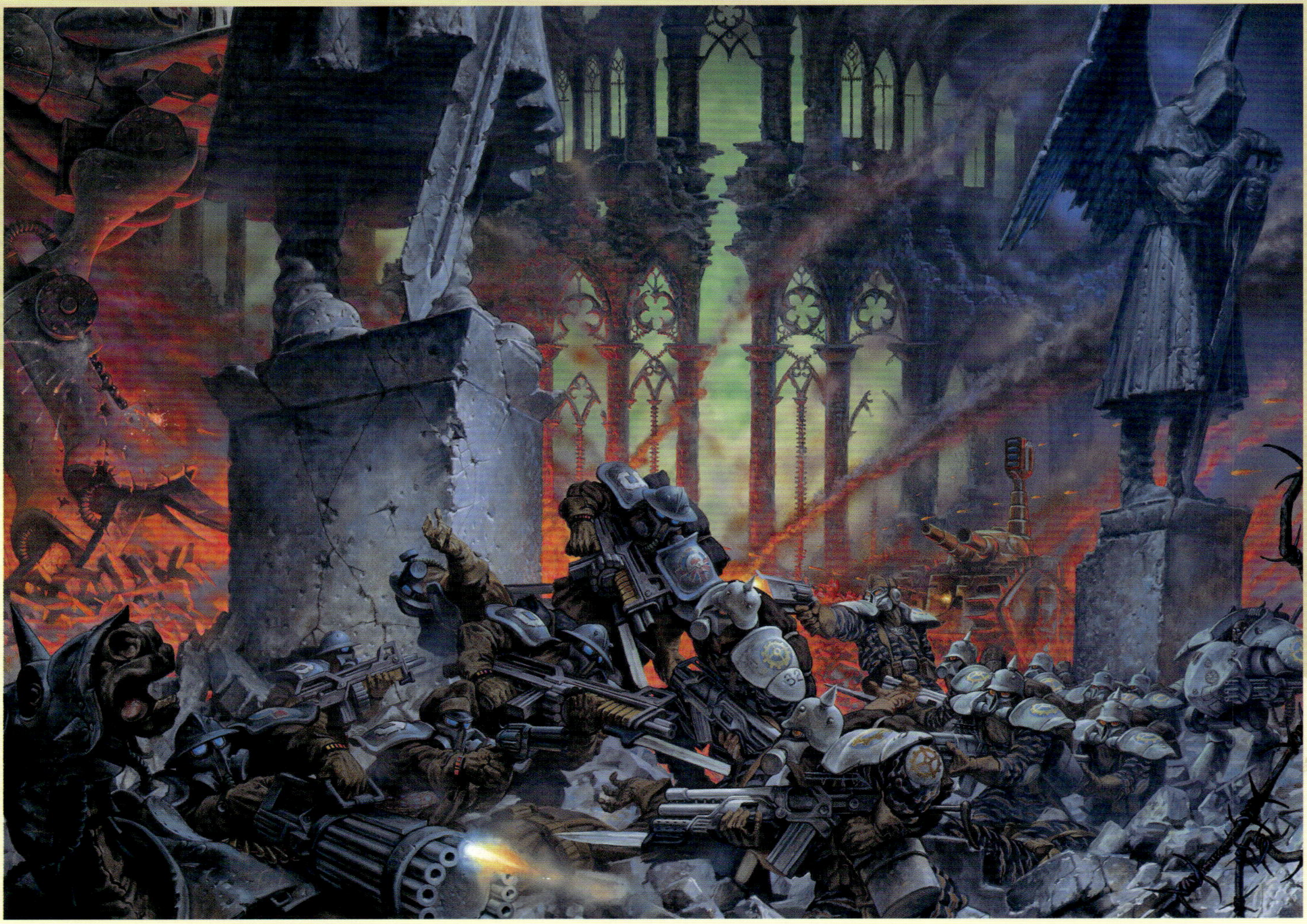

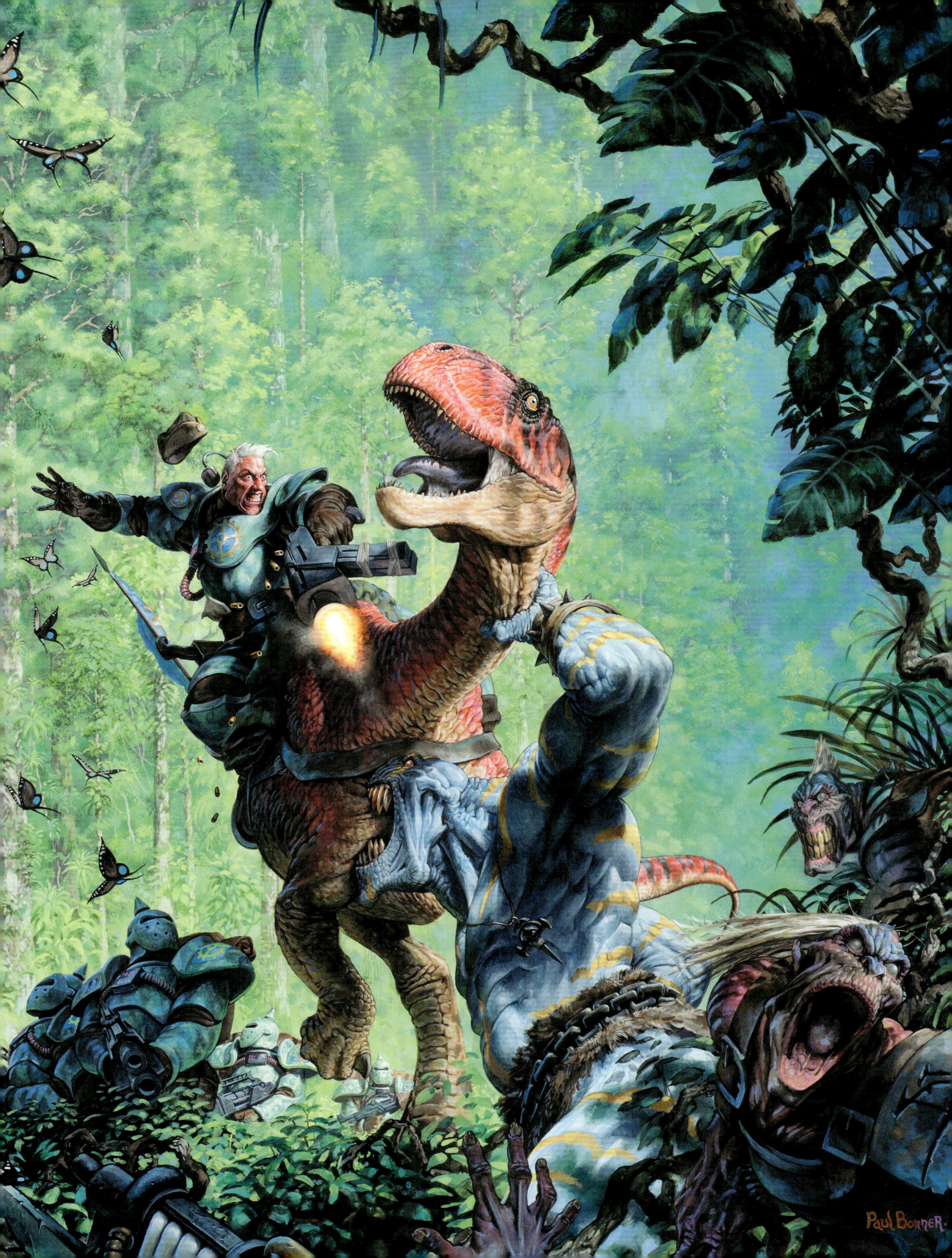
Paul Bonner.

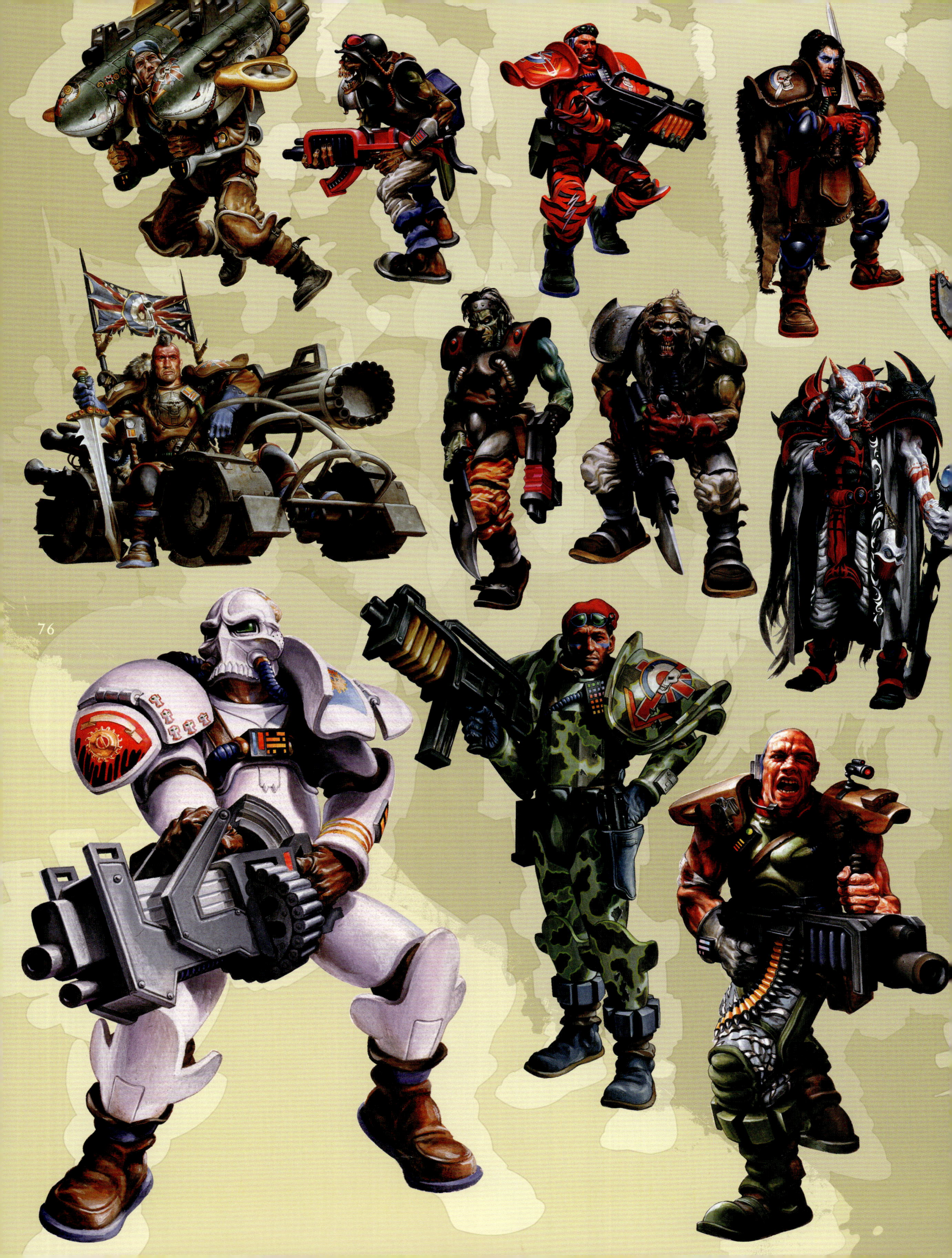

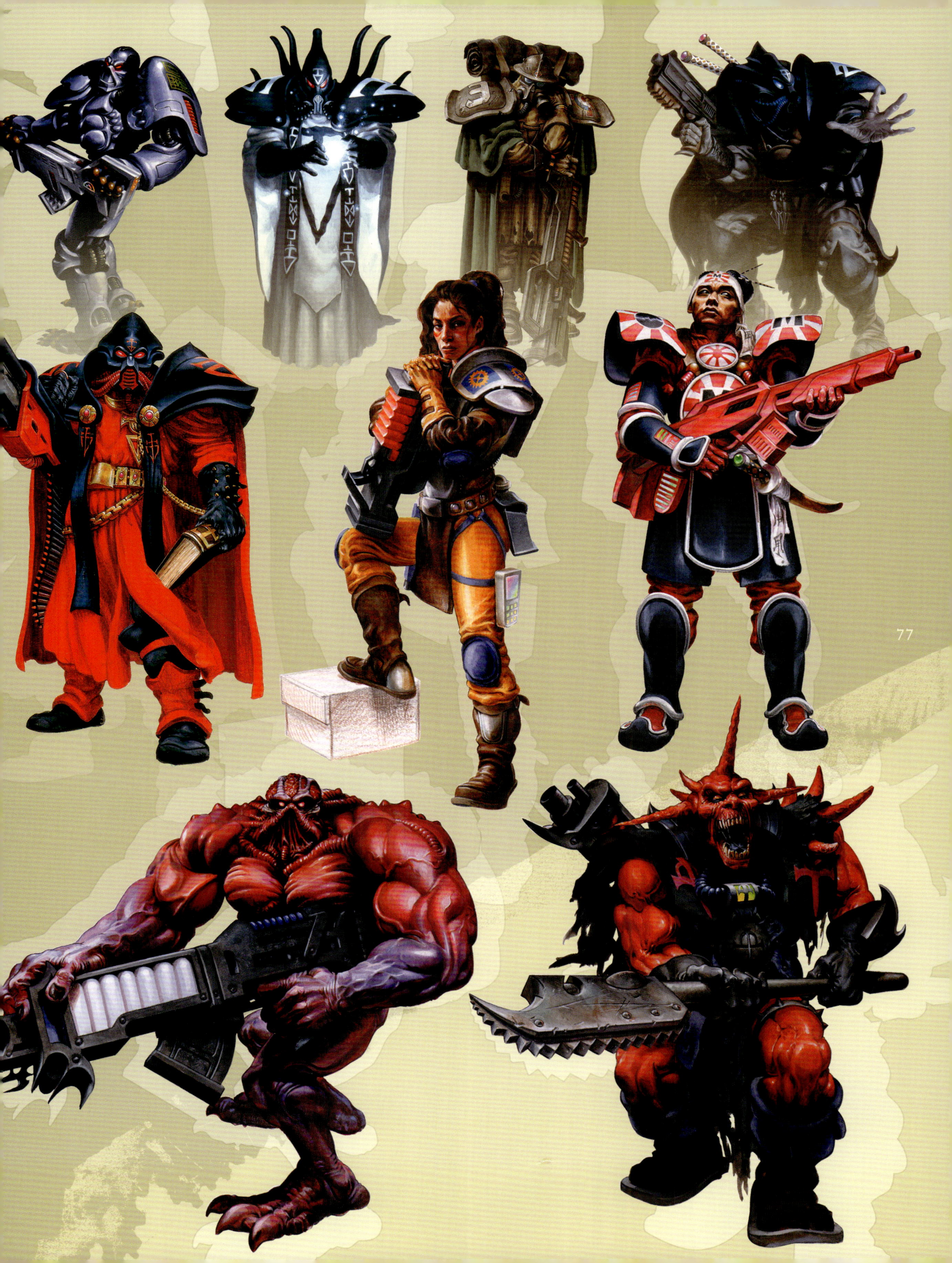

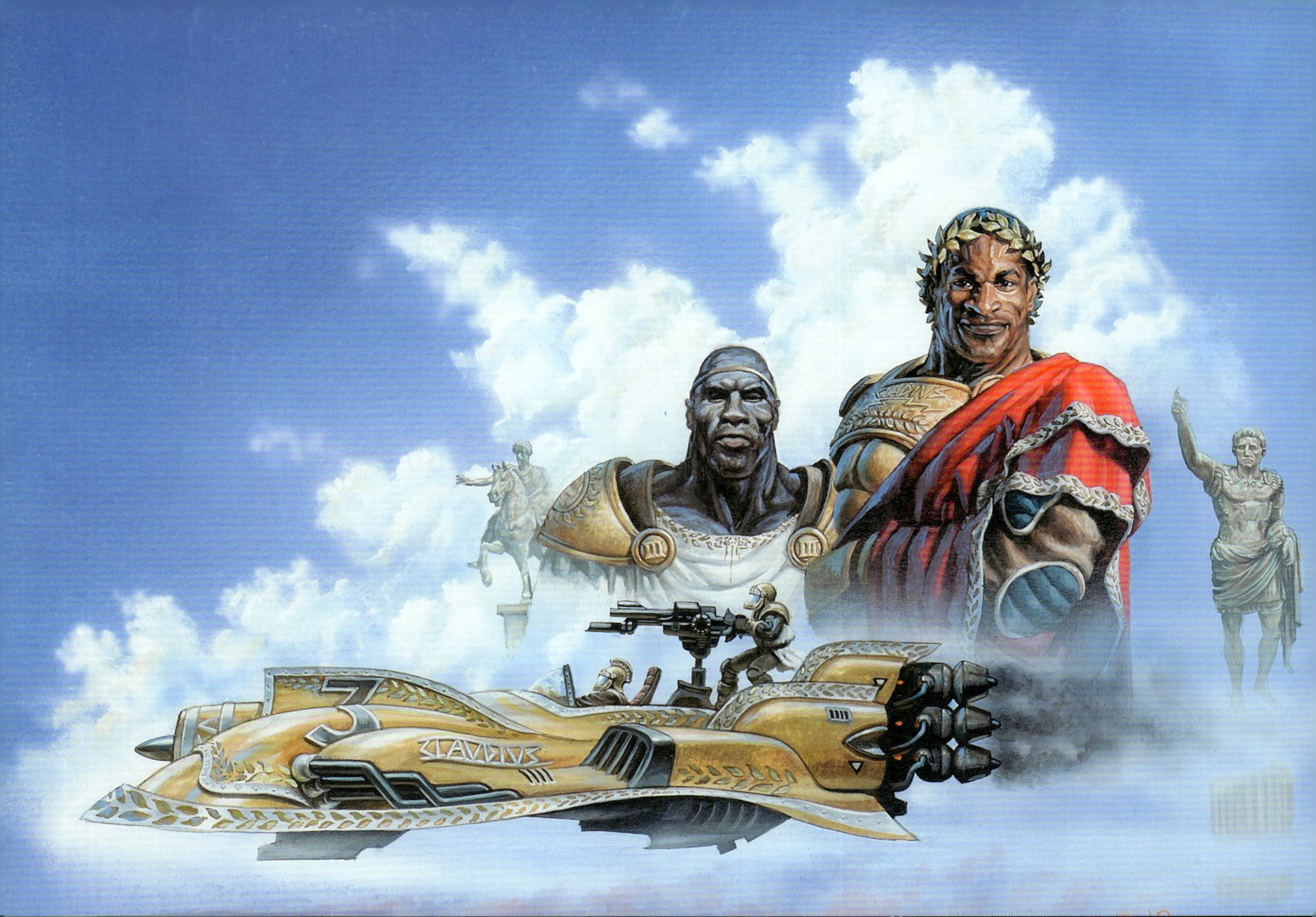

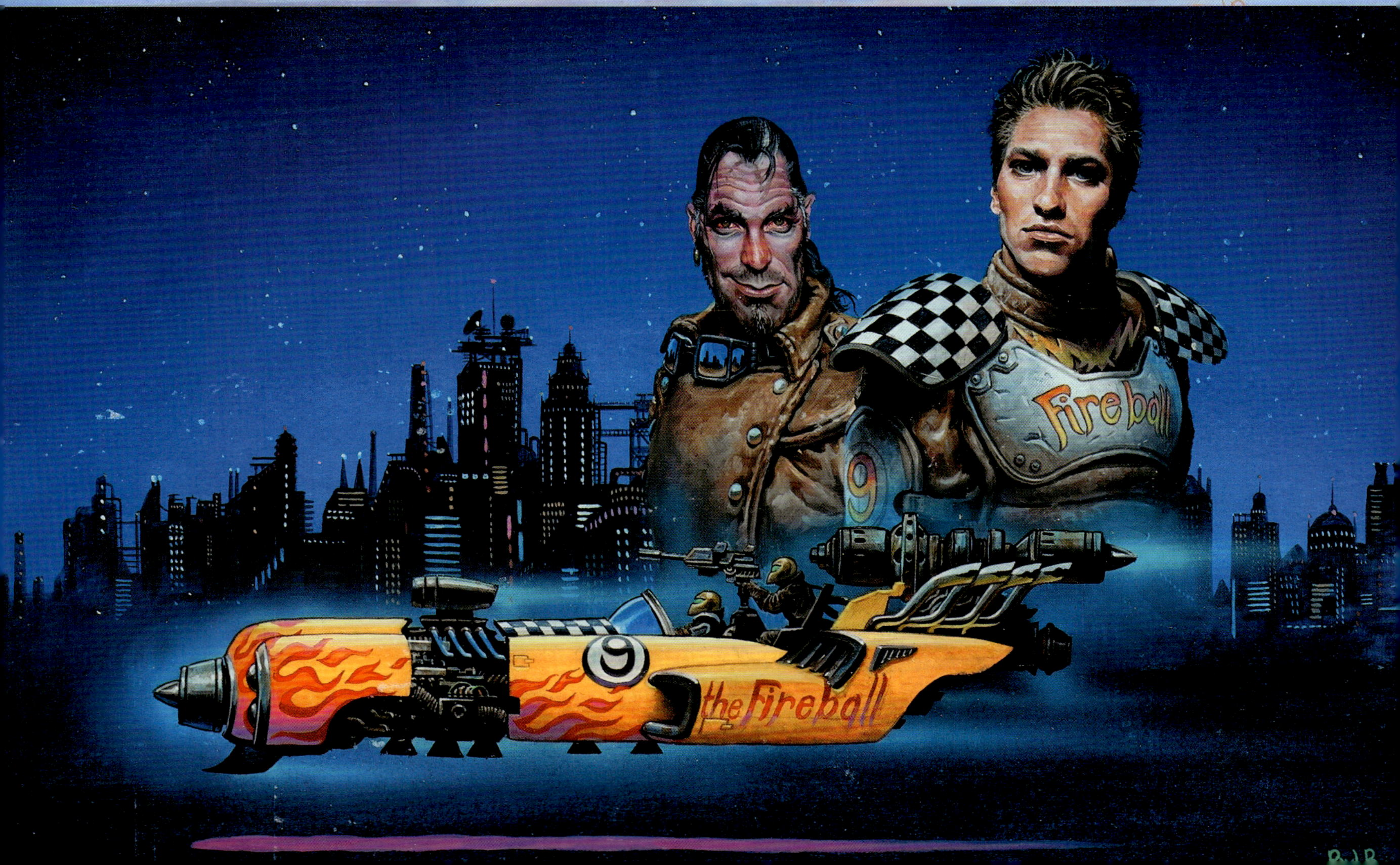

CLAVDIVS
Fireball
the Fireball

CONCEPTS FOR A FILM PROJECT. SORT OF *DEATHRACE 2000* CROSSOVER WITH *MAD MAX*.

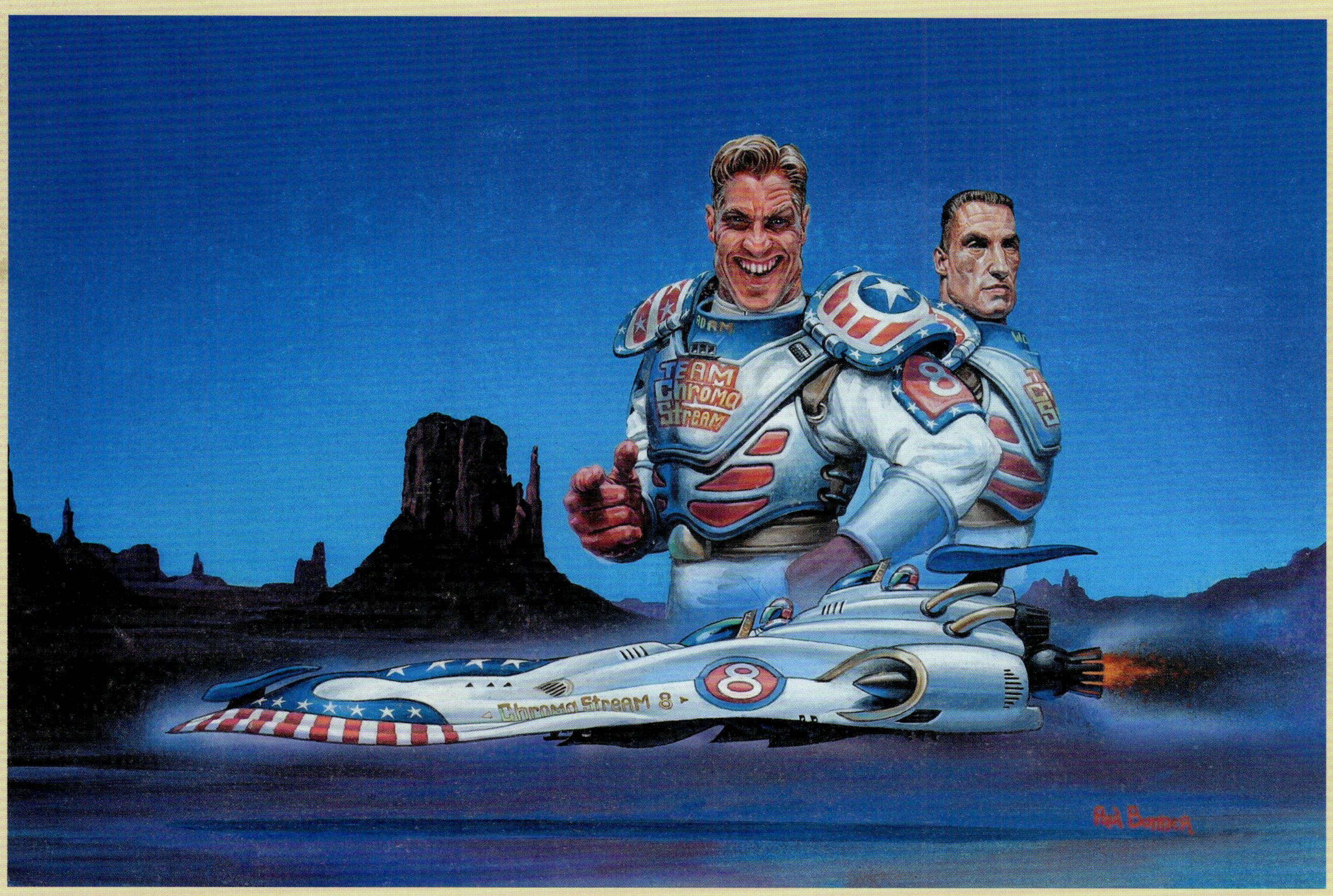

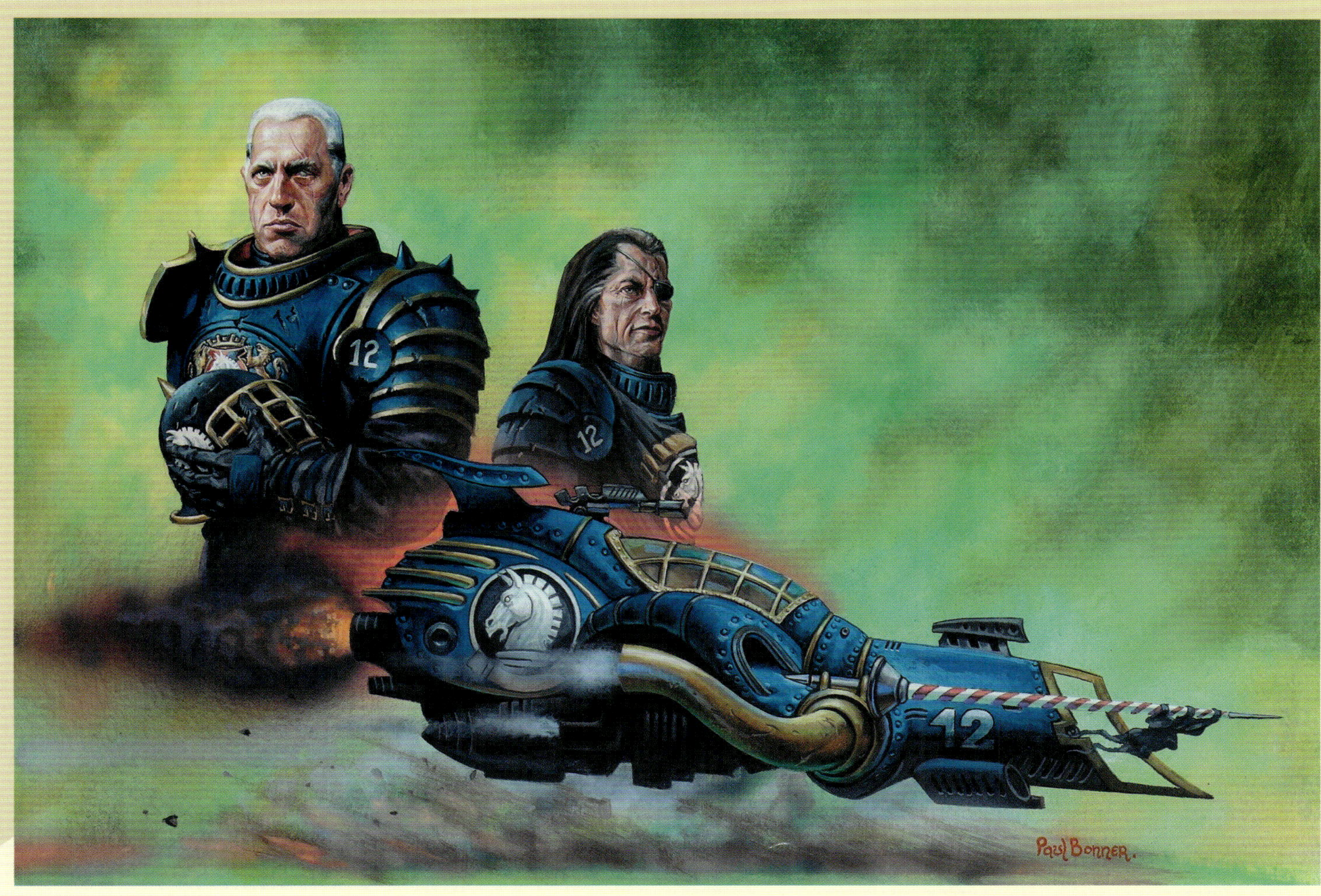

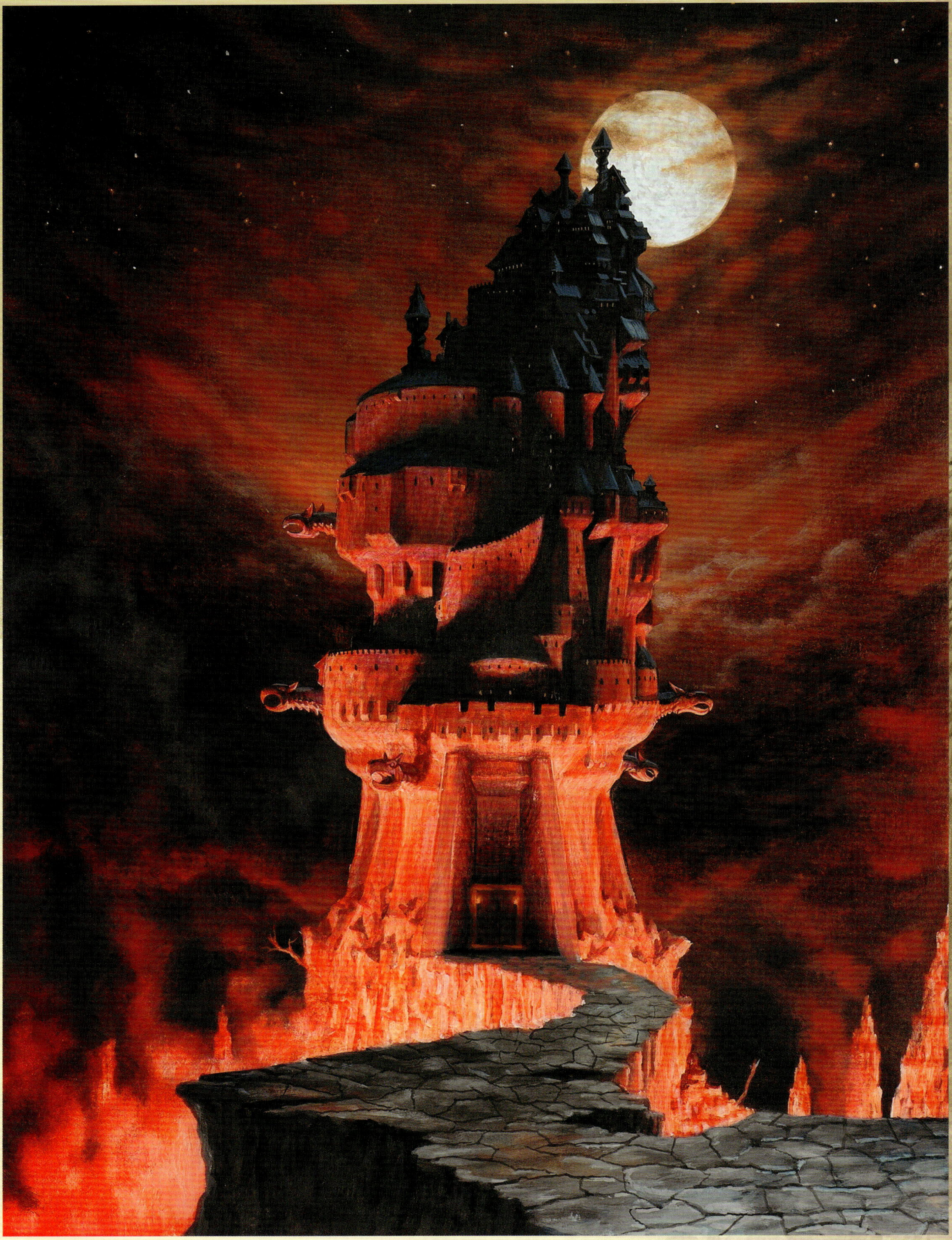

Cover project for a video game.

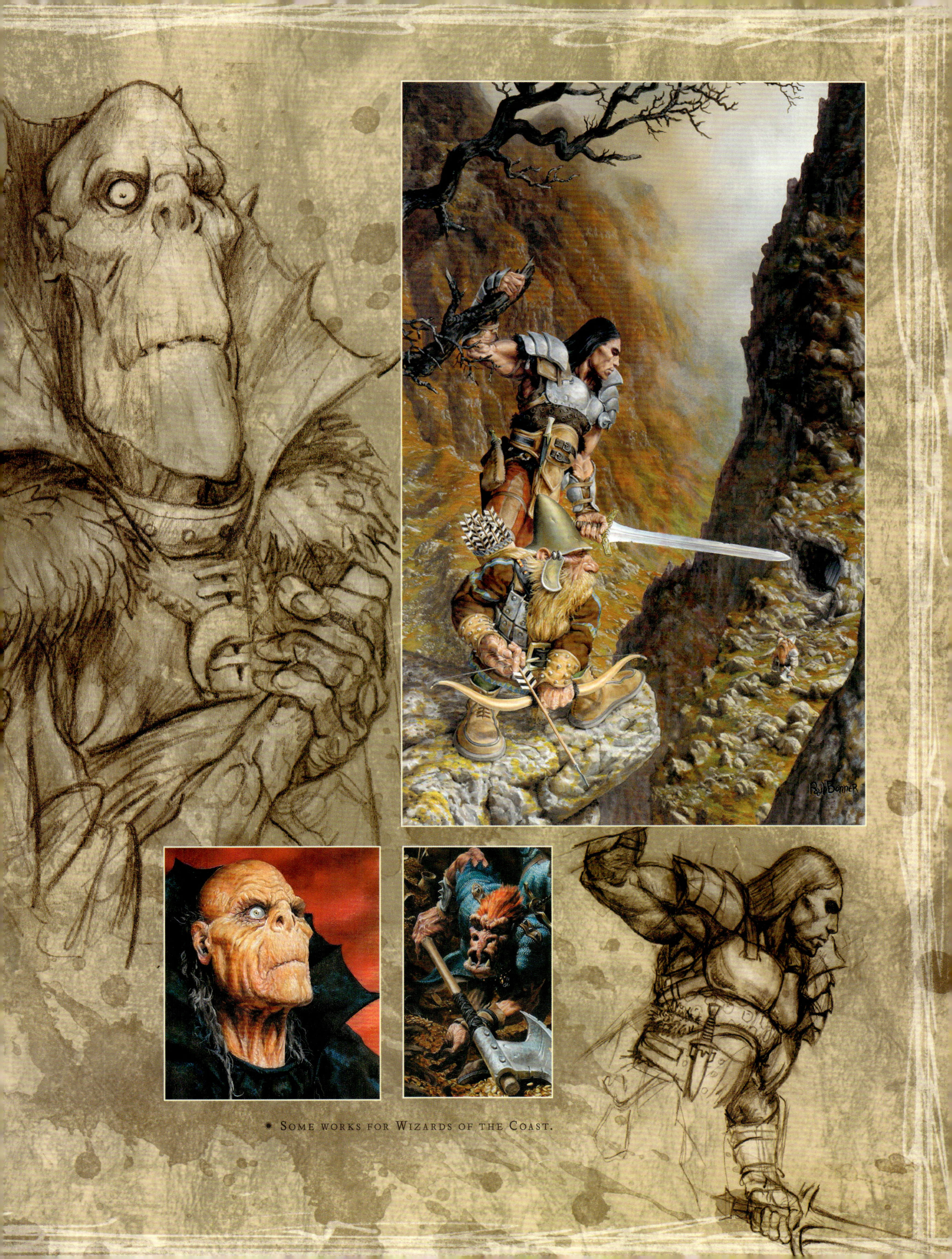

• Some works for Wizards of the Coast.

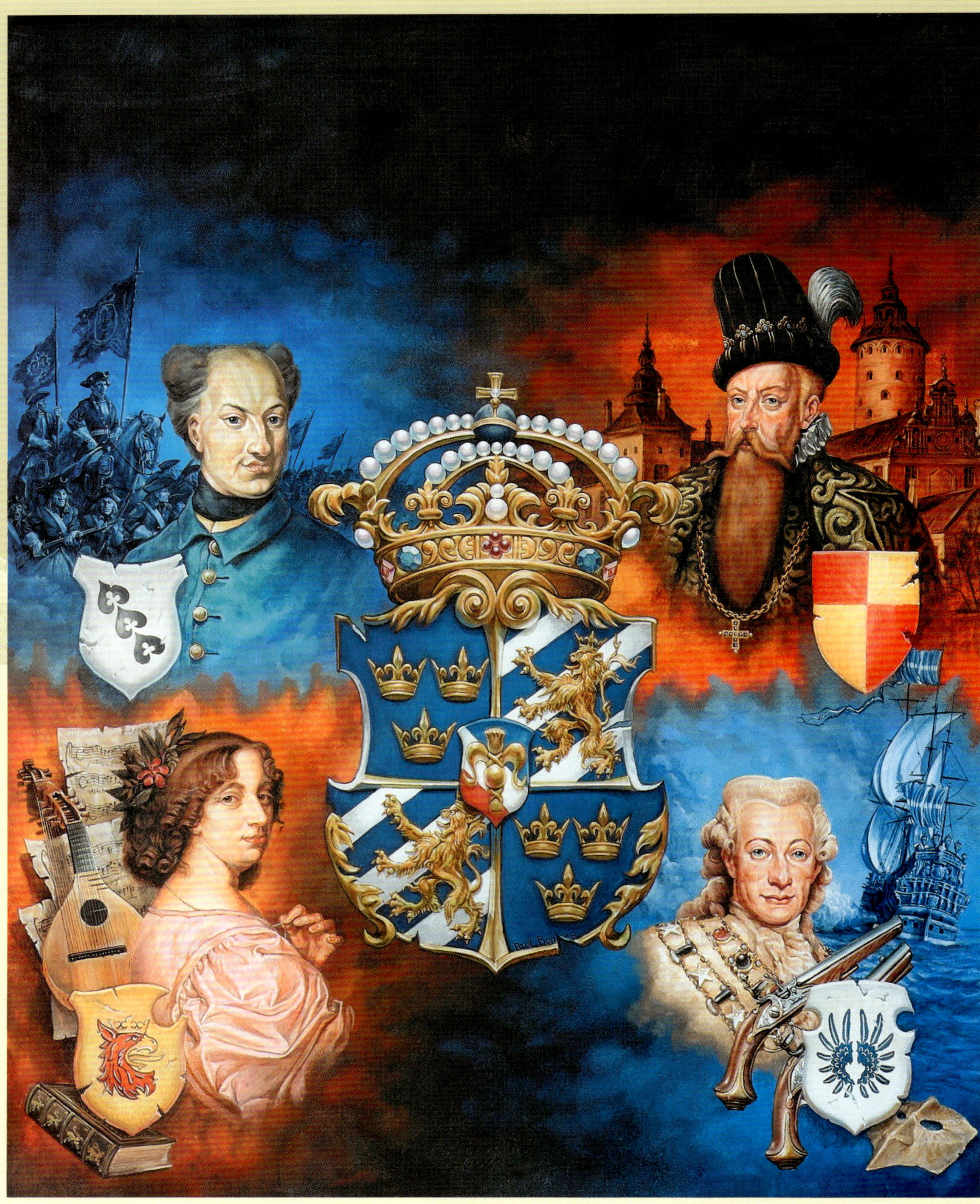

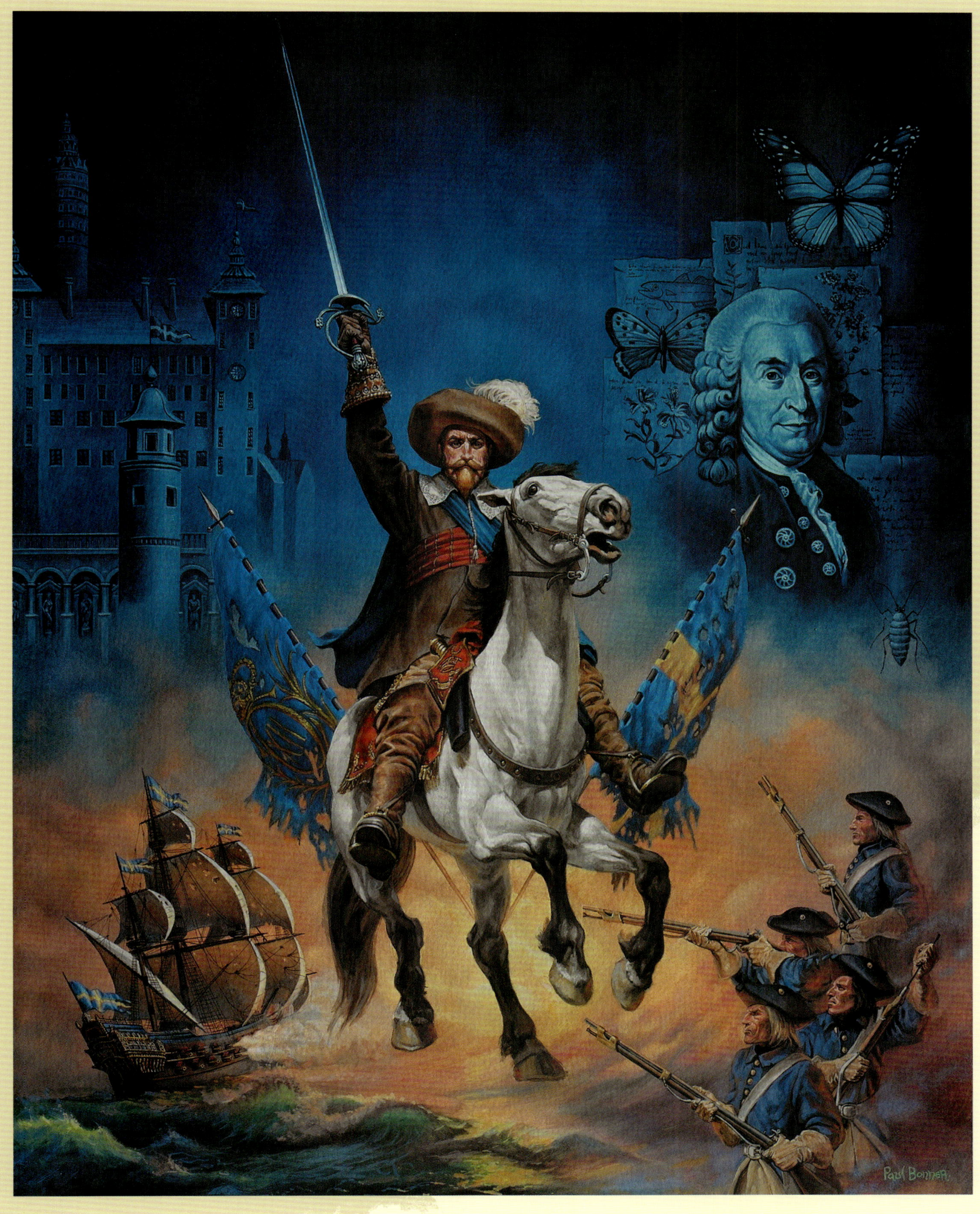

Svea Rike. Video game cover. A game based on Swedish history.

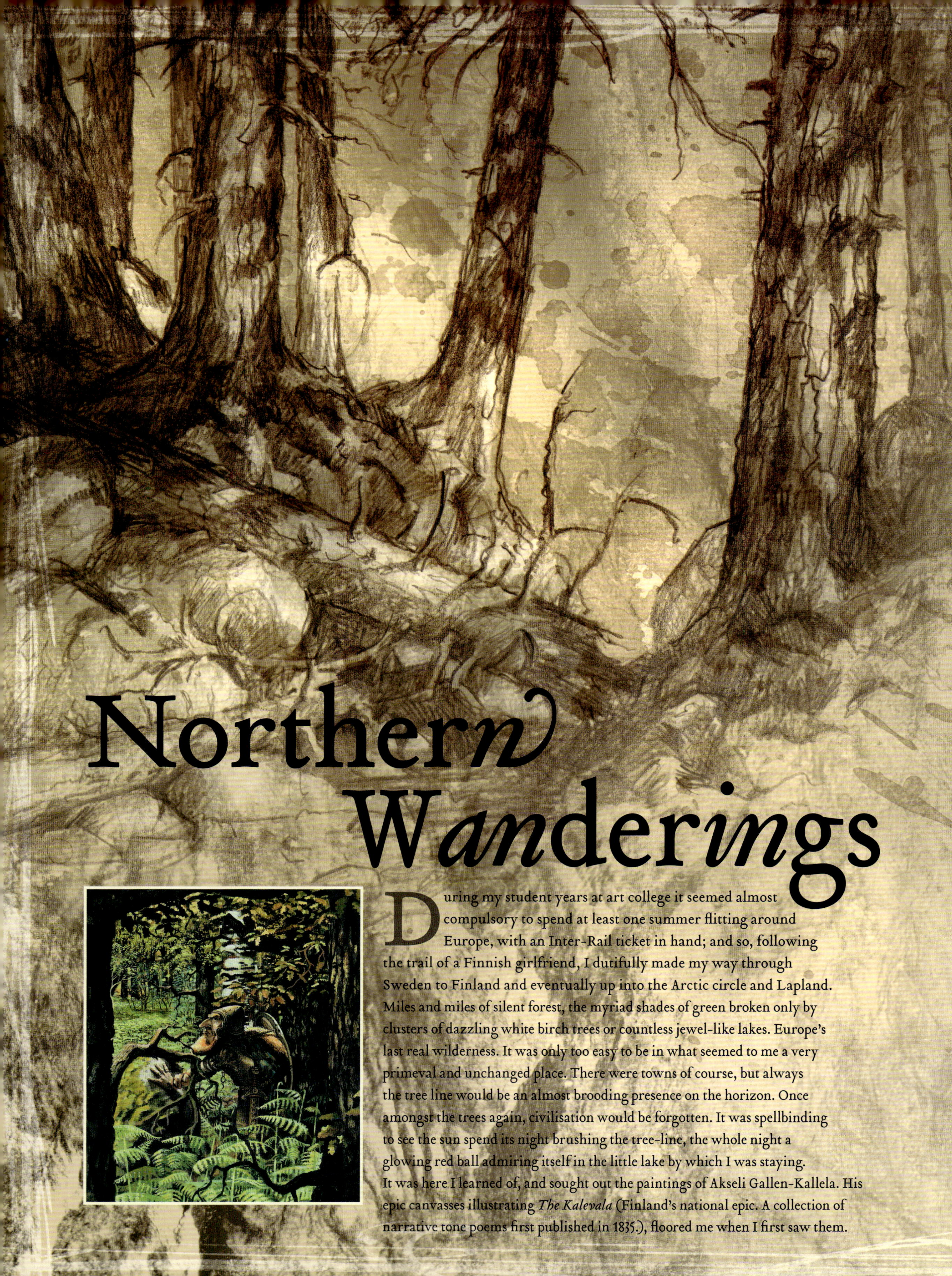

Northern Wanderings

During my student years at art college it seemed almost compulsory to spend at least one summer flitting around Europe, with an Inter-Rail ticket in hand; and so, following the trail of a Finnish girlfriend, I dutifully made my way through Sweden to Finland and eventually up into the Arctic circle and Lapland. Miles and miles of silent forest, the myriad shades of green broken only by clusters of dazzling white birch trees or countless jewel-like lakes. Europe's last real wilderness. It was only too easy to be in what seemed to me a very primeval and unchanged place. There were towns of course, but always the tree line would be an almost brooding presence on the horizon. Once amongst the trees again, civilisation would be forgotten. It was spellbinding to see the sun spend its night brushing the tree-line, the whole night a glowing red ball admiring itself in the little lake by which I was staying.

It was here I learned of, and sought out the paintings of Akseli Gallen-Kallela. His epic canvasses illustrating *The Kalevala* (Finland's national epic. A collection of narrative tone poems first published in 1835.), floored me when I first saw them.

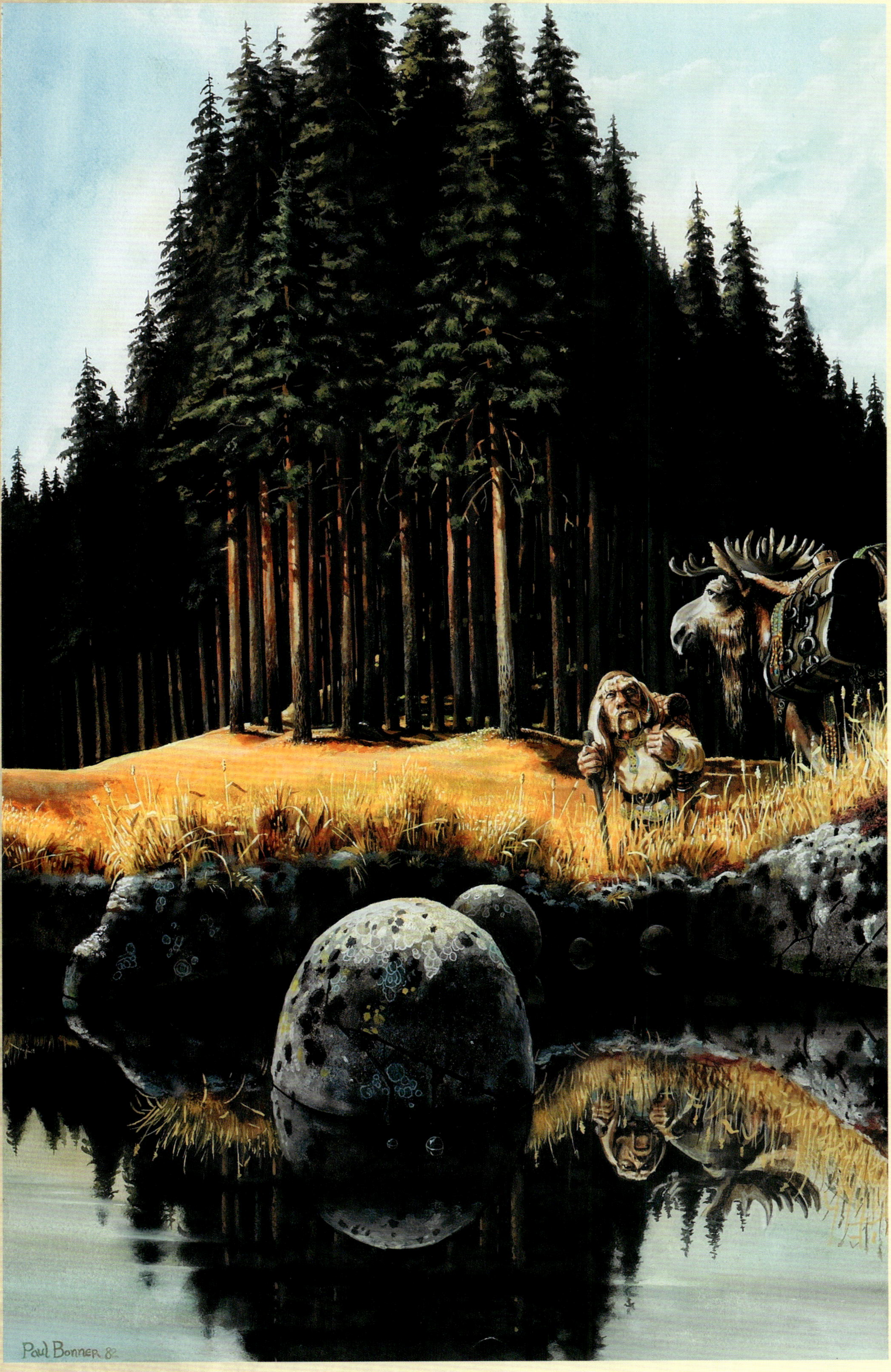

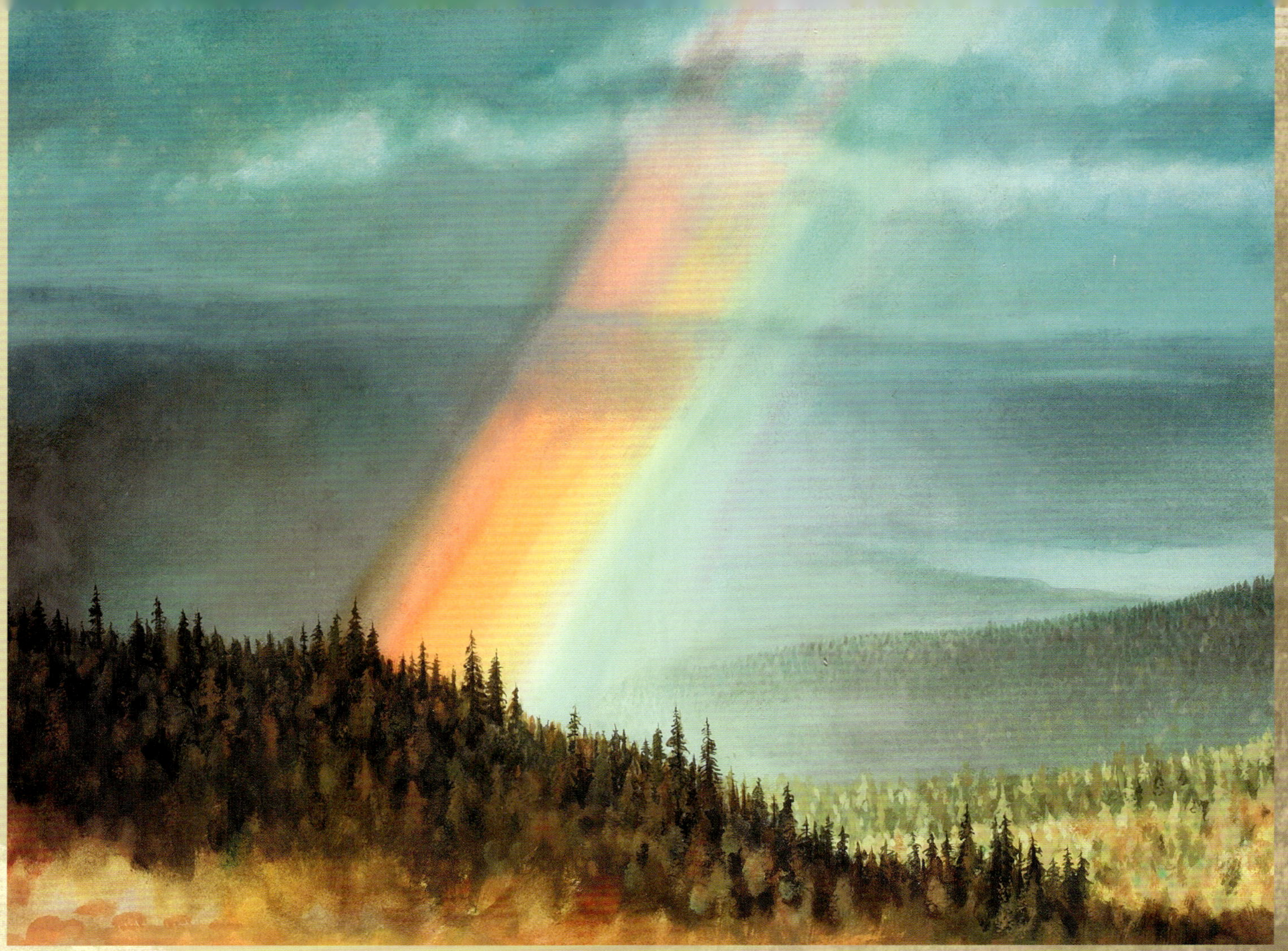

A masterful amalgamation of technical ability, colour, emotion and story-telling, the whole painted with a conviction rarely seen. Surrounded by the nature that had inspired him to so lovingly portrayed it, I got busy storing images away. Mental pictures, sketches and some photos; all were stored away for future reference.
I remember it was a culture shock coming back to the bustle and routine of life in London, but I itched to find a way to condense the impressions that I had accumulated into some definitive images which would try and capture all I had seen.

With no one looking over my shoulder, they actually came very easily, and with almost no forethought or actual preparatory scribbling - one leading to the next as the images grew from each other and suggested themselves. Some never got finished, as a better idea pushed them aside, or an occasional job turned up that my financial circumstances wouldn't allow me the luxury of refusing.
The initial idea was to come up with some definitive images that captured the essence of my travels, and then somehow try and tie them together to create my own epic little folk tale. I have always found it both easy and necessary to weave narratives around my paintings, providing a background for characters and the settings they find themselves in. It provides a justification and visual necessity for body language and facial expressions, which in turn create a reality that, hopefully, should reverberate through the picture. Something has to be taking place. Shining armour, axes the size of bulldozers and a last minute pump of the biceps won't get you a walk-on part in my world. You better have something to say, something on your mind, or dirty knees. I need someone or something with a story to tell.
Telling my own story was another matter. Each separate painting had a little narrative going on, but I was never able to persuade them to join forces and get together something that resembled a heroic epic. Actually, the fact that each one has its own little story, and exists independently from the others, leaves me with a rather reassuring feeling that somewhere some doors are open and that who- or whatever is free to come and go as they please. Again, it is about trying to capture one single moment, whilst at the same time providing furtive glances at the past, and hints of a possible future.

Having struck upon an outlet for my own energy, I found an increasing dissatisfaction with the commercial jobs my poor agent tried to rustle up for me. He tried, but he could never really pry me out of my own world. Caught up in this world, I would put off doing jobs until the last minute, and found it more and more difficult to work up any enthusiasm for the cosy world of children books that I could feel myself being herded towards. Working on my own paintings caused one or two stretched deadlines, and the growing conviction that I needed to be able to follow my own musings.
This lead to the obvious step of becoming a part-time gardener. It paid my bills, which, as well as freeing my conscience from having to nag me about turning down jobs, gave me the freedom to do my own work, as well as healthy doses of fresh air.

Paul Bonner

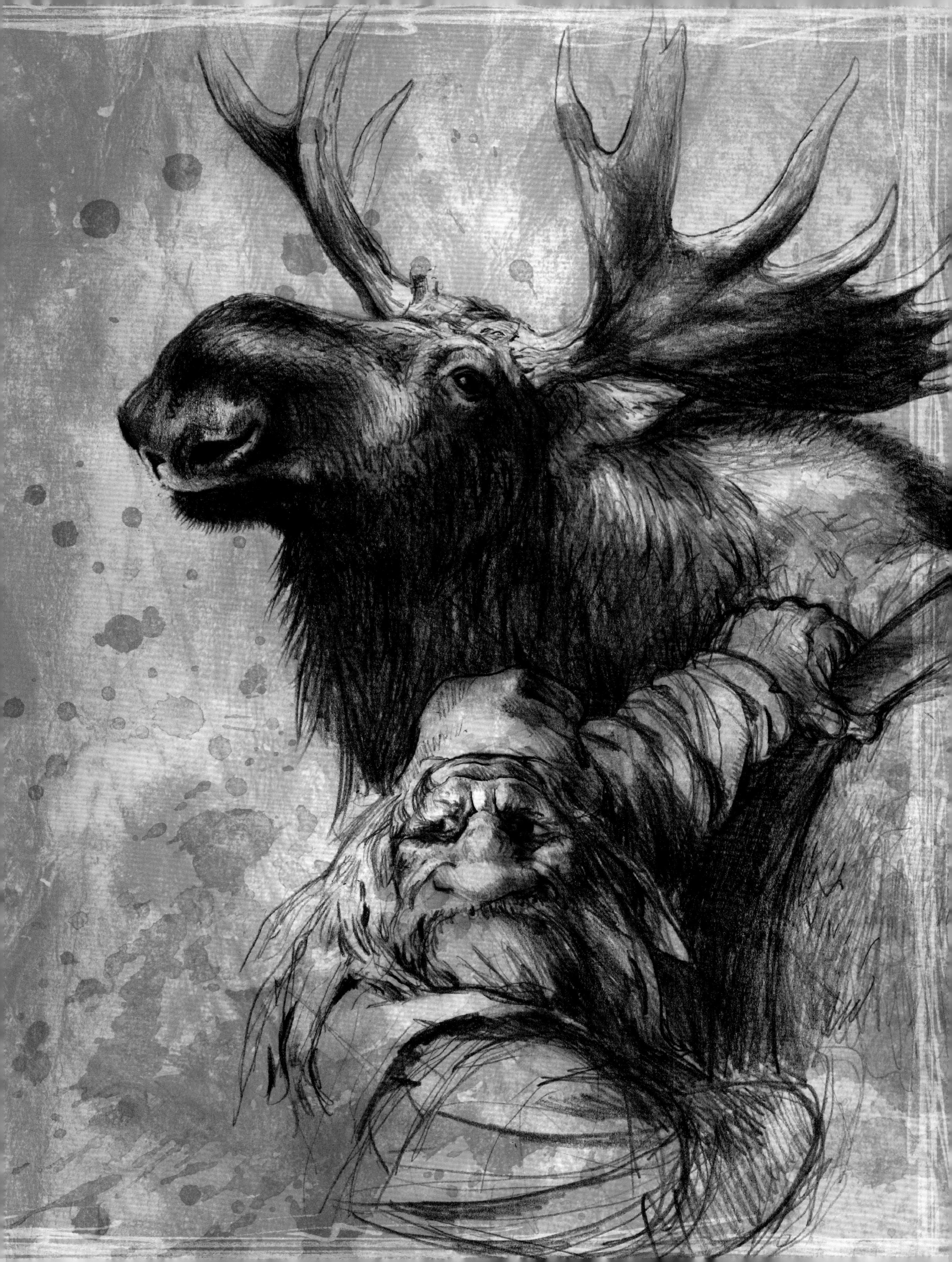

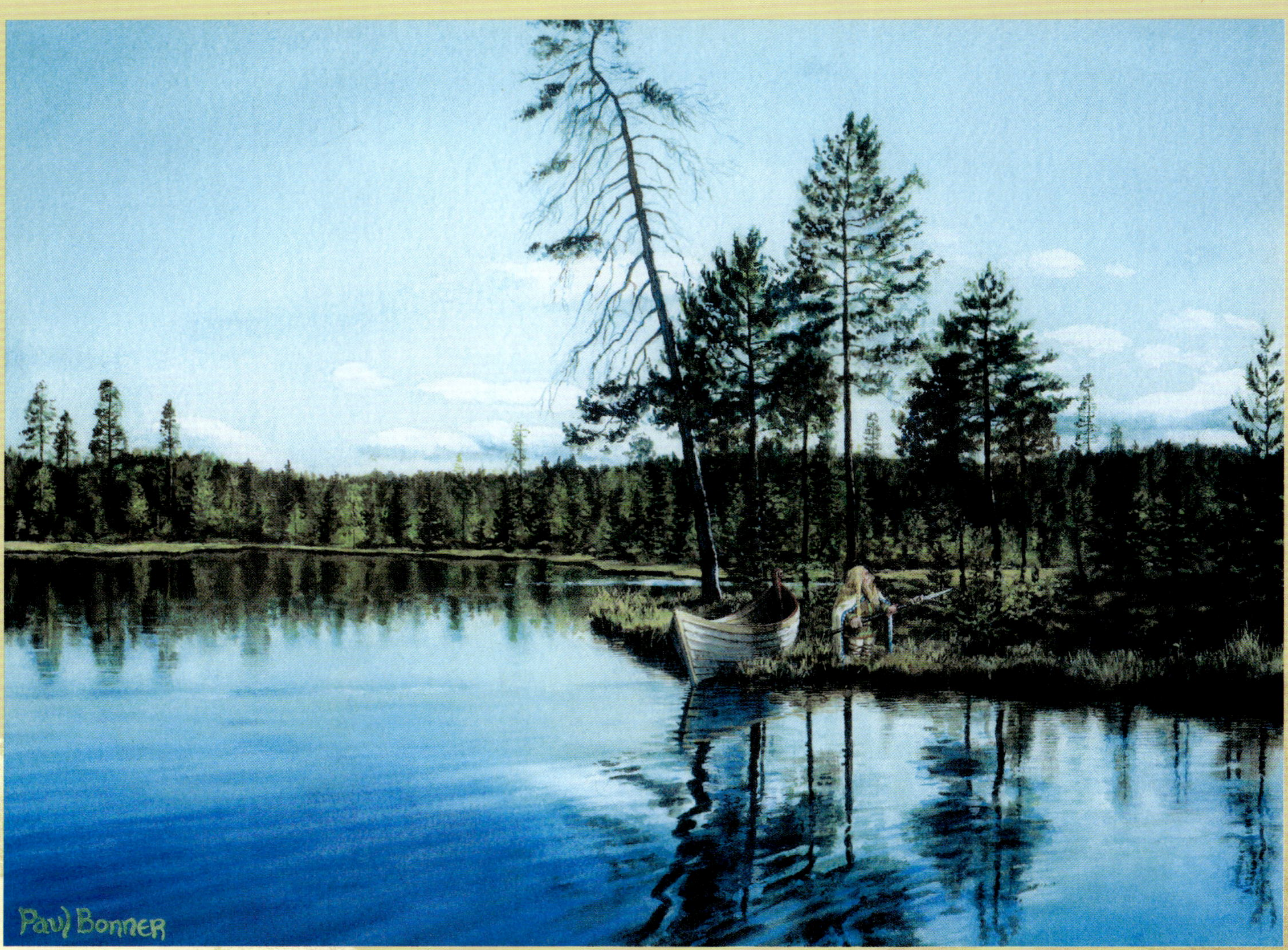

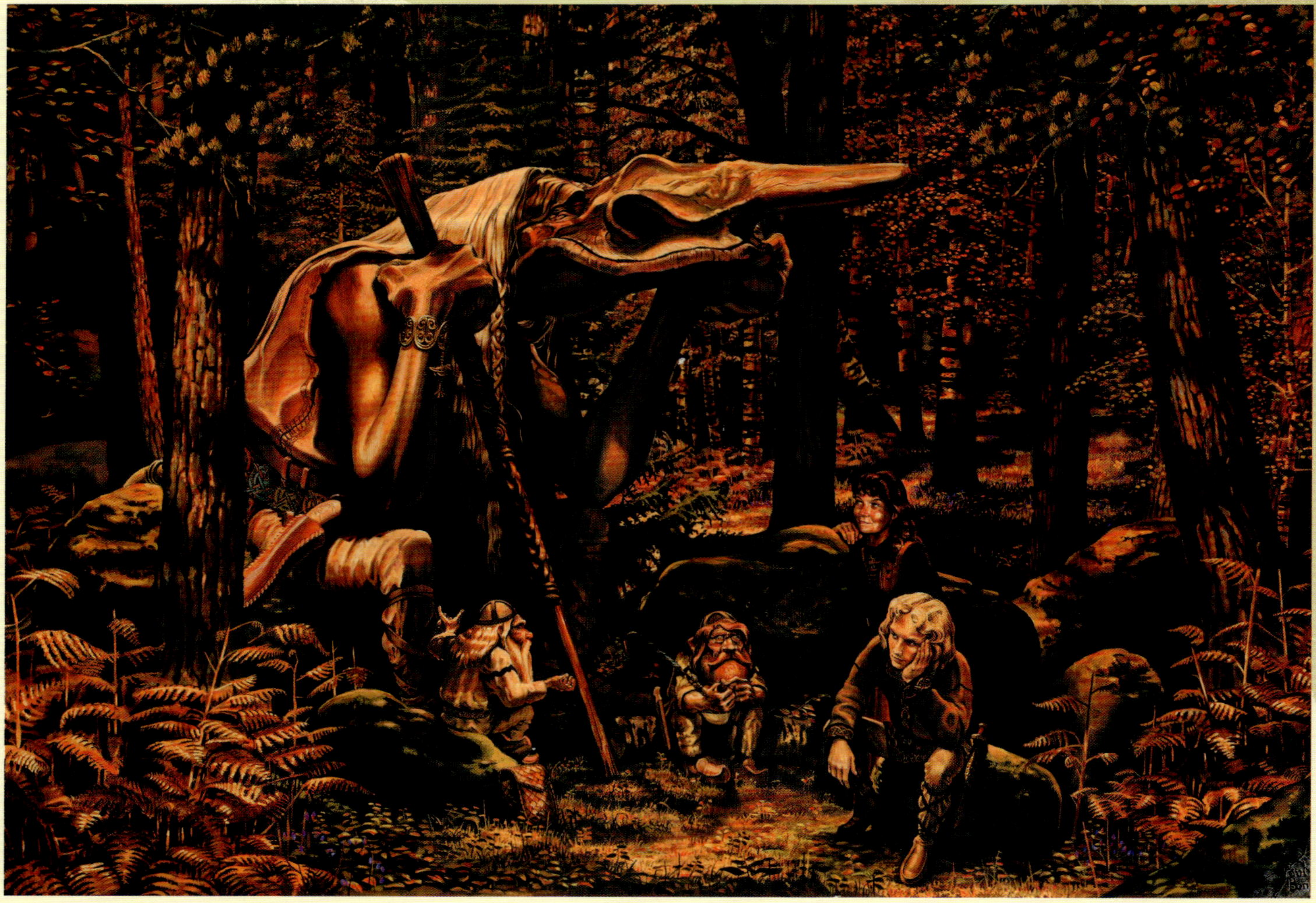

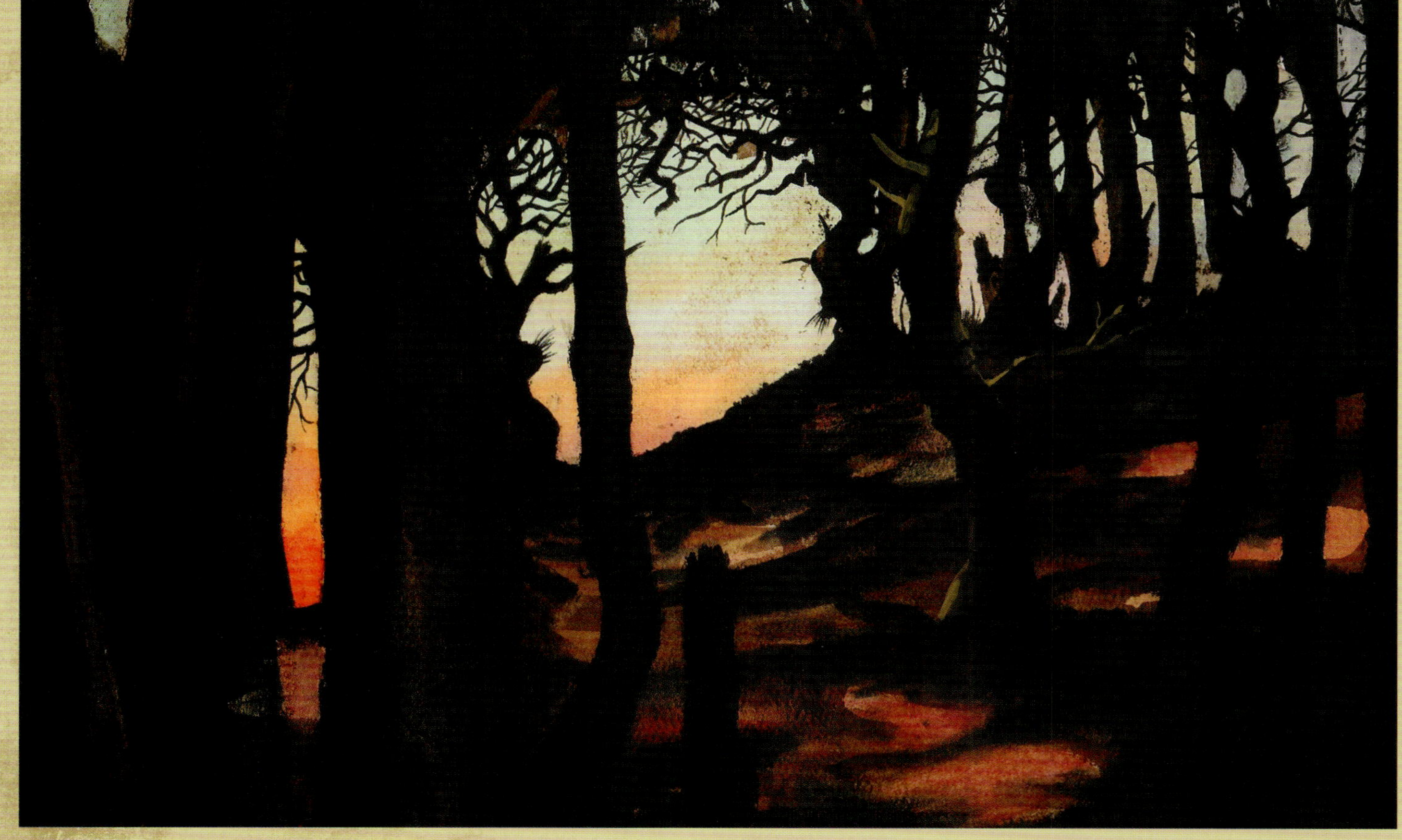

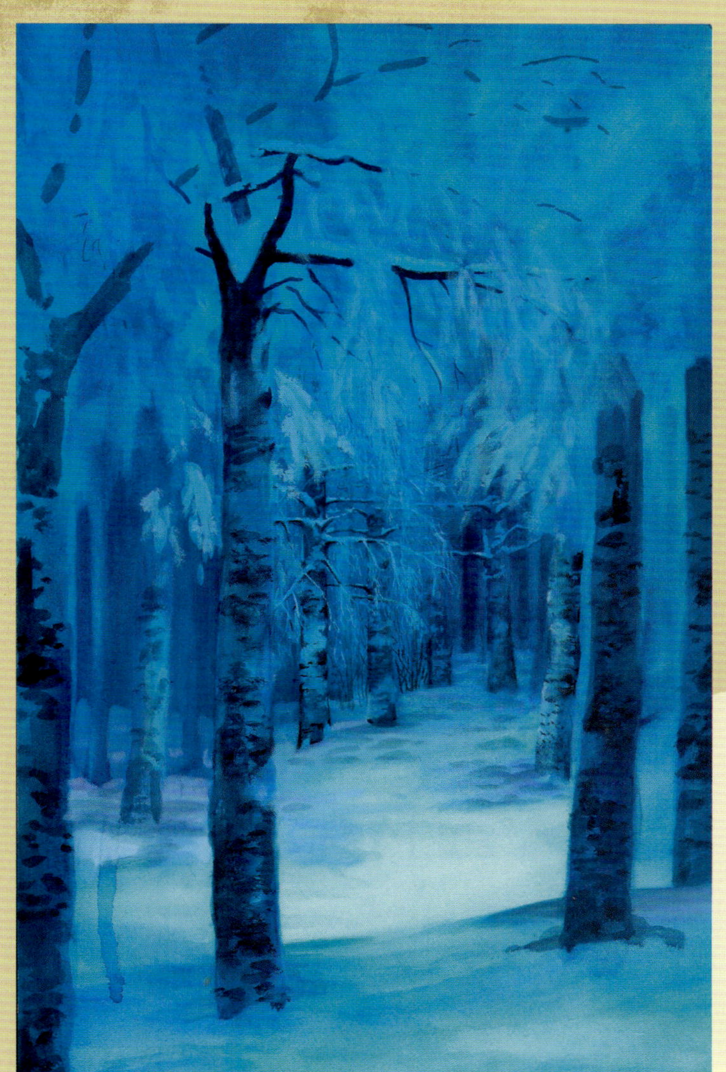

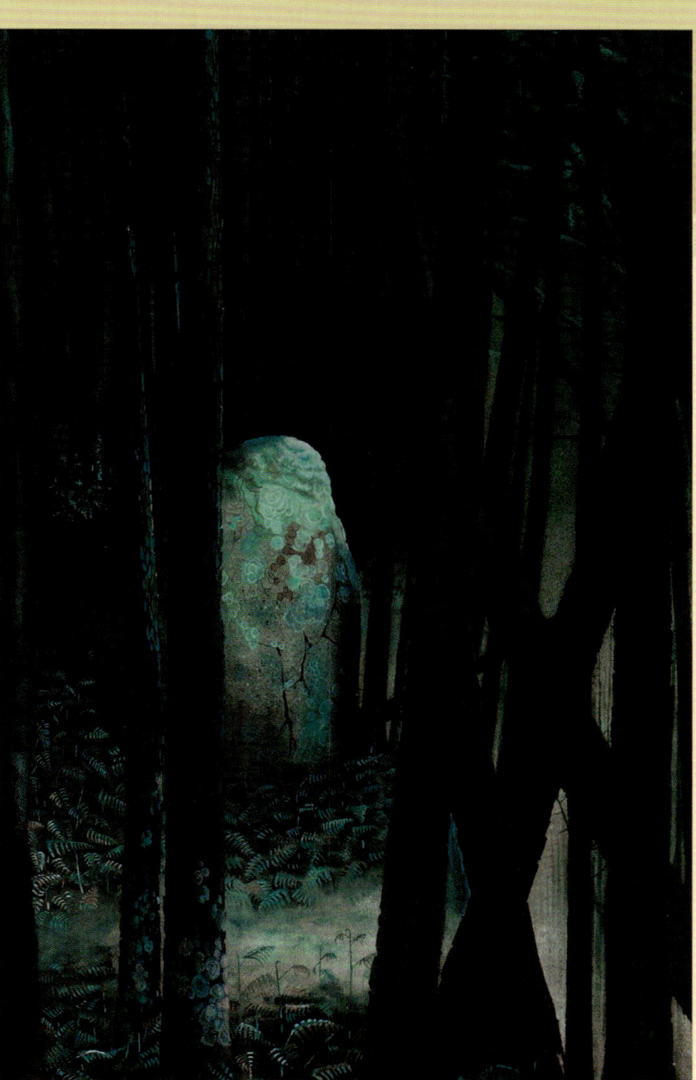

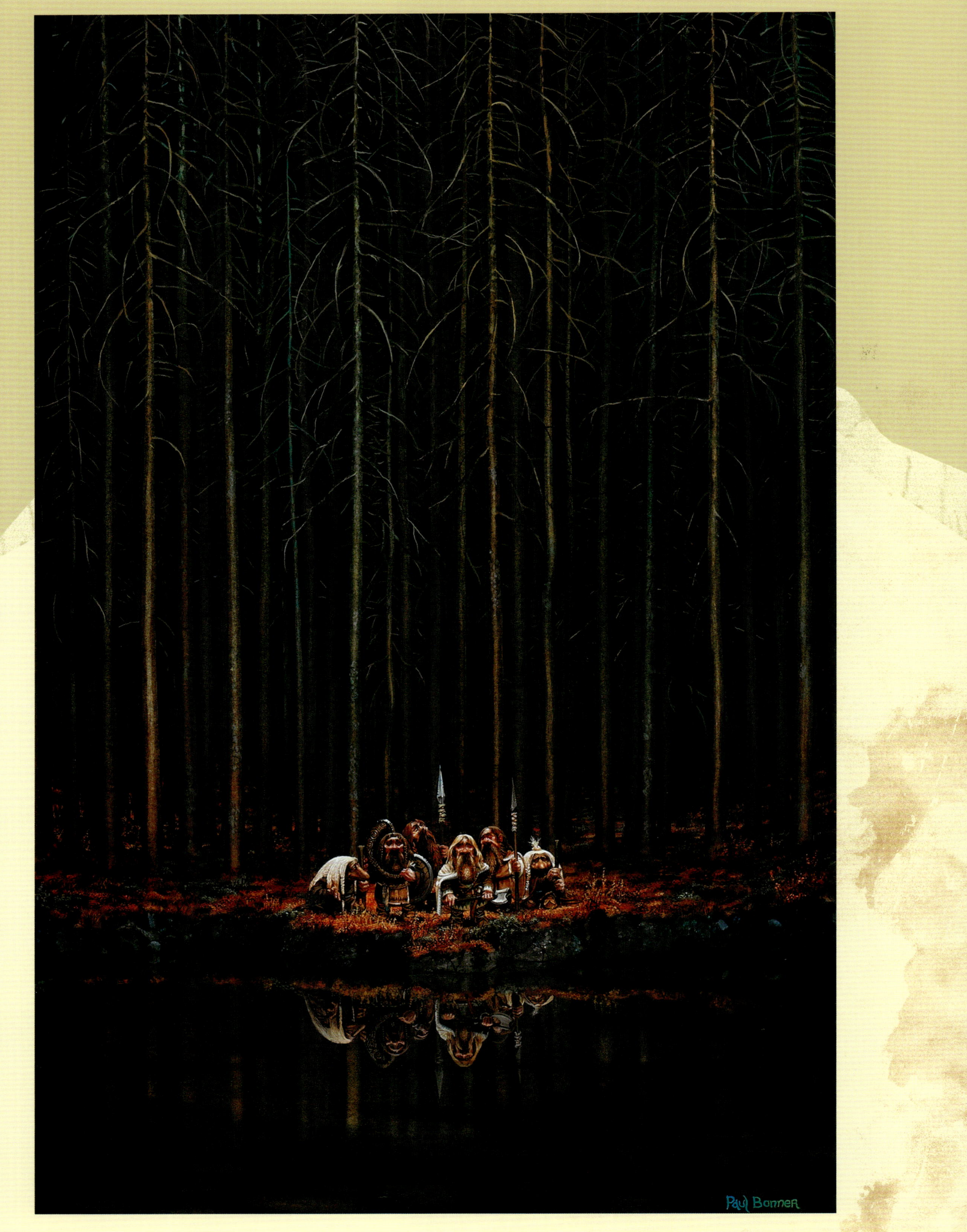
Paul Bonner

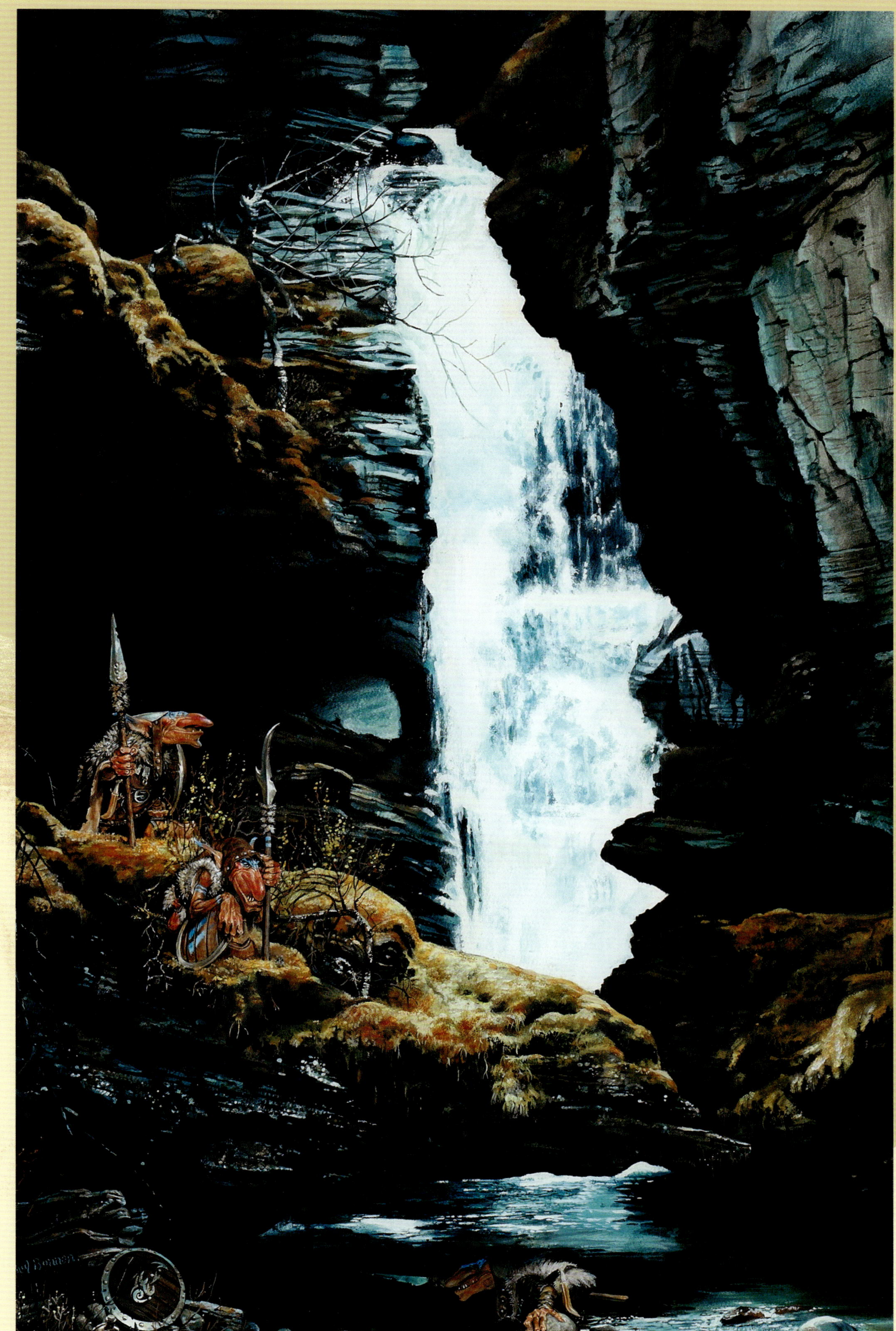

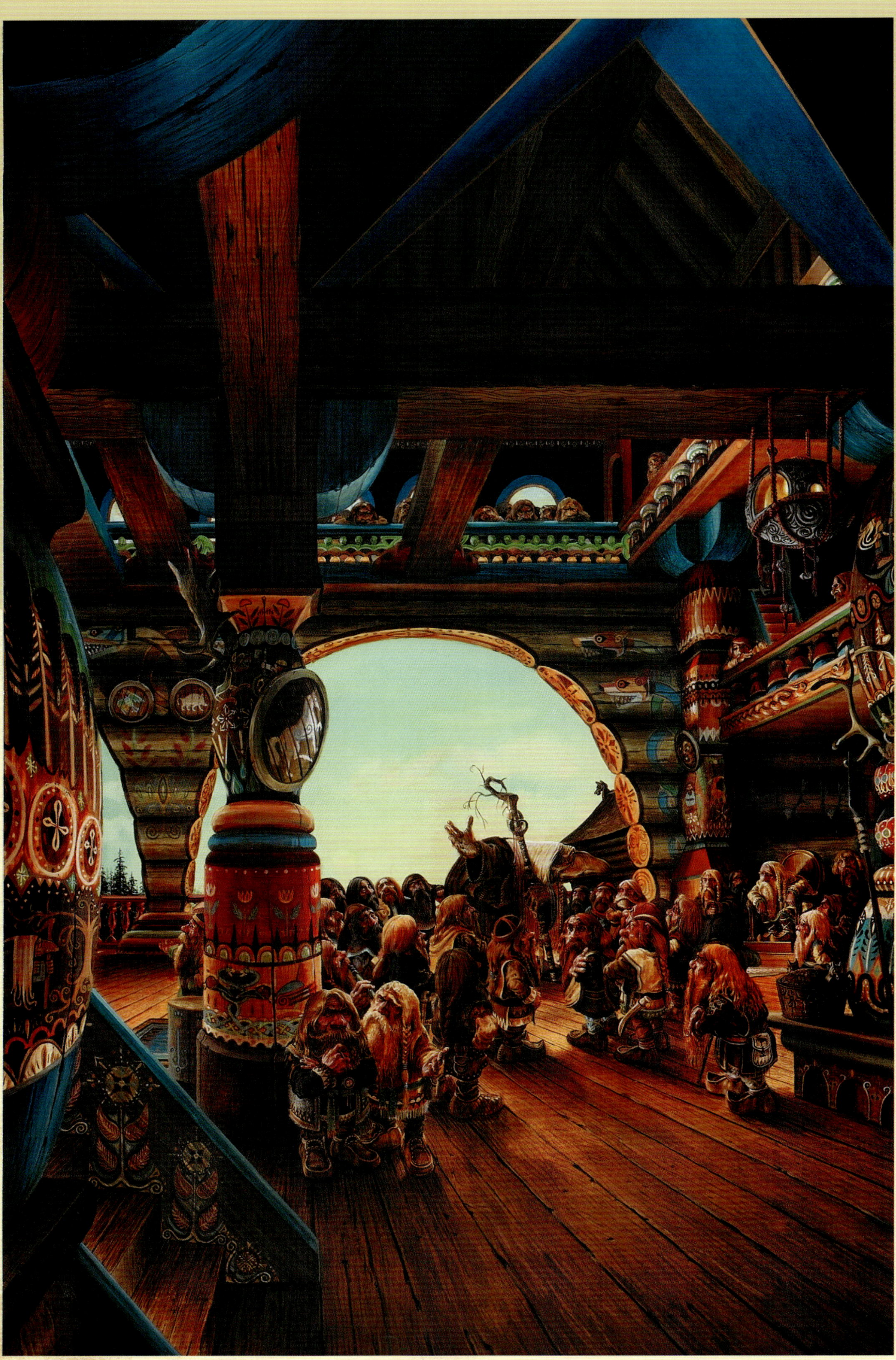

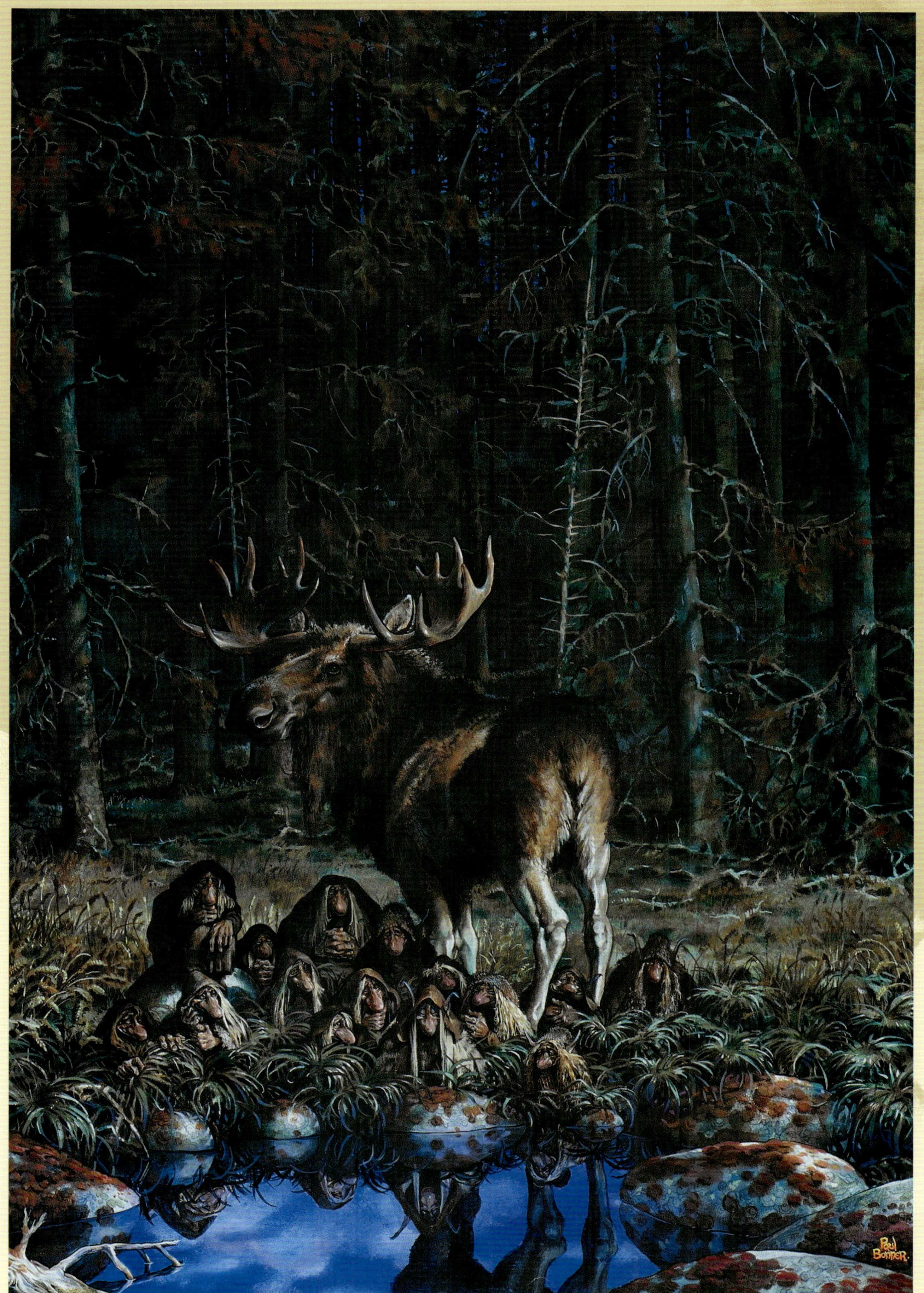
Paul
Bonner.

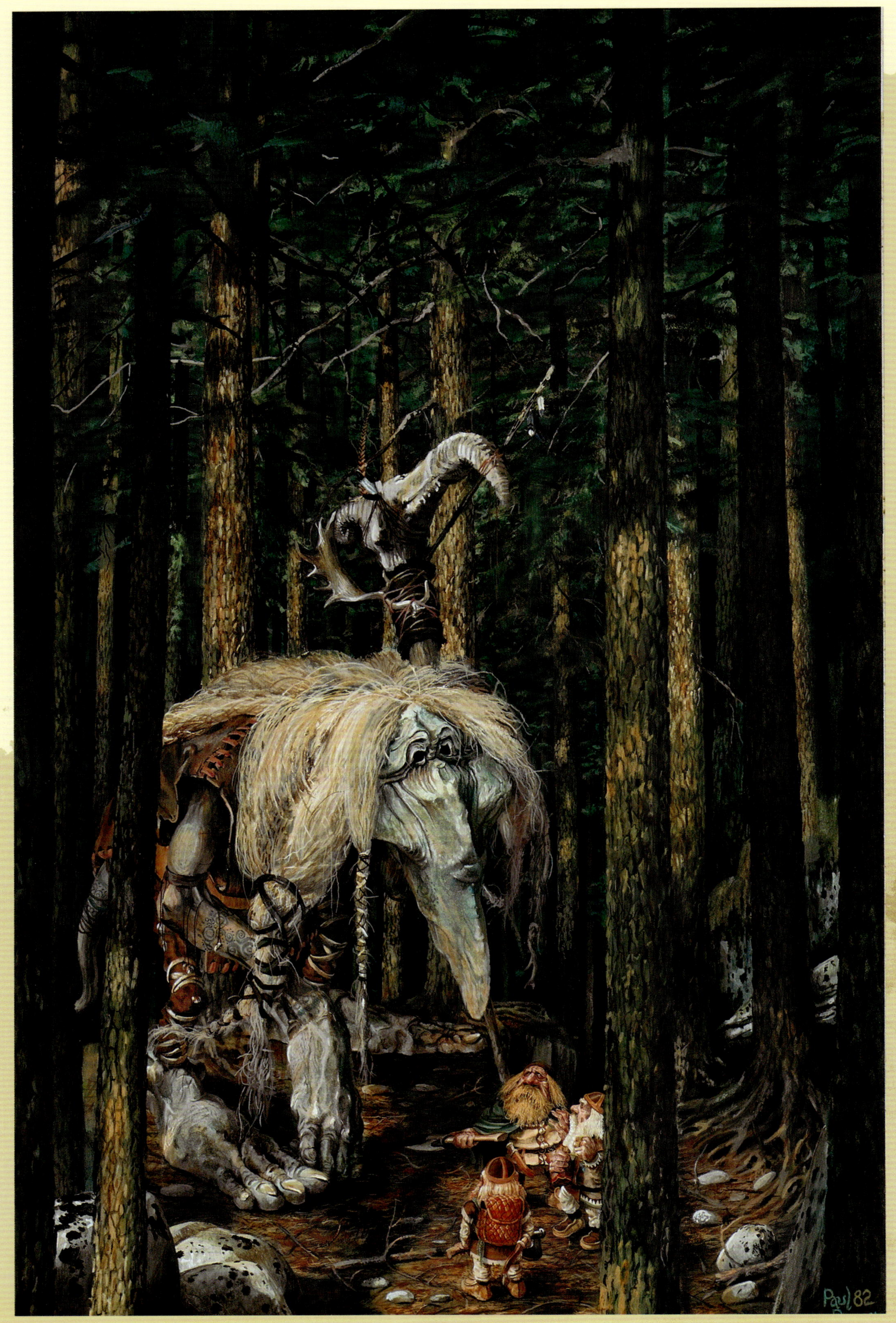
Paul 82

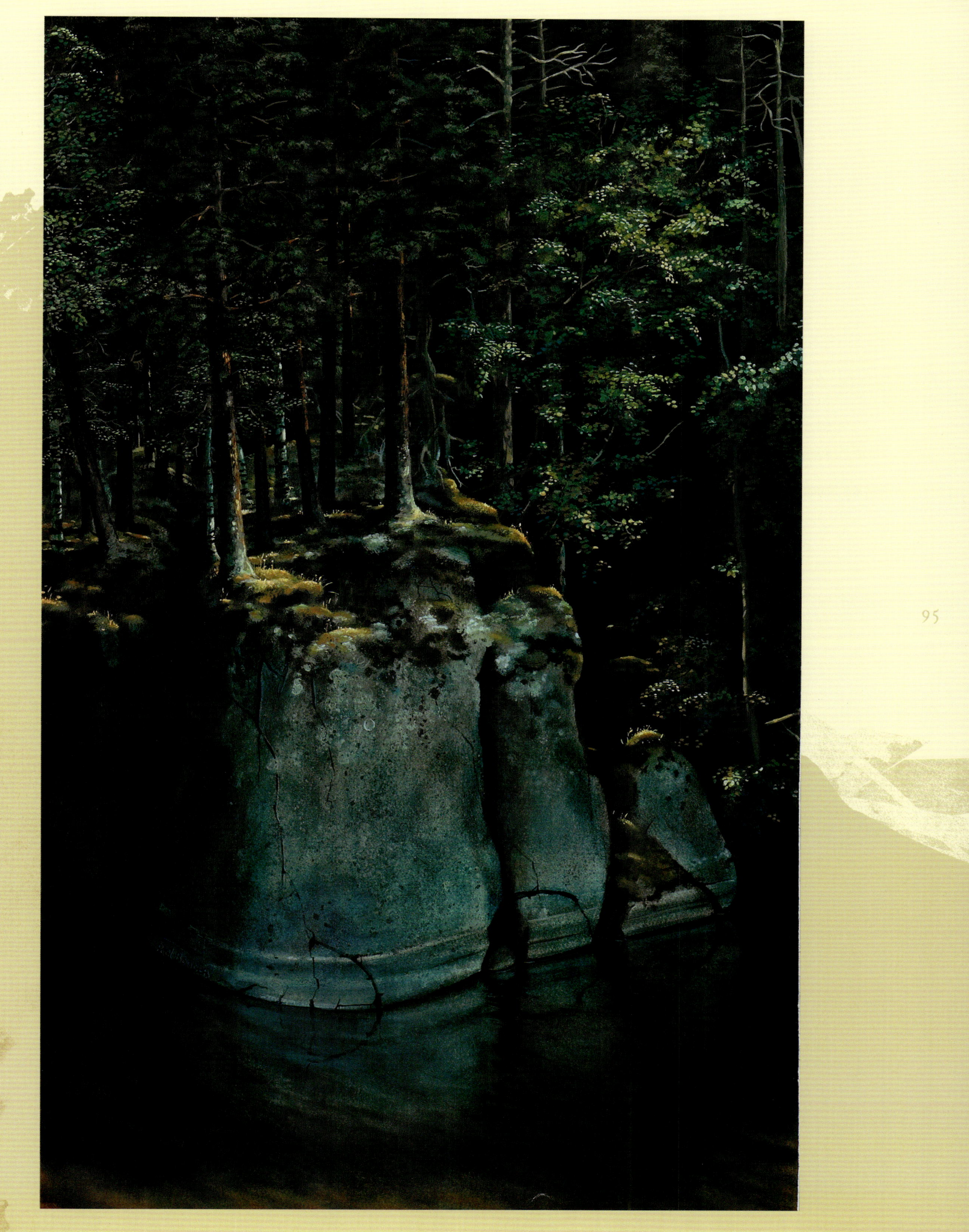

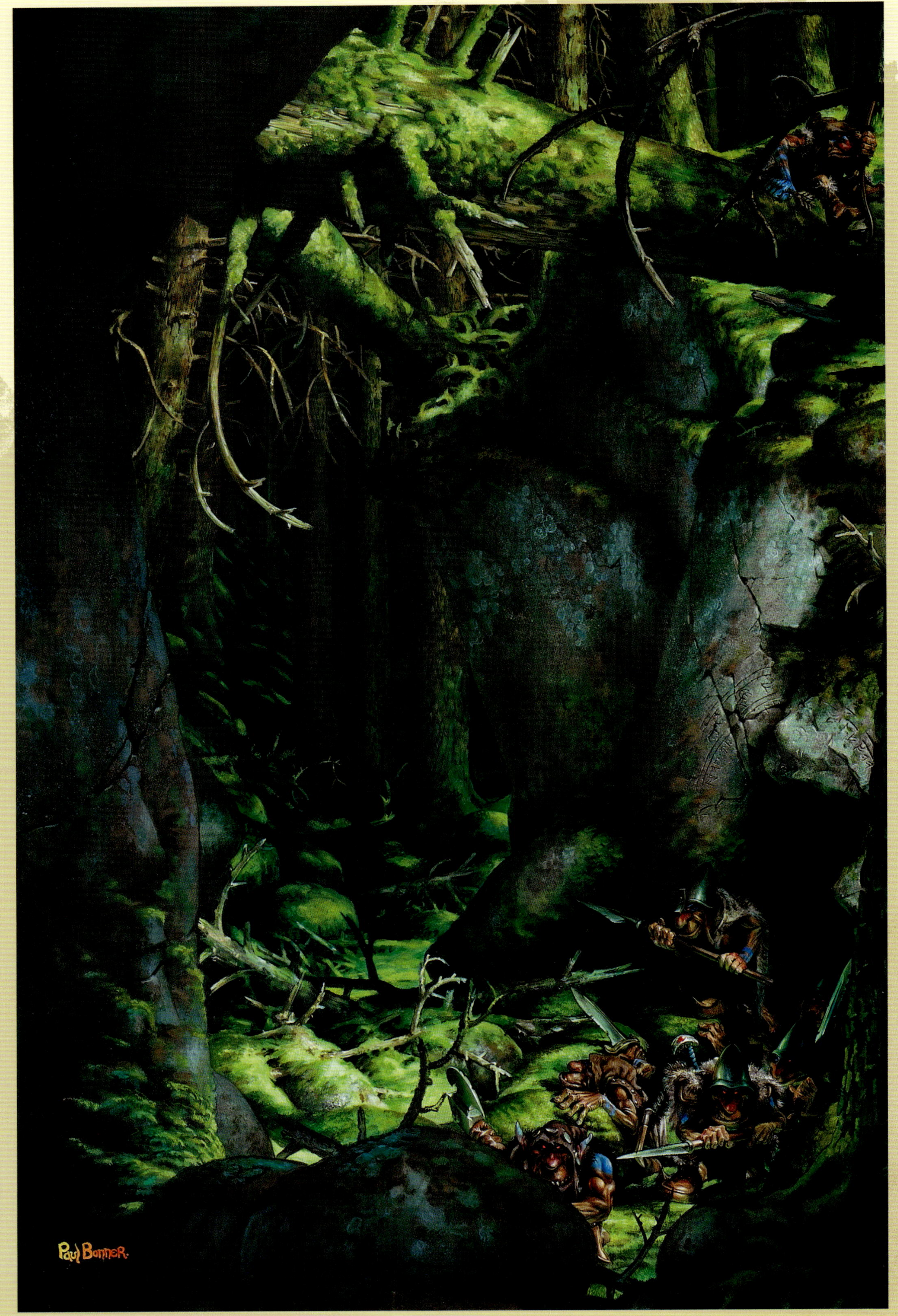
Paul Bonner.

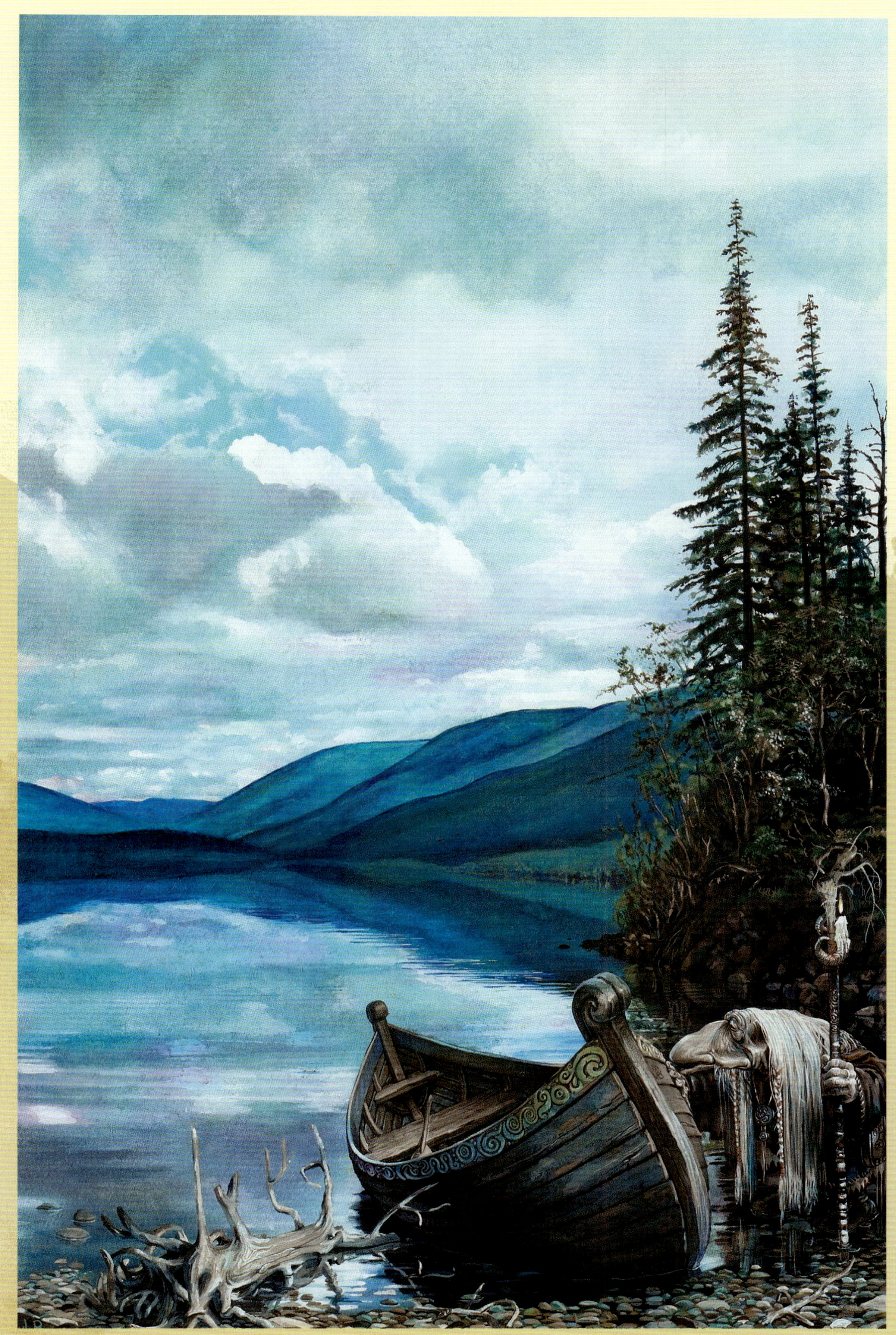

97

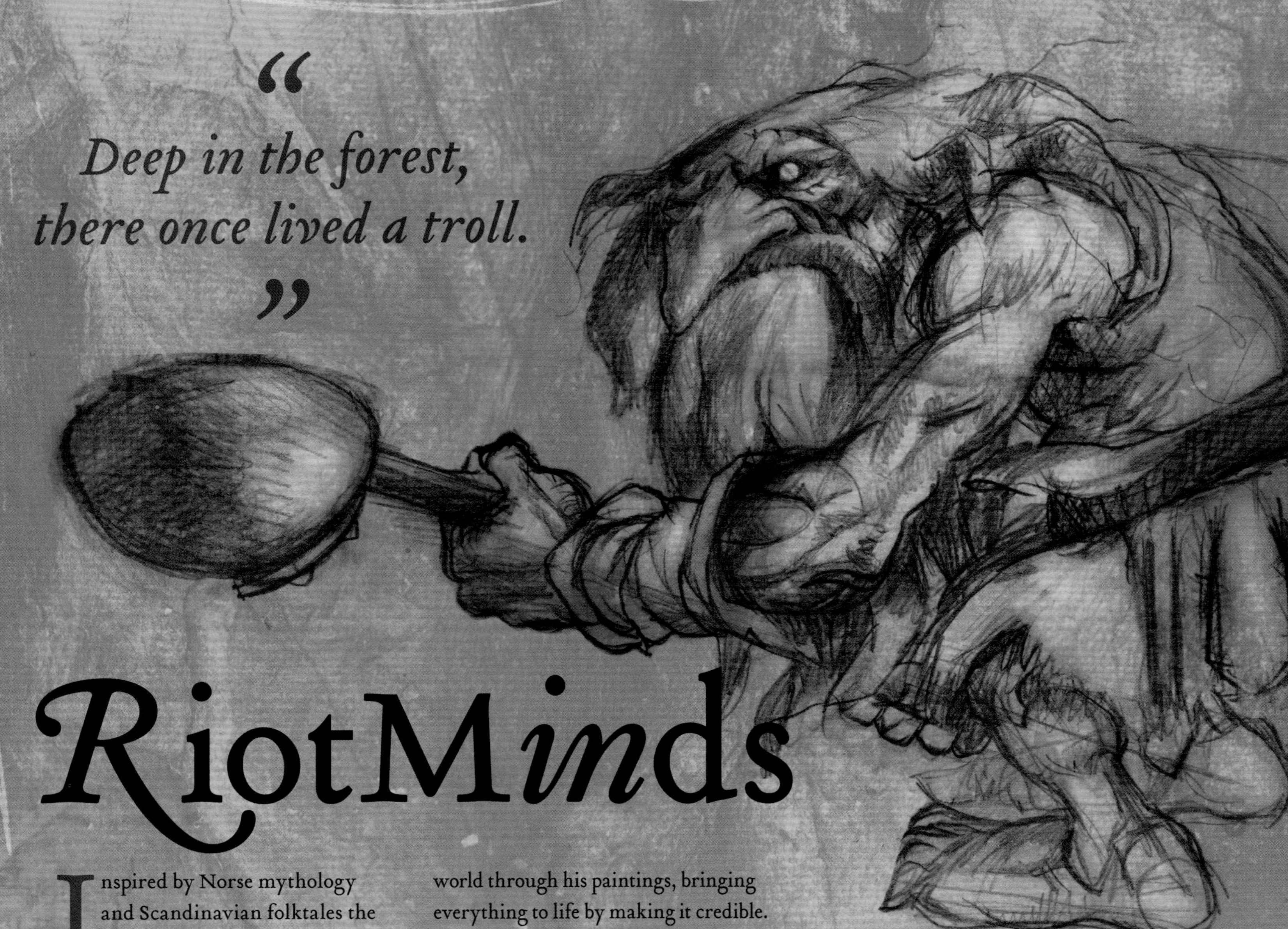

"Deep in the forest, there once lived a troll."

RiotMinds

Inspired by Norse mythology and Scandinavian folktales the fantasy world of Trudvang is unique in many ways. The landscape of mystic waterfalls, deep forests and moss-covered stones plays as important a role as the trolls and other beasts dwelling there.

At first I didn't know that Paul was intrigued and inspired by the sagas and legends of Norse mythology. Sure, I'd seen his fantastic paintings for Mutant Chronicles and some of his early black-and-white illustrations for Games Workshop, but when I first saw a few unpublished paintings based on Scandinavian themes, I knew he would be the perfect cover artist for us. His wonderful take on trolls, the deep forests and the mythical tone – they just had everything we wanted. However, over the years Paul has become more than a cover artist for us. His designs and ideas have inspired us, helping us to carve out the various setting in our world through his paintings, bringing everything to life by making it credible.

Paul is second to none when it comes to details and design. Looking at his paintings you'll find so many beautiful intricacies, not only in terms of a figure's accoutrements, anatomy and expression, but also how the light plays with the surroundings, how the shadows shroud the forest and how it all reflects from a dark pool. This wealth of attention plays a key role in his paintings. I have always loved how Paul can make a painting interesting and believable, yet avoiding the all too predictable fantasy settings. Trudvang is not about streaming fireballs, or knights in glimmering armour and flaming sword, its about down-to-earth heroes trying to battle nature as much as trolls and other fabulous beasts taken from the Scandinavian myths. Few other artists that I have met have understood this. Paul creates a perfect balance of the epic and the simple, the heroic and the ordinary. Every painting Paul has done for us is different. It would be impossible to compare them with each other, or to say one is better that another. My personal favorite though – and one which I think encapsulates everything we want for Trudvang – is the image depicting a few heroes in a boat looking at two trolls. Take a close look at this one, you'll see so much detail in the water, the moment is so perfectly captured, that you feel you are there. Just look at the rune dragon on the stone wall, it seems ancient, who did that, when and why? This painting has so few of the standard modern fantasy elements in it but so many of the old traditional Scandinavian fantasy paintings. Arthur Rackham, Akseli Gallen-Kallela and John Bauer – all of them had mastered the art of making the Scandinavian folktales come alive. Paul Bonner truly keeps that tradition alive with his wonderful paintings.

Théodore Bergquist – *RiotMinds*

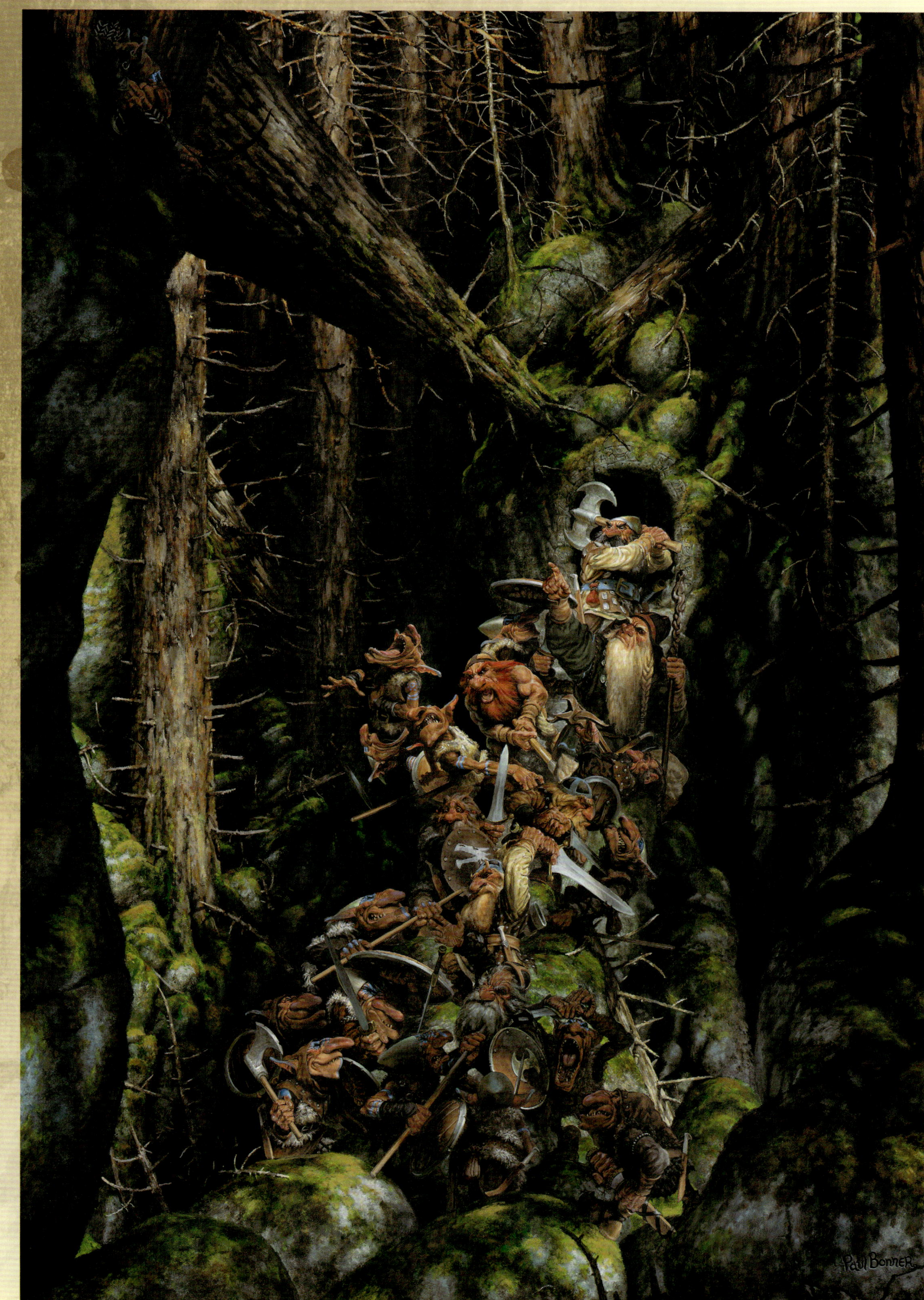
Paul Bonner

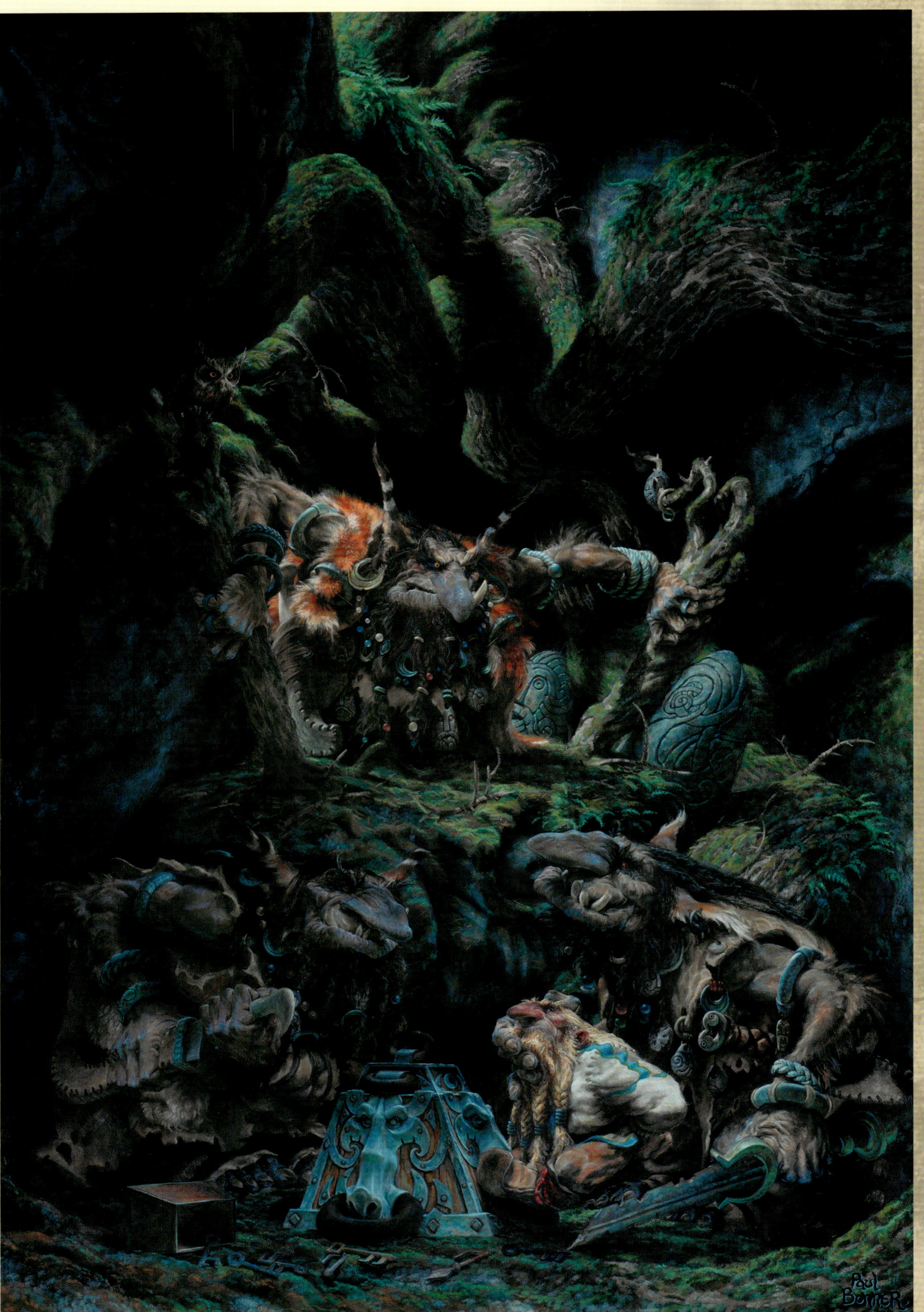
Paul
Bonner

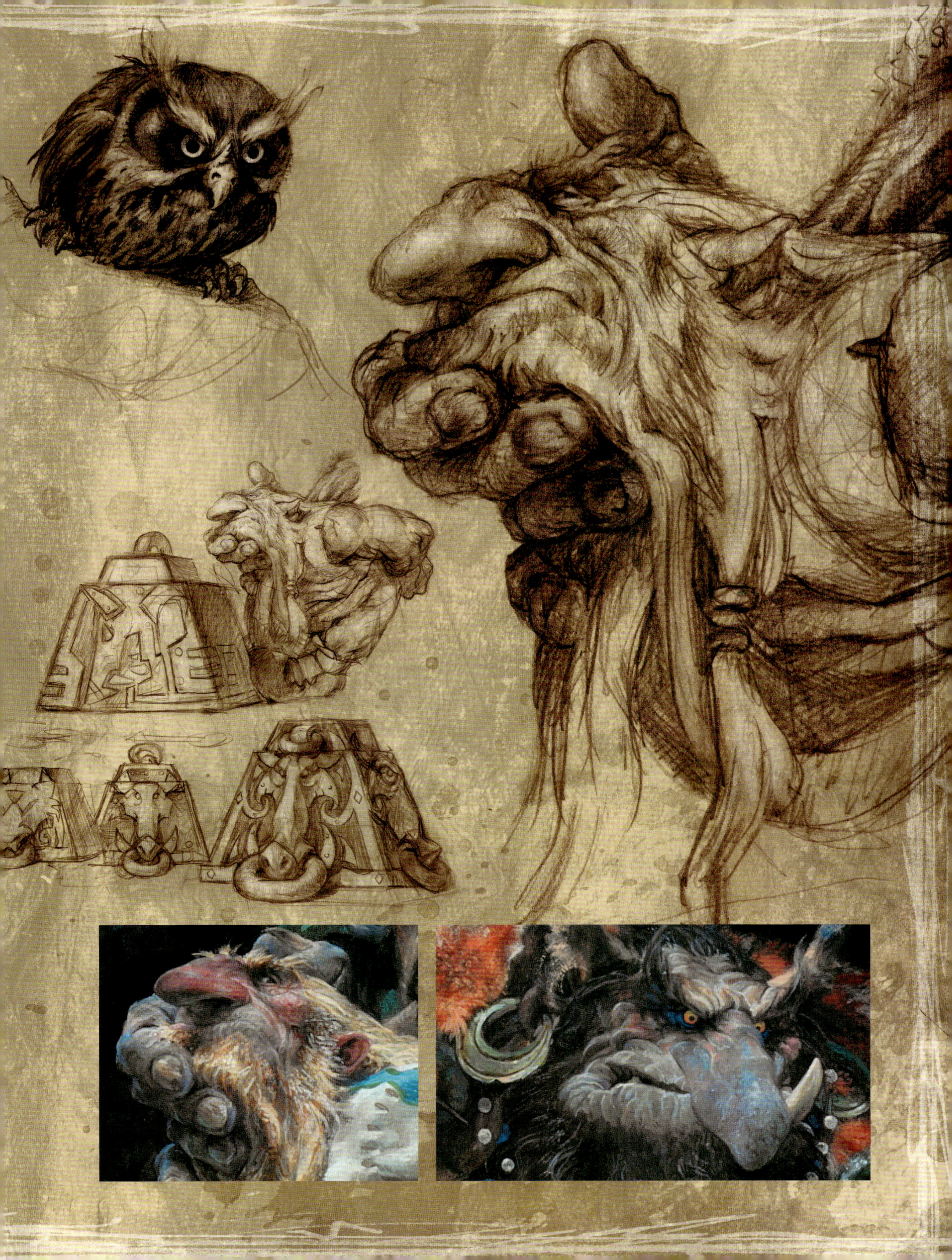

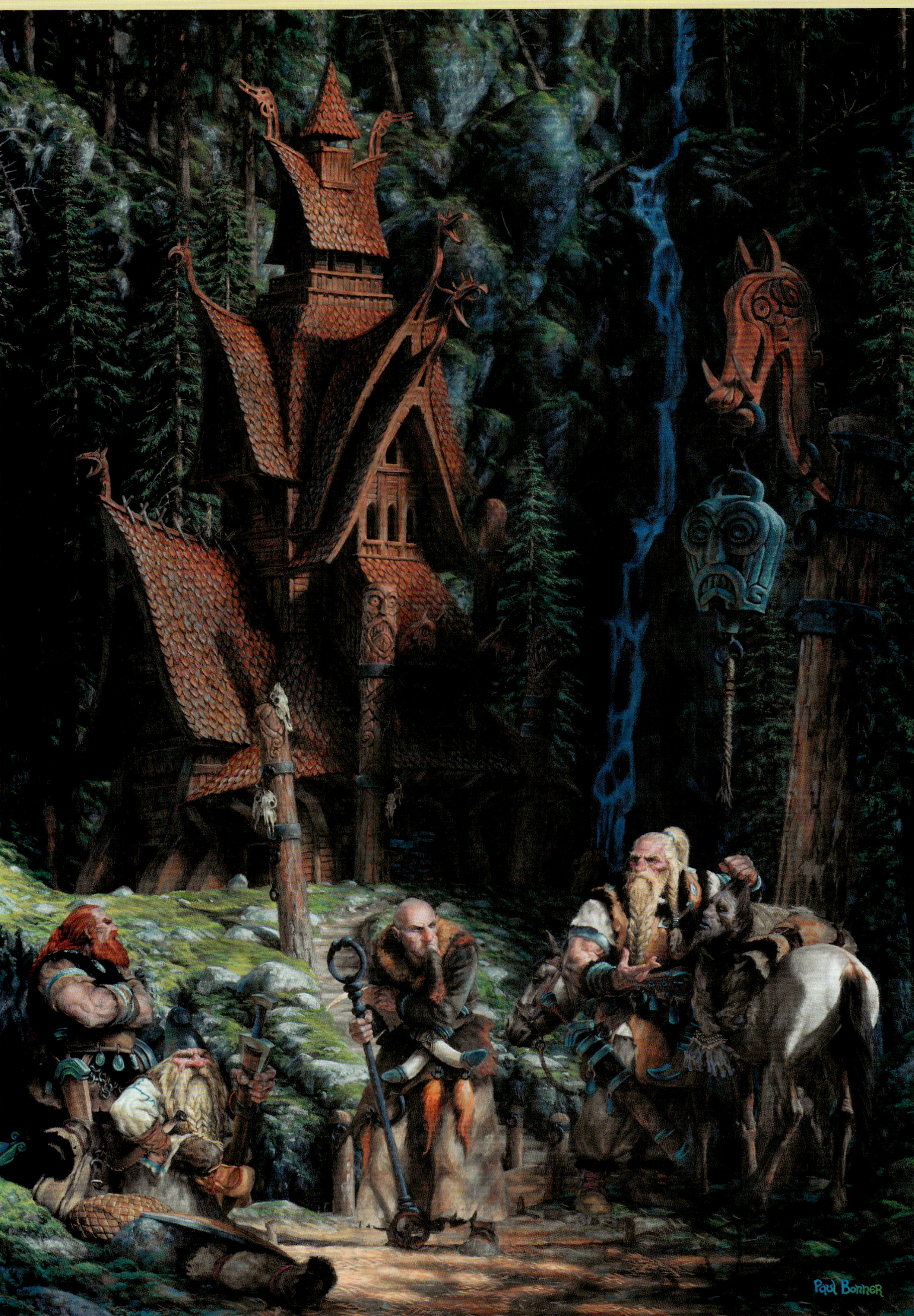
Paul Bonner

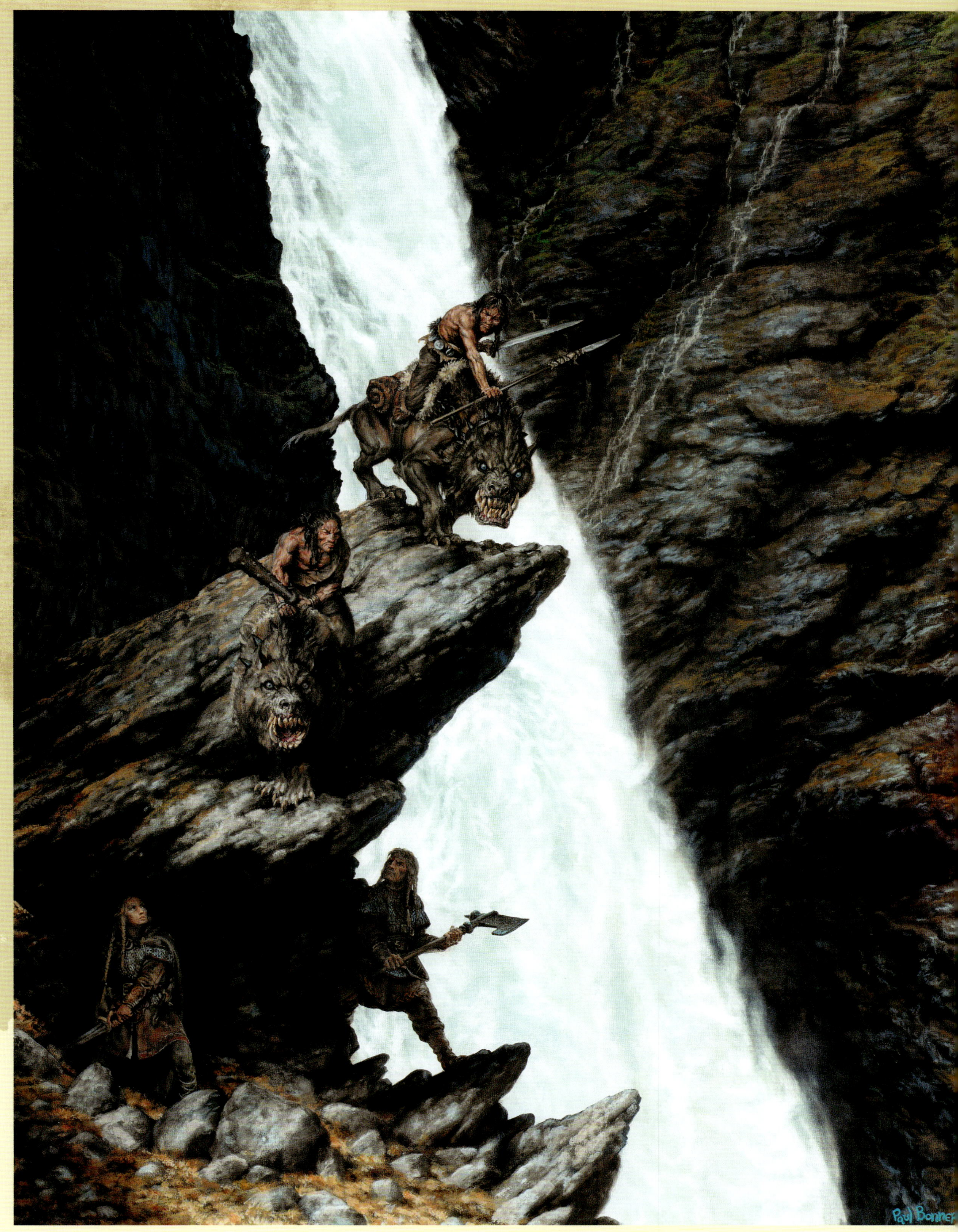
Paul Bonner

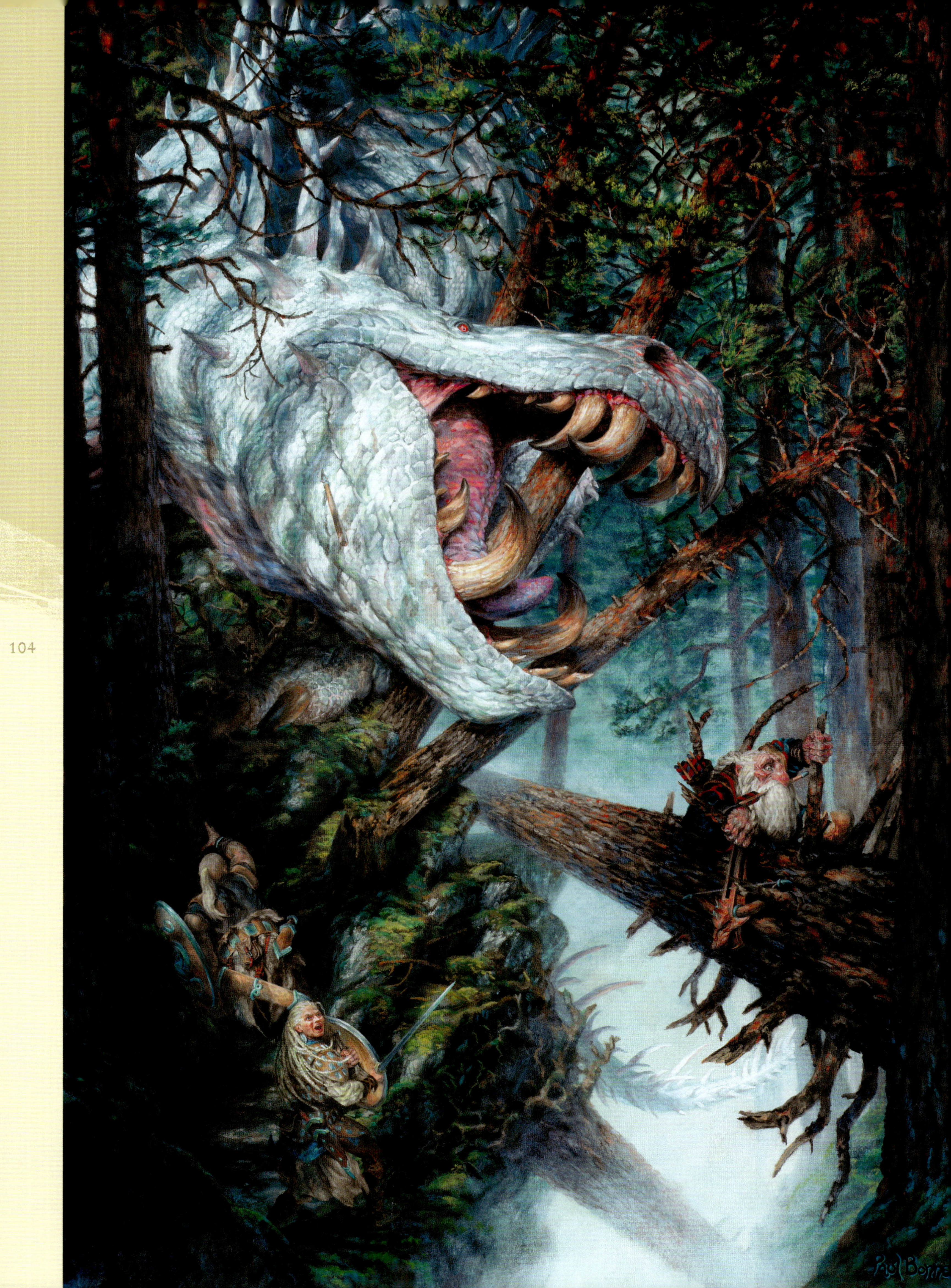
Paul Bonner

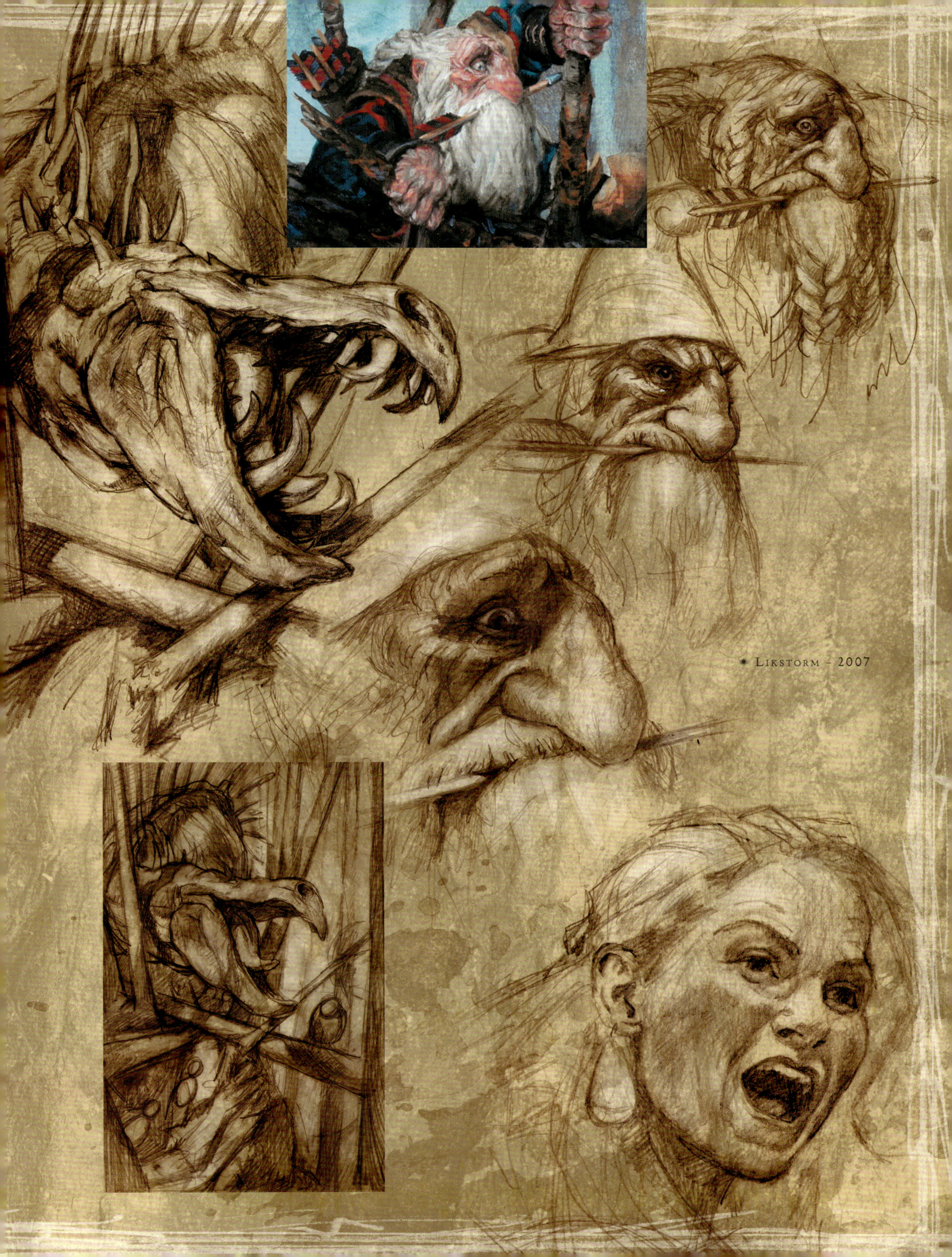

✶ Likstorm - 2007

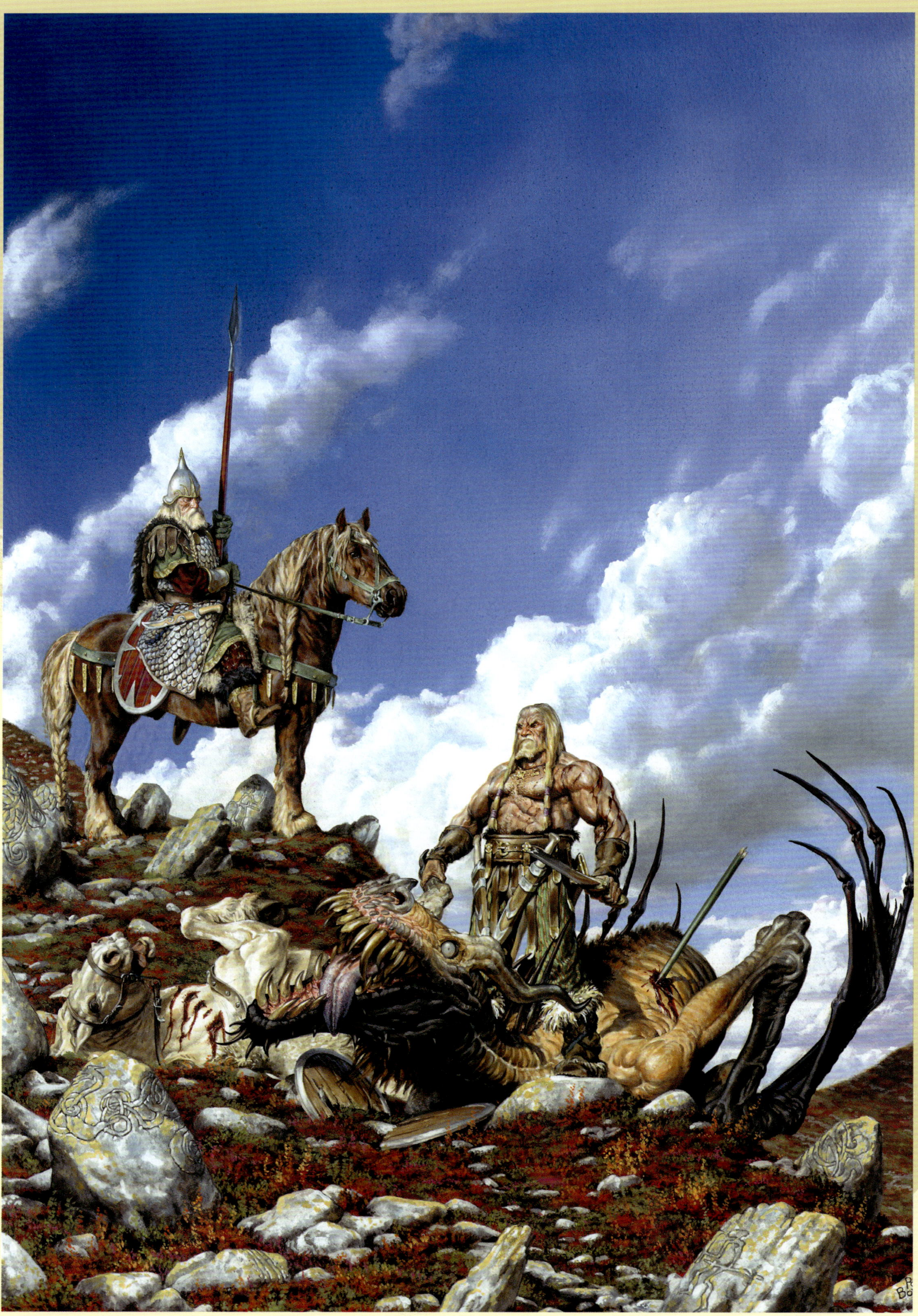

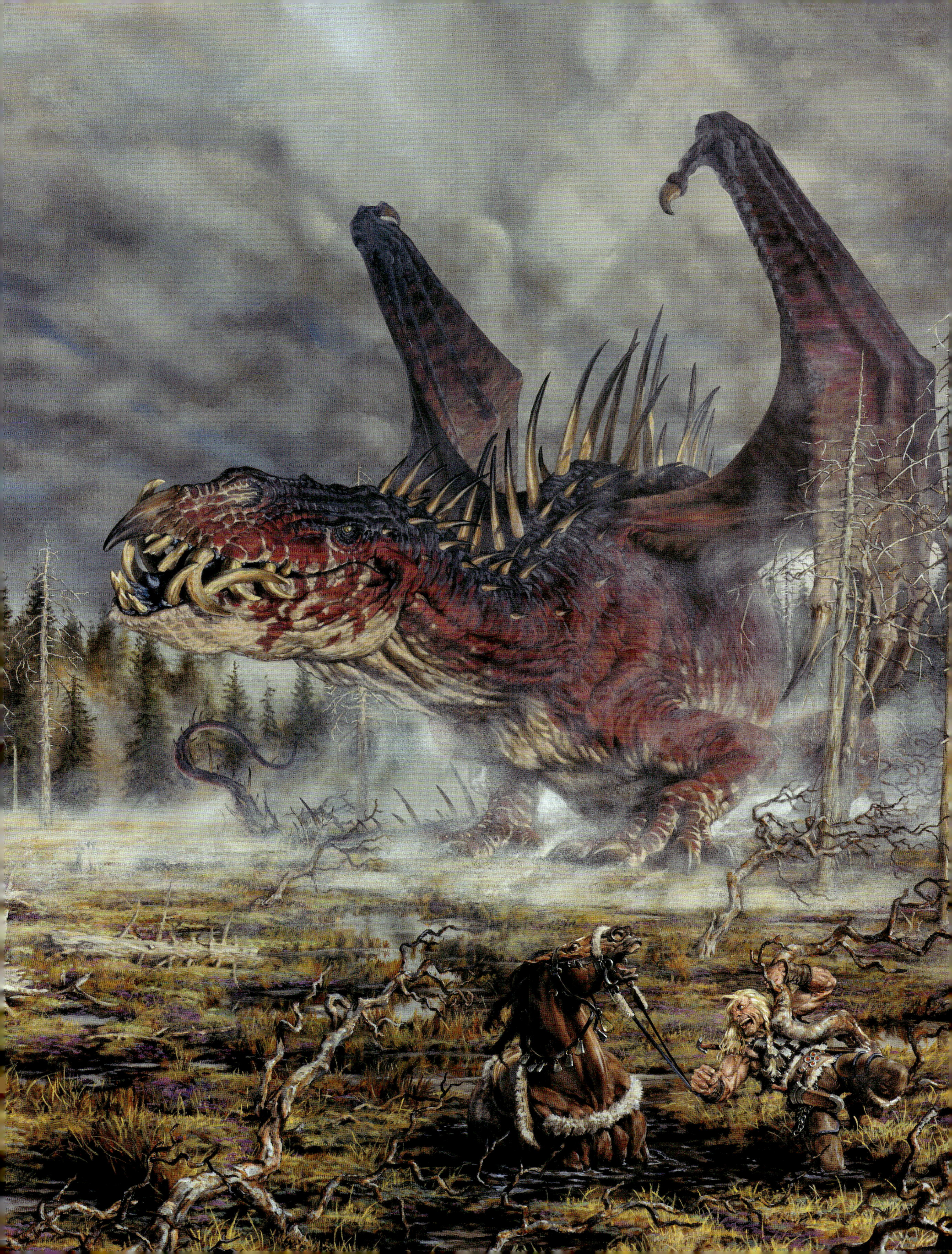

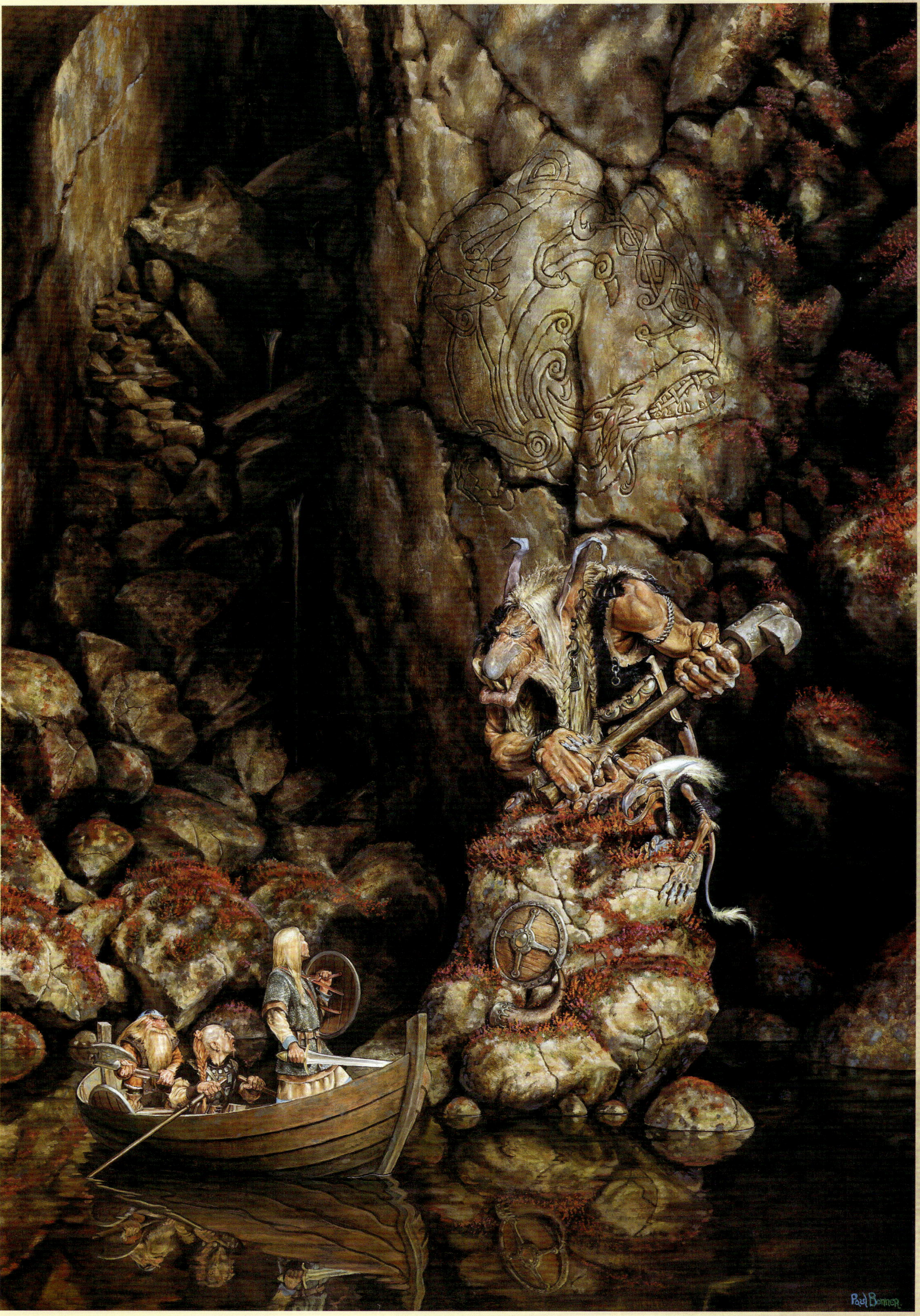
Paul Bonner

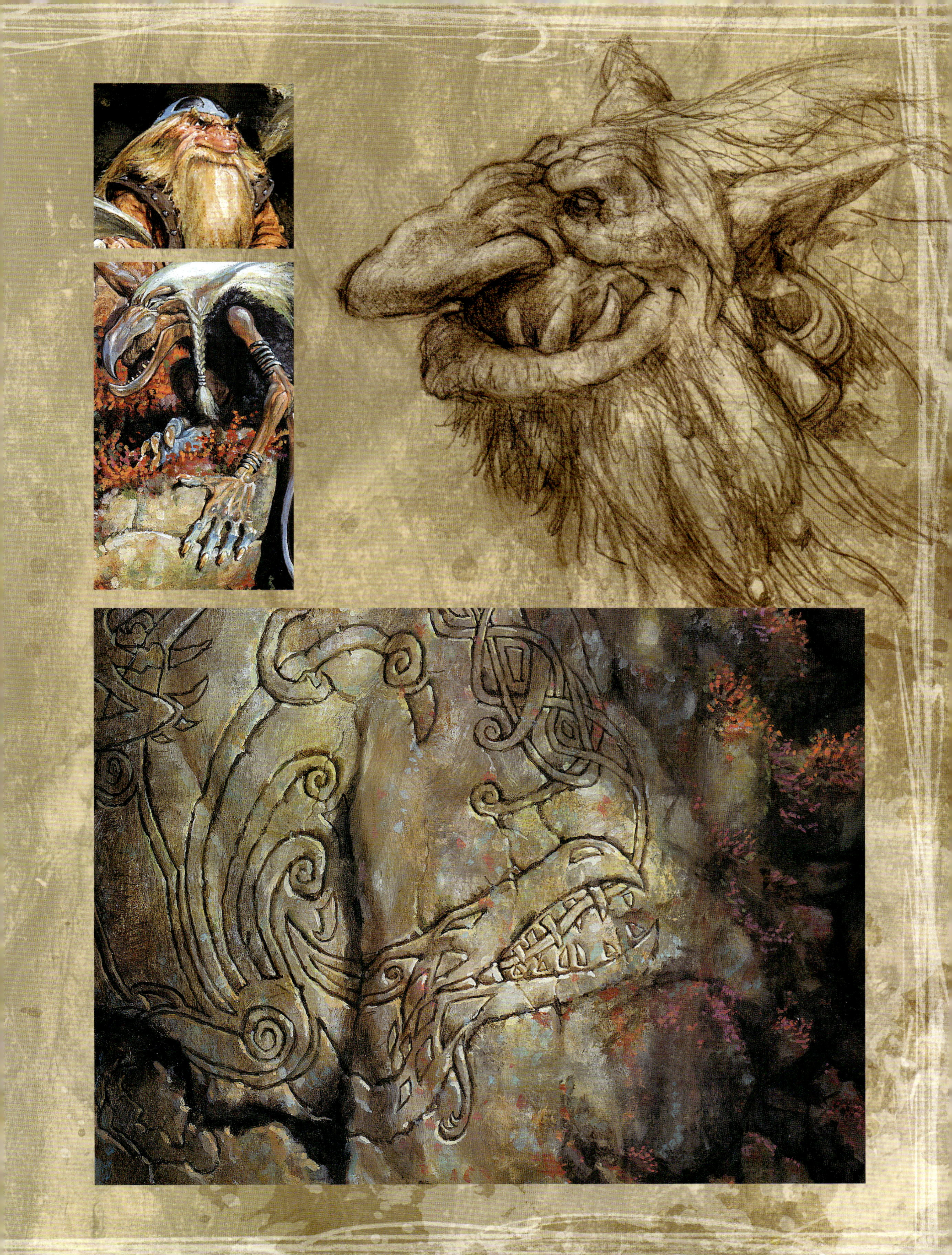

* Snösaga - 2002

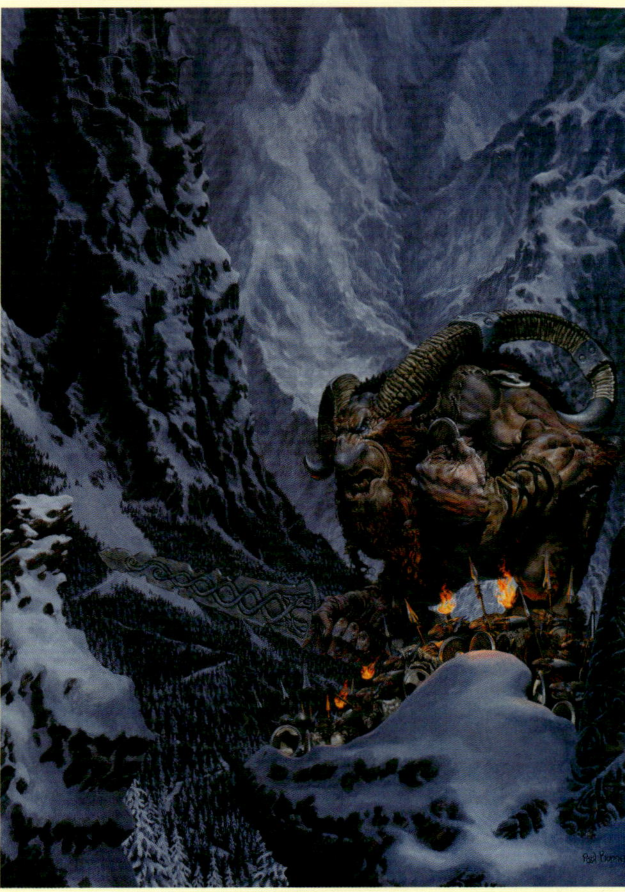

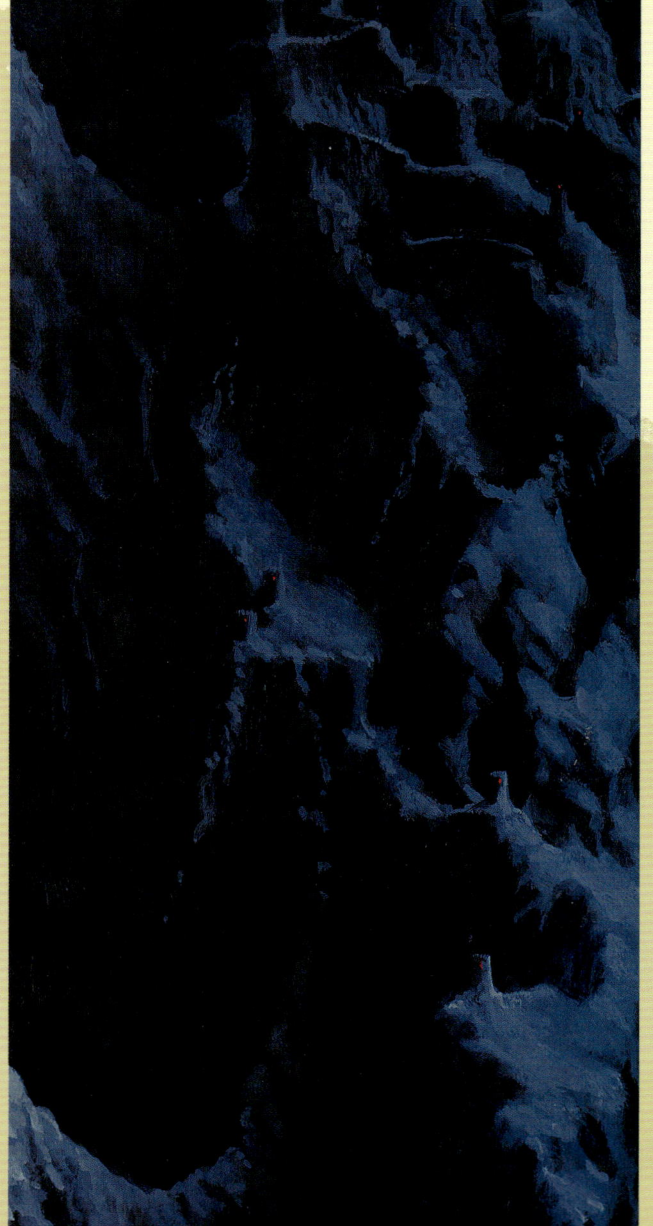

Another phone call - another chance to roam strange lands and mingle with their inhabitants. Ones more familiar this time. A bunch of dwarves; a bunch of goblins; a big fight... in a deep forest. Do you think you might be interested? Well... I'll see what I can do. That was the first one, and they have just kept on coming. Suitably iconic landscapes with a compatible collection of inhabitants. Even a dragon or two. A direct line, way back to that first reading of *The Hobbit* when, as an 8 or 9 year old, some kind of internal machinery shifted gears, clicked into motion and steadfastly began to propel me forward along the path that I still find myself contentedly travelling on. On the same path I met up with Drakar and Demoner. A world that has stepped out of, after having been steeped in, the collective and primal folk culture and memories of Scandinavia. Happily for me, Theo, like Jean Bey from Rackham, is another shining example of how to be an art director. Plant a couple of ideas and leave me alone. I do provide him with a scribble (using the word sketch would be a trifle misleading). One is always enough, and over the years he has developed a remarkable ability to catch glimpses of finished paintings in the rather abstract markings I present him with. Once he has that glimpse, he is content to let me get on with it, trusting me to come up with the painting hidden somewhere within. This gives me the freedom to wander around the landscapes I have been in, and those easily accessible in my imagination, until I find a place where I can stop and admire the view. Their beginning points are nearly always based upon some kind of reality, from my wanderings in Scandinavia, or my own native Lake District. It becomes an attempt to create, out of an assortment of different visual ideas, an image that suggests a stopping off place on that line receding into the mists, where all those primitive roots and origins lie hidden. After all, it is precisely these landscapes that have given a background, or stage, to centuries of sagas, myths, folktales and legends from Northern Europe. Whether deep, silent fir forests or windswept and lonely mountains and moors, they have all provided a home to the gods, spirits and heroes that our ancestors accepted as a very real and integral part of their daily existence. These iconic landscapes have also provided the settings for some of the more compelling literature to come out of Northern Europe; from *Beowulf* to the *Kalevala* and through to Middle Earth. Having being strongly influenced by these and many other books, I am very much aware of being bound to this rich vein, and am constantly trying to tap into it, elusive as it sometimes is. I'm helped greatly in this by the drawings of Alvaro Tapia, an elusive freelancer who seems effortlessly able to conjure up the essence of these tales and sagas. Imbued with many rich details and wonderfully believable characters, his drawings have given me many a much needed shove when my own visual musings have deserted me. After each painting is finished, there is always a feeling of expectancy upon packing my brushes away and travelling back to the terminal, where I gather information for the next journey. I've usually pushed Theo into giving me a few hints as to the subject matter of the next painting. So, even though I tend to alternate and begin a painting for Rackham, it is comforting for me to know that somewhere in the forests a little part of me has set up a tent and is happily tramping around, waiting to stumble across the next scenario.

Paul Bonner

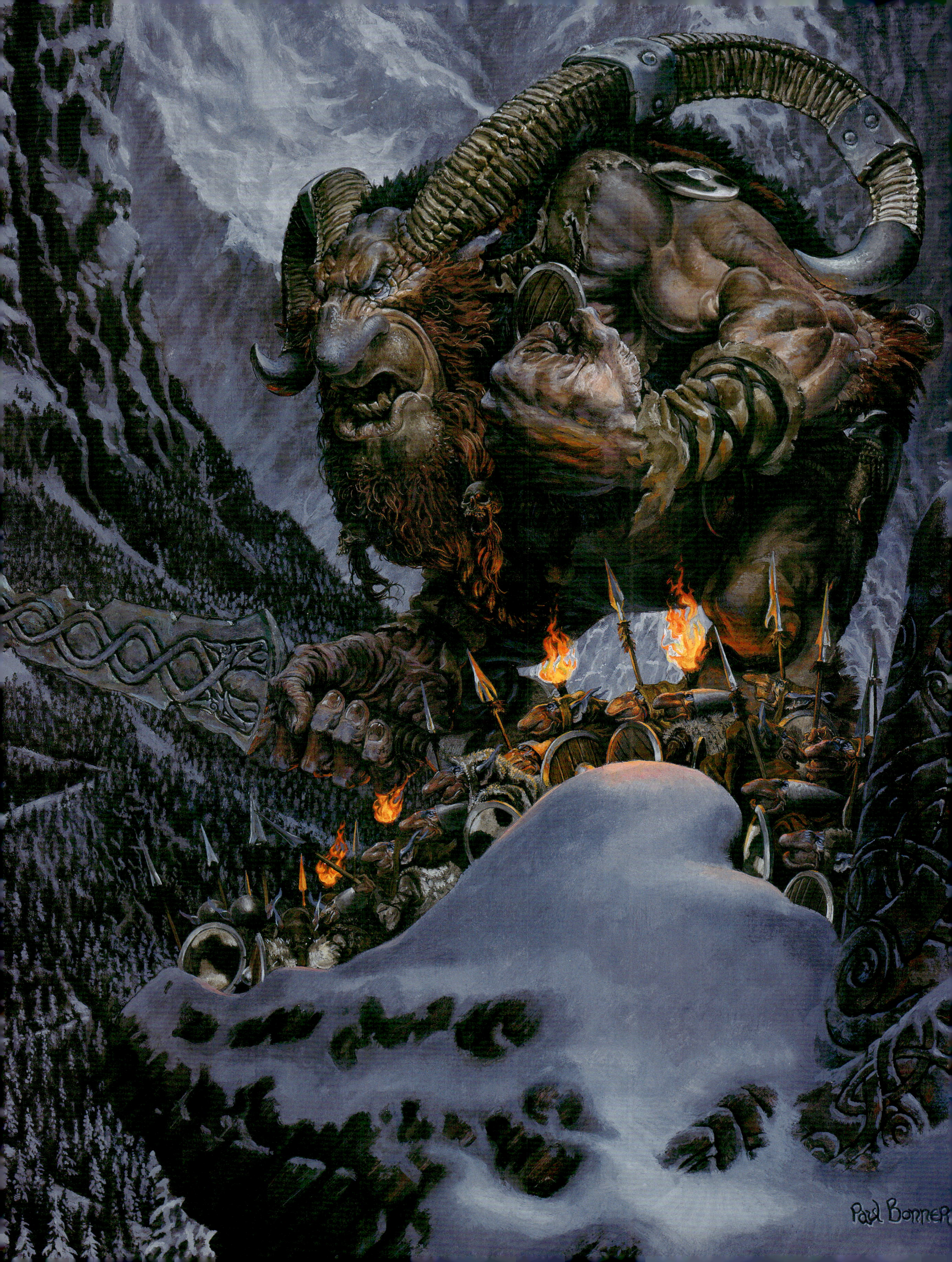
Paul Bonner

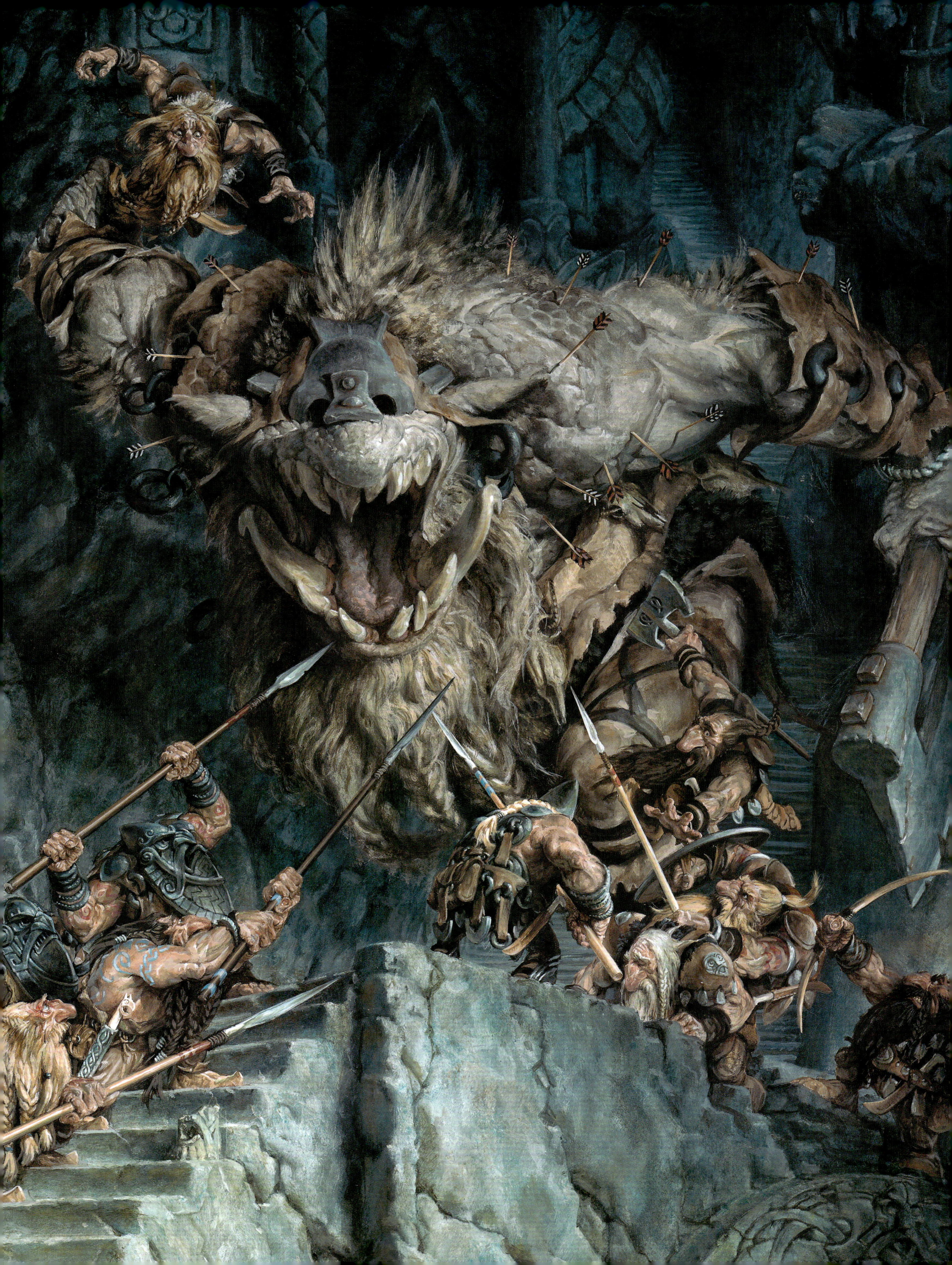

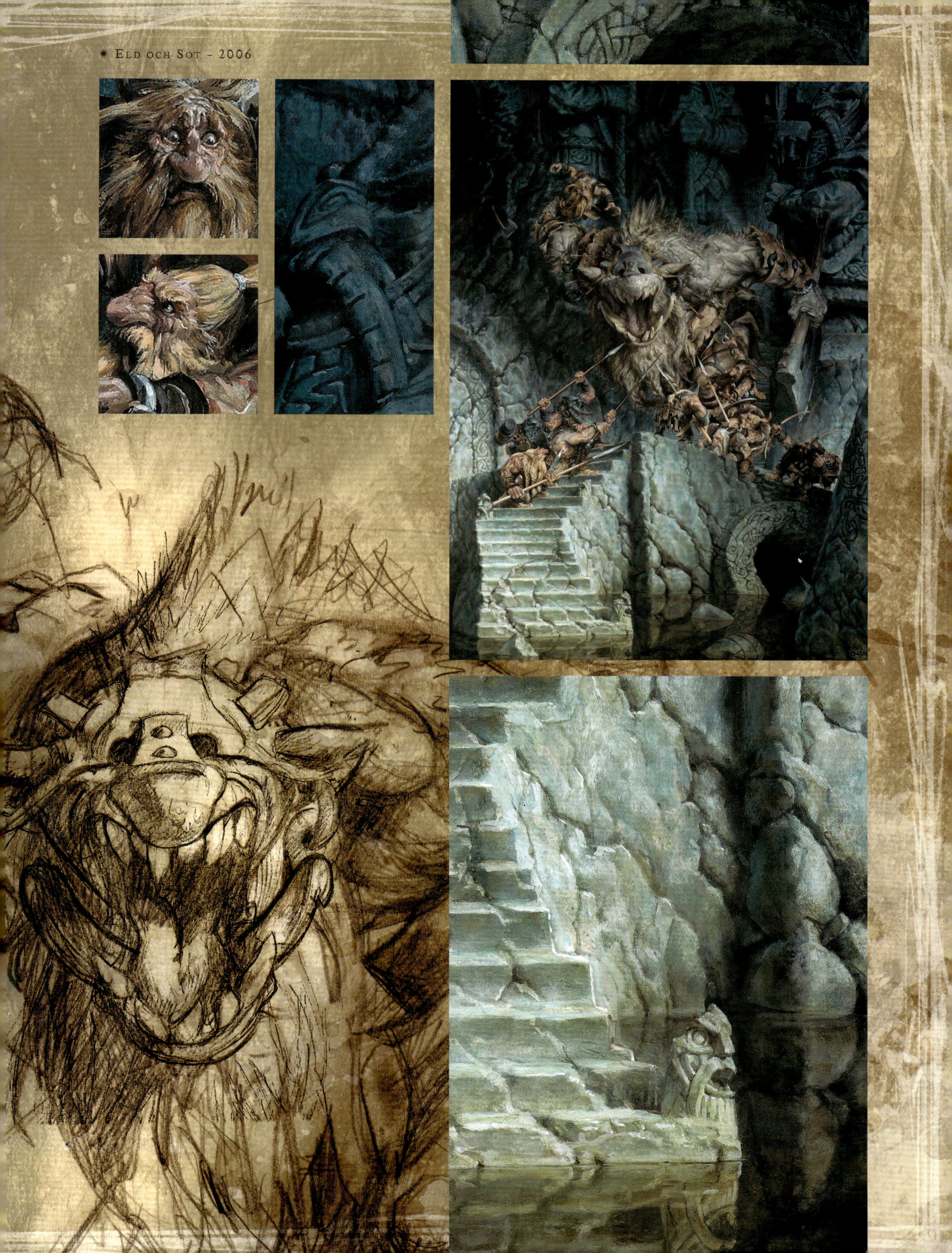

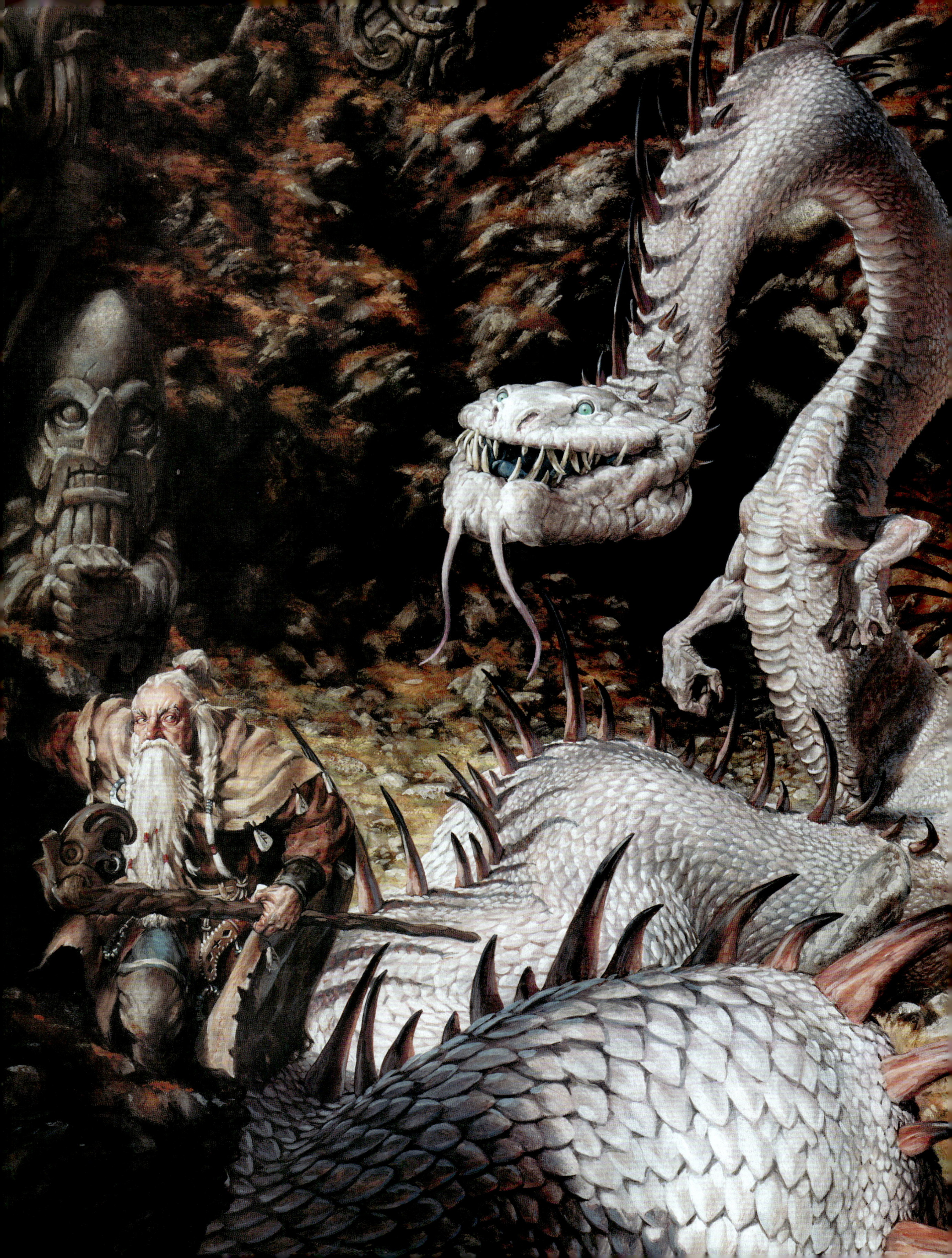

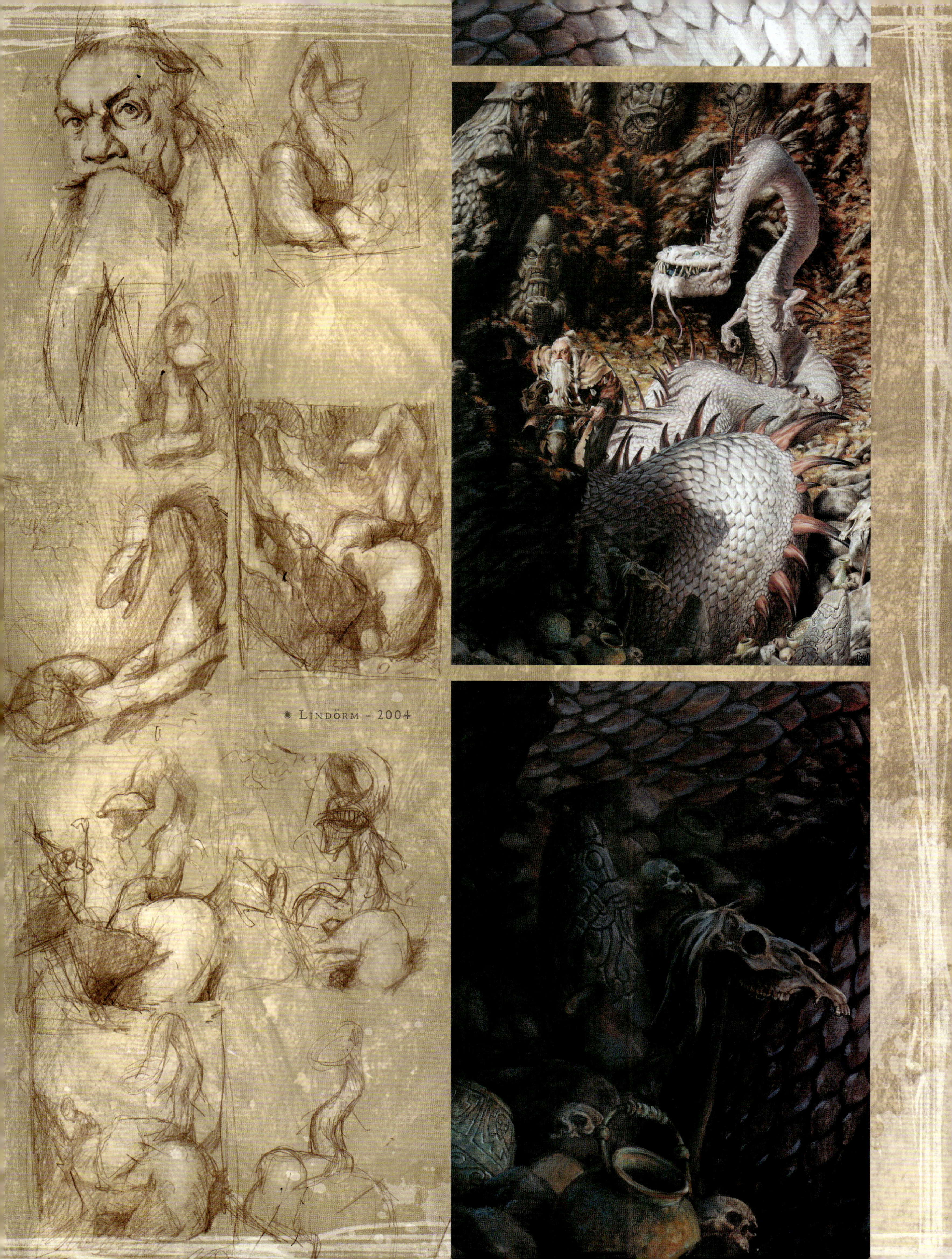

• Lindörm – 2004

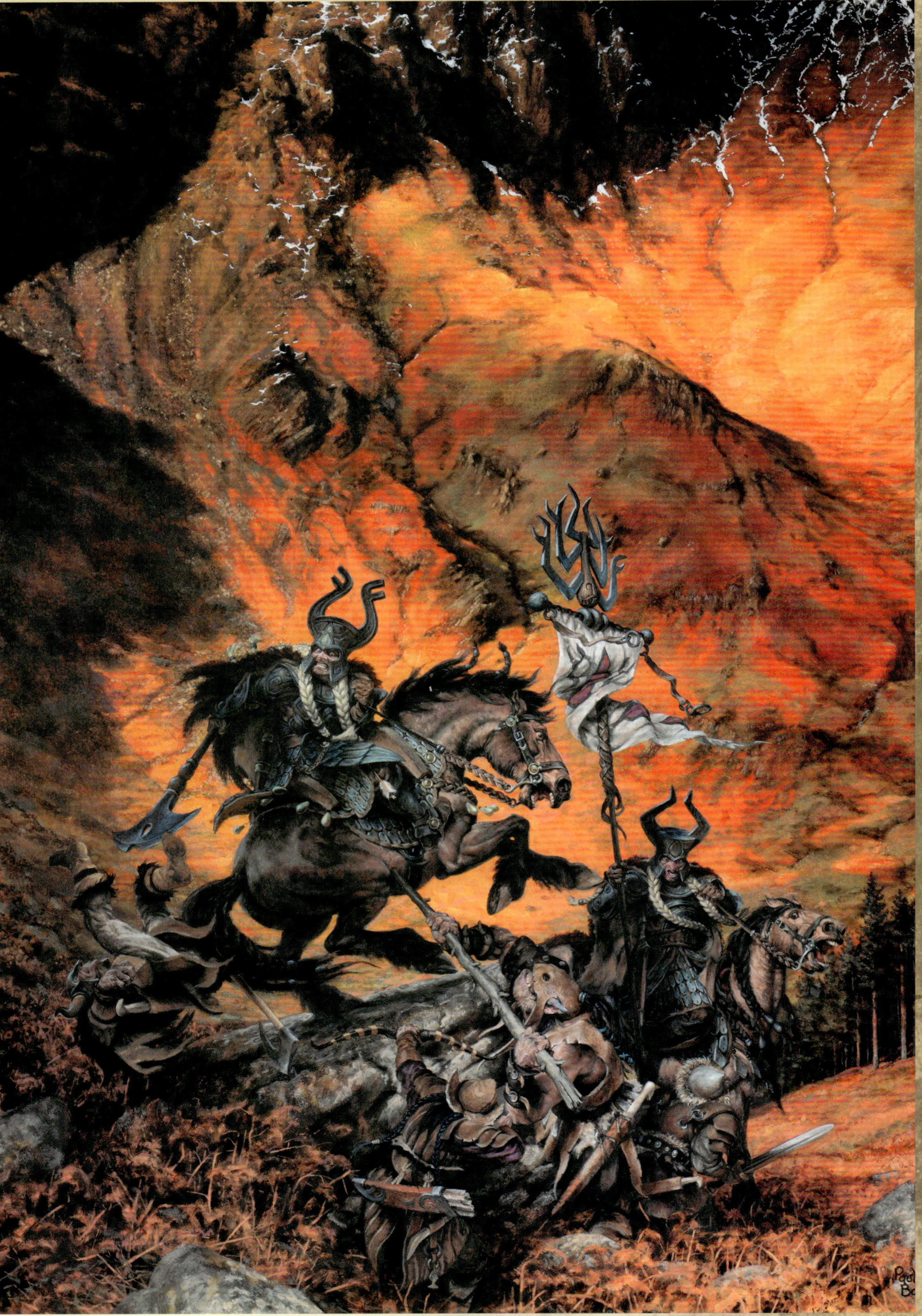

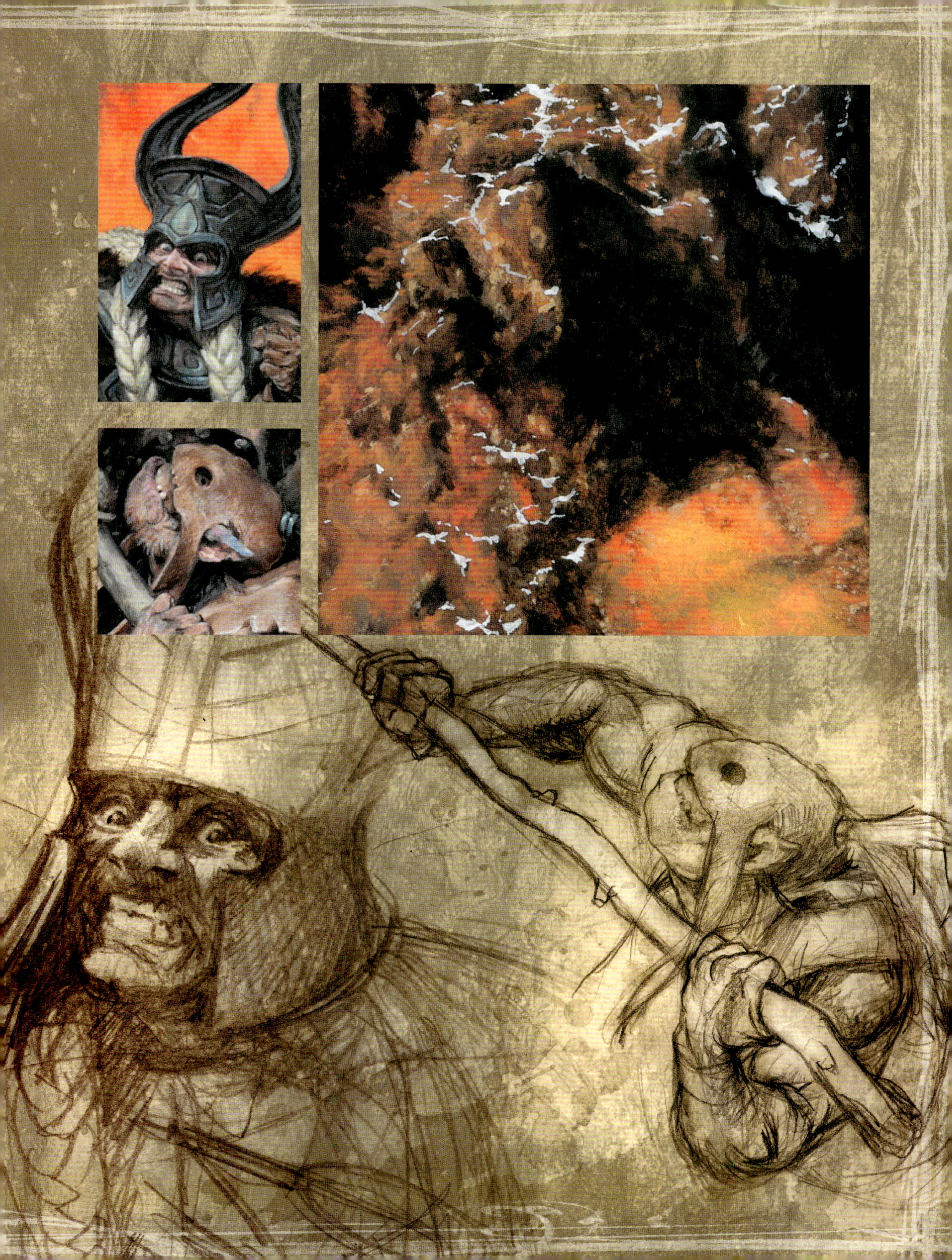

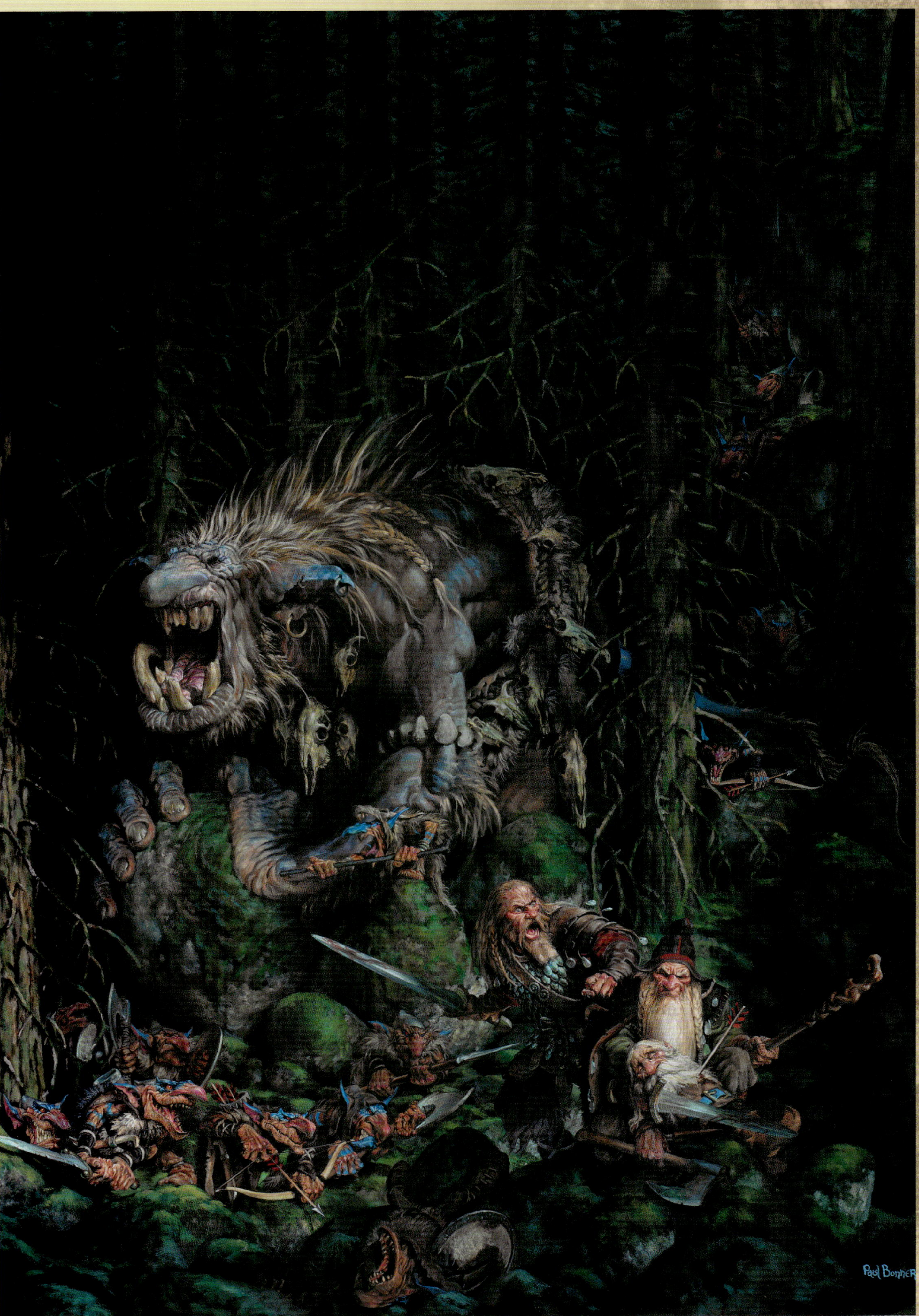
Paul Bonner

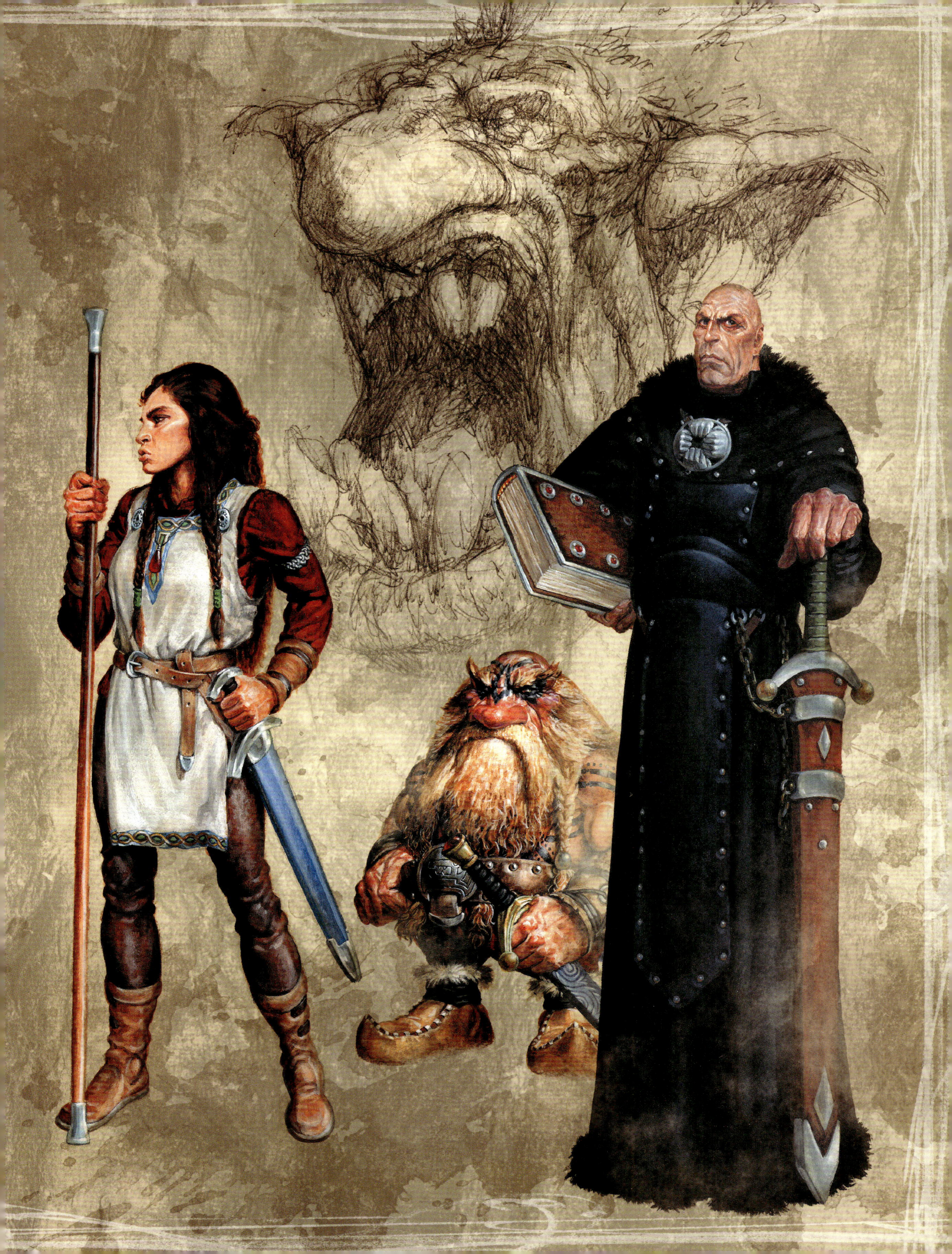

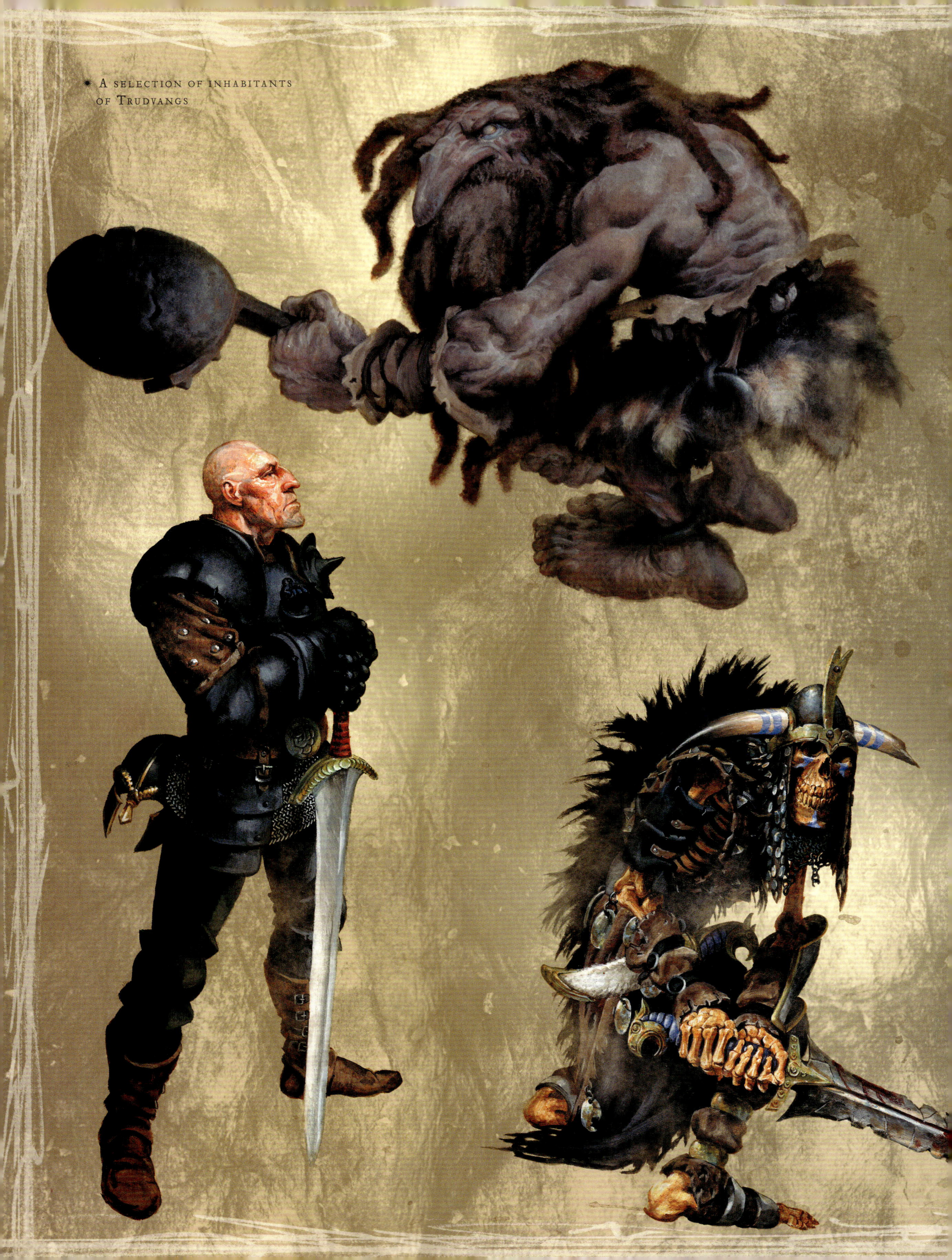

A selection of inhabitants of Trudvangs

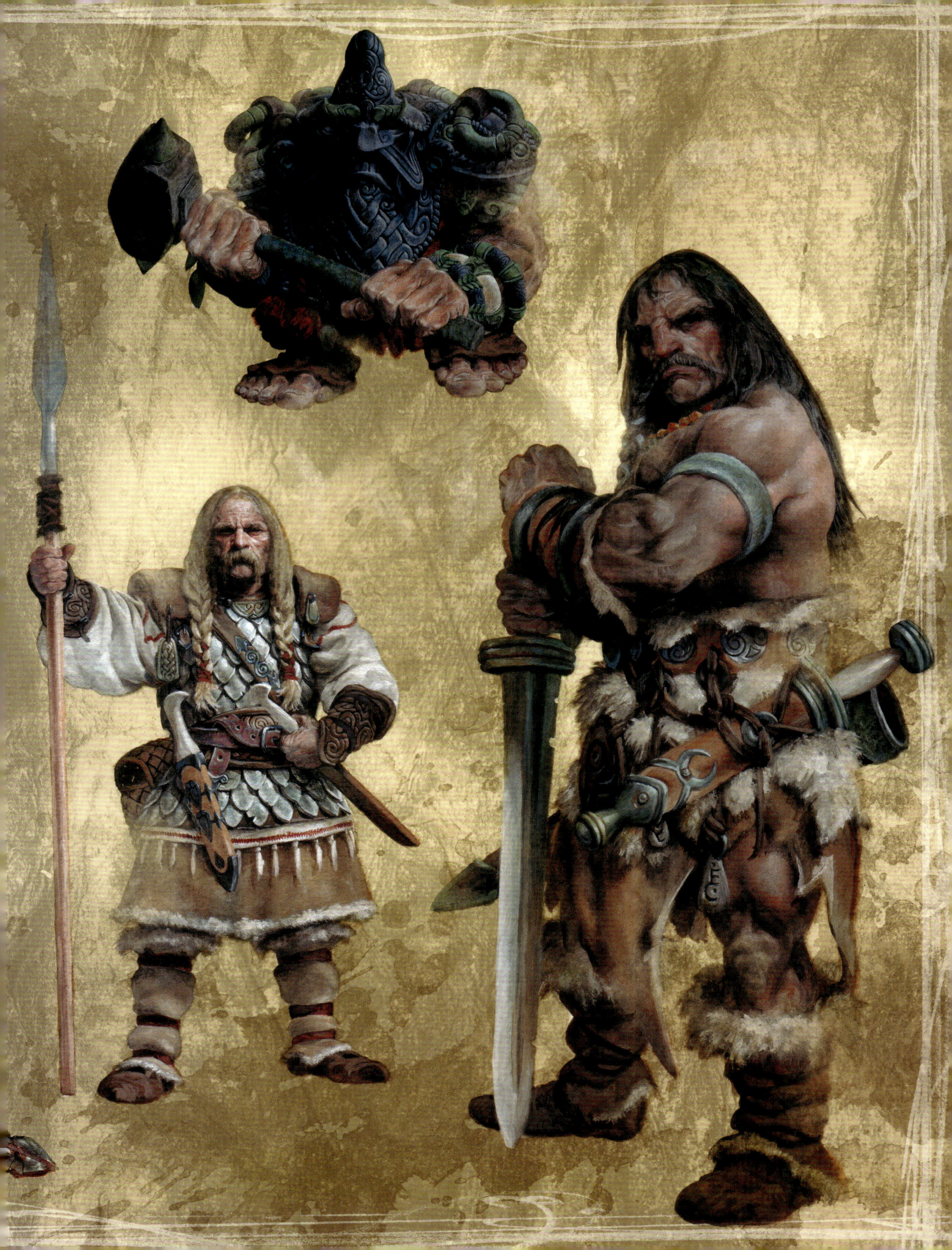

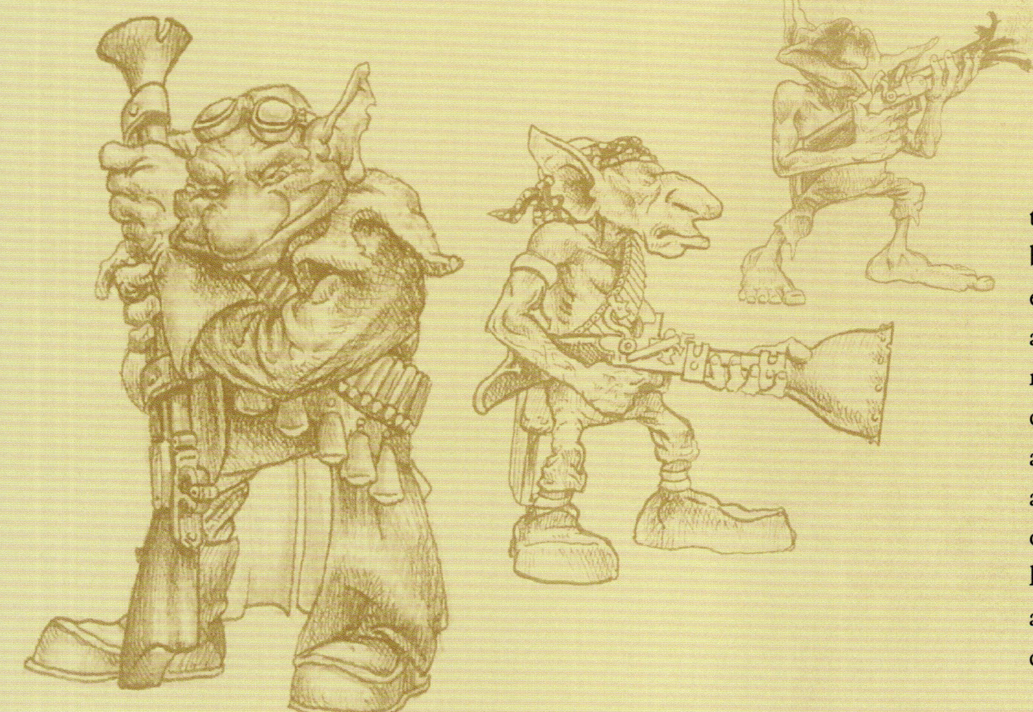

their lands were as real as they were for me. Thus it became the era of the full page illustration, and Paul established himself as an artist who could create robust and colourful windows that opened right onto these new worlds. There is many an echo of turn-of-the-century illustrators such as Bilibin, Neilson, DuLac and, of course, Arthur Rackham. Masters like Surikov and Shishkin can also be seen lurking in the shadows of his paintings. Paul brings all these influences to life with a very accomplished ability not only in form and dynamic energy but also with a strong sense of colour and balance that has matured with time.

Games Workshop

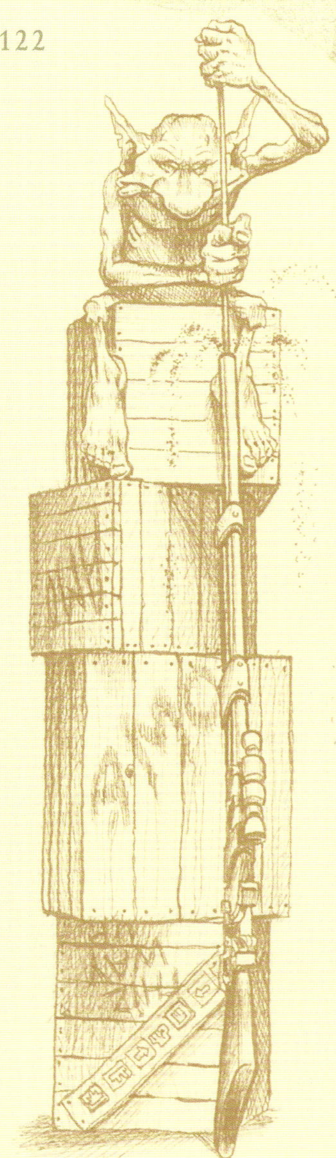

Somewhere deep within us all resides a well of sublime emotions which hark back to our ancestral roots and primitive origins. Sweeping forested mountains and gurgling streams are laced with swirling mists and racked by driving rain – this is the very stuff that can evoke an immediate emotional response within us all. For me these feelings also come from looking at Paul's work. Yet his art goes far beyond a mere interest in imagery, but is instead a direct tap into a shared and inherited knowledge that carries with it a strong vision of Northern European folklore. His work drips with the ogres, trolls, orcs and sorcerers who inhabit that primeval forest of the North.

The rapid growth of Games Workshop in the 1980s led the embryonic Design Studio to expand the imagery of the game Warhammer and its bleaker brother Warhammer 40,000. The painters and illustrators began to produce work that transcended simple representations of the miniatures they depicted. In this period Games Workshop established a much imitated vision of dark, brooding medieval and apocalyptic worlds. These evocations went far beyond mere illustration of warriors and battles – they delved deep into a rich narrative background which gave the games a resonance and made them as vivid and interesting as history itself. It became a time of dwarves, orks and elves who inhabited worlds that almost existed, and I am sure that for many gamers these creatures and

My favourite piece of his from this period is a colour painting depicting Freebooter orks. Within this piece there is dynamic action, bestial warriors, big guns and pirate clothes. It is a succinct summing-up of the visual elements that excite miniature collectors and gamers. Though it has left an indelible mark, it is not just this image of Paul's that has been an inspiration to me over the years. What has fired my imagination is not the guns nor the snarling maws, but something that is intangible which I can only describe as Dickensian or Shakespearean. It has something to do with character, for Paul is unmatched in his ability to create a cast of motley individuals, each one with his origins in a mythology that harkens back many generations to ages of superstition and conflict.

I always look forward to seeing new works from Paul and look upon them with feelings of wonder and admiration which, I am sure, others journeying through this tome will experience. Sharing a house with him in another age has left me with an impression of this gentle Englishman that resembles a Scandinavian warrior who would play a certain record by a famous Swedish pop-combo every evening before retiring to dream of the dark forests of the North.

John Blanche
February 2007

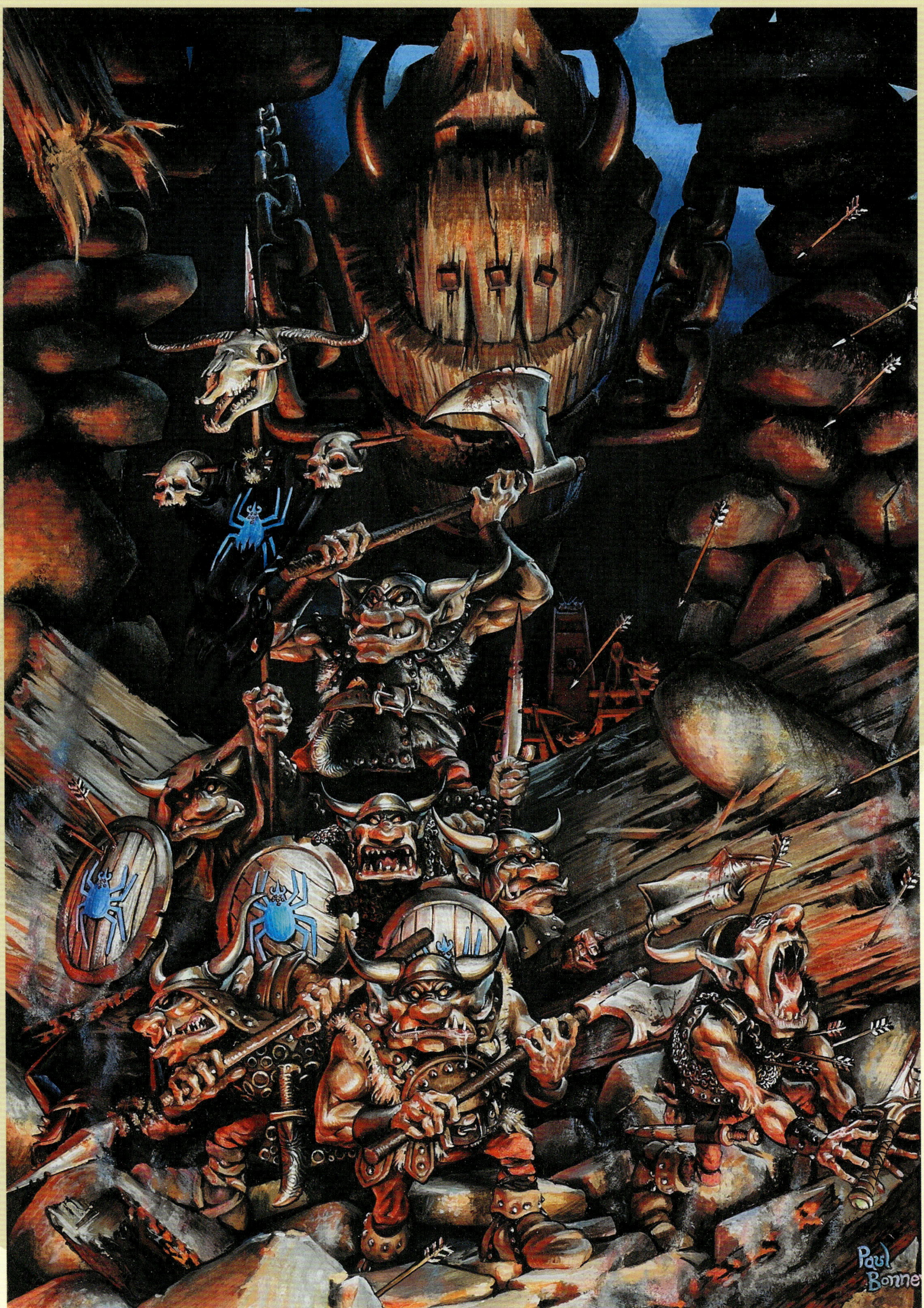
Paul
Bonner

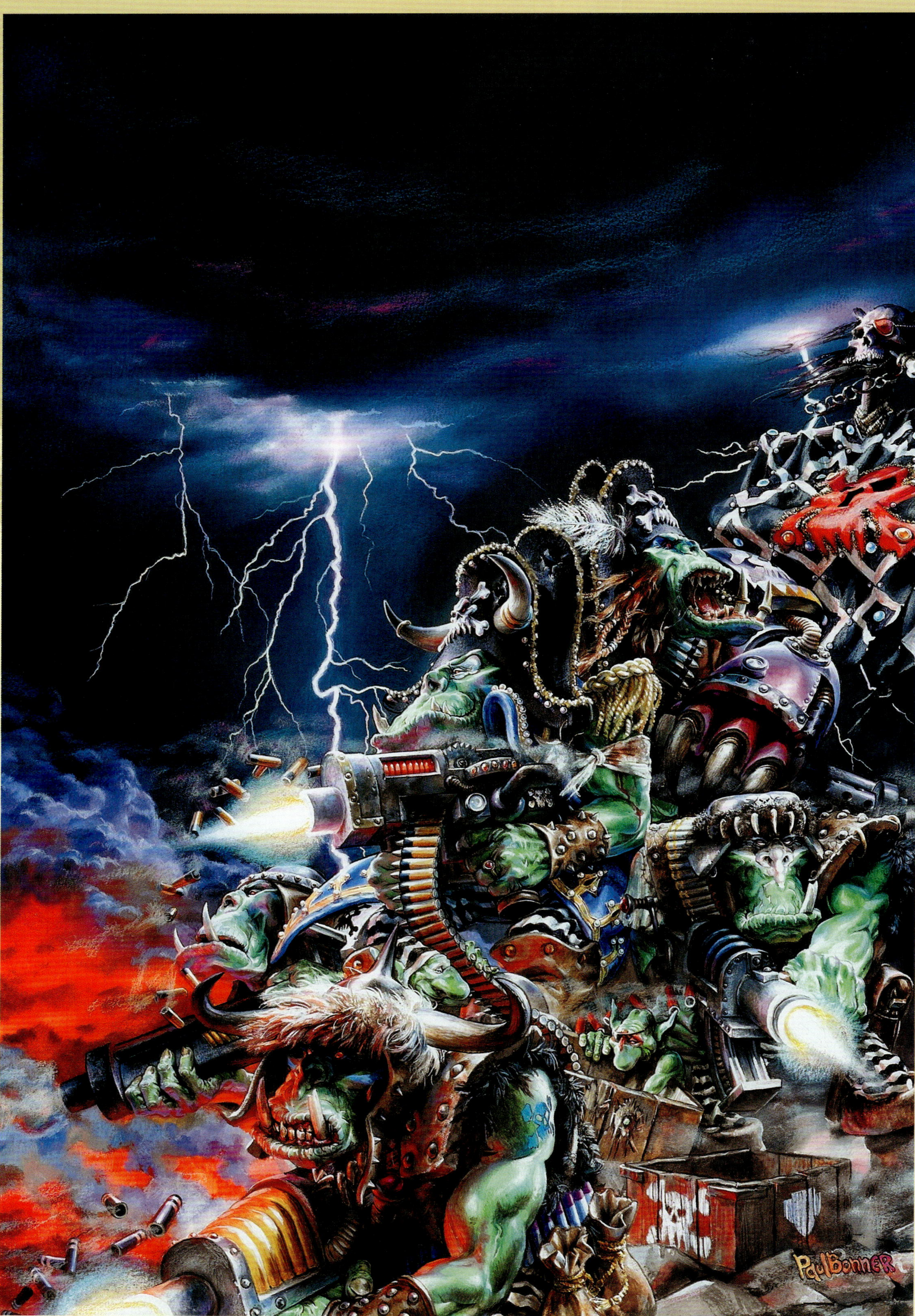
PaulBonner

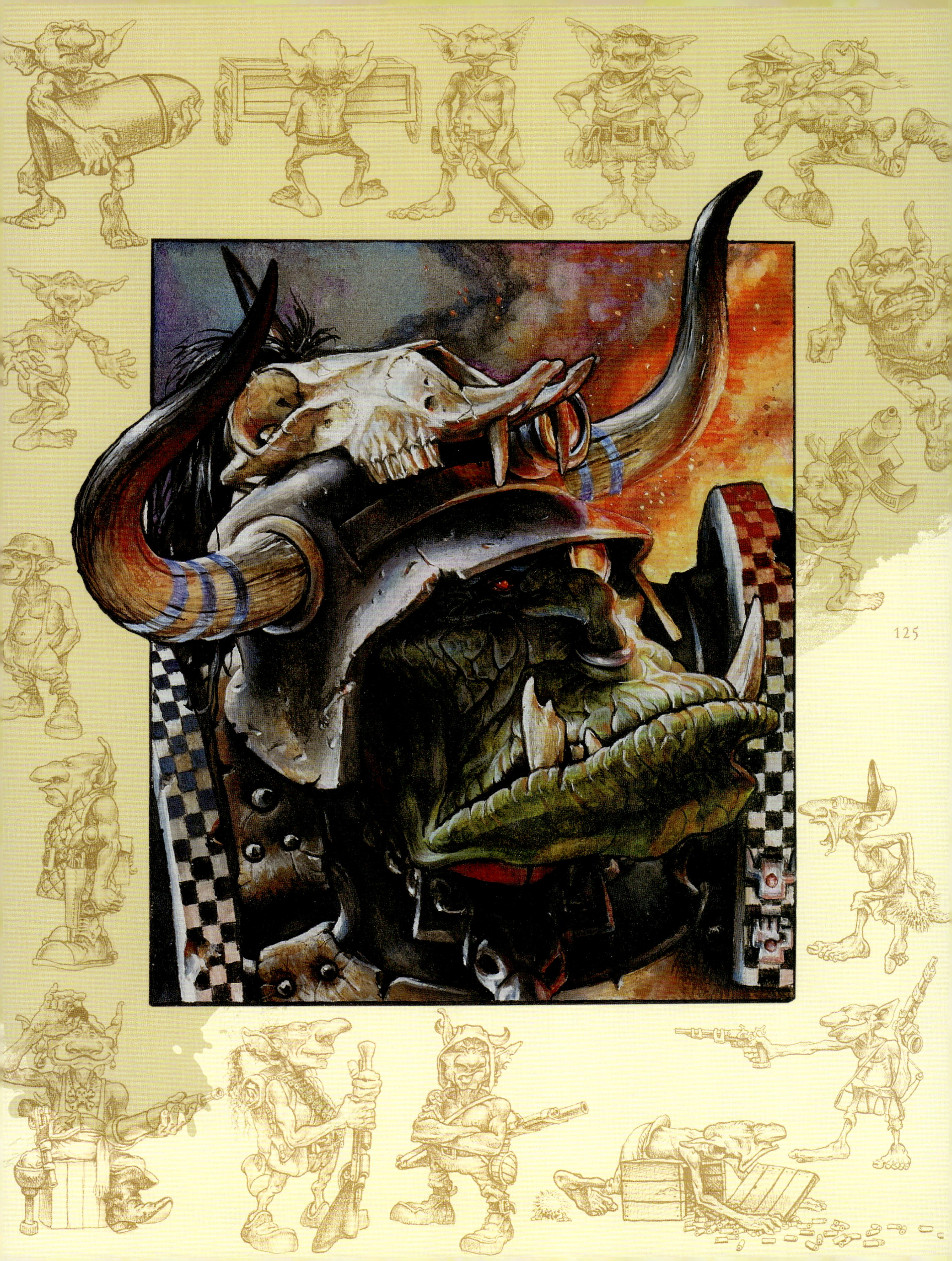

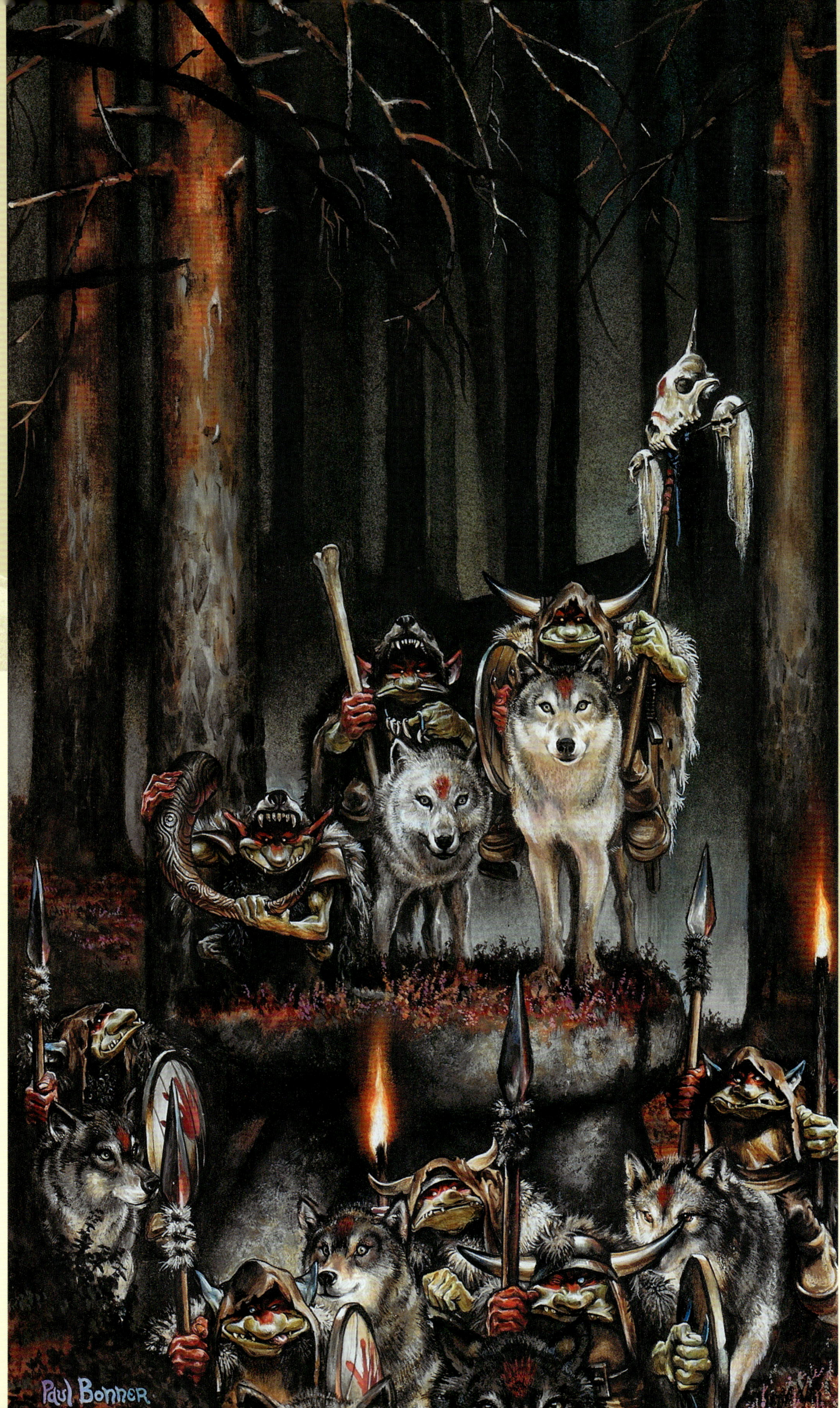
Paul Bonner

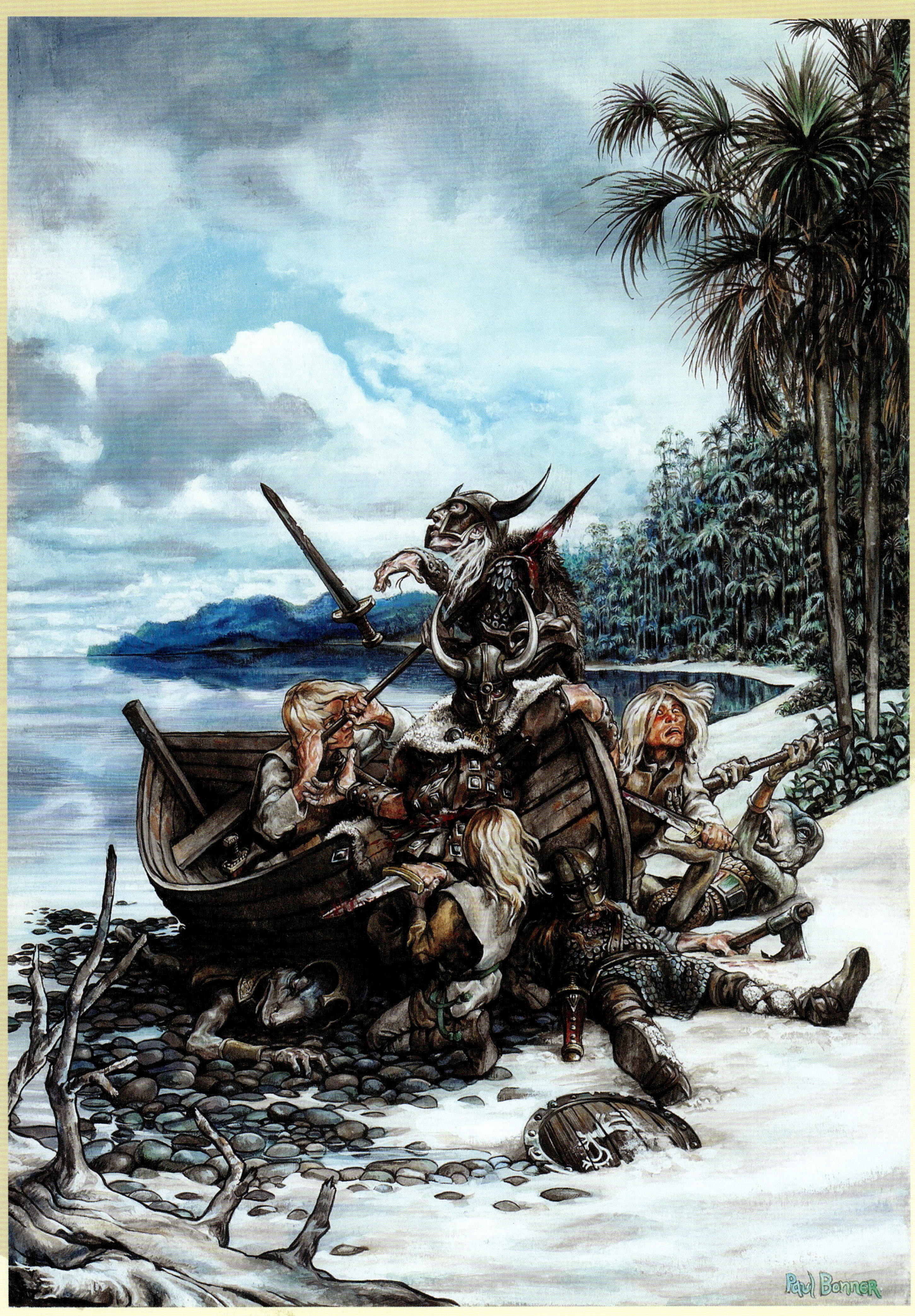

◆ With apologies to Akseli Gallen-Kallela

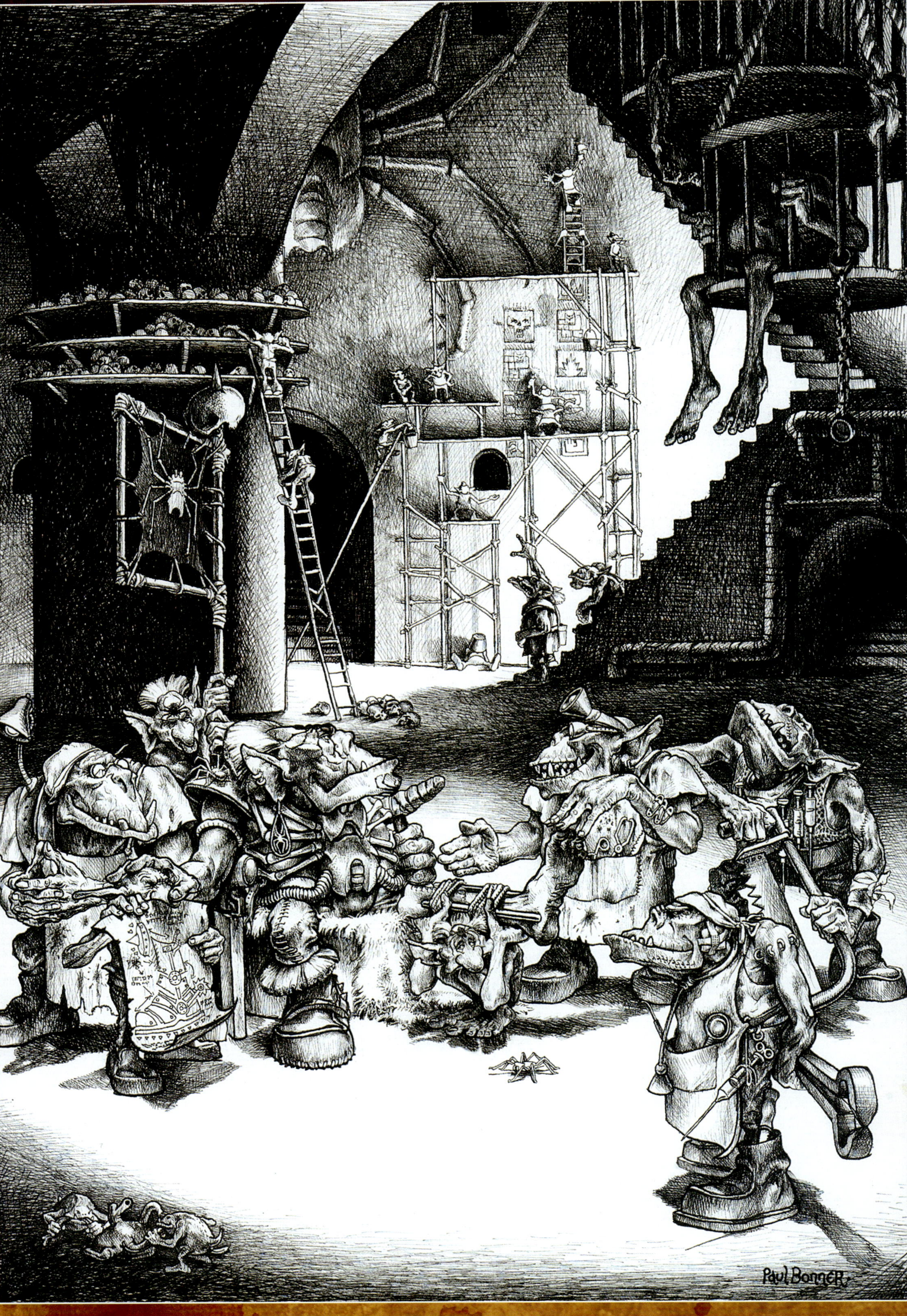
Paul Bonner

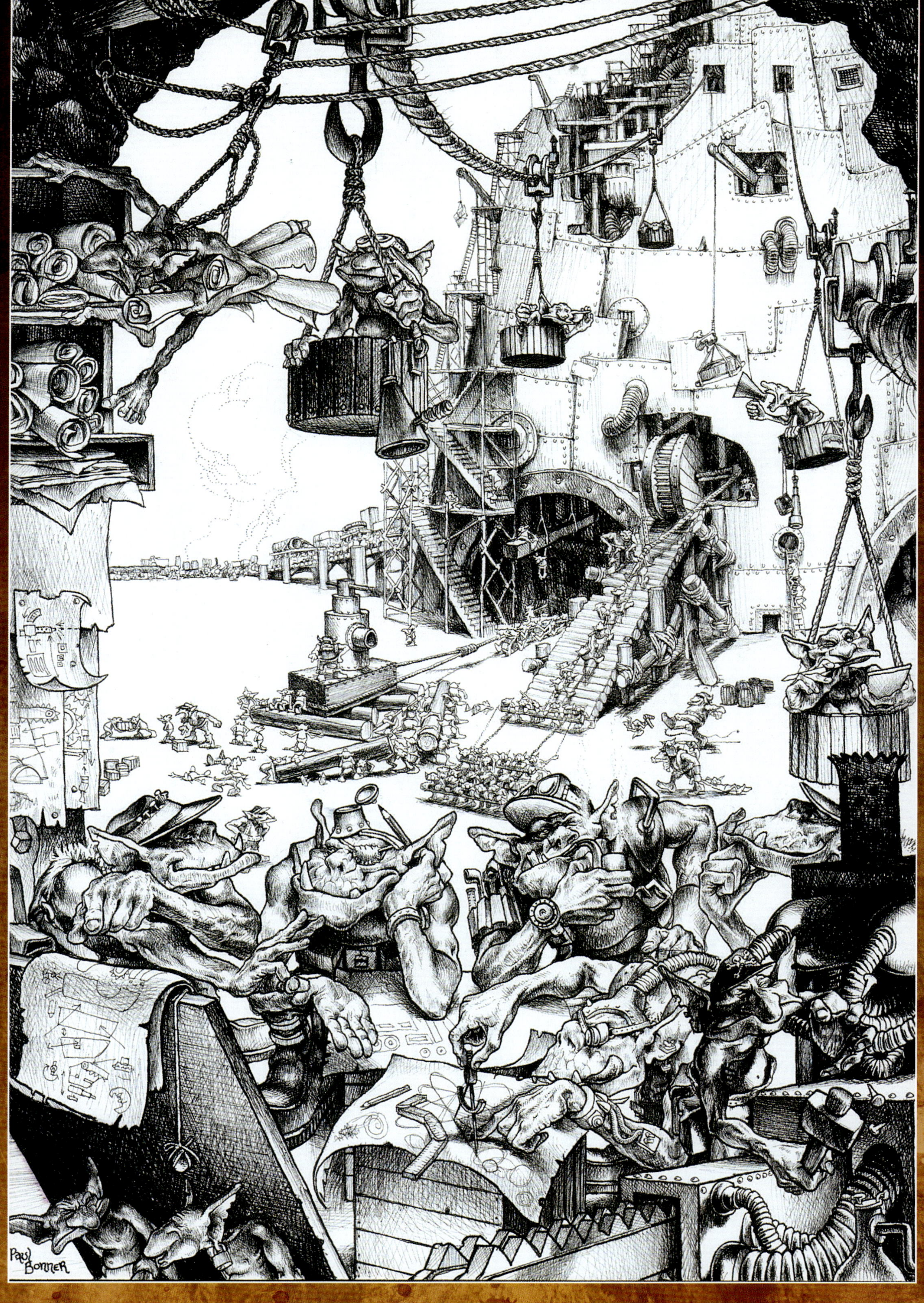
PAUL BONNER

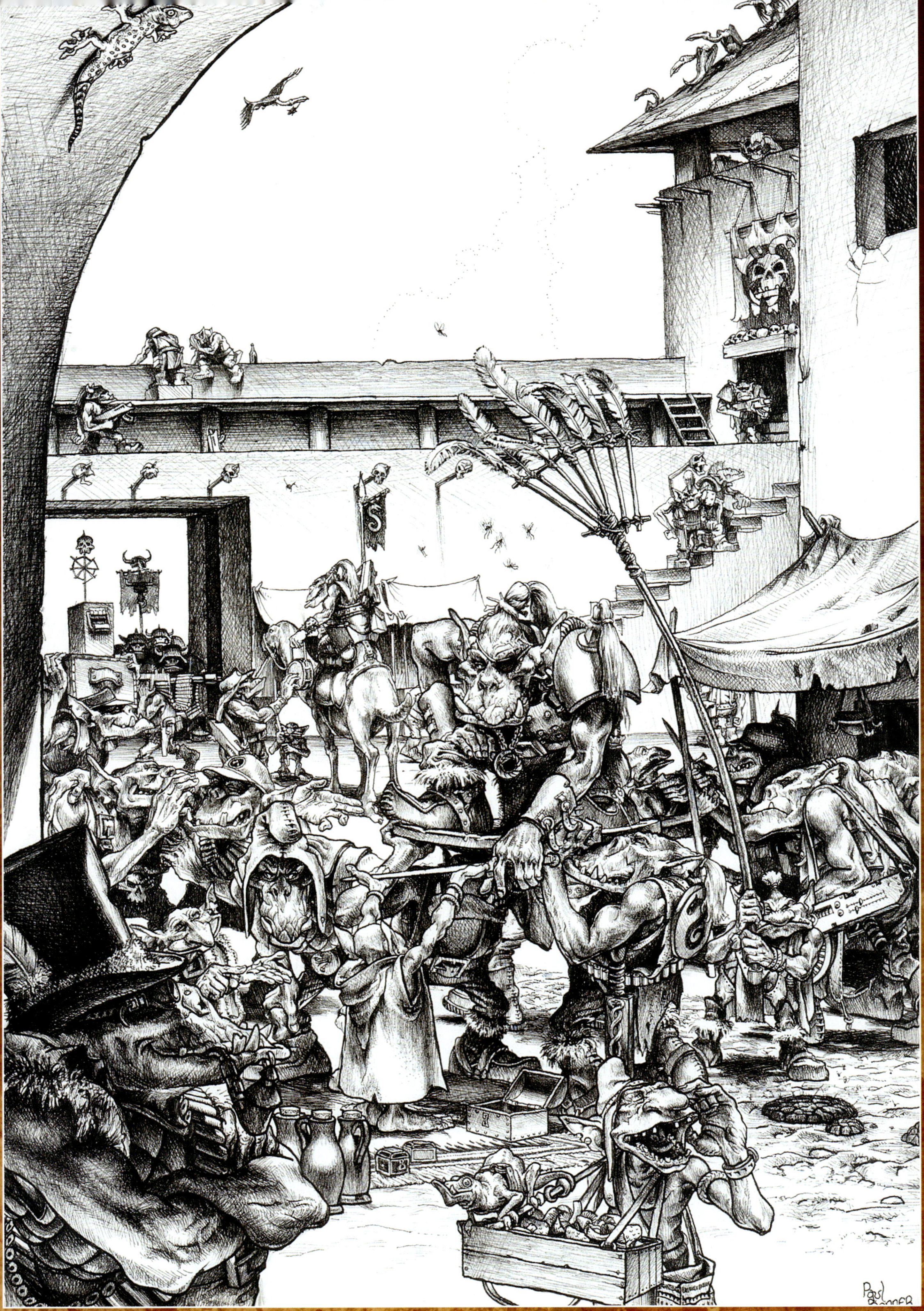

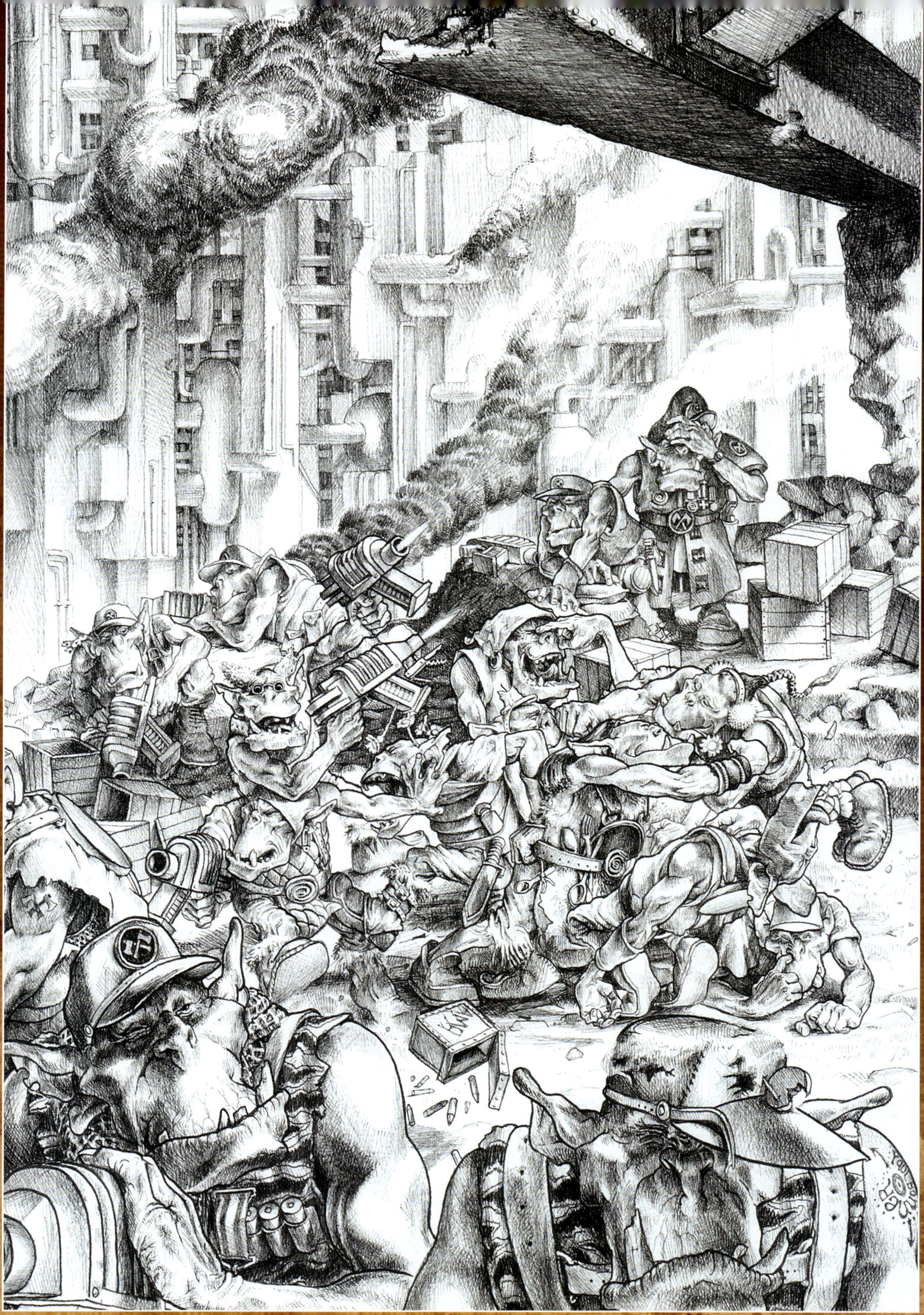

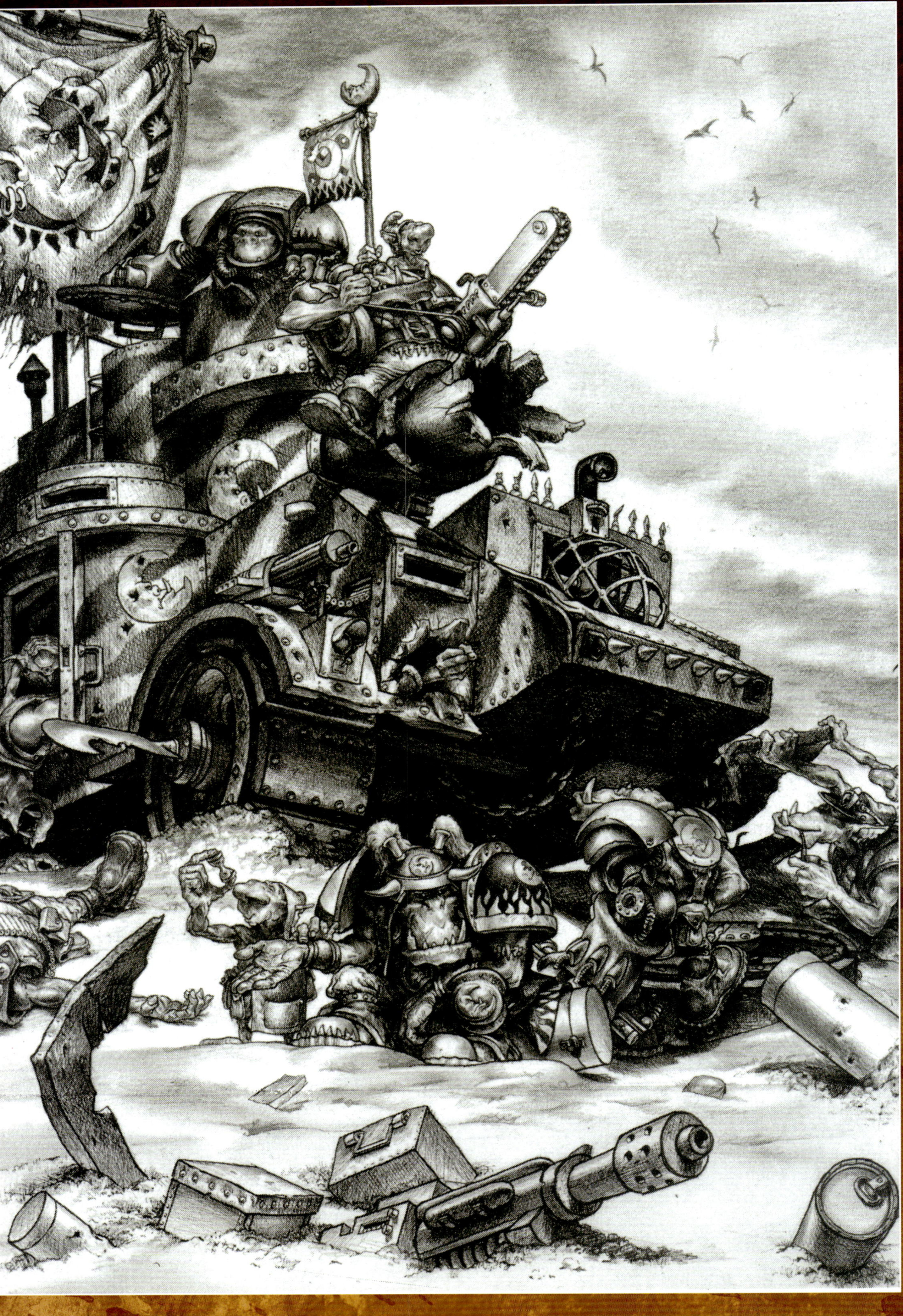

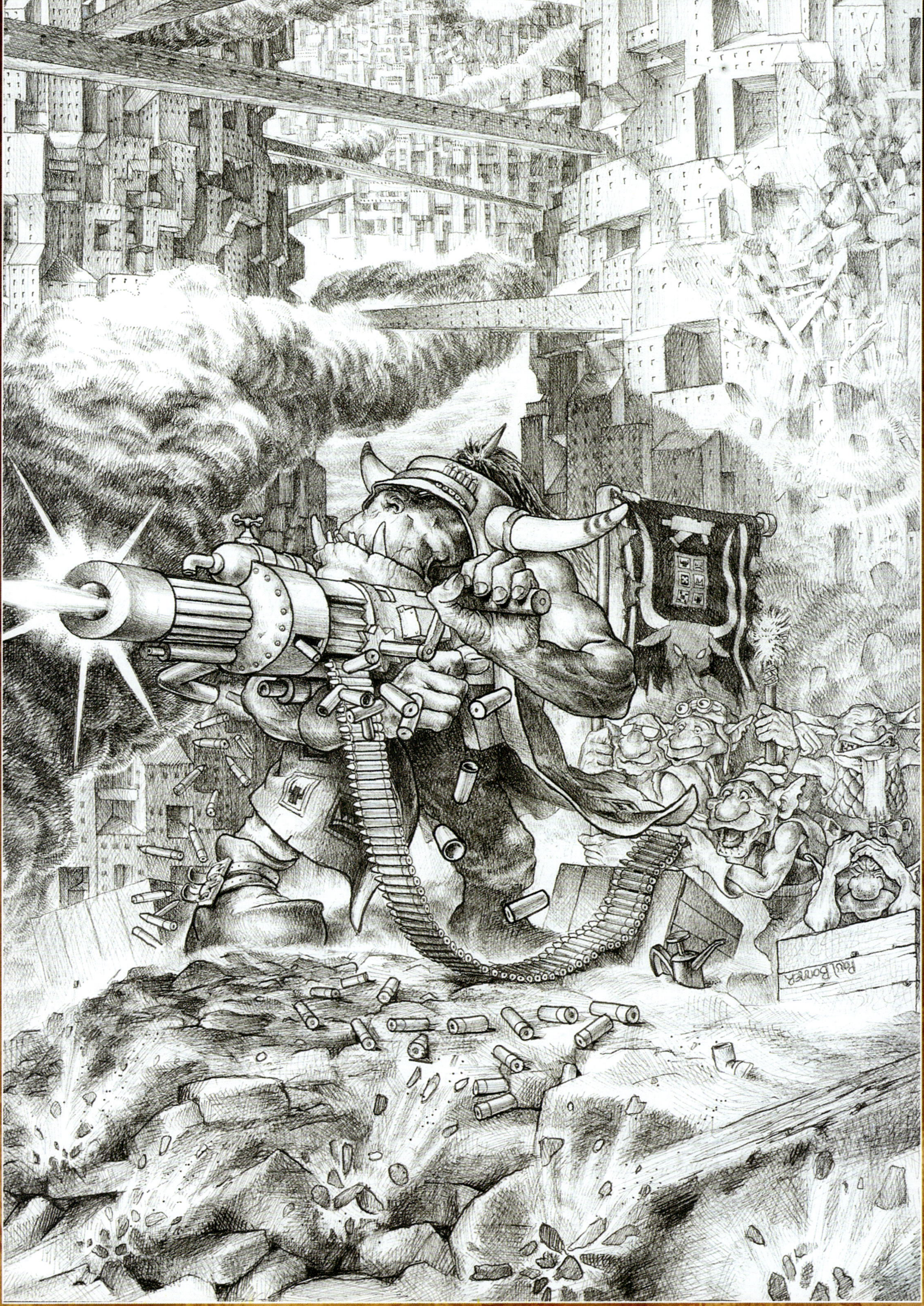

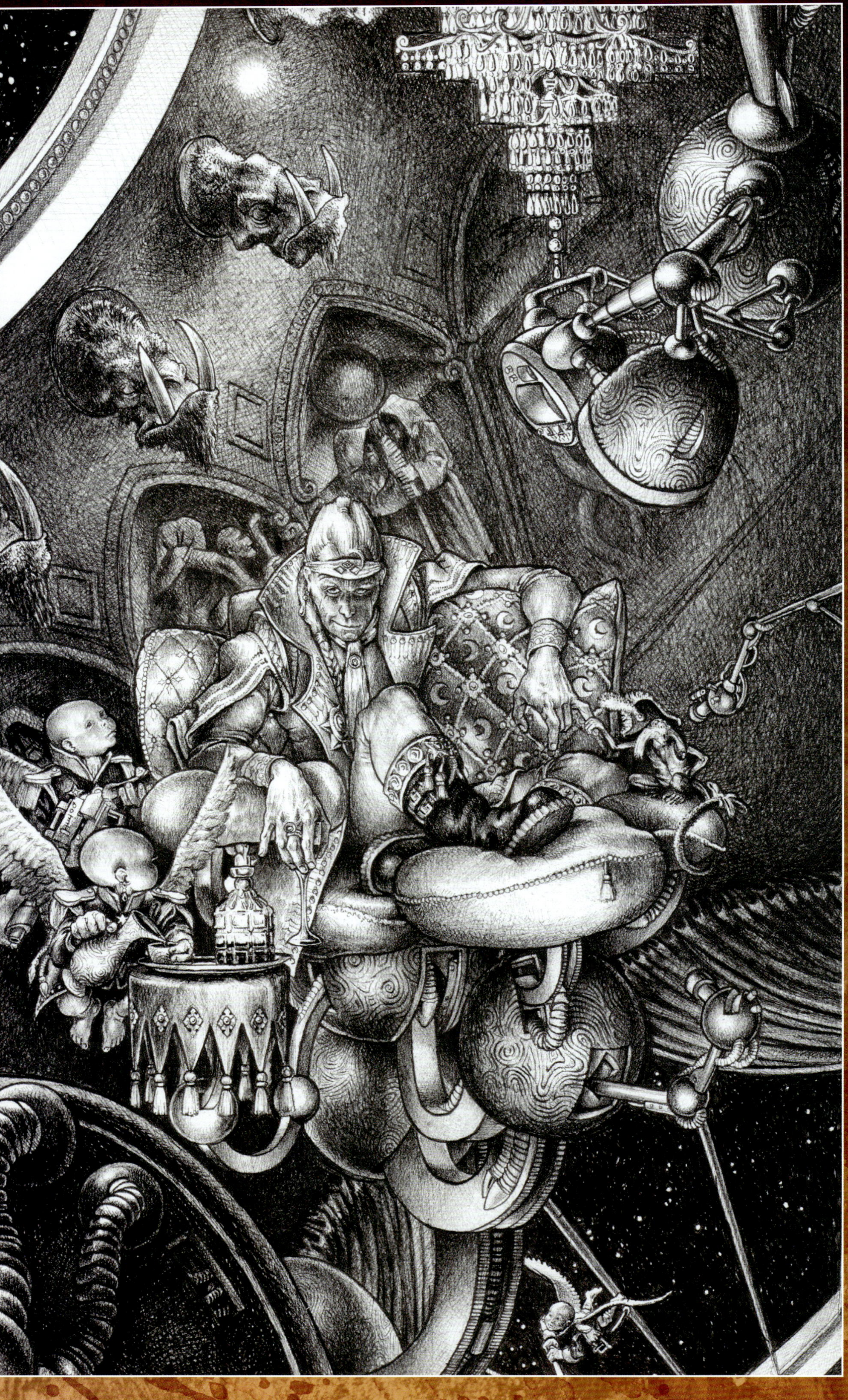

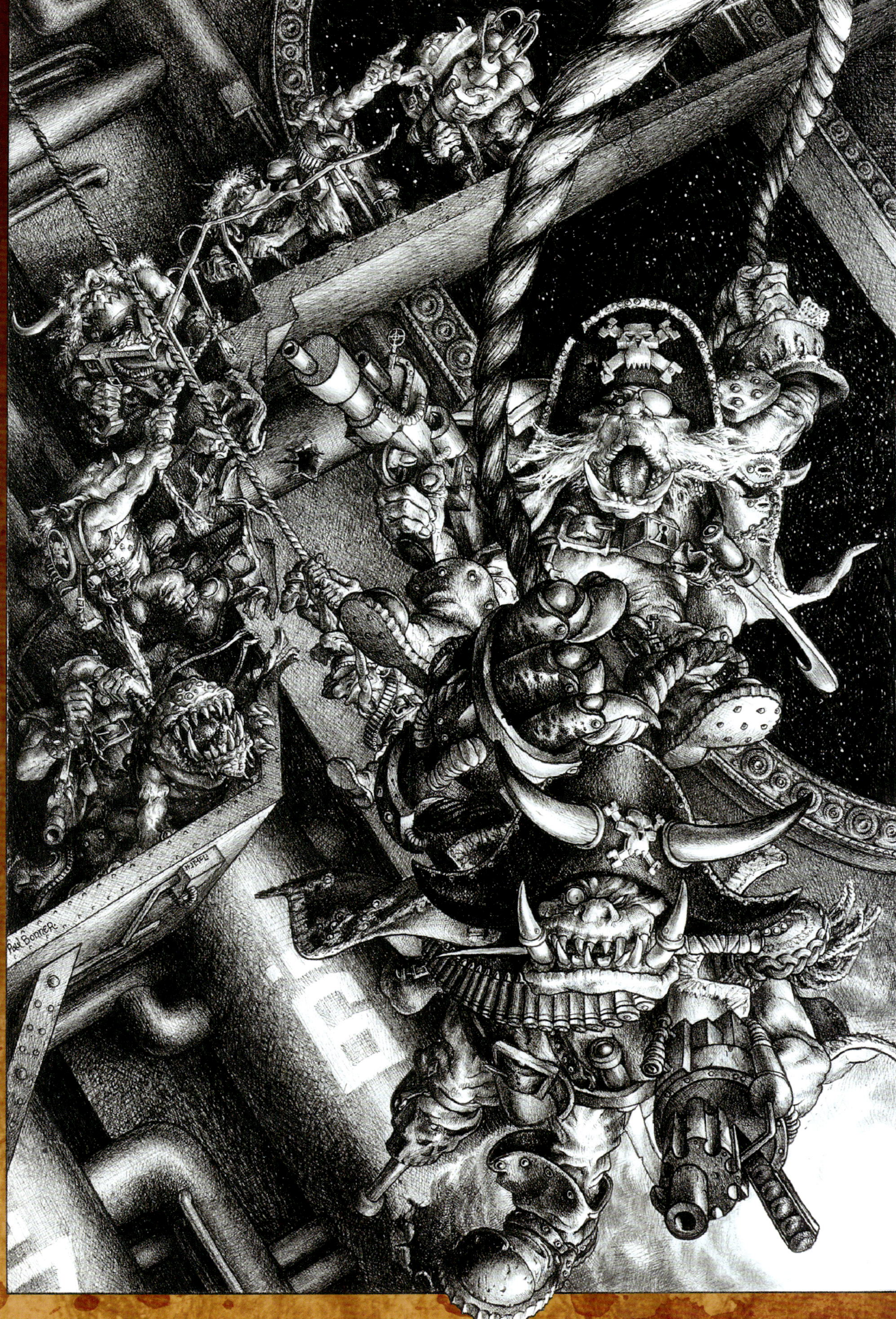

At some point or other I started doing some freelance black and white illustrations for GW's *White Dwarf* magazine. I can't recall how I stumbled across into this world, but it provided a glimpse of other people enthusiastically creating something they loved, and more importantly, they were happy to let me in.

I did a couple of colour pieces amidst lots of black and white work, and eventually their art director John Blanche, who almost alone visually defined the unique look of their universe, offered me a full time job. This would entail a move to Nottingham, the hub of their fledgling empire, to their design studio. At first I was unsure. I was so used to working alone that I couldn't really imagine how it would be to work alongside other like-minded souls. However, I knew I was never going to push myself any further upon London's commercial art world, so I packed my bag, brushes and cat, and moved to Nottingham.

I shared a house and studio with John, Wayne England, Stephen Tapin, and with a young Adrian Smith soon to join us. The studio was an exhilarating place to work. A

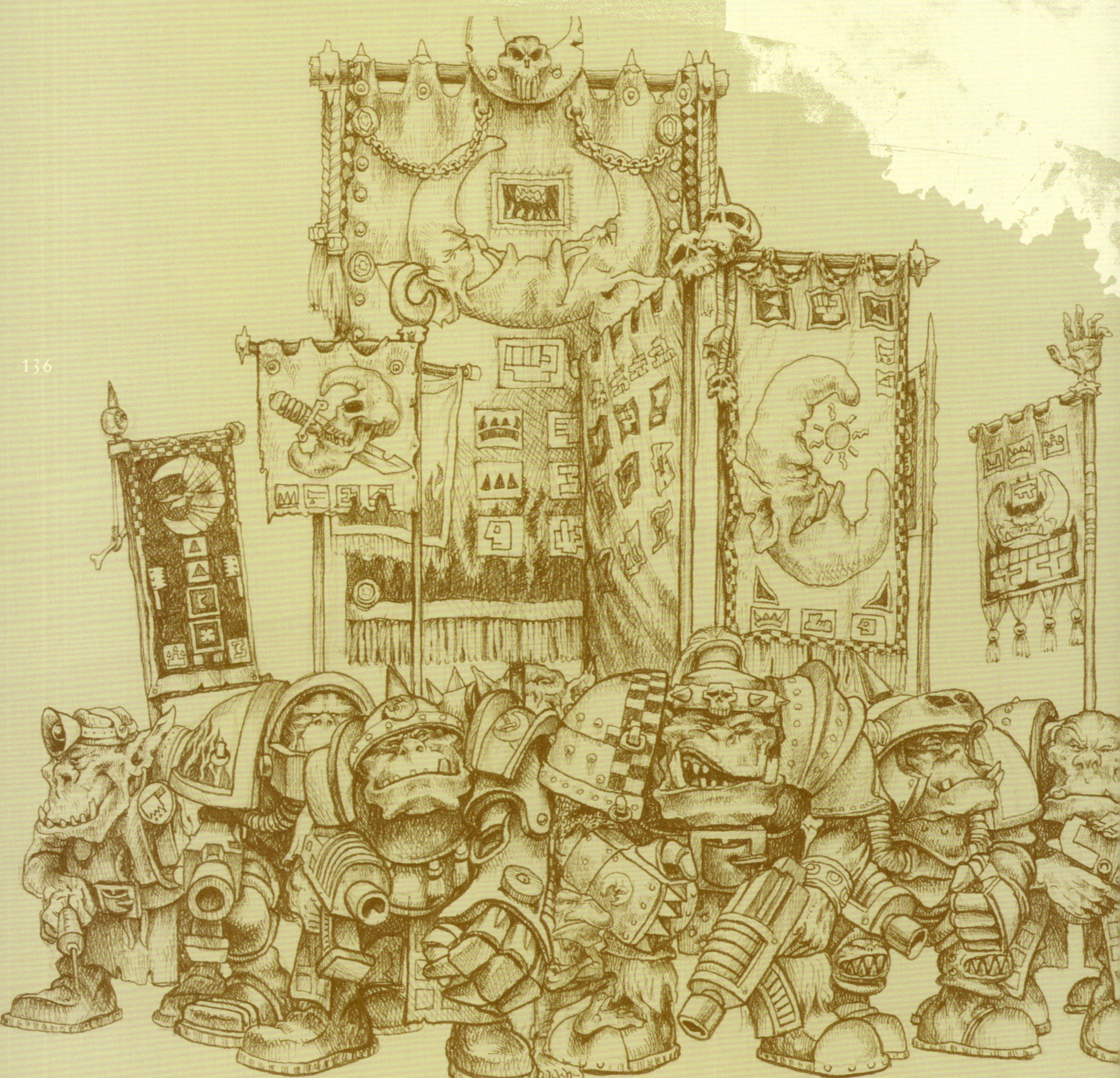

hive-like place with a hive like mentality, people busily immersed in their goal of giving birth to the myriad ideas and impulses that buzzed constantly around the building.

We worked closely together, feeding eagerly off each other's triumphs, and just as eagerly, each other's disasters. Biologically impossible elbows and knees; sausage fingers and an incredible array of blasphemous attempts at anatomy all caused much derision and hilarity. Meaning well, but merciless, it spurred us on to attempt betterment with each new drawing. Never knowing when someone might be peering over my hunched shoulders, hardly bothering to suppress their mirth at what was taking place on the paper, made the use of threats and whips redundant.

The world that Games Workshop was creating, to me, was a new direction I had never being in. Brooding and apocalyptical, it was a dark, gothic universe without much hope. It took me a while to find my way, but with leadership and enthusiastic encouragement from John, I was soon able to immerse myself in it. Having only worked as a hermit so far, I found that living and working with other artists steering towards the same vision left little time for the somewhat more lyrical worlds I had previously inhabited. However, I soon found that the visual intensity and harsh, violent nature of the Warhammer 40K universe provided its own irresistible momentum. A visceral energy pulling us along with it, to whatever dark future was waiting. The excitement of being part of this, at the time, even compensated for my palette suffering the restrictions of being limited to black and white. Not being able to work things gradually up in paint from loose sketches, I was forced to adopt a more direct and reckless approach, putting definitive marks down right from the beginning. Looking back, it was actually an incredible learning curve involving incessant drawing without the cosmetic luxury of using colour to coax a semblance of life onto the ever-waiting blank white paper.

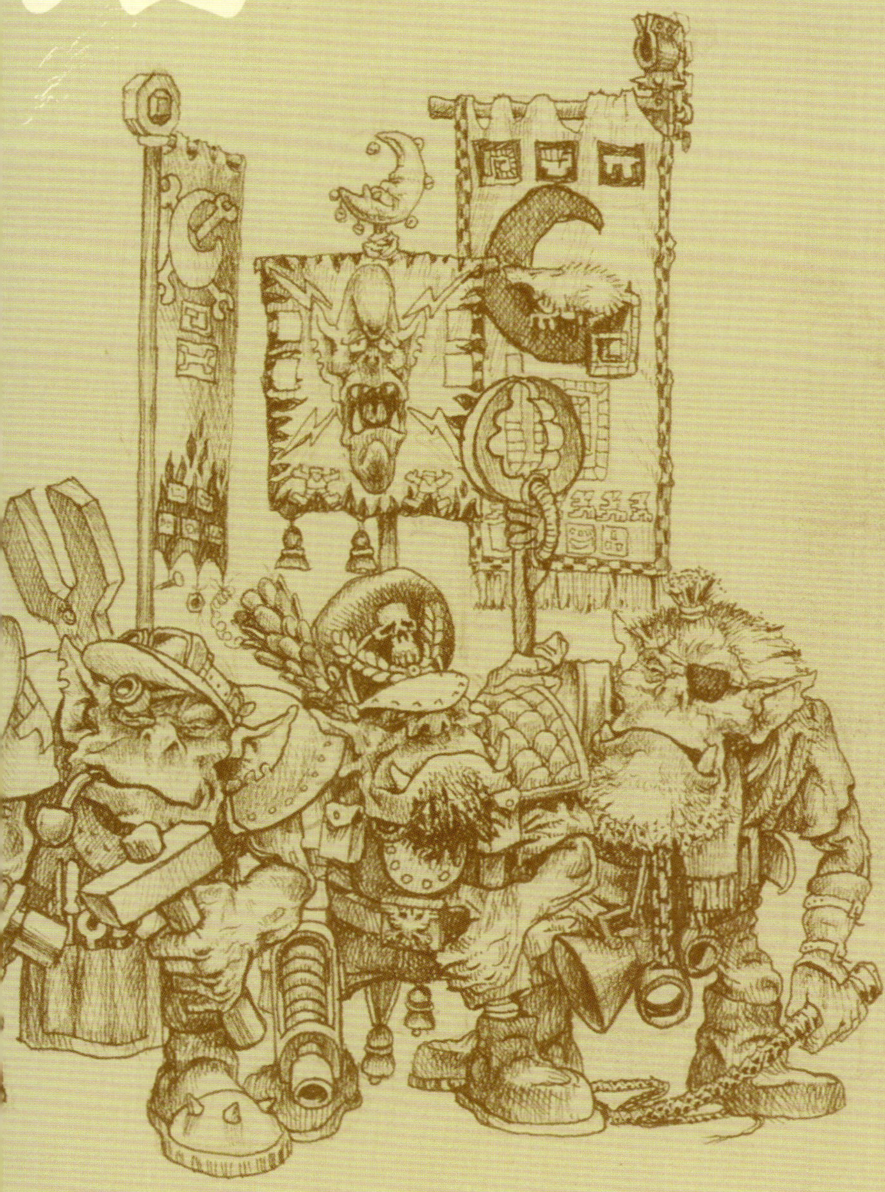

The creation of the Warhammer 40K universe necessitated an incredible amount of attention spent on detail. At times this could be frustrating; trying to give some narrative and life to a drawing, while all the time having to constantly check specifics of uniform, armour and insignia. John would give me relative freedom in providing a narrative for my drawings, letting me try and make them character driven, rather than constant visions of some apocalyptical firefight in another dark and bleak corner of the universe. This indulgence from John helped balance the need for constant referral to the rule book to check on what the intergalactic despots and warmongers regarded as the day's fashion

Over a period of time, the sheer volume of information required for the illustrations to be of any use seemed to overwhelm the spontaneity needed to create an image of any artistic merit. Looking at what GW produce now, their vision has become even more powerful and centred. The darkness and violence inherent in both Warhammer and 40K is even more iconic and powerful. Fearsome in its bleakness even.

For me it had been two years of constant inspiration, stimulation and creativity, both in and out of the studio. There was, however, a layer of dust over my brushes and paints which I wasn't given an excuse to get rid of. After living in a black and white world I was desperate to paint again.

It was not to be though, and so, after having maybe drawn one too many orc banner or glyph, with only more on the horizon, I was somewhat reluctantly forced to the conclusion that I would have to move on.

Paul Bonner

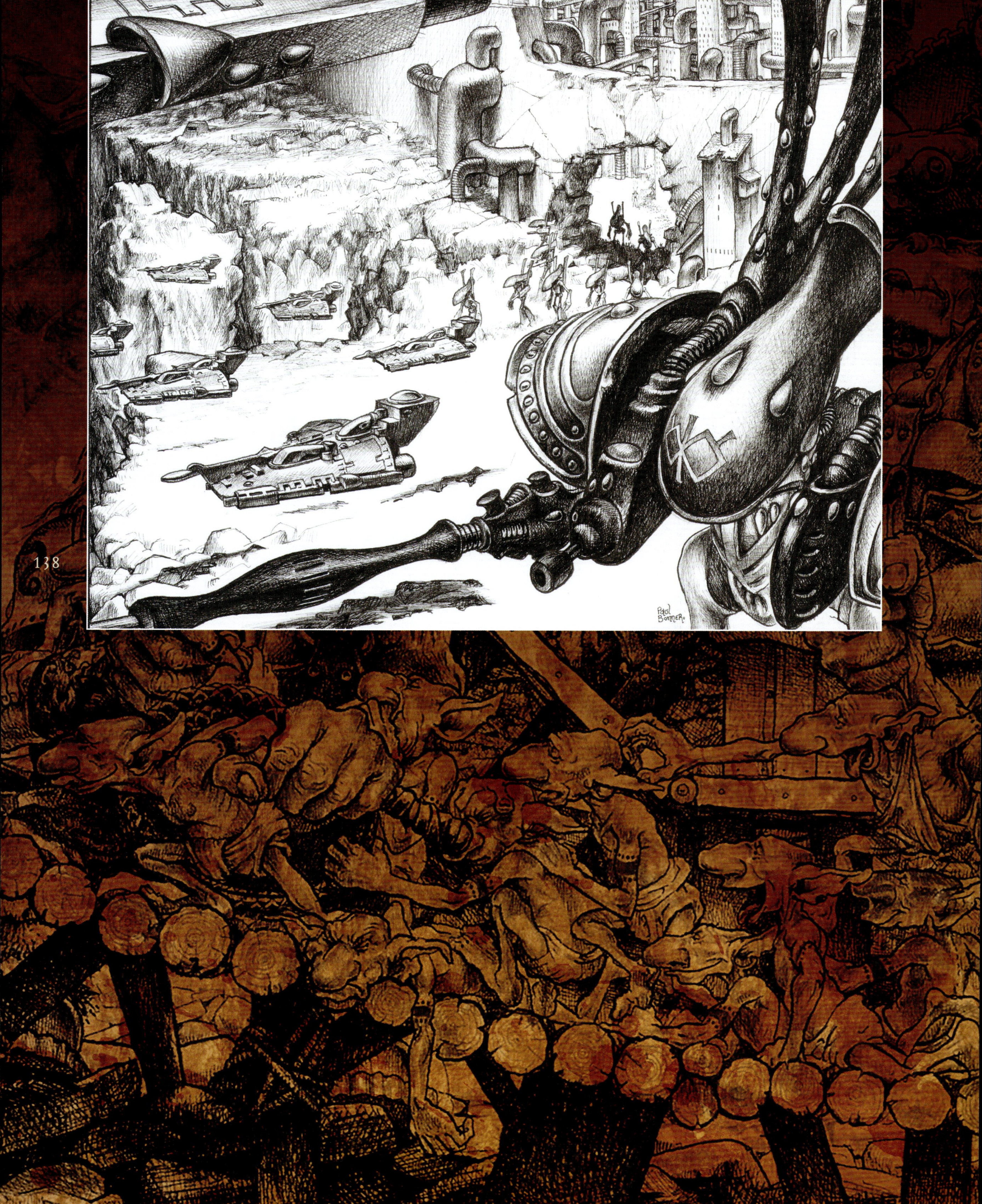
Paul Bonner

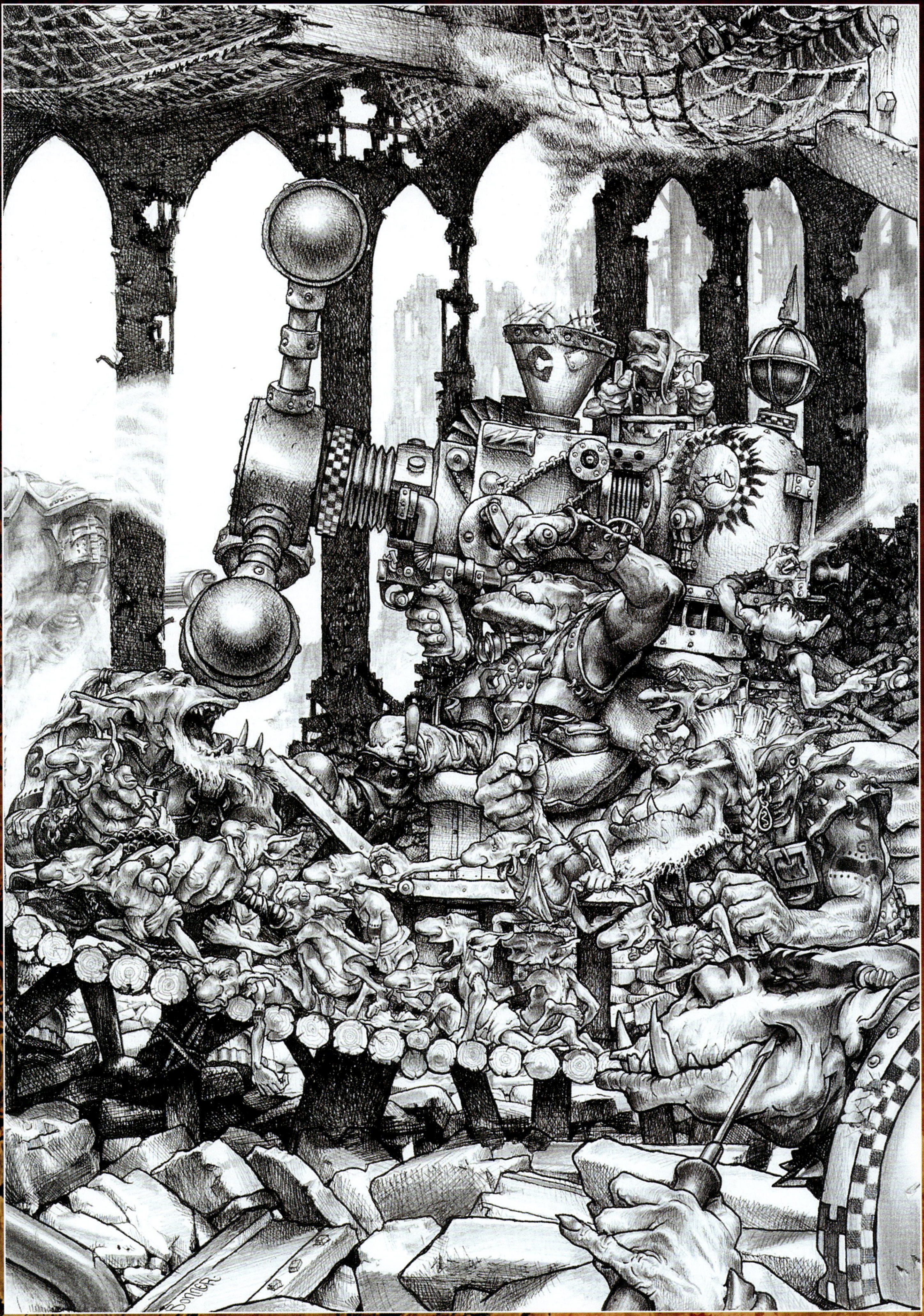

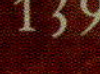

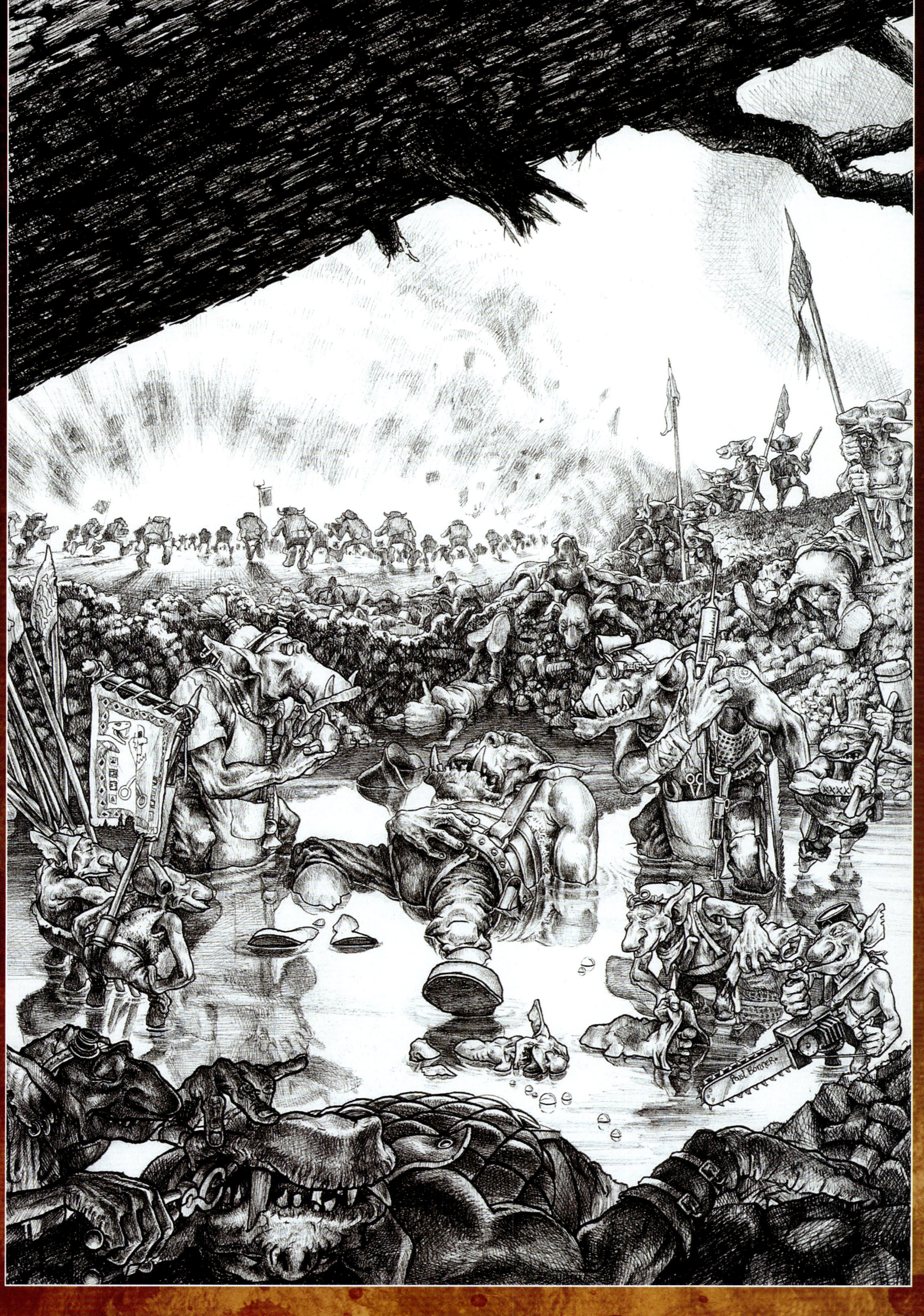
Paul Bonner

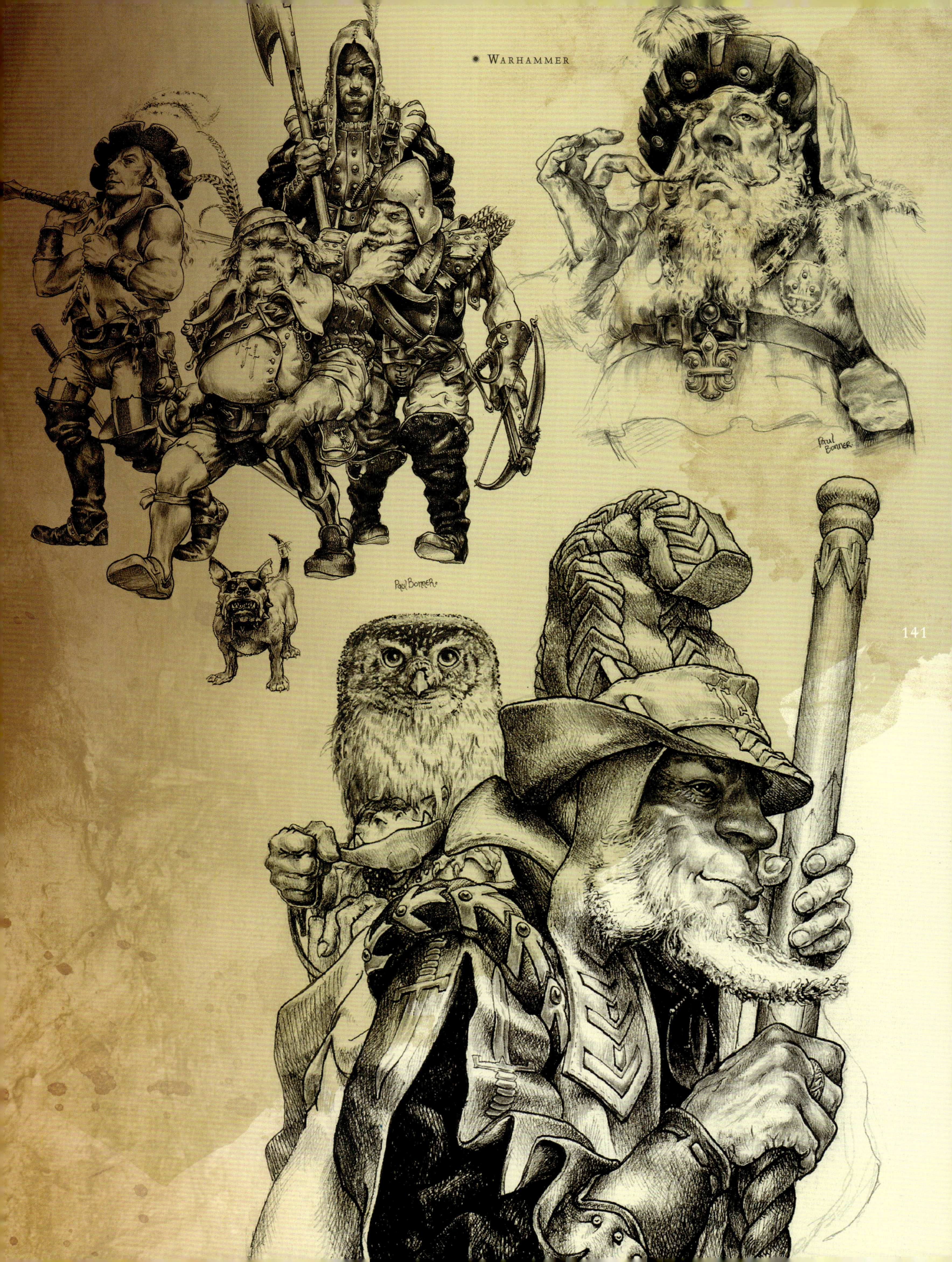
Paul Bonner
Paul Bonner

You should know this about Paul Bonner: he is humble. I recall a phone conversation we had in 1999 in which he was wondering if he should submit work to the juried annual *Spectrum: The Best in Contemporary Fantastic Art*. He seemed concerned about whether his work would be good enough to make it into the publication. I encouraged him to submit a few pictures, thinking to myself that he would certainly get in the book and would probably win an award. Sure enough, the following year he was represented by 3 paintings in *Spectrum 7* and won a silver award for one of his efforts, a spectacular painting of a Tyrannosaurus Rex attacking a herd of Edmontosaurs.

fasa

I was introduced to Paul's work by a friend and co-worker named Mike Nielsen. We worked in the art department at FASA Corporation, a Chicago-based game company, and Mike was a fan of Paul's work for Games Workshop and his covers for Target's Mutant Chronicles™ books. I was immediately impressed by the work and later, when we were developing a card game based on FASA's Shadowrun® role-playing game, we decided to contact Paul about doing some card artwork. As a longtime fan, Mike did the honors and we were thrilled when Paul agreed to paint some cards for us.

The work he did was superb. The Shadowrun world is a mixture of the mythological and the technological. The game features traditional races and creatures of myth and high fantasy in a nontraditional setting: a high-tech future. Paul captured both the fantasy and science fiction elements of the game with ease. More importantly, he was able to breathe life into the characters he painted, particularly non-human characters like dwarves, trolls and orks.

That's what Paul does. He breathes life into his pictures. In fact, he does much more than that. In an industry filled with artwork depicting larger than life beings and creatures, his work stands out because his creations have character. They are endowed with a spark of life that is often missing in fantastic art. Expressions and anatomy aren't simply exaggerated in Paul's art, they are amplified, given a presence within the picture that commands the viewer's attention. You can believe the dwarves, trolls and beasties in Paul's work are real because they look as if they have lived. The lines on their faces suggest experience. They appear as multi-dimensional individuals with distinct quirks and personalities. You can imagine them in battle (as they are often depicted) but you can also see them as moving, thinking, emotional creatures and, because they are painted with a genuine understanding of anatomy, they are utterly believable. The environments in Paul's work, like the creatures, contain the spark of life. His command of light and shadow enables him to place his creations in surroundings that are convincing to the viewer. In fact, these environments often have as much character as the strange and wonderful beings who inhabit them. You can almost smell the decaying leaves or feel the rough surface of carved, ancient stones in a Bonner painting. Each picture has a distinct atmosphere, a sense of place. Paul can infuse even the toughest, nastiest subject matter with a touch of whimsy. It's not an easy trick to pull off but he does it with flair and it's important. Games should be fun and the artwork associated with them, even the roughest and darkest of the lot, should remind us that they're fun. Paul's paintings do that and it's why I wanted as many of them as I could get on FASA products. He painted some of the most memorable covers we published and he's the kind of artist that makes an art director's job easy by bringing a fresh, imaginative perspective to a project every time. Give him an idea to illustrate and he'll not only run with it, he'll improve upon it. It's a gift.

Enjoy this book. You're looking at the work of a truly inventive artist in complete control of his craft. His imagination will take you to places you never expected to visit. Believe me, you'll want to go back again and again.

Jim Nelson
March 2007

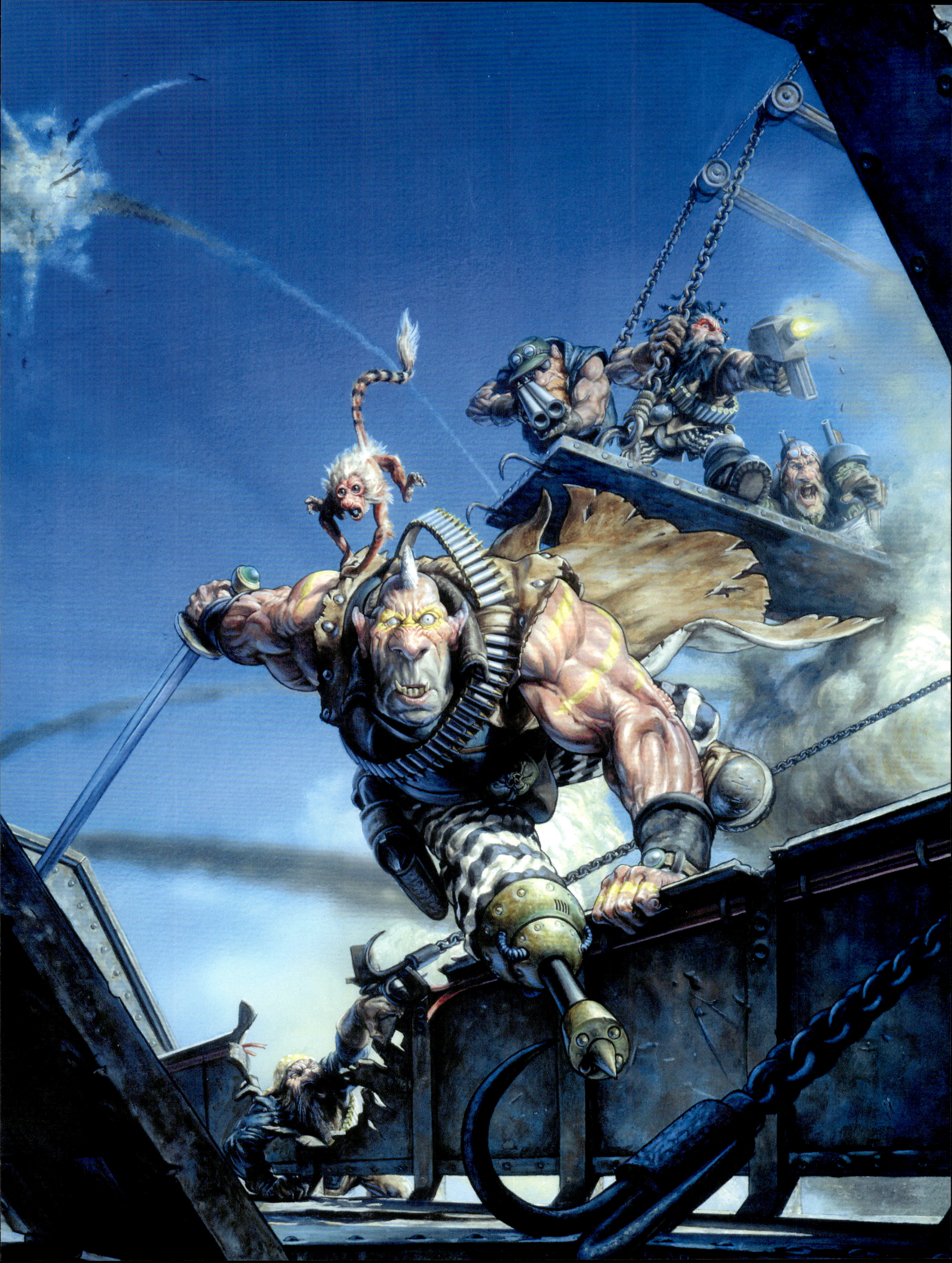

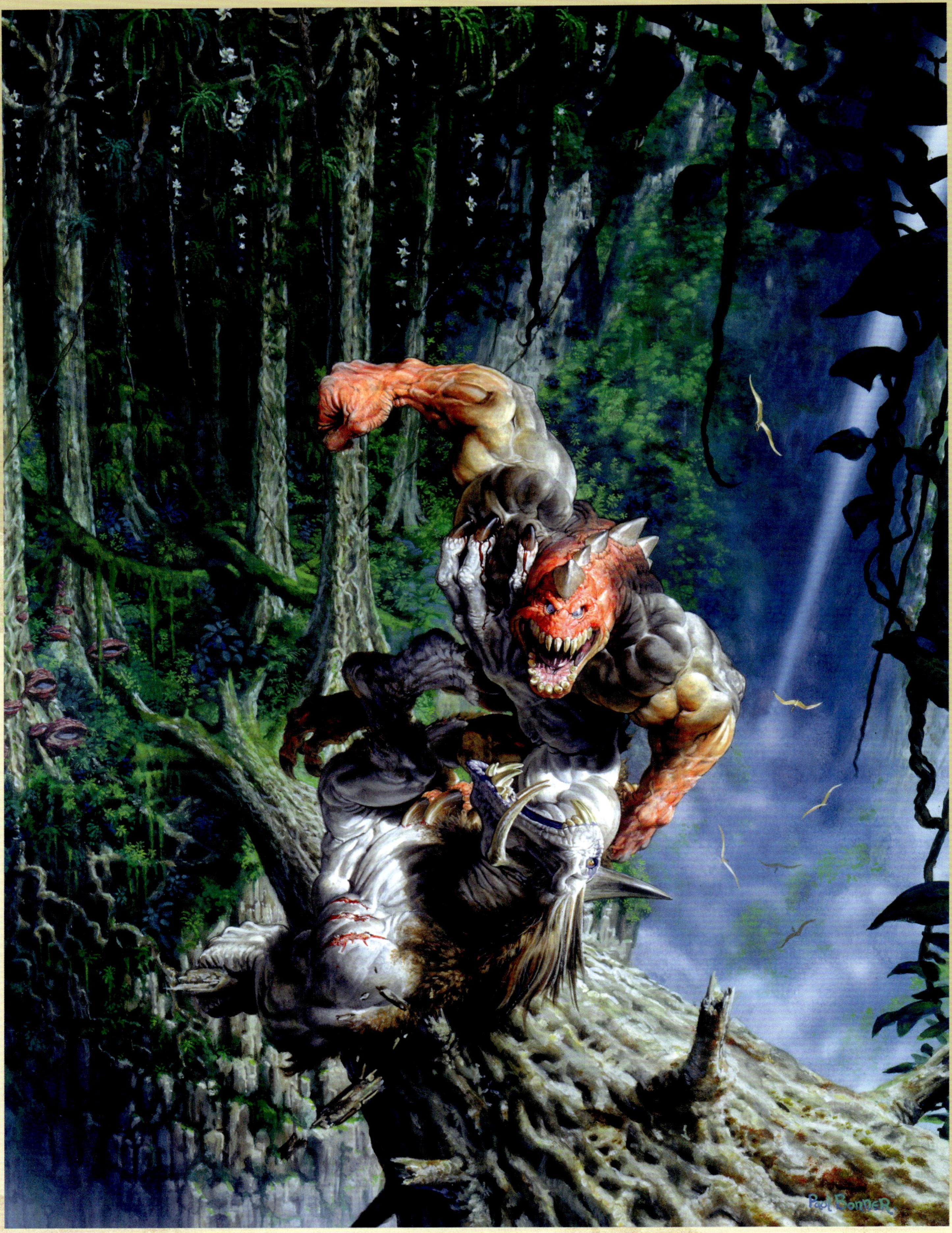

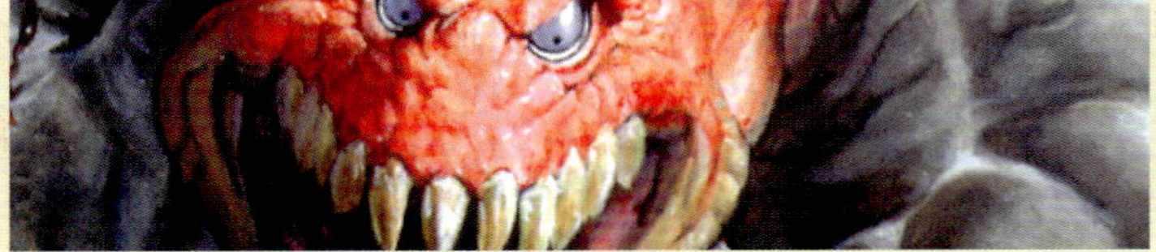

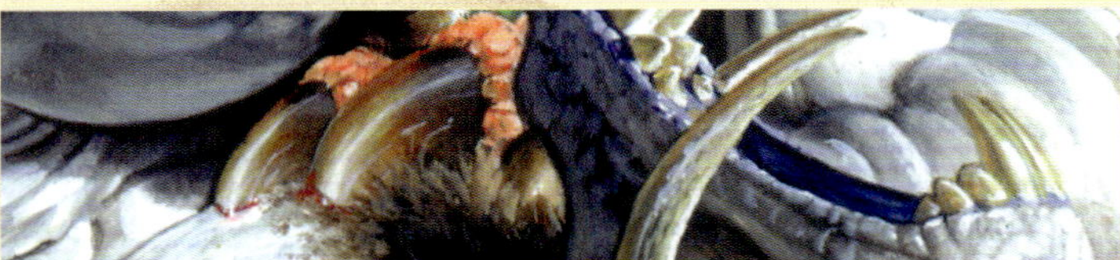

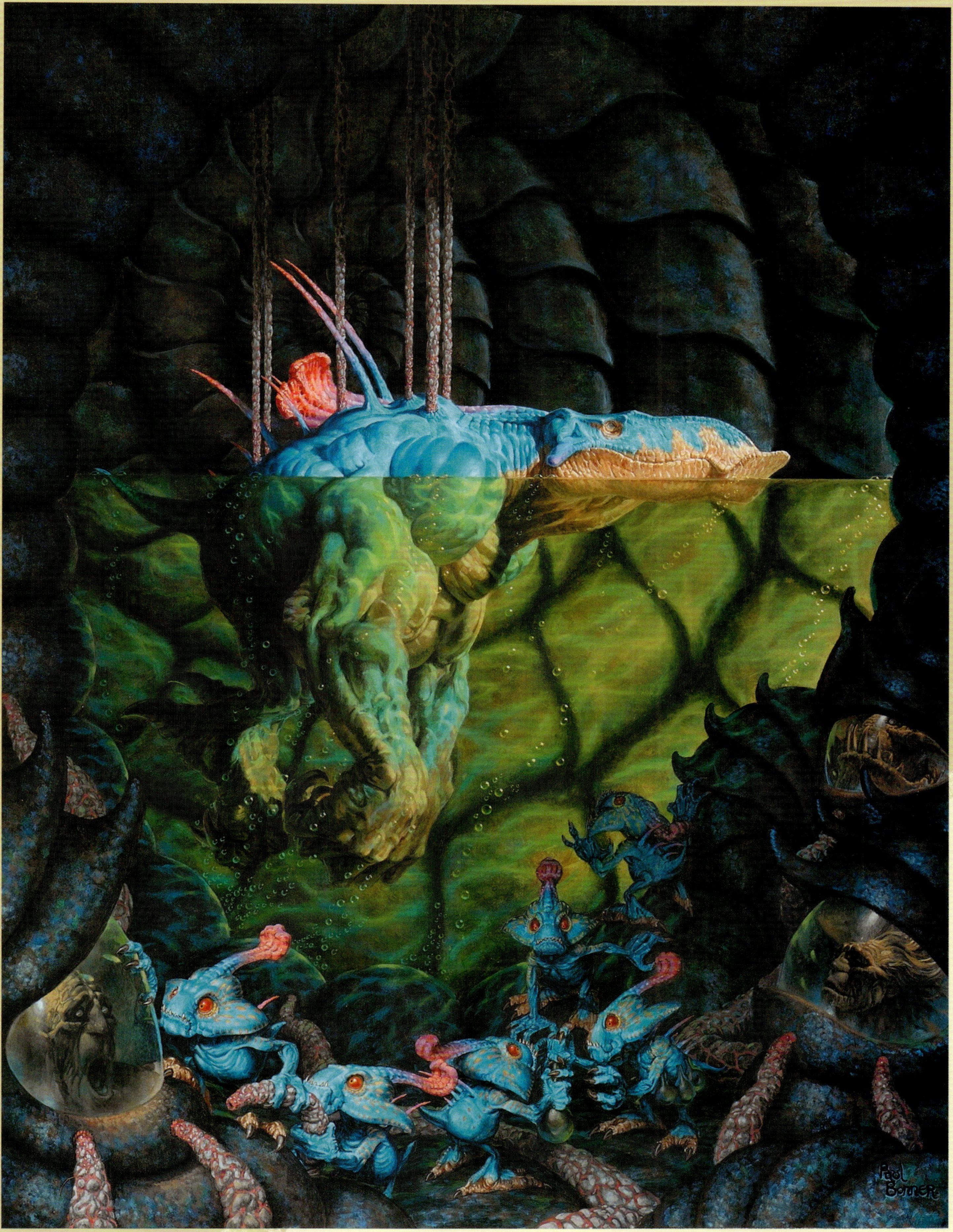

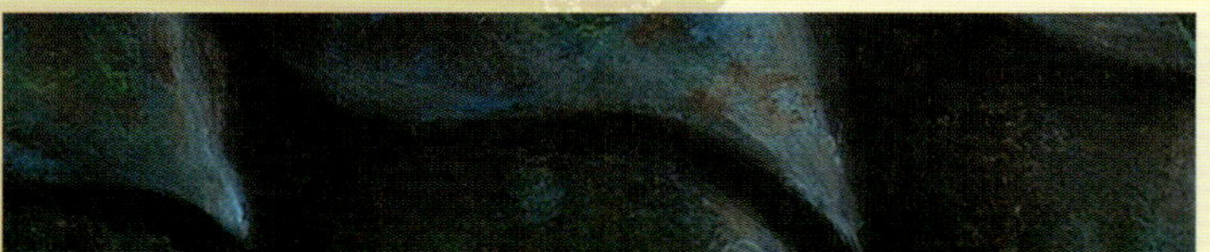

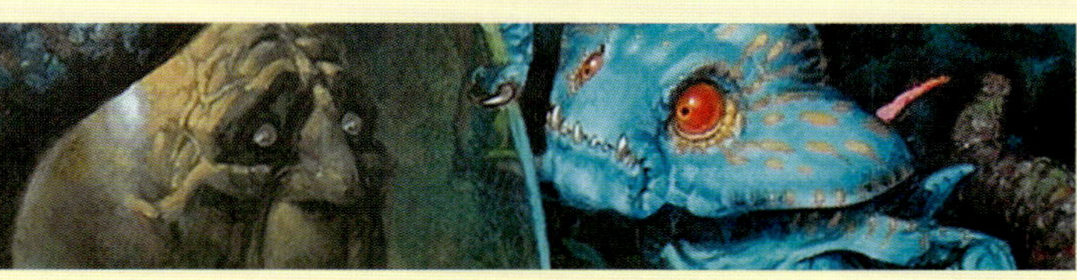

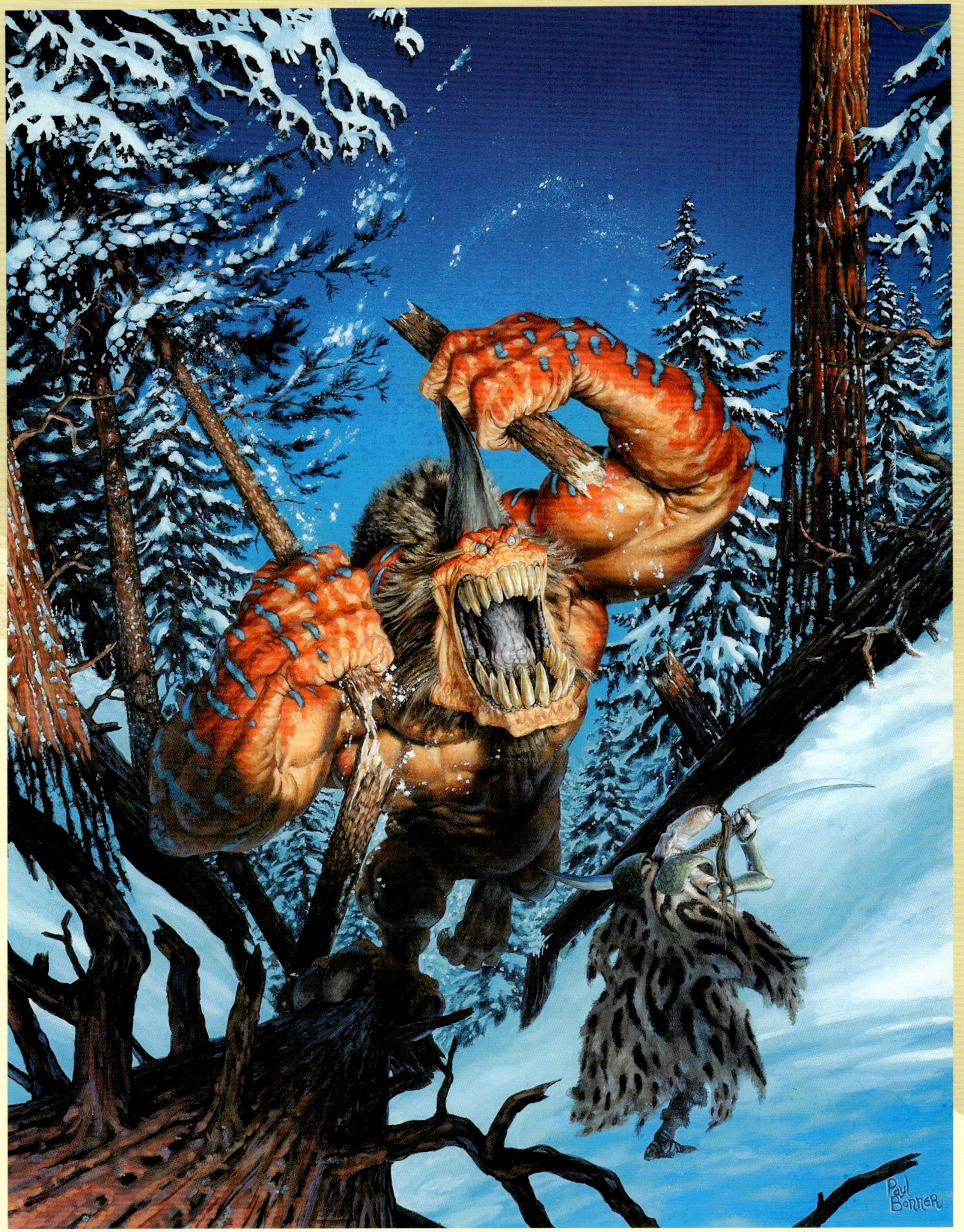

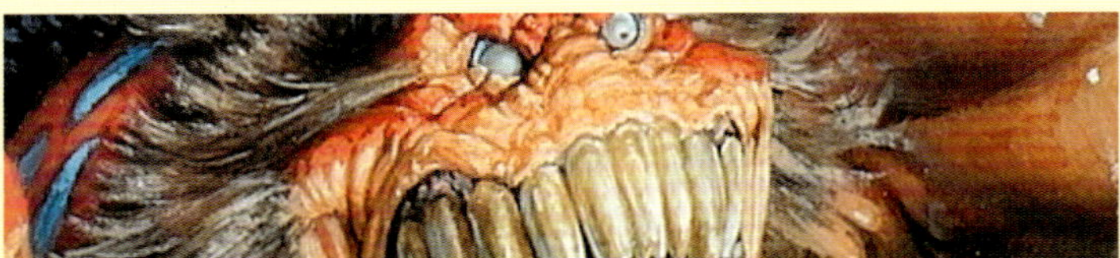

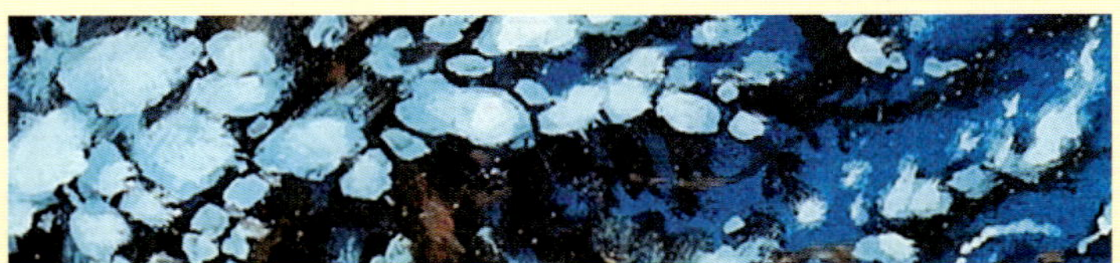

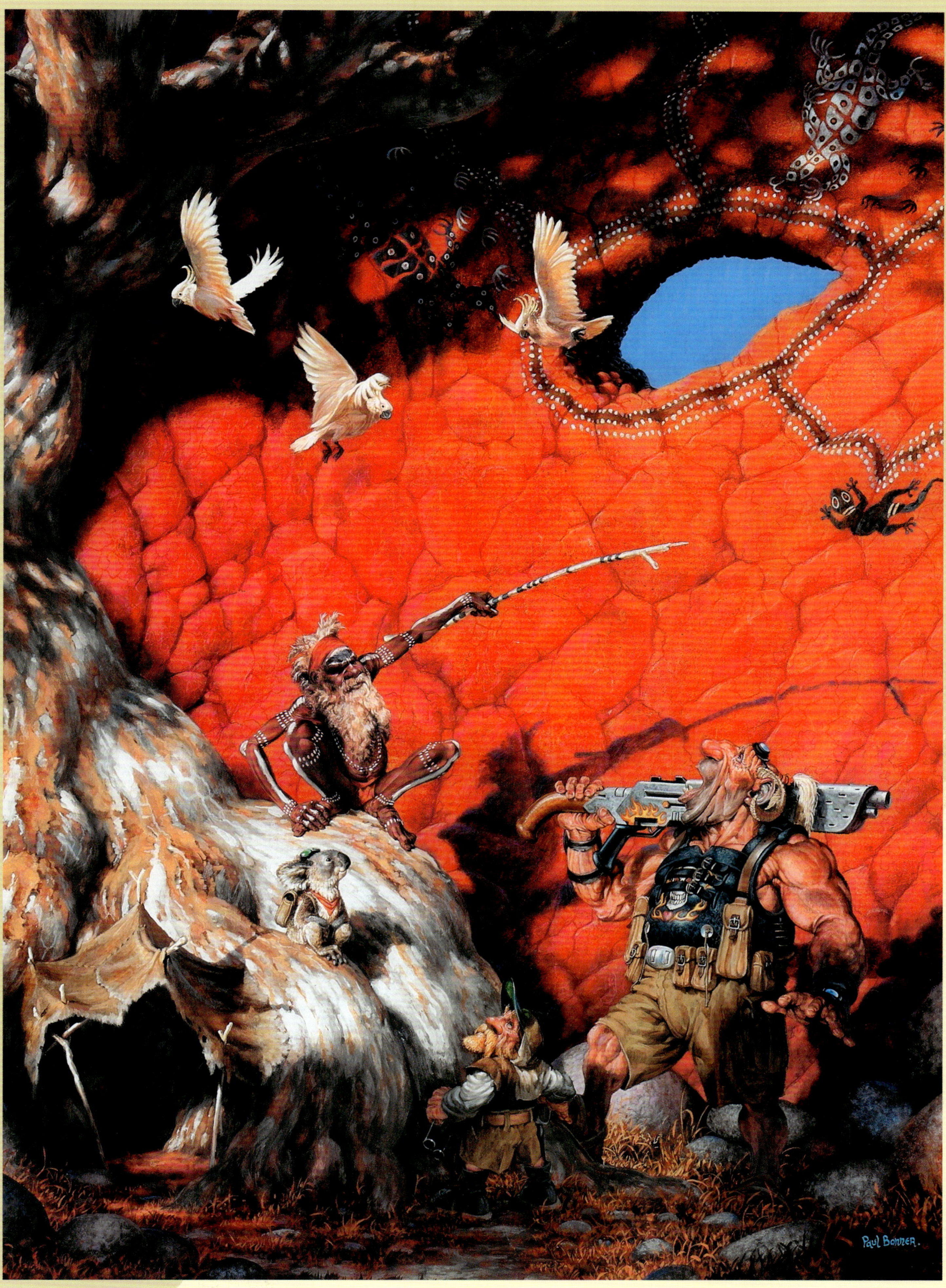

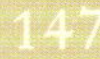

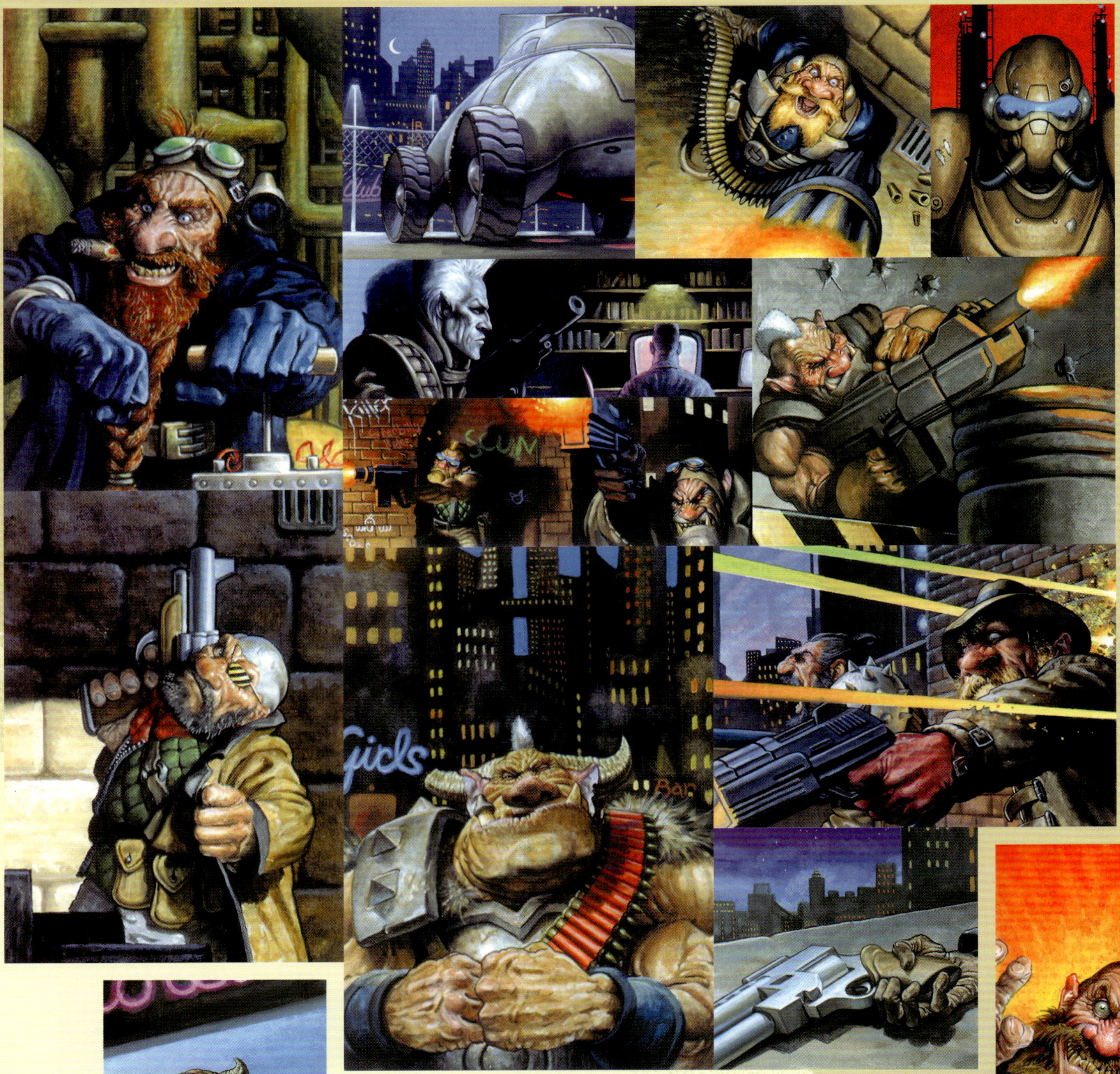

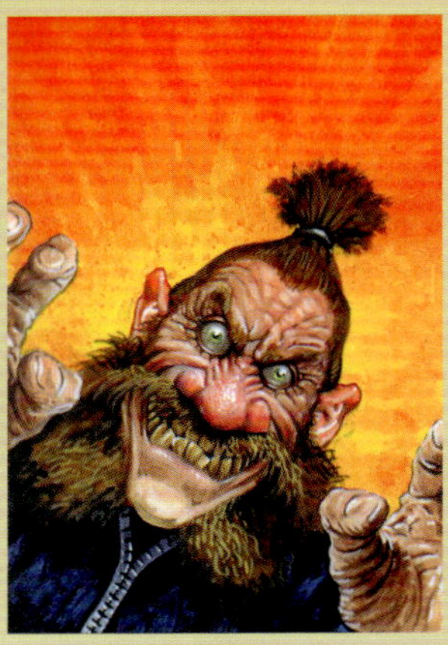

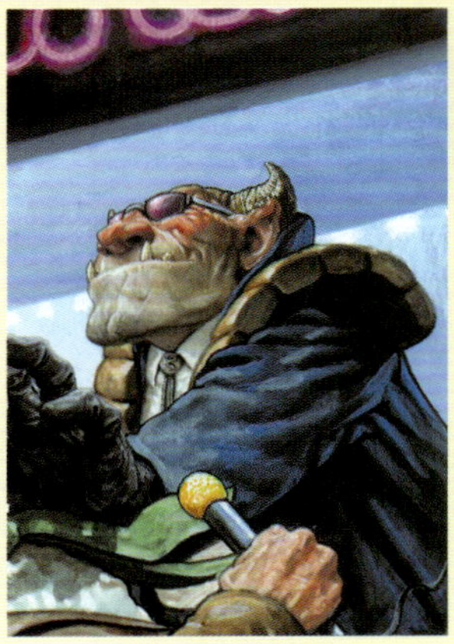

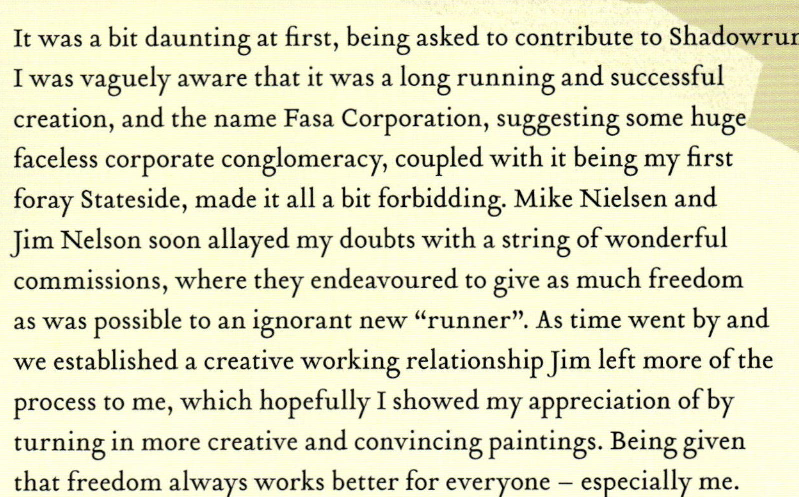

It was a bit daunting at first, being asked to contribute to Shadowrun. I was vaguely aware that it was a long running and successful creation, and the name Fasa Corporation, suggesting some huge faceless corporate conglomeracy, coupled with it being my first foray Stateside, made it all a bit forbidding. Mike Nielsen and Jim Nelson soon allayed my doubts with a string of wonderful commissions, where they endeavoured to give as much freedom as was possible to an ignorant new "runner". As time went by and we established a creative working relationship Jim left more of the process to me, which hopefully I showed my appreciation of by turning in more creative and convincing paintings. Being given that freedom always works better for everyone – especially me.

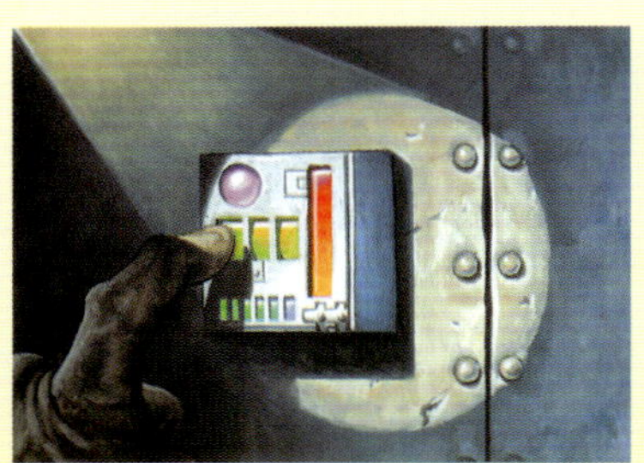

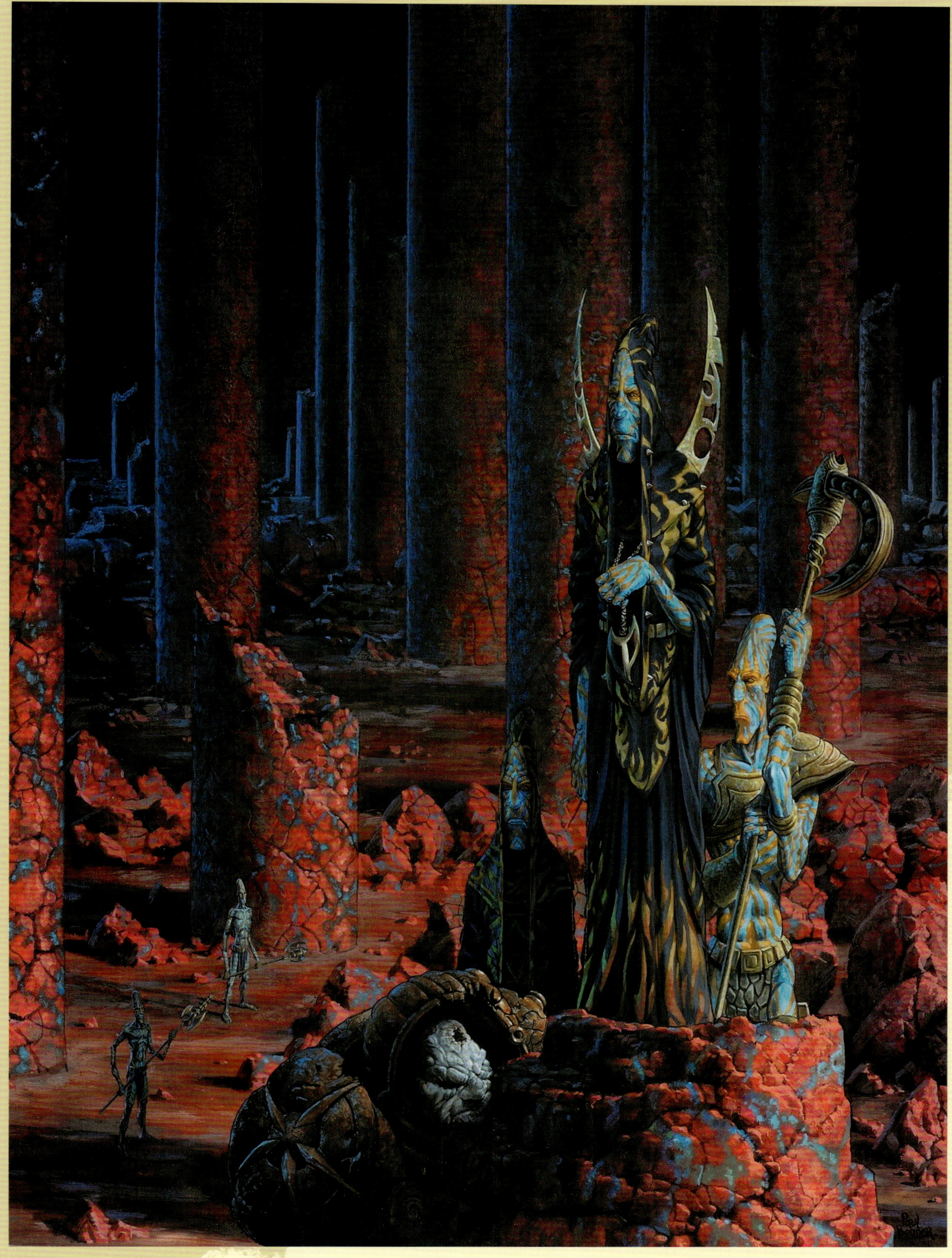

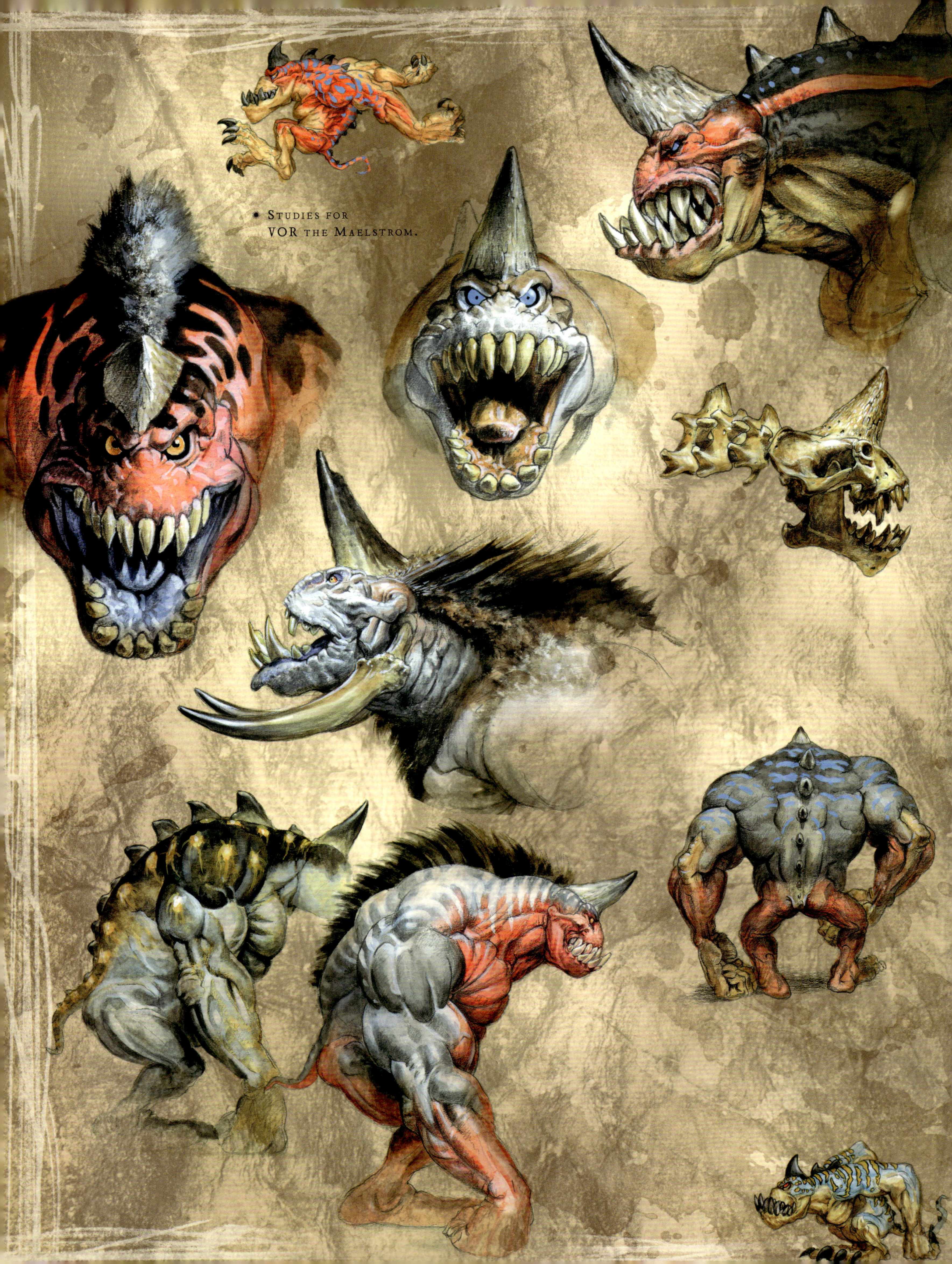

Studies for VOR the Maelstrom.

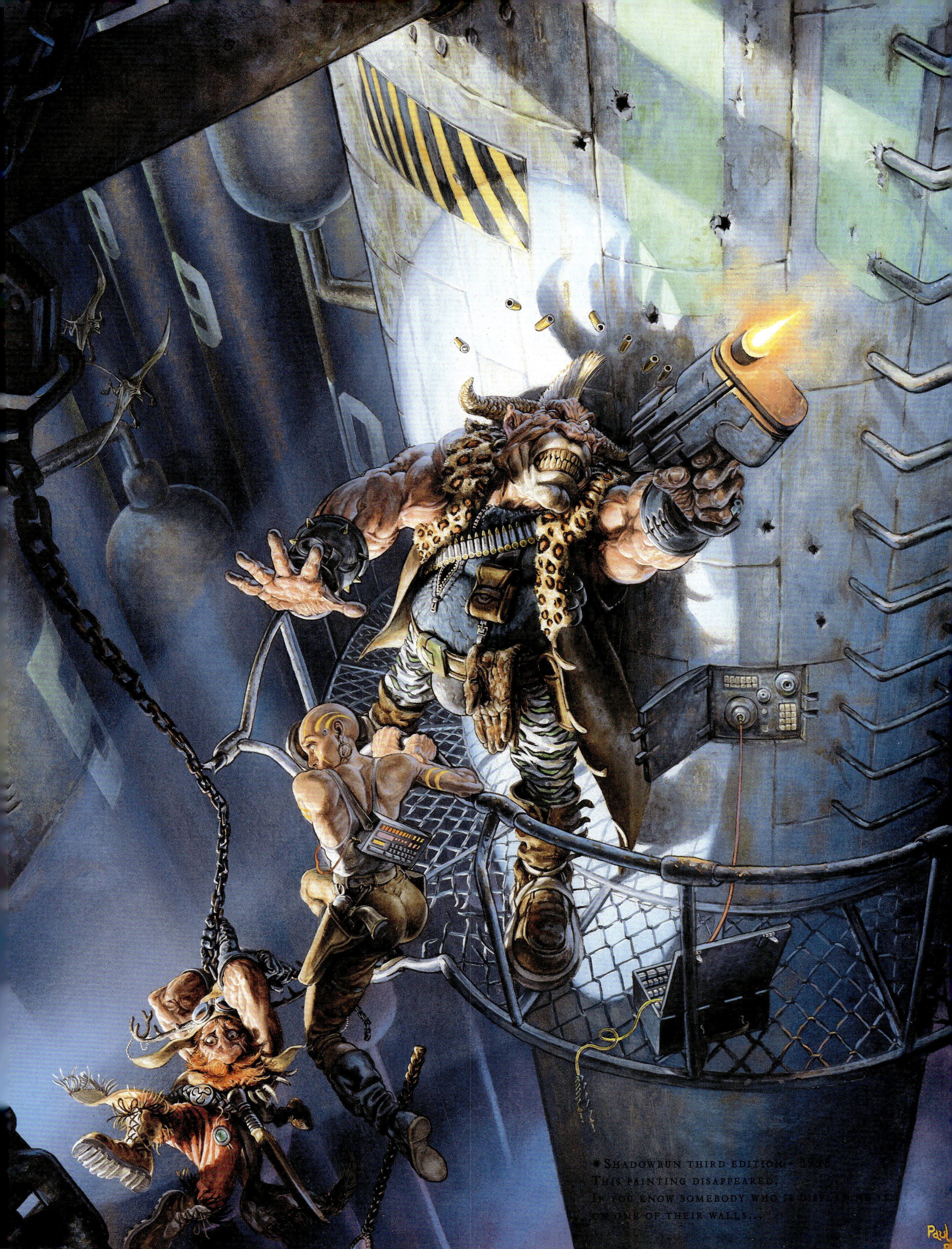

• Shadowrun third edition - 1998.
This painting disappeared.
If you know somebody who is displaying it
on one of their walls...

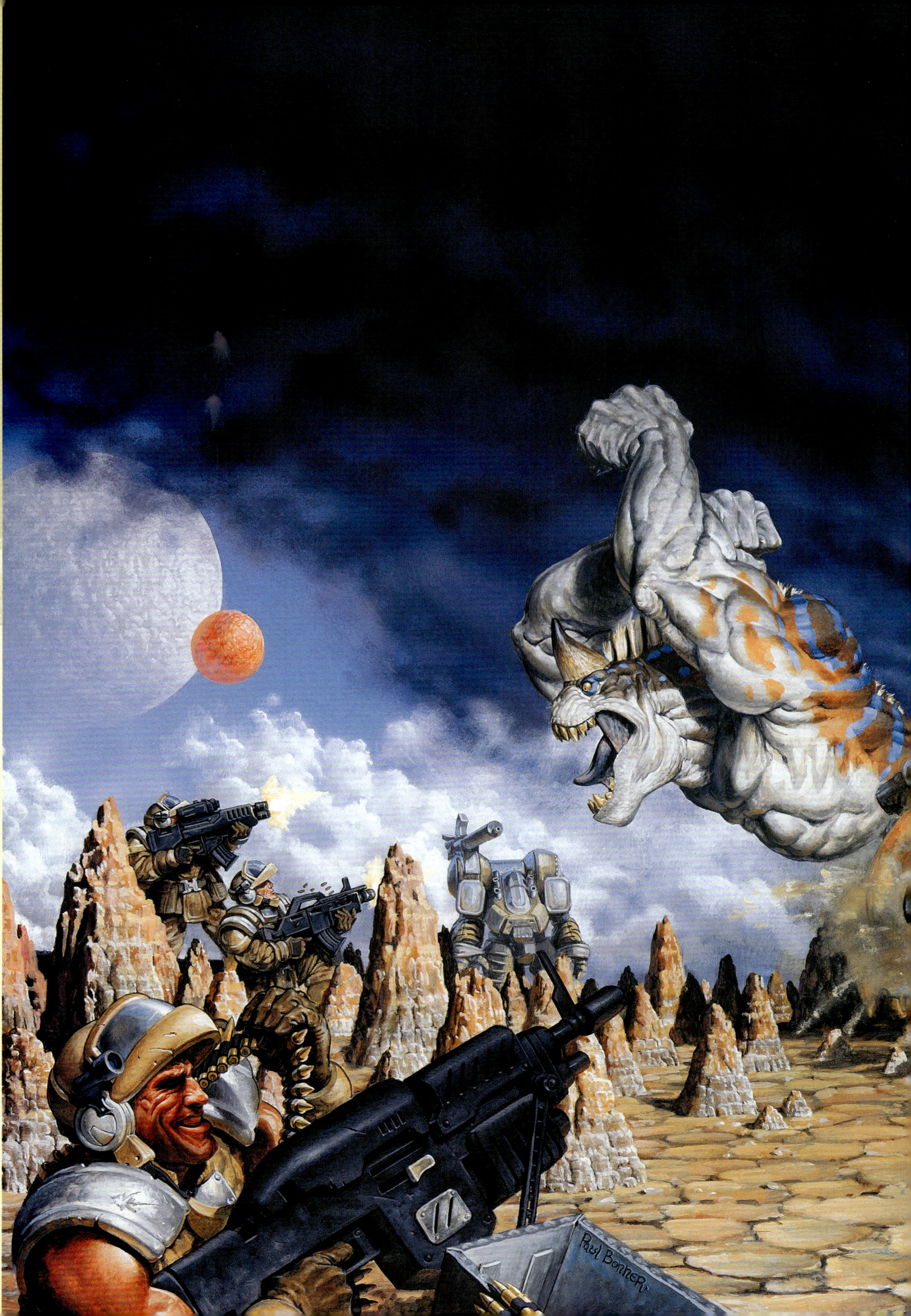

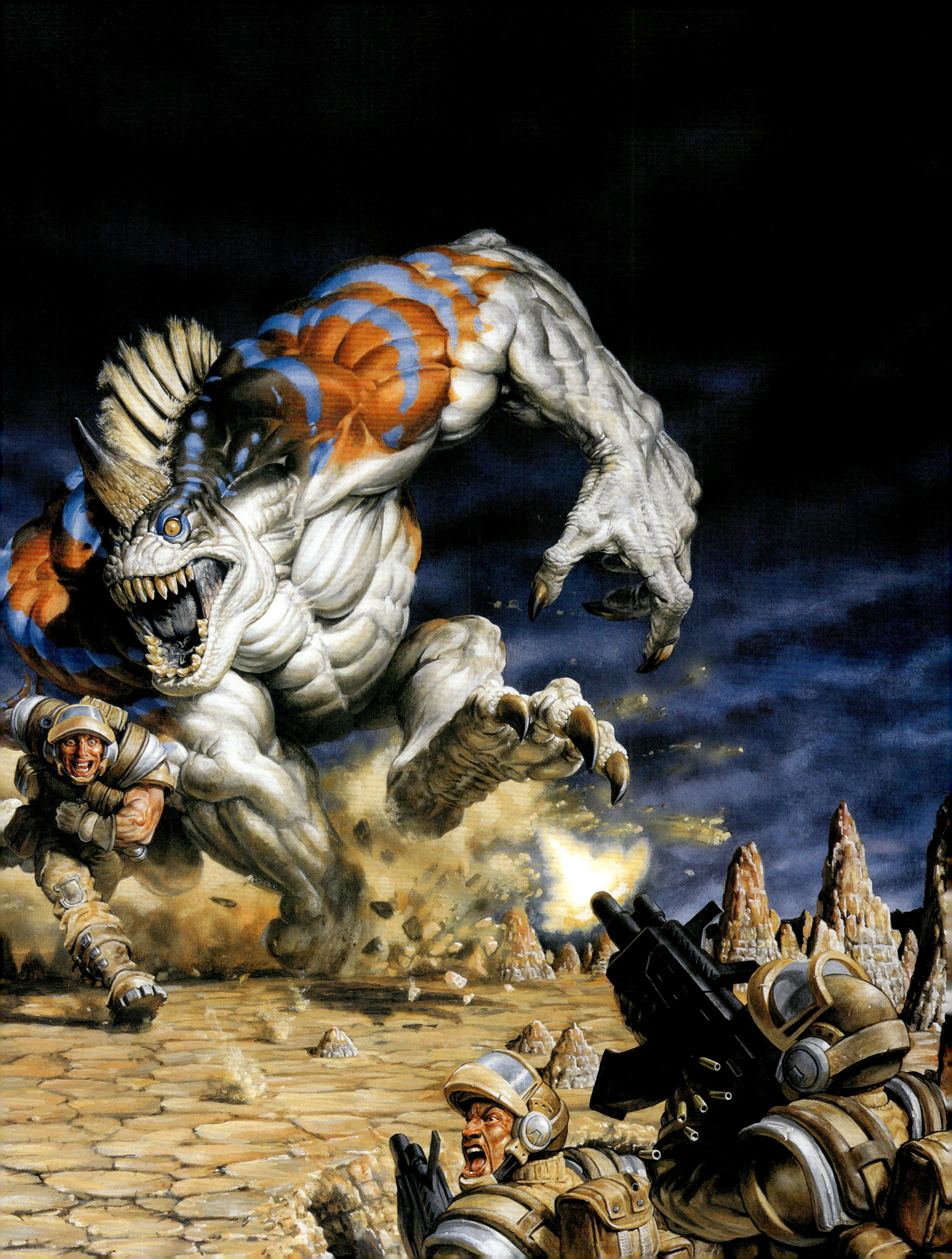

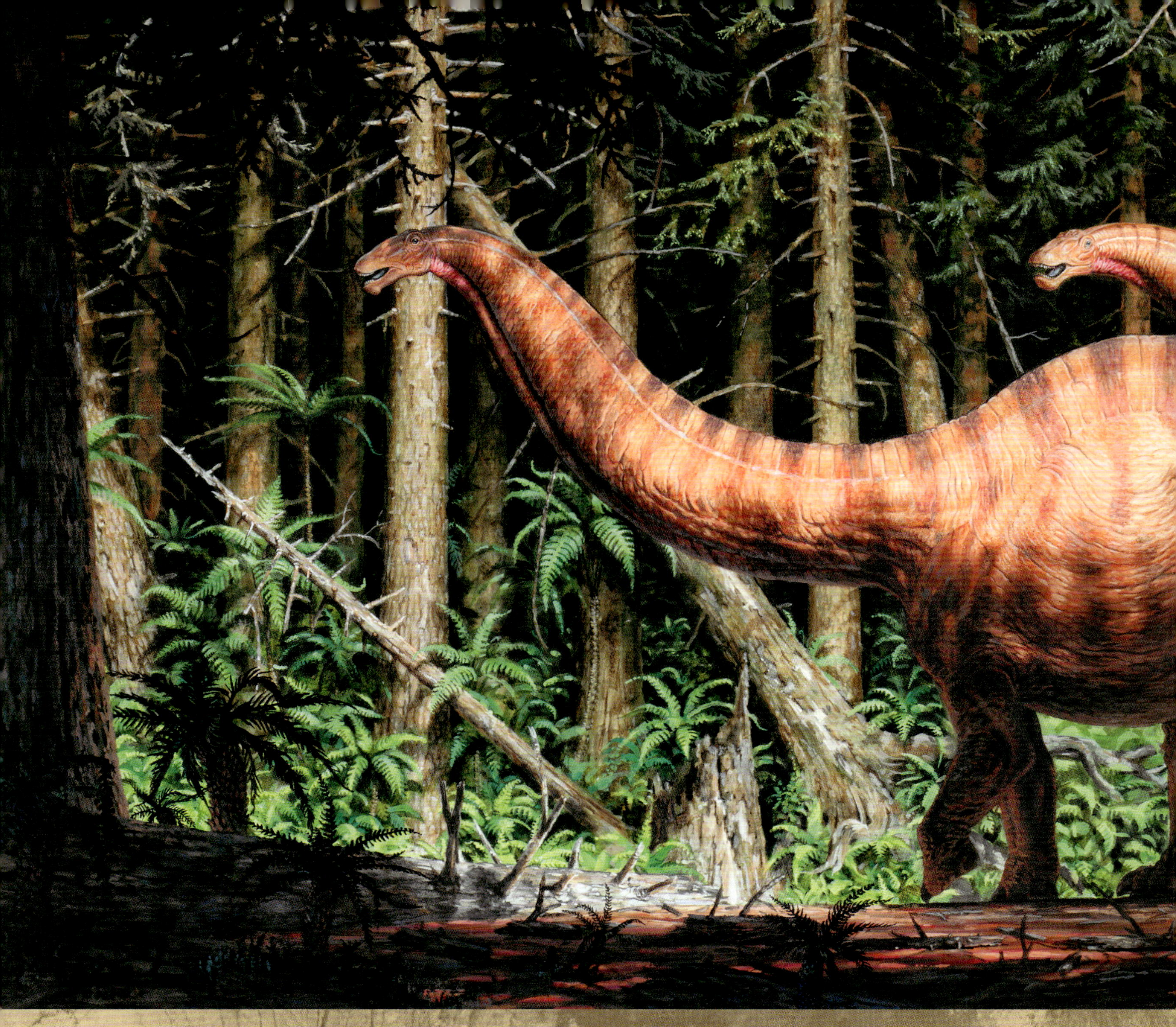

Dinosaurs

Apart from the plasticine boulders fired from my siege engines, my long-suffering knights had to also contend with the rather unwelcome attentions of a whole range of psychotic and perpetually hungry dinosaurs.

While my knights have long since passed into the eager hands of younger clan members, the dinosaurs that managed to avoid capture or extinction have actually established a much larger colony that remains firmly in my possession.

Again, my parents, especially my father, must bear some of the responsibility for these past times and interests. It must have been him that took me to see *Fantasia*, where I have vague memories of being awestruck by the primordial dinosaur sequence (it must be said that in those formative years there was no video, DVD, movie merchandising, or multiplexes. Every visual treat came from a huge screen, behind velvet curtains, in a cathedral like building).

...

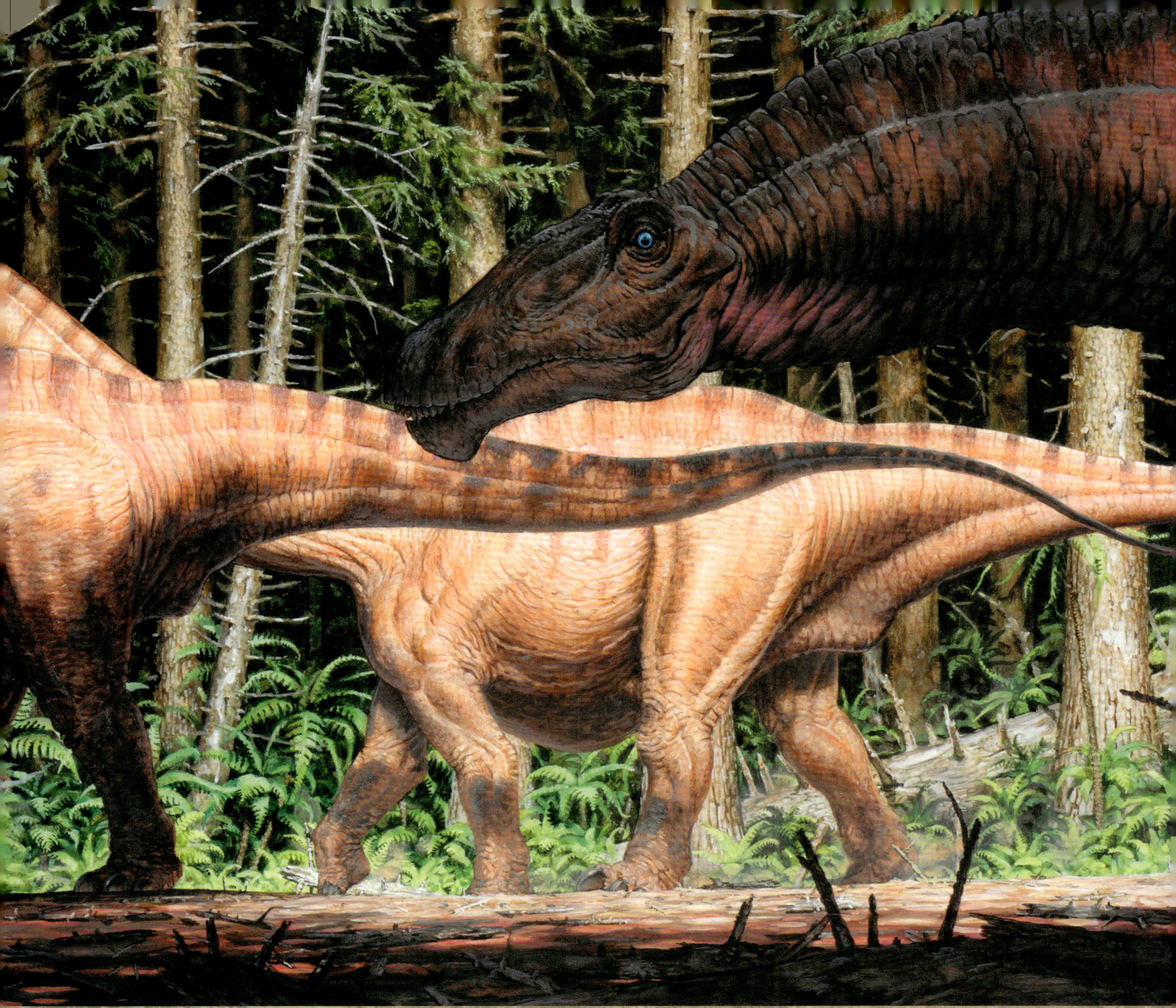

Apatosaurs

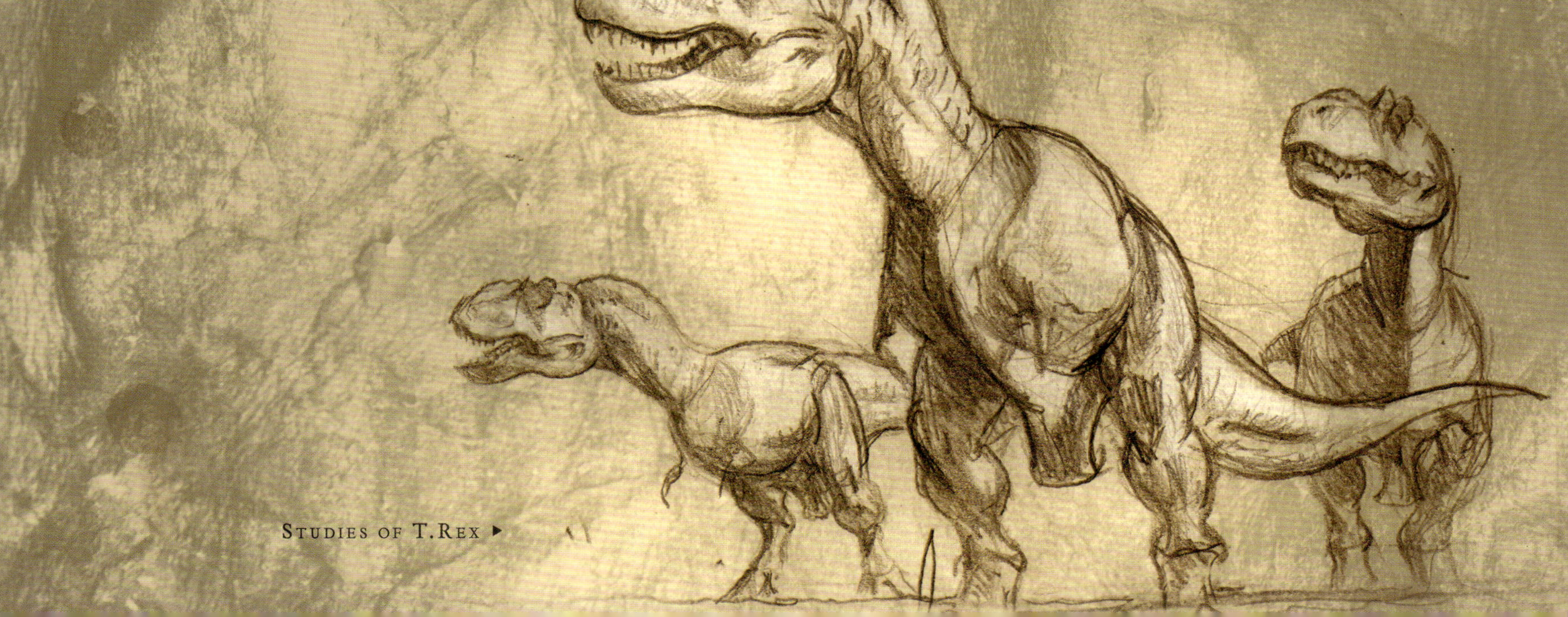

Studies of T.Rex

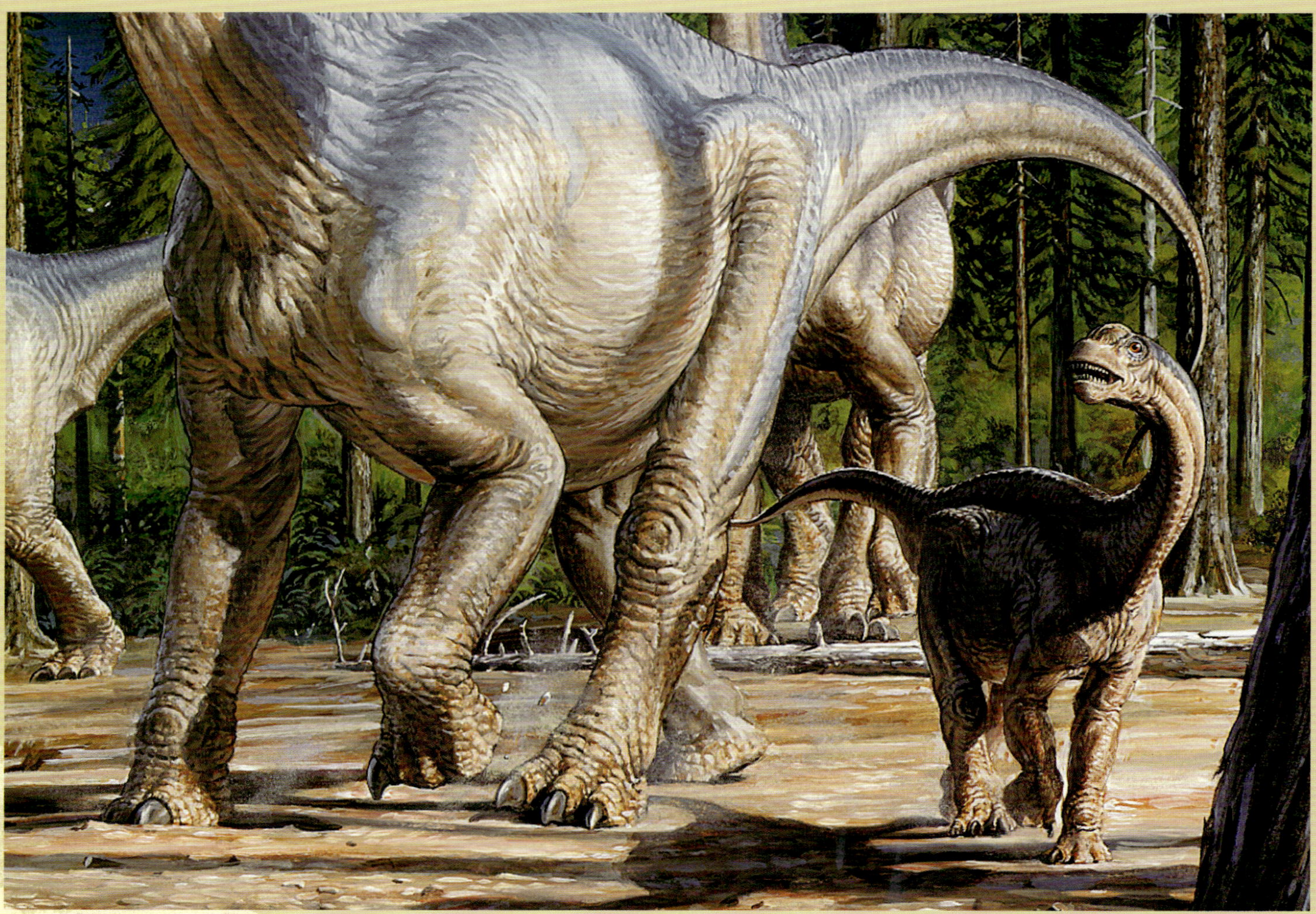

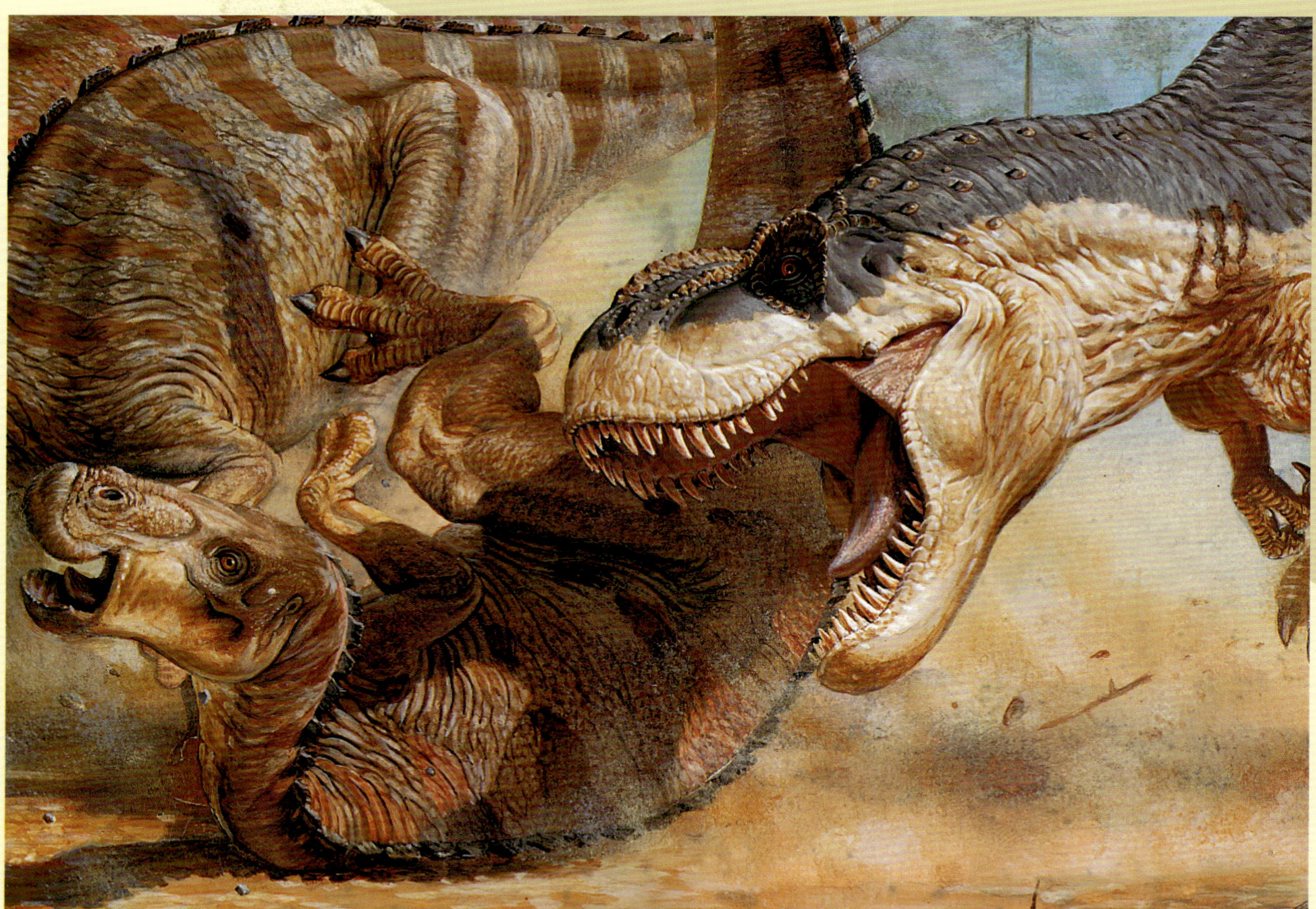

✷ Tyrannosaurus and Edmontosaurs – 1997

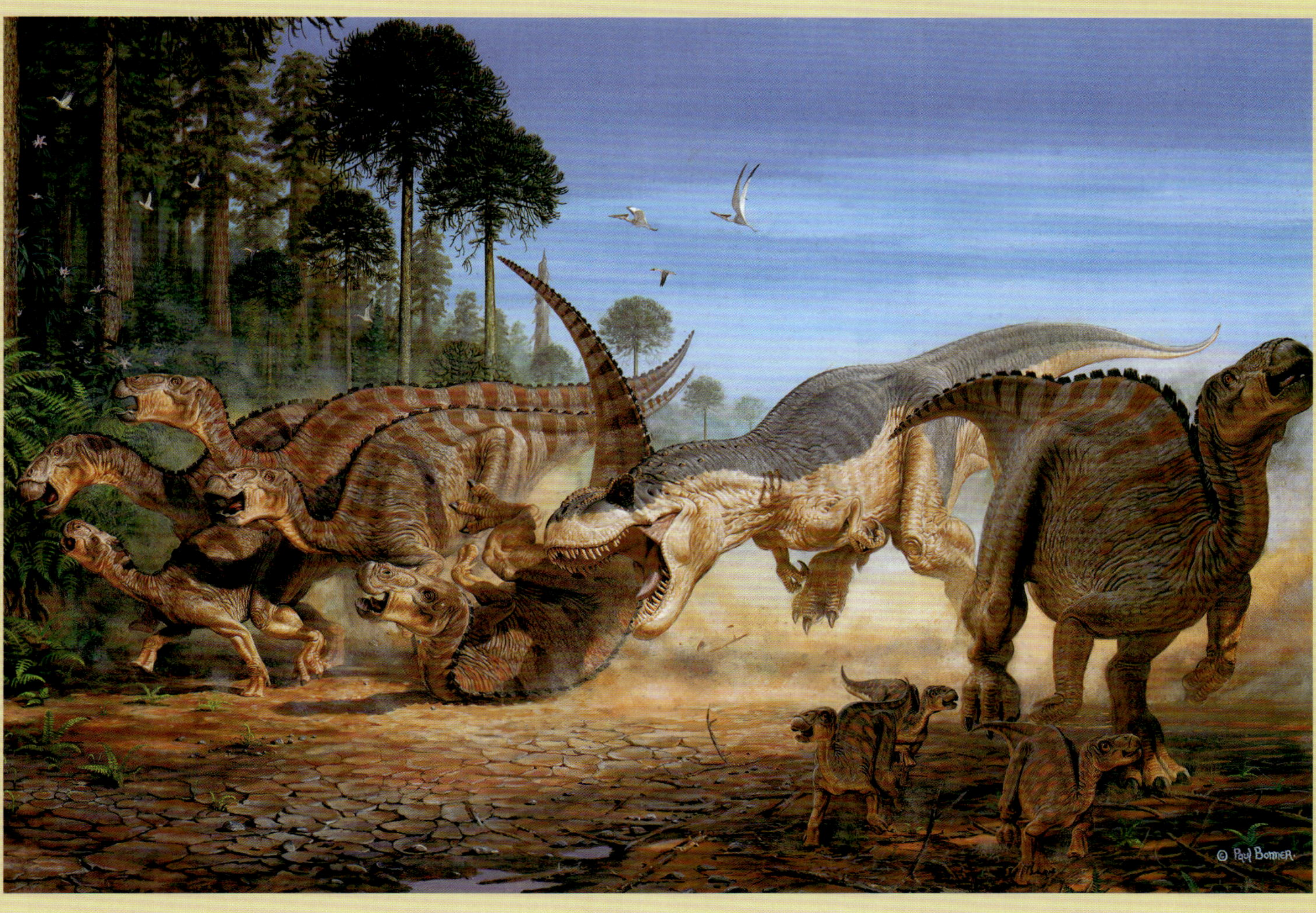

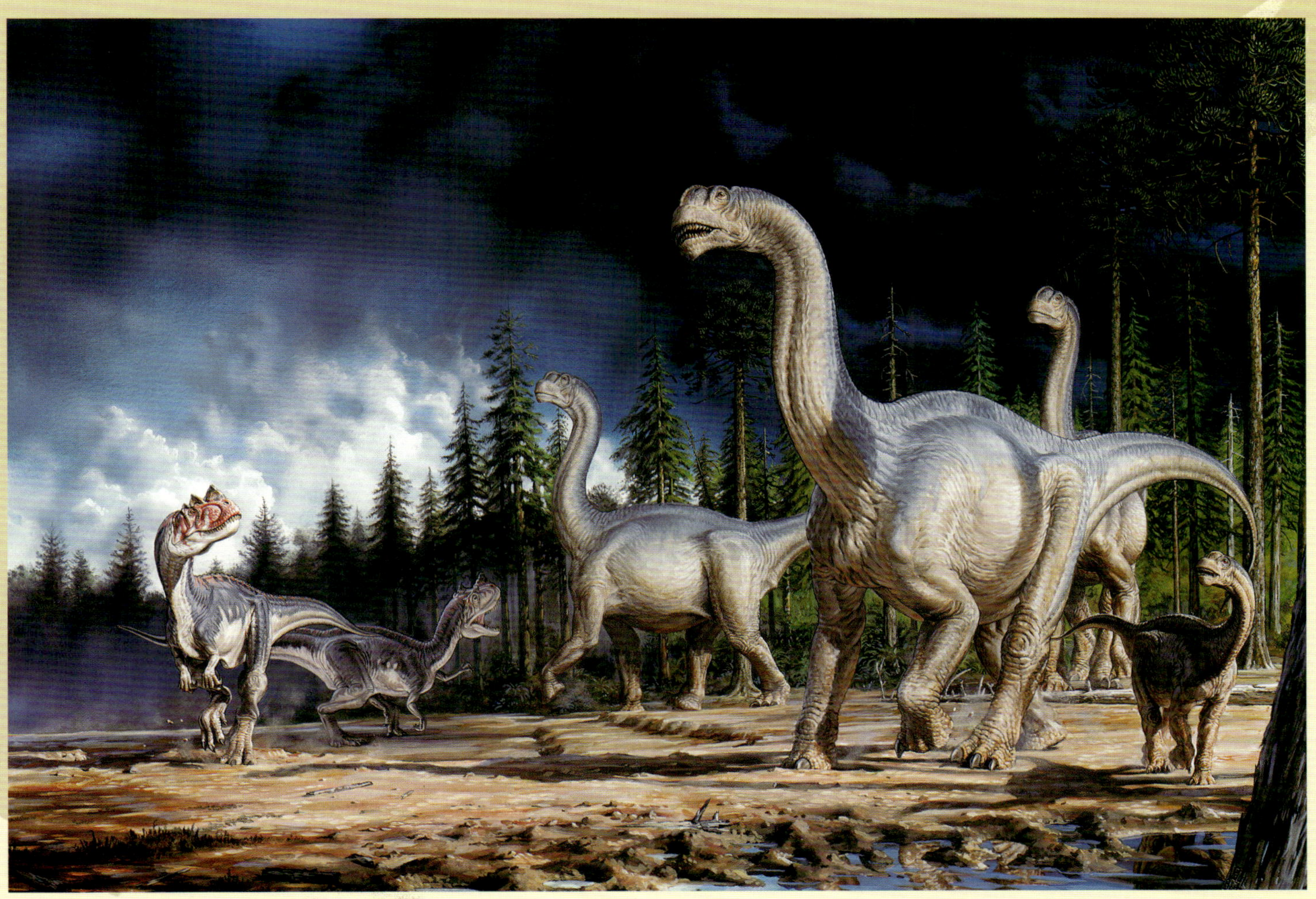

✷ Ceratosaurs and Camarasaurs – 1998

Albertosaur

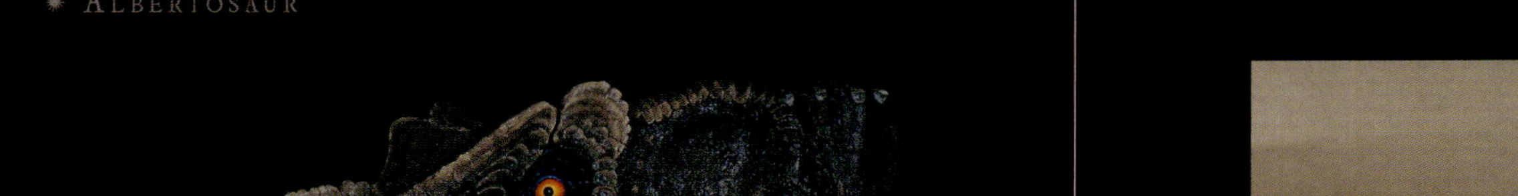

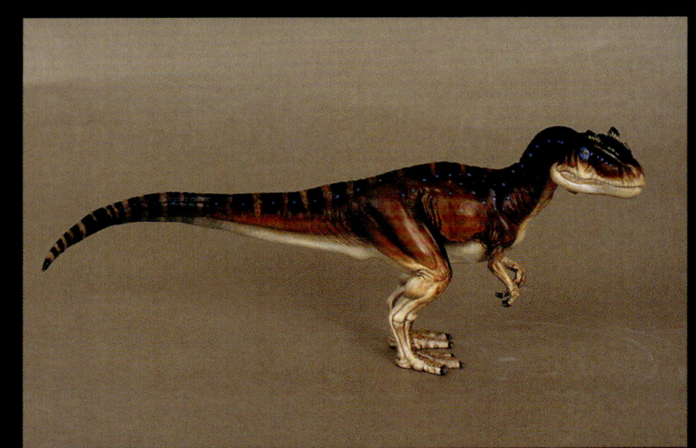

Tyrannosaurus

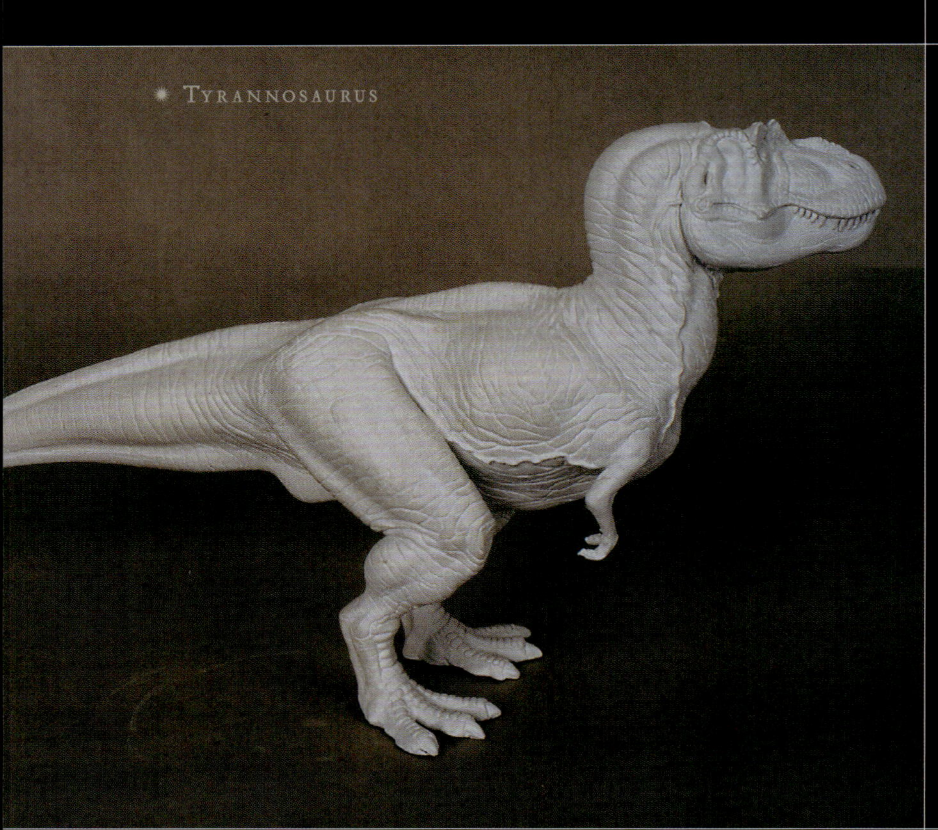

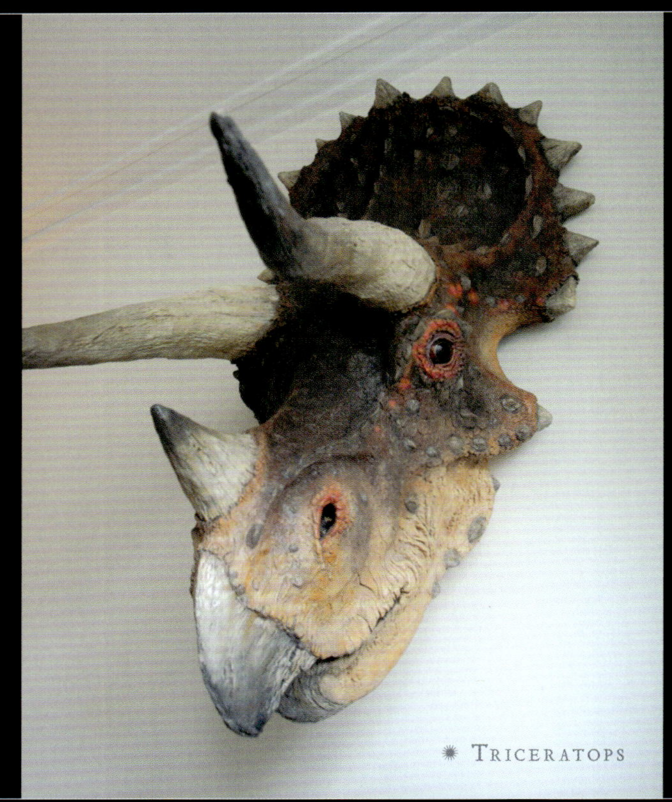

Triceratops

Stegosaurus

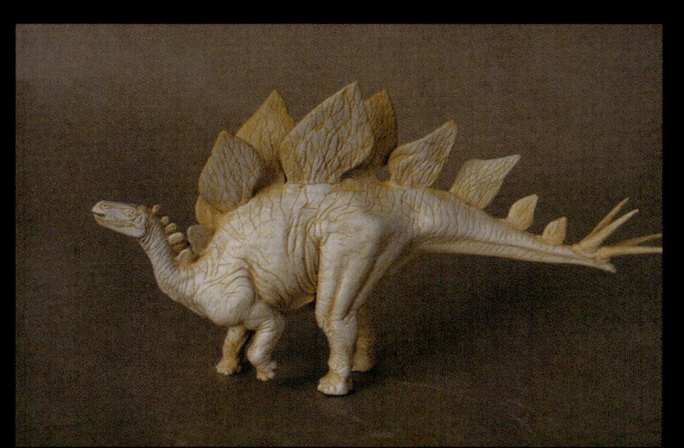

Allosaurus

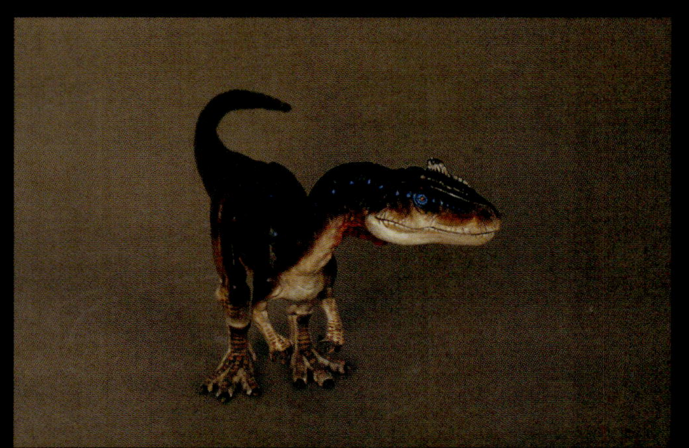

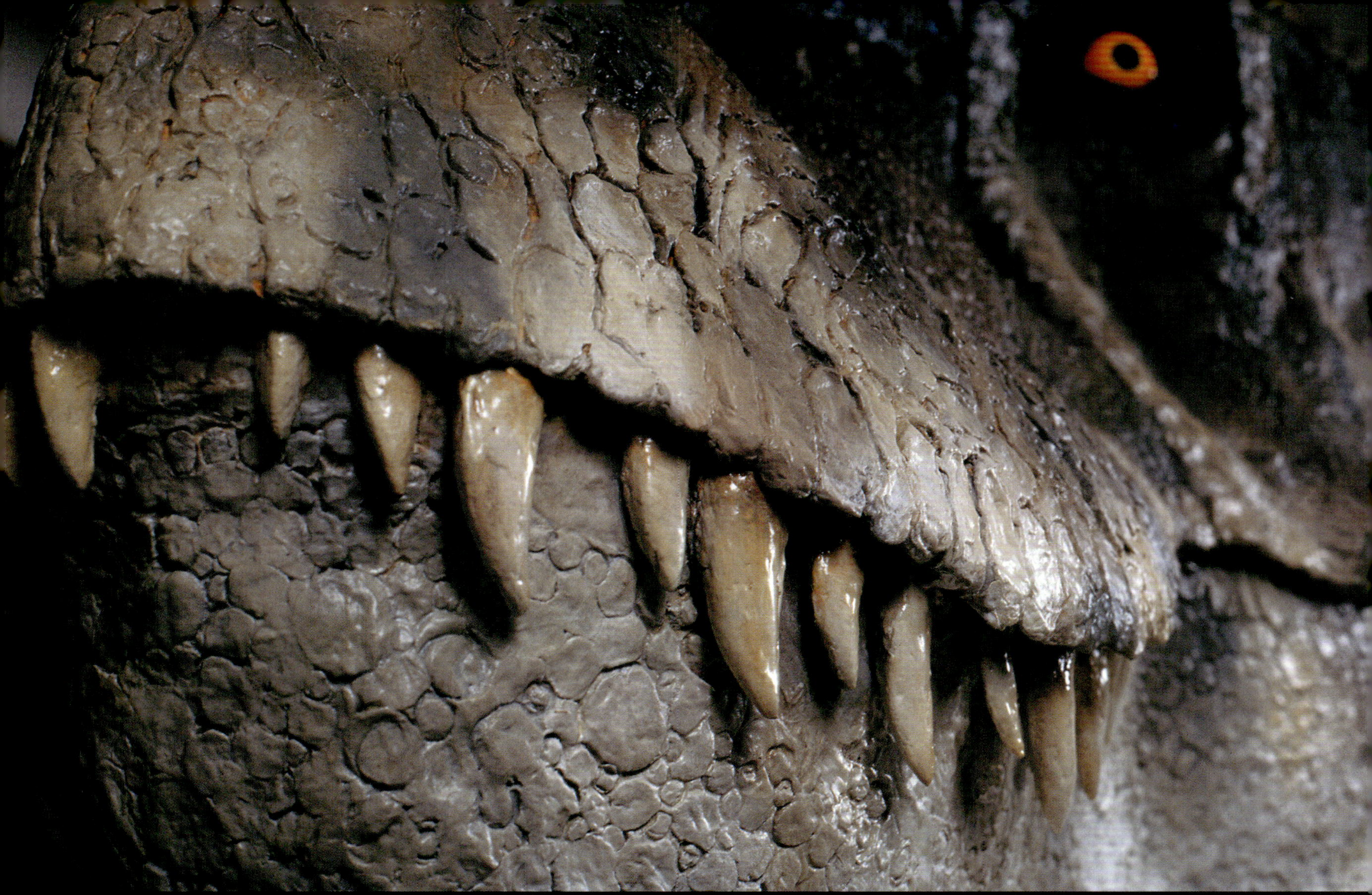

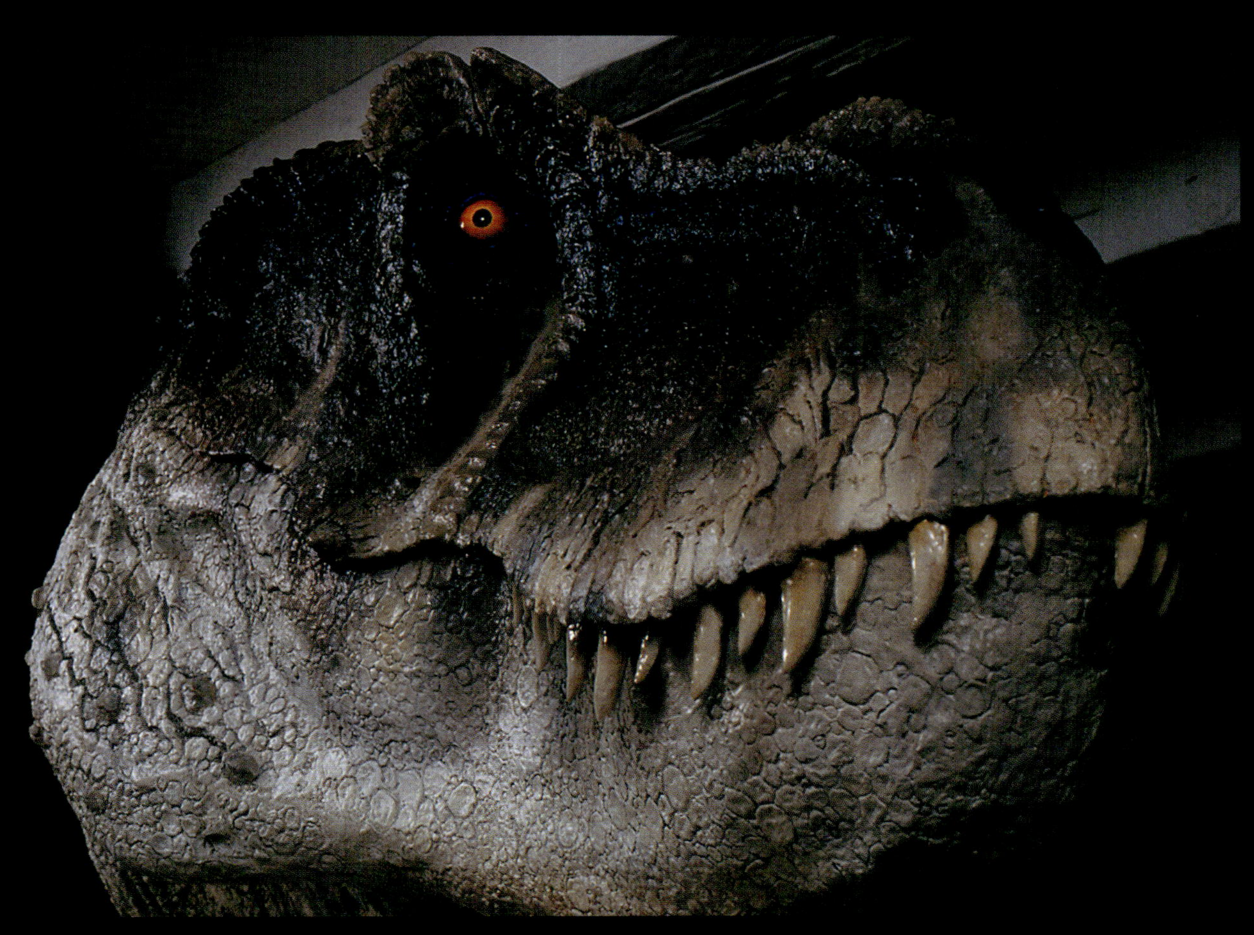

• Albertosaur

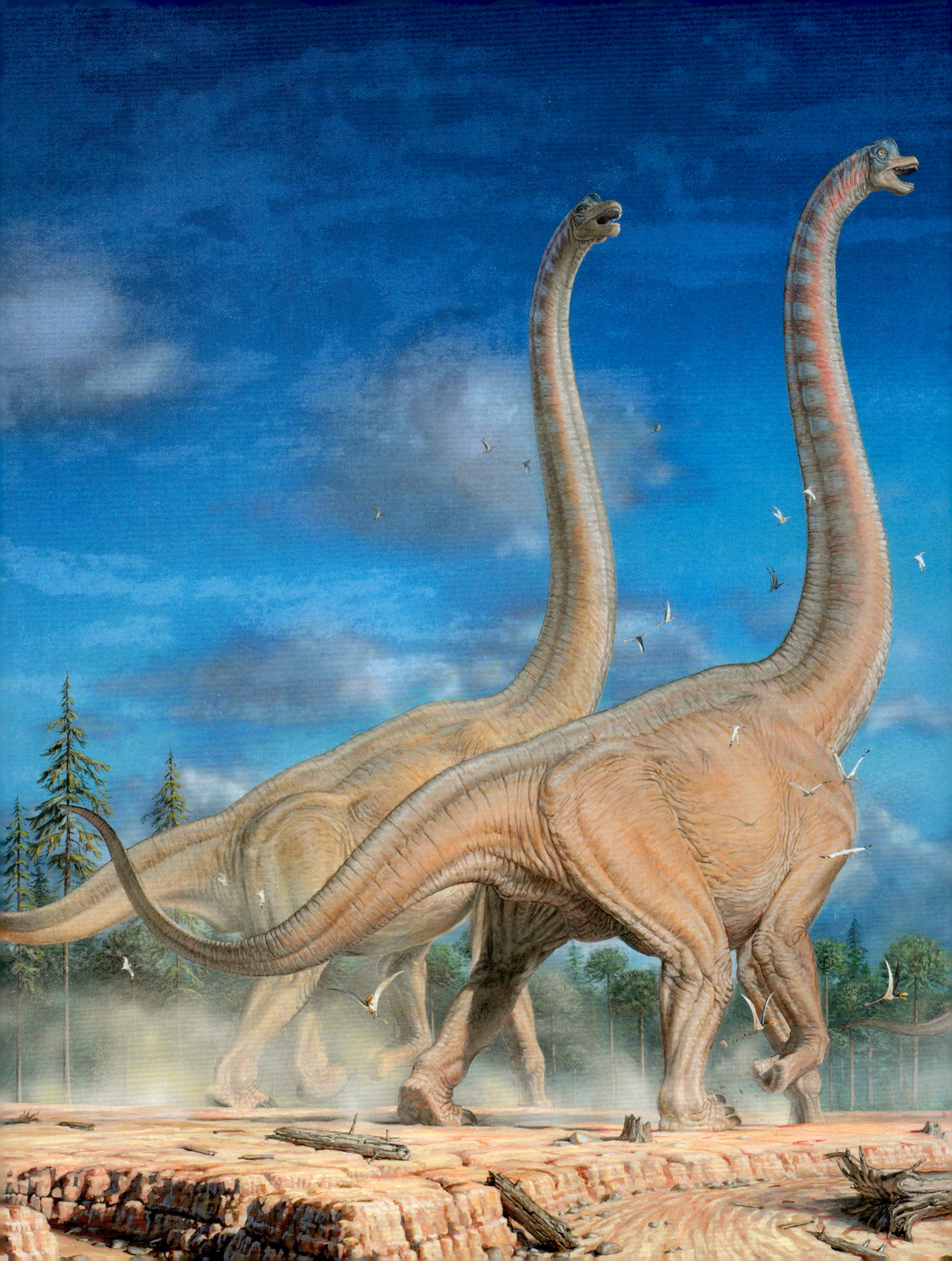

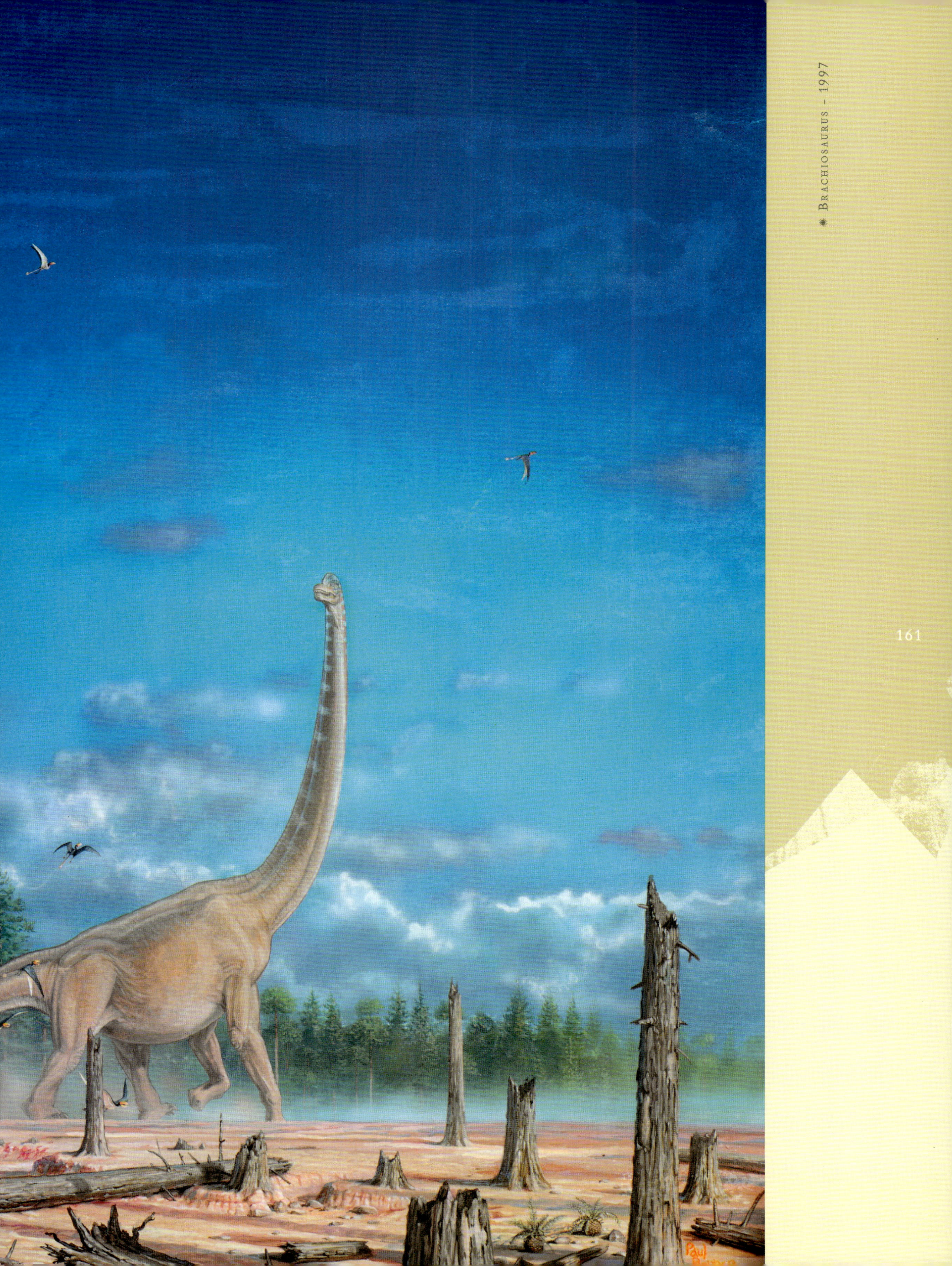

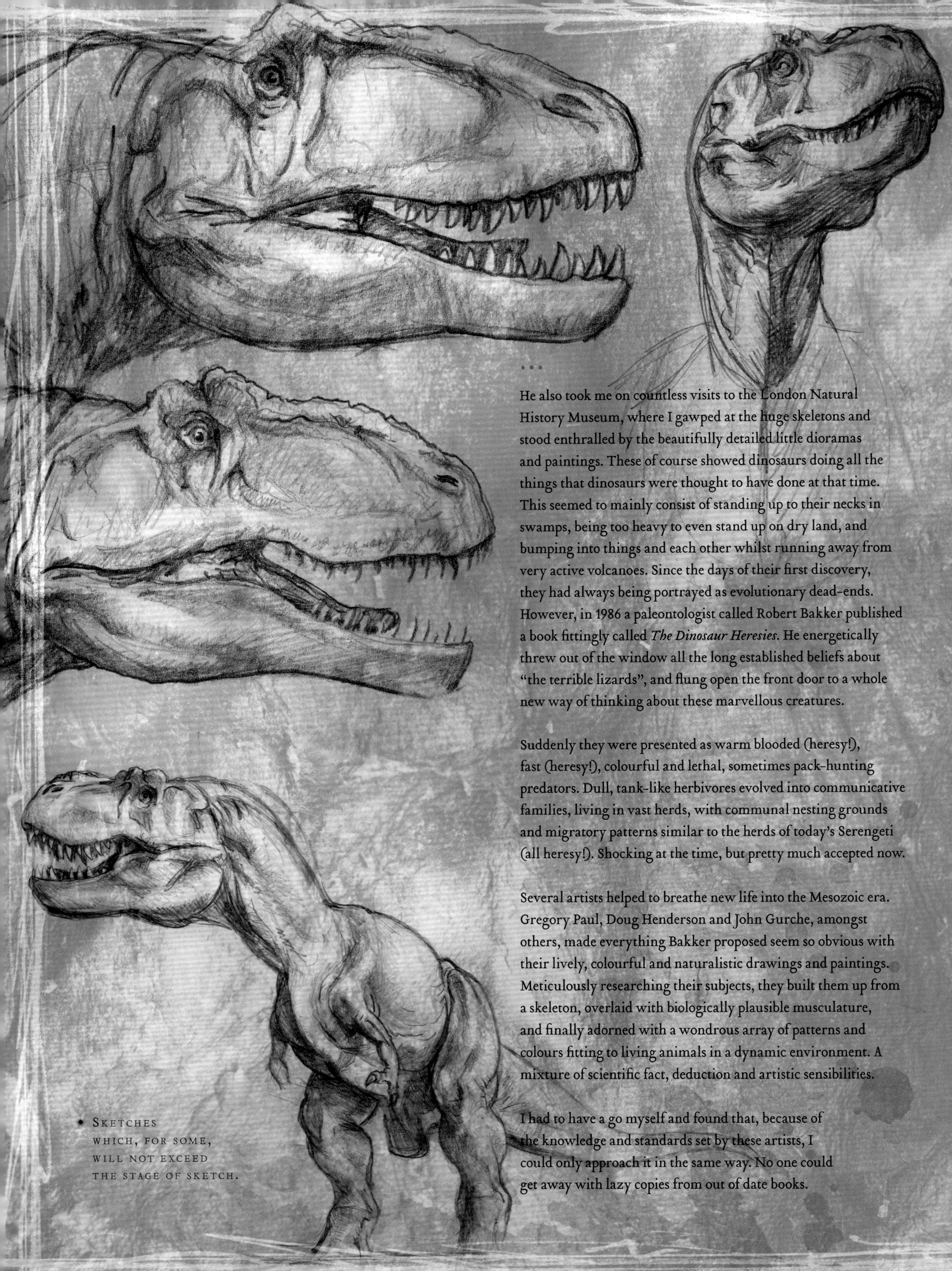

He also took me on countless visits to the London Natural History Museum, where I gawped at the huge skeletons and stood enthralled by the beautifully detailed little dioramas and paintings. These of course showed dinosaurs doing all the things that dinosaurs were thought to have done at that time. This seemed to mainly consist of standing up to their necks in swamps, being too heavy to even stand up on dry land, and bumping into things and each other whilst running away from very active volcanoes. Since the days of their first discovery, they had always being portrayed as evolutionary dead-ends. However, in 1986 a paleontologist called Robert Bakker published a book fittingly called *The Dinosaur Heresies*. He energetically threw out of the window all the long established beliefs about "the terrible lizards", and flung open the front door to a whole new way of thinking about these marvellous creatures.

Suddenly they were presented as warm blooded (heresy!), fast (heresy!), colourful and lethal, sometimes pack-hunting predators. Dull, tank-like herbivores evolved into communicative families, living in vast herds, with communal nesting grounds and migratory patterns similar to the herds of today's Serengeti (all heresy!). Shocking at the time, but pretty much accepted now.

Several artists helped to breathe new life into the Mesozoic era. Gregory Paul, Doug Henderson and John Gurche, amongst others, made everything Bakker proposed seem so obvious with their lively, colourful and naturalistic drawings and paintings. Meticulously researching their subjects, they built them up from a skeleton, overlaid with biologically plausible musculature, and finally adorned with a wondrous array of patterns and colours fitting to living animals in a dynamic environment. A mixture of scientific fact, deduction and artistic sensibilities.

I had to have a go myself and found that, because of the knowledge and standards set by these artists, I could only approach it in the same way. No one could get away with lazy copies from out of date books.

✷ Sketches which, for some, will not exceed the stage of sketch.

The paintings were very time consuming, because of the research, and I only wished my "paid work" allowed me more time, but though I loved having them tramp around in my imagination, they were no help in keeping me fed. I must also confess to a slight disenchantment, after the extraordinary success of *Jurassic Park* led to a sudden glut of dinosaurs. If you knew where to look, they were jumping out of books and leaping out of art studios all over the place.

To try and give them more life than a two-dimensional representation could ever give, I thought I would try my hand at sculpture, and so just before malnutrition took hold, I made some little clay models and some rather bigger "trophies". Messing around with a secret mix of two-ply toilet paper, wallpaper paste and chicken wire proved an immensely rewarding experience. In part I suspect this was due to not having to deal with the problems of creating the illusion of three dimensions in only two dimensions. It already exists, as it were. One can see mistakes straight away and it is often glaringly obvious how to correct them. Happy days.

A liberating endeavour, and one I will always have in the back of my mind to try and return to. The results of these little excursions into the world of three dimensions, due to their size, hang in my shared studio, where, apart from having to suffer brief attacks with a duster, they perform the dual task of fascinating and terrifying any toddlers who happen by.

So, the childhood passion and interest is still there, and I'm sure it will need to push itself out onto paper at some time in the future. As subjects for art, they are just so ascetically pleasing on every level imaginable. Until then – an occasional book is added to the shelf and, to the delight of my own little boy, the number of toy plastic replicas in the big box slowly grows, hopefully ensuring their survival into another era.

Paul Bonner

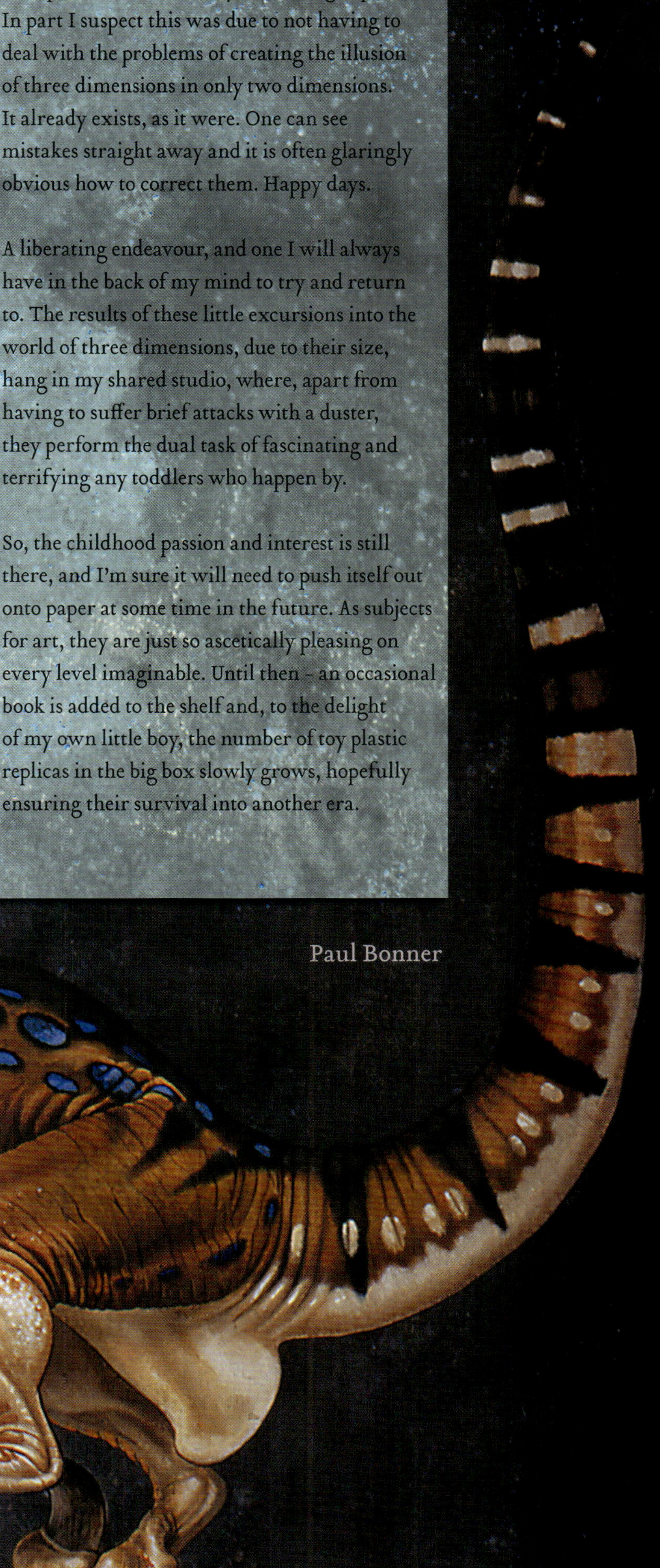

• Velociraptor – 1997

After College

At my diploma show, before leaving the rather wonderful confines of art college, an artists' agent offered to take me under his wing, and so we joined forces determined to take London's commercial art world by storm.

I was firmly convinced that I would soon be paying my way in the world by painting goblins, dwarves and trolls for all and sundry... but it was not to be.

There simply was not the market that there is today, and it wasn't long before my characters began to take on a rather more wholesome and rosy cheeked appearance than I ever intended. Following my own inspirations, I had already painted myself into a corner, which in spite of game attempts at some rather clean cut children's books, I became determined to stay in. Attempting to branch out, broaden my appeal, and in some respects water down my own visions, only helped convince me to stick with what made me happy.

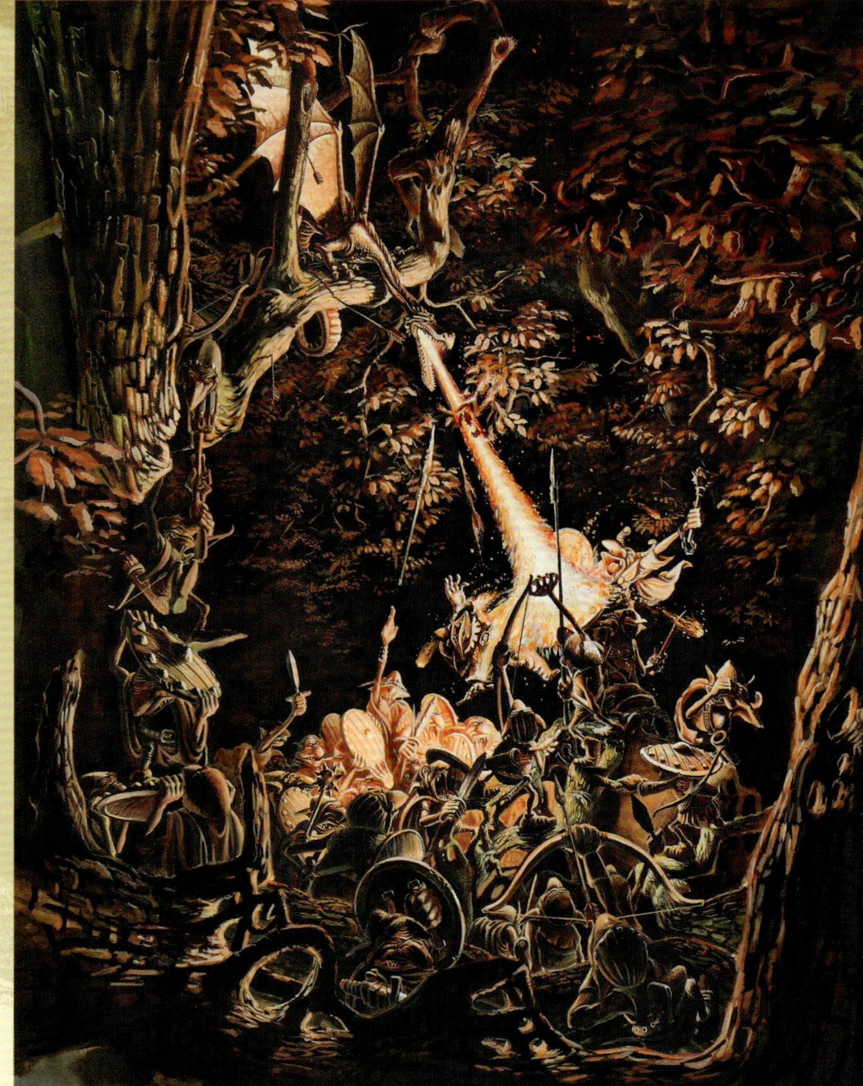

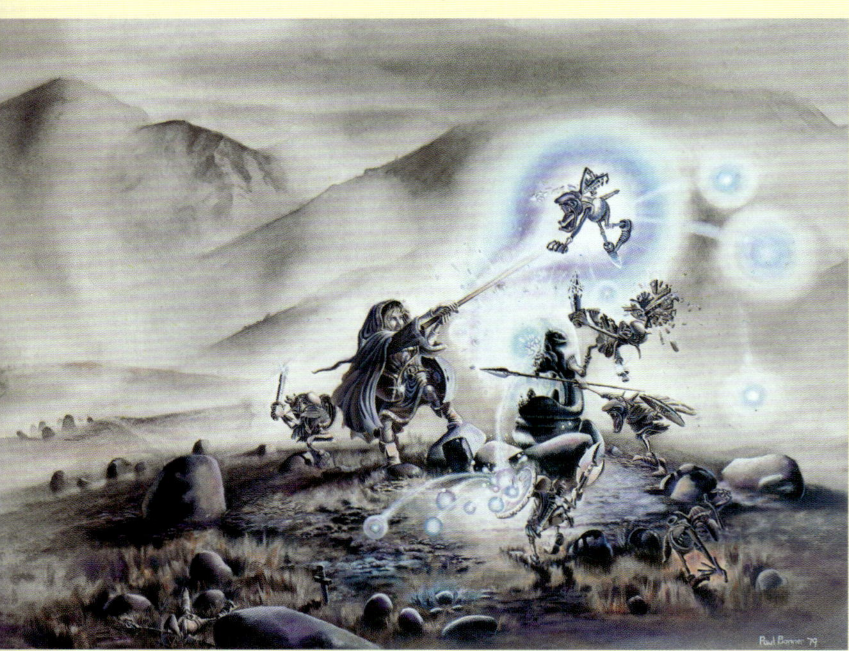

These two examples were the most enjoyable paintings that my agent persuaded a client to let me loose on. I remember there being very little interference from the client. I like to think that seeing my own paintings showed them that I was better left alone with the subject matter. A luxury and act of faith not often repeated.

Paul Bonner

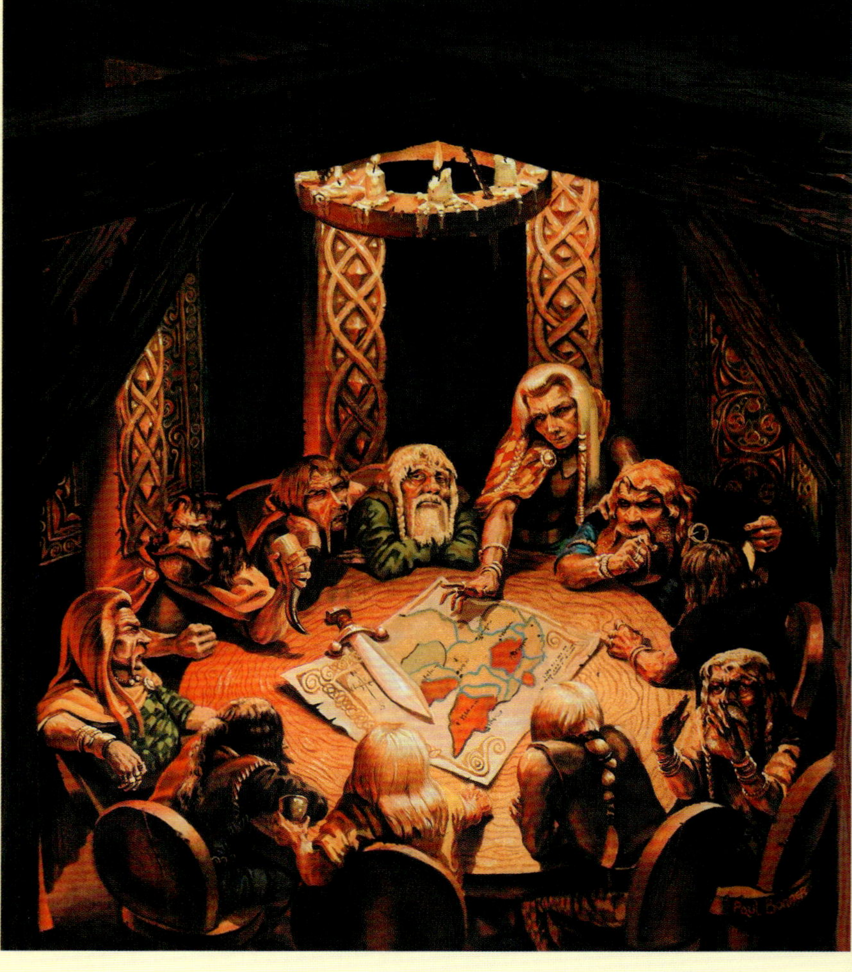

Covers of a magazine on King Arthur - the Eighties

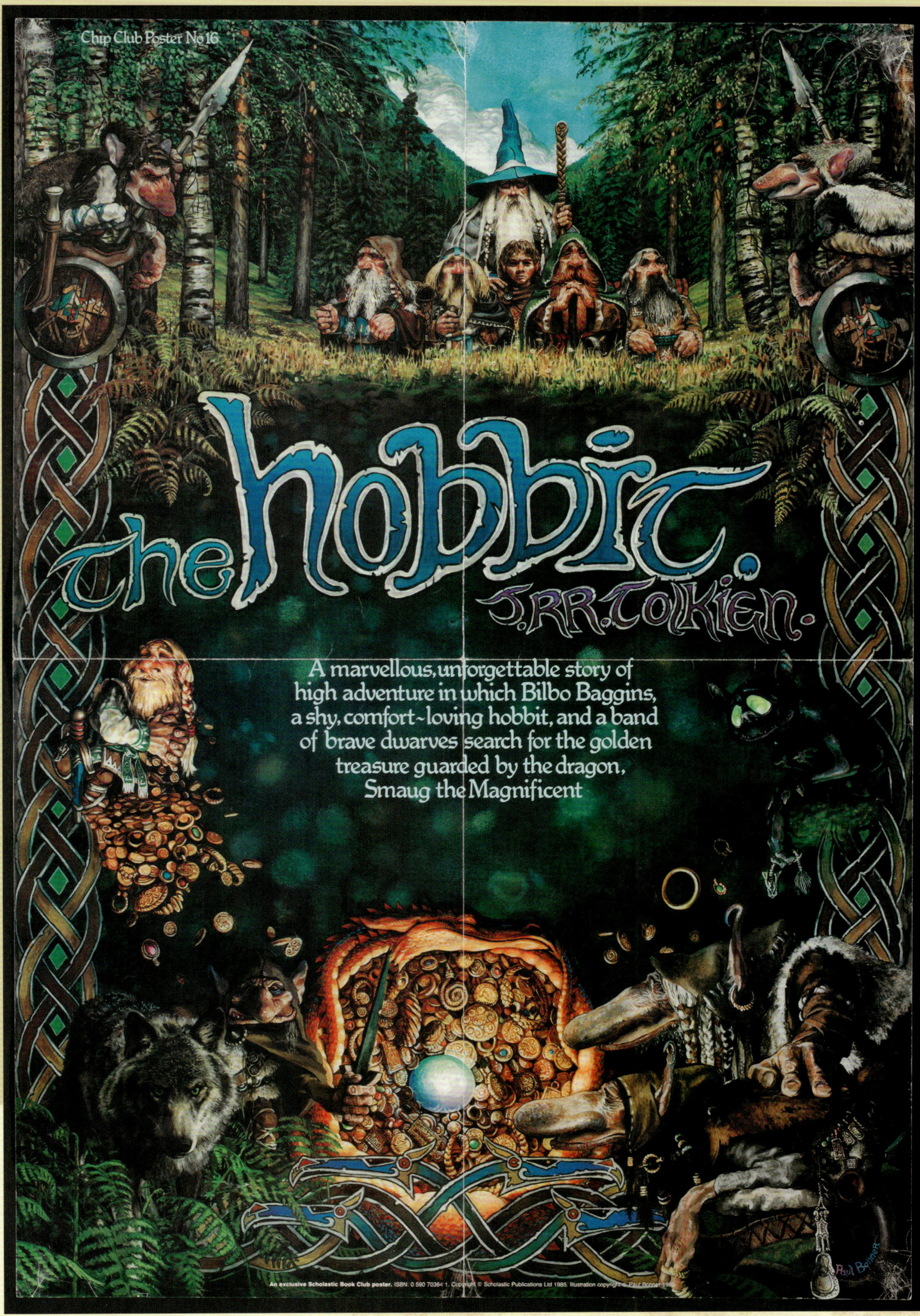
Chip Club Poster No16
The hobbit.
J.R.R.Tolkien.
A marvellous, unforgettable story of
high adventure in which Bilbo Baggins,
a shy, comfort-loving hobbit, and a band
of brave dwarves search for the golden
treasure guarded by the dragon,
Smaug the Magnificent
Paul Bonner
An exclusive Scholastic Book Club poster. ISBN: 0 590 70364 1. Copyright © Scholastic Publications Ltd 1985. Illustration copyright © Paul Bonner 1985

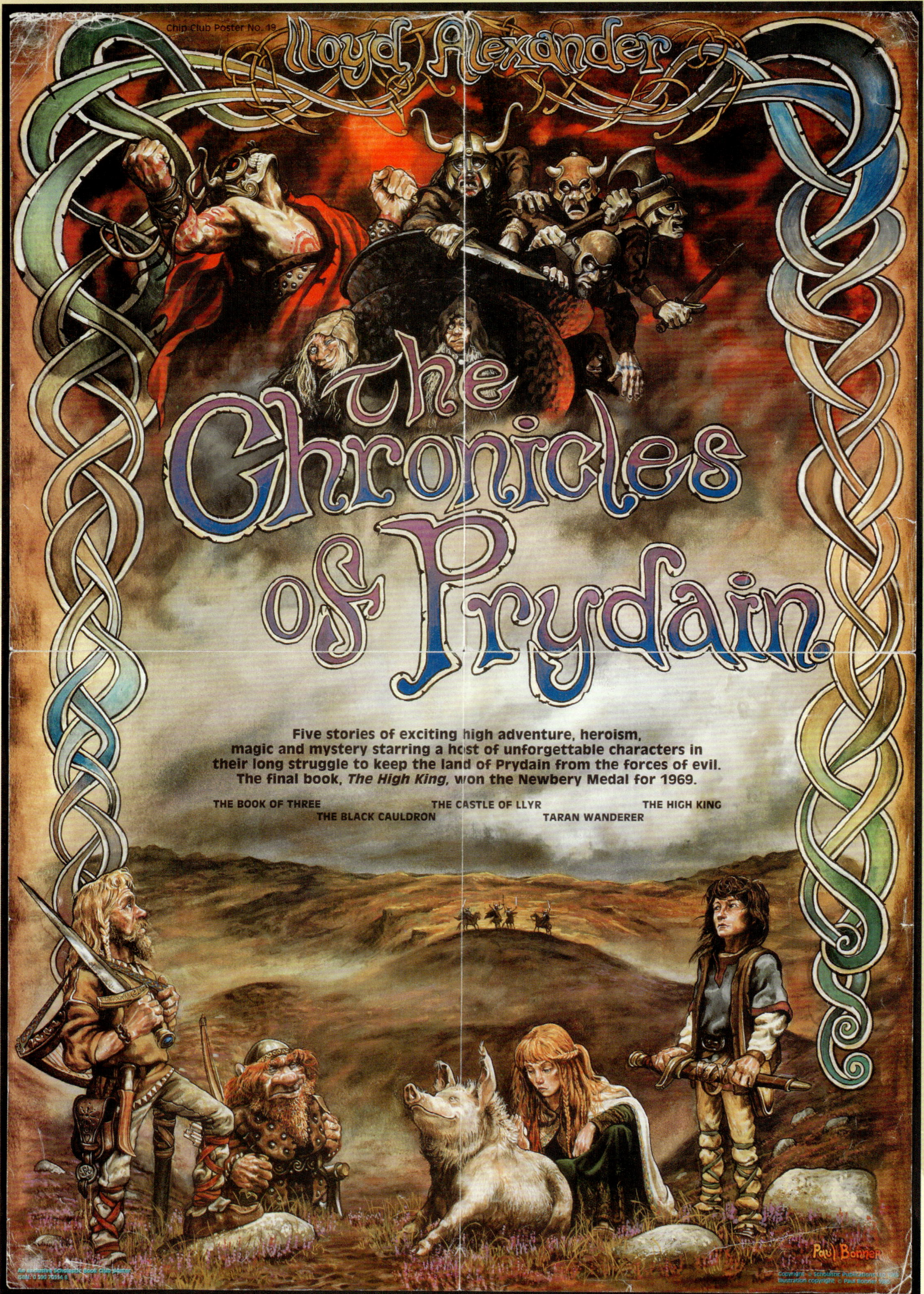
Chip Club Poster No. 19
Lloyd Alexander
The Chronicles of Prydain
Five stories of exciting high adventure, heroism, magic and mystery starring a host of unforgettable characters in their long struggle to keep the land of Prydain from the forces of evil. The final book, The High King, won the Newbery Medal for 1969.
THE BOOK OF THREE
THE BLACK CAULDRON
THE CASTLE OF LLYR
TARAN WANDERER
THE HIGH KING
Paul Bonner
An exclusive Scholastic Book Club Poster
ISBN: 0 590 70514 8

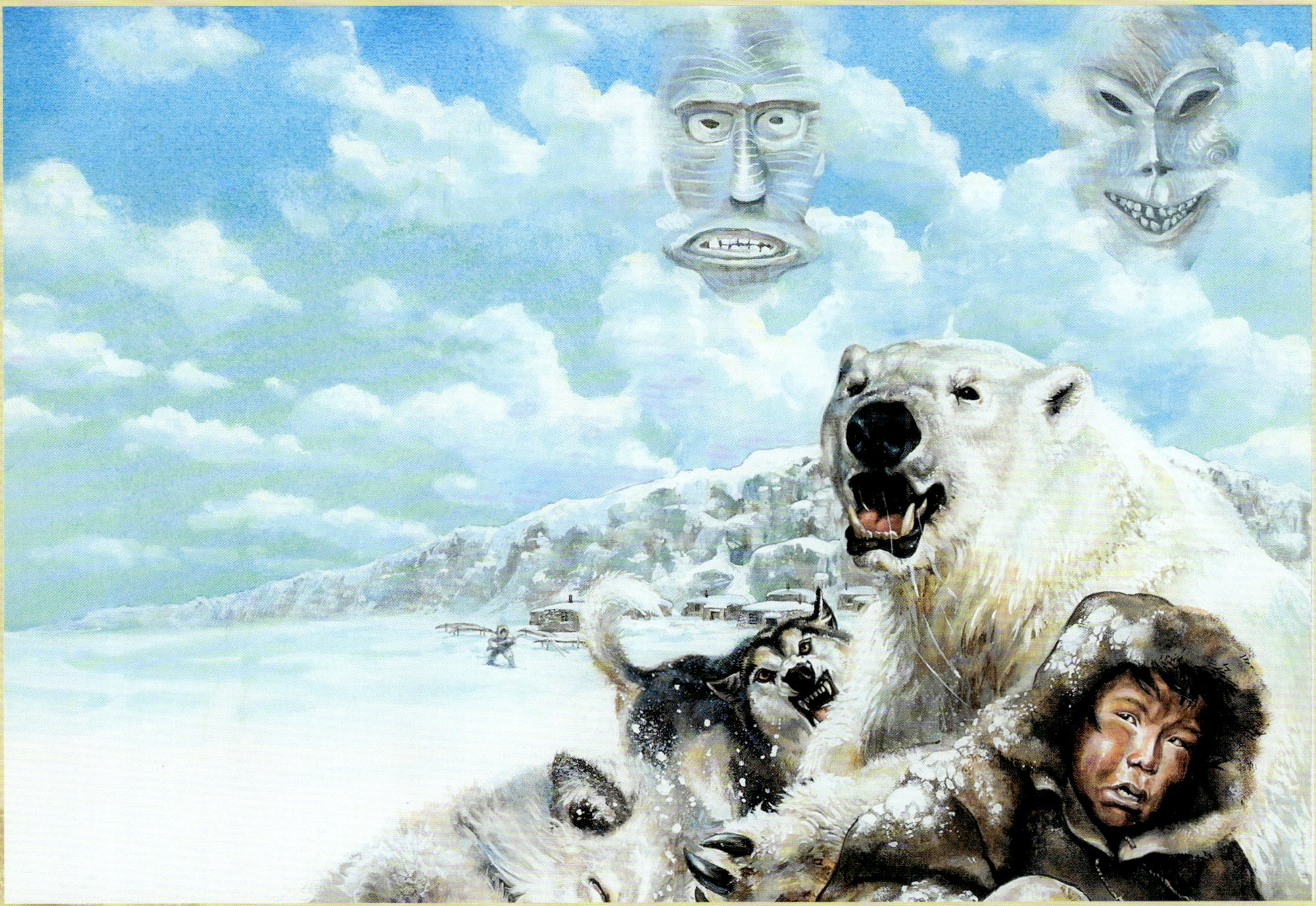

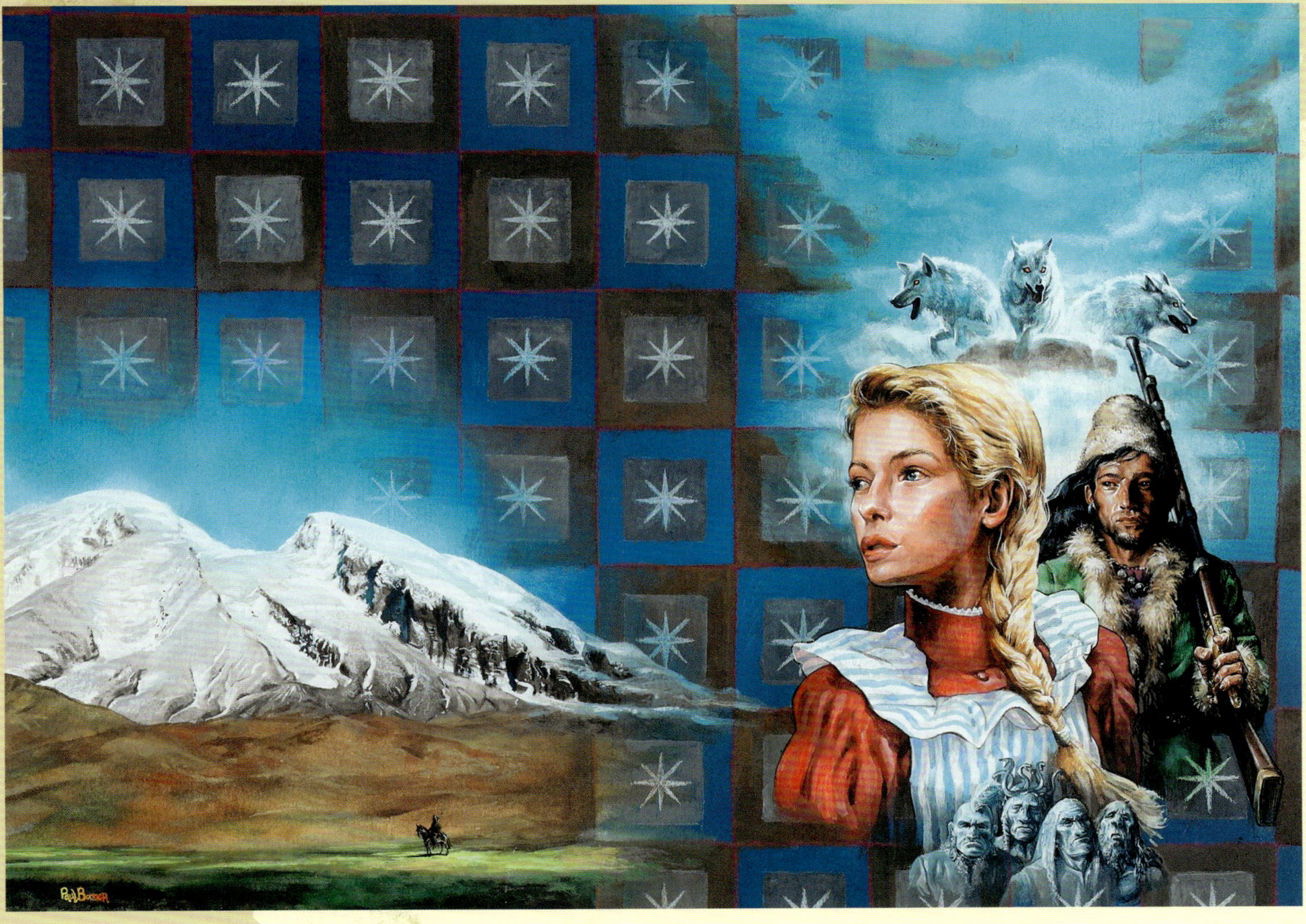

✷ Some of the covers I did for children's books that helped pay the bills when I first moved to Denmark. Some were fun, but I did miss the spiky shoulderpads.

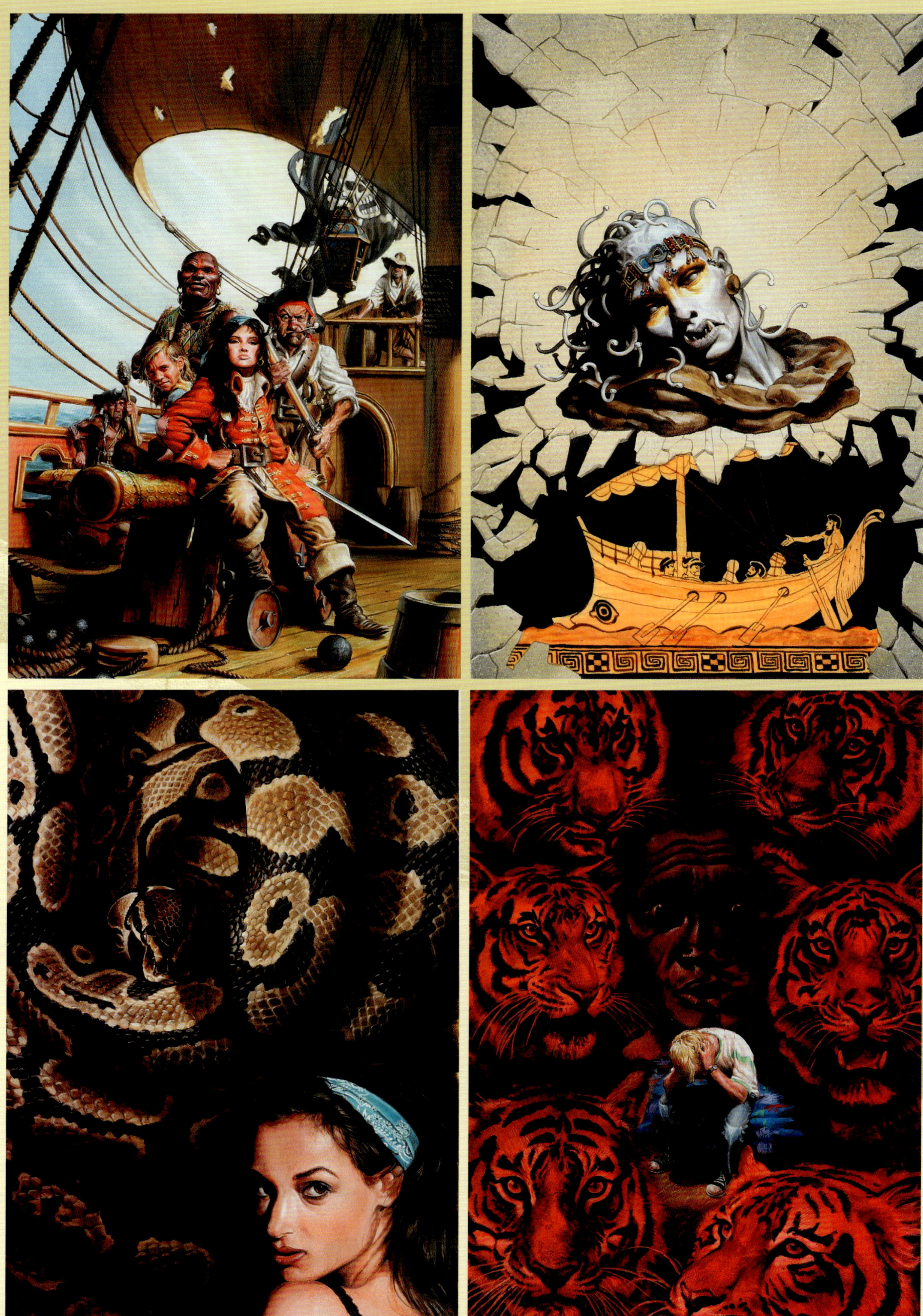

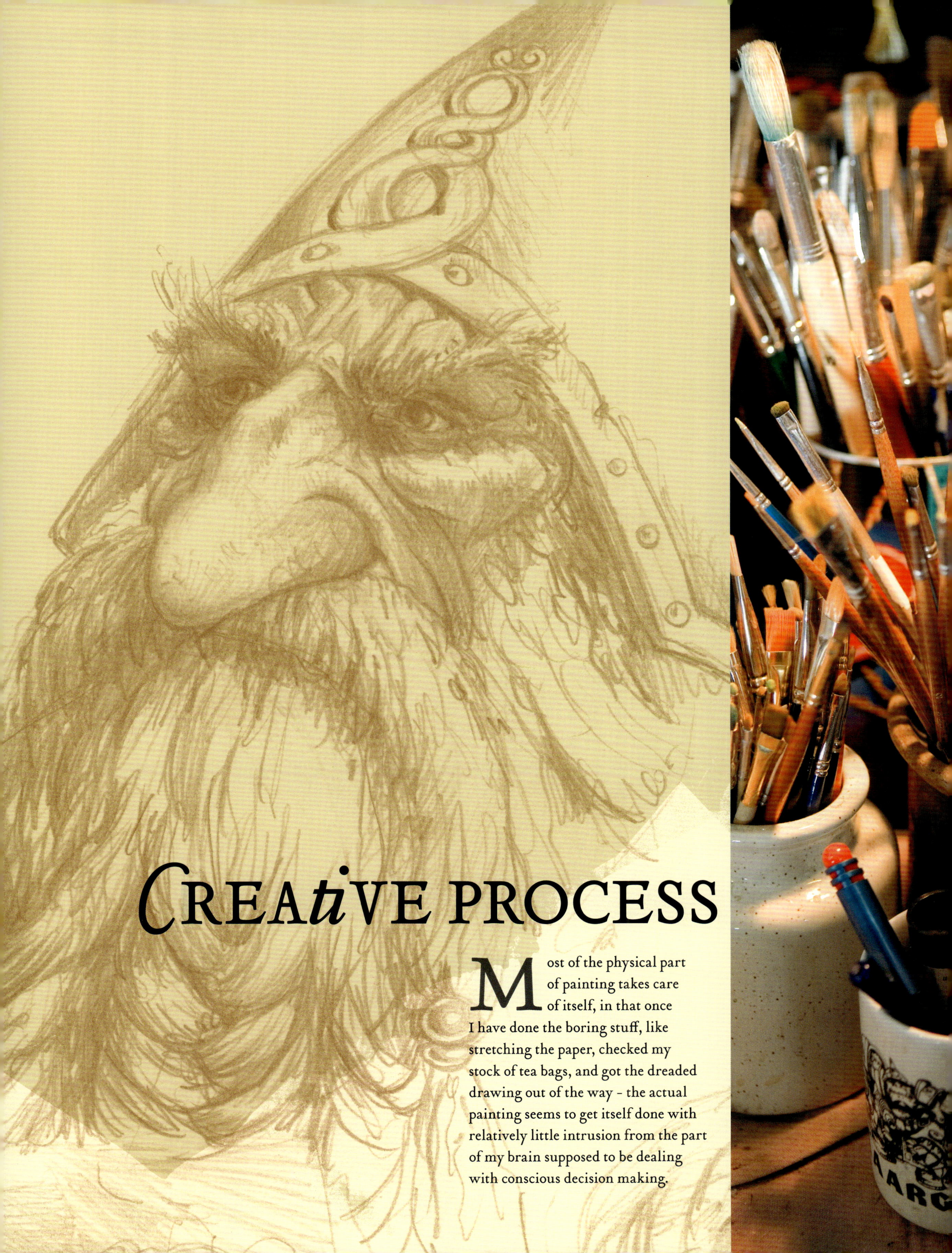

CREATIVE PROCESS

Most of the physical part of painting takes care of itself, in that once I have done the boring stuff, like stretching the paper, checked my stock of tea bags, and got the dreaded drawing out of the way – the actual painting seems to get itself done with relatively little intrusion from the part of my brain supposed to be dealing with conscious decision making.

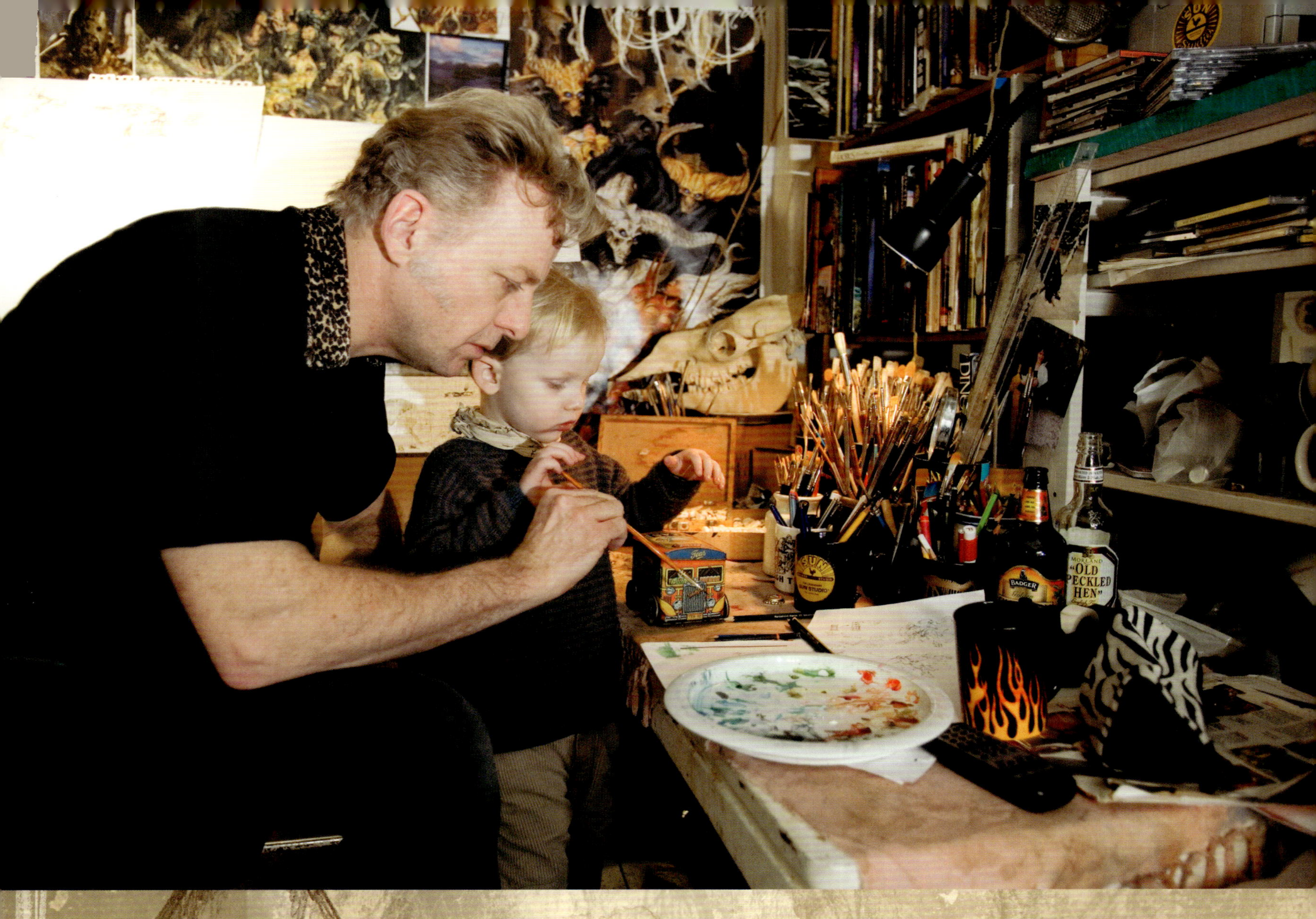

I really don't look forward to the drawing. I don't consider myself naturally good at it, one of those fortunate souls who seem able to conjure up exquisite drawings with just a few deft flourishes of the pencil. It is a laboured struggle for me to translate my imagination on to a blank piece of paper, especially so when those images are constantly shouldering their way to the front of my consciousness, demanding that I pick up a brush and get on with the fun business of painting them. Certain things, no matter how many hundreds of times I have drawn them, present the same or fresh problems each time. When I'm itching to get on with the task of trying to give some life to my imaginings and start splashing some paint around, it can be a real test of character. I know how I want things to look, but getting them there is always the hardest part. The tiniest adjustments to the tilt of a head, or just how much a hand is clenched can alter the body language of a character completely, and, in turn, its relationship to everything else... so it is a perplexing search for the perfect solution. Or at least what seems perfect at the time.

Equally tricky to come up with - and equally crucial - is choosing which precise moment the painting should try and capture. A flurry of fervent action or a few heartbeats later, where some kind of respite provides more tension and drama. Or maybe the quiet contemplative mood of nothing happening in particular (a firm favourite, although I'm not often allowed to get away with this option). Choosing one frozen moment from what is, in effect, a film playing in the theatre of my imagination, requires

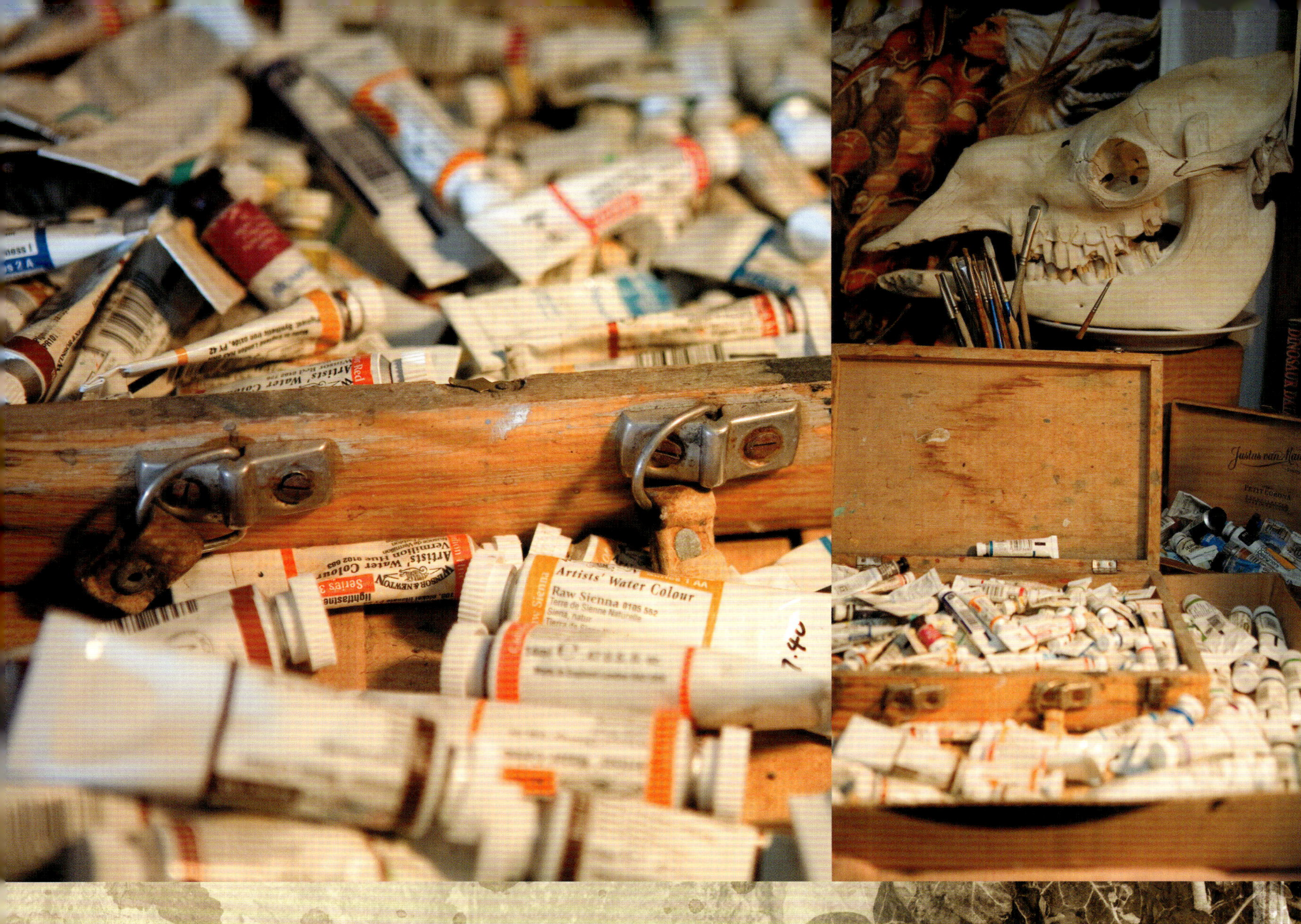

many playbacks, fast forwards and freeze frames, until one moment more than others begins to lodge itself into the "distinct possibilities" area. Each time little incentives present themselves seductively... Oooooh! I get to paint a forest with this one! Aaaaah! Big, cracked rocks festooned with mosses and carvings with this one! Ha! Maybe I could get a dead horse into this one! (It's usually the trees that do it for me.)

It's the same process for whoever or whatever has to walk or stomp into the landscape provided for them. Finding some nuances in character and posture that create exciting possibilities and fresh challenges. First, however, these inhabitants have to have an enviroment that they can have journeyed to, in and from. It was there before they arrived - and will be there after they have done whatever the story requires of them and wandered on again. Unless, of course, one of the story's requirements happens to involve dying. In my earlier days I never bothered so much with the backgrounds, always considering the protagonists far more important, and much more fun to do. Now, however, I find painting the background so rewarding that often, when it comes to the characters, it feels like they are an intrusion upon a stage that was getting on perfectly well without them. It happens often in reality, that whilst tramping around in some of natures more arresting landscapes, one is suddenly prey to the very same feeling of having rather nervously trespassed.
Before I can get close to unleashing myself on a background, I must painstakingly scribble my way through the planning and drawing process.

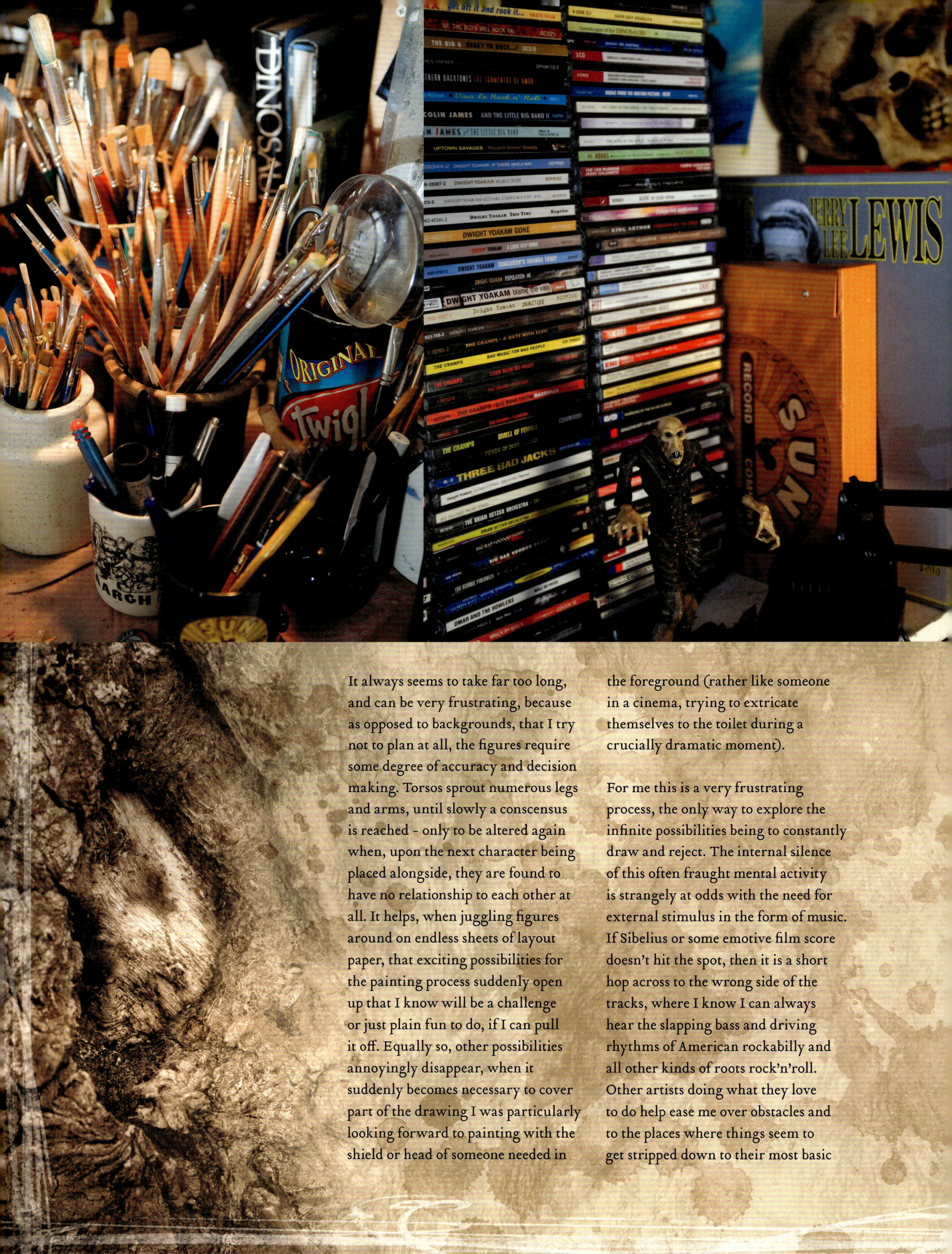

It always seems to take far too long, and can be very frustrating, because as opposed to backgrounds, that I try not to plan at all, the figures require some degree of accuracy and decision making. Torsos sprout numerous legs and arms, until slowly a conscensus is reached - only to be altered again when, upon the next character being placed alongside, they are found to have no relationship to each other at all. It helps, when juggling figures around on endless sheets of layout paper, that exciting possibilities for the painting process suddenly open up that I know will be a challenge or just plain fun to do, if I can pull it off. Equally so, other possibilities annoyingly disappear, when it suddenly becomes necessary to cover part of the drawing I was particularly looking forward to painting with the shield or head of someone needed in the foreground (rather like someone in a cinema, trying to extricate themselves to the toilet during a crucially dramatic moment).

For me this is a very frustrating process, the only way to explore the infinite possibilities being to constantly draw and reject. The internal silence of this often fraught mental activity is strangely at odds with the need for external stimulus in the form of music. If Sibelius or some emotive film score doesn't hit the spot, then it is a short hop across to the wrong side of the tracks, where I know I can always hear the slapping bass and driving rhythms of American rockabilly and all other kinds of roots rock'n'roll. Other artists doing what they love to do help ease me over obstacles and to the places where things seem to get stripped down to their most basic

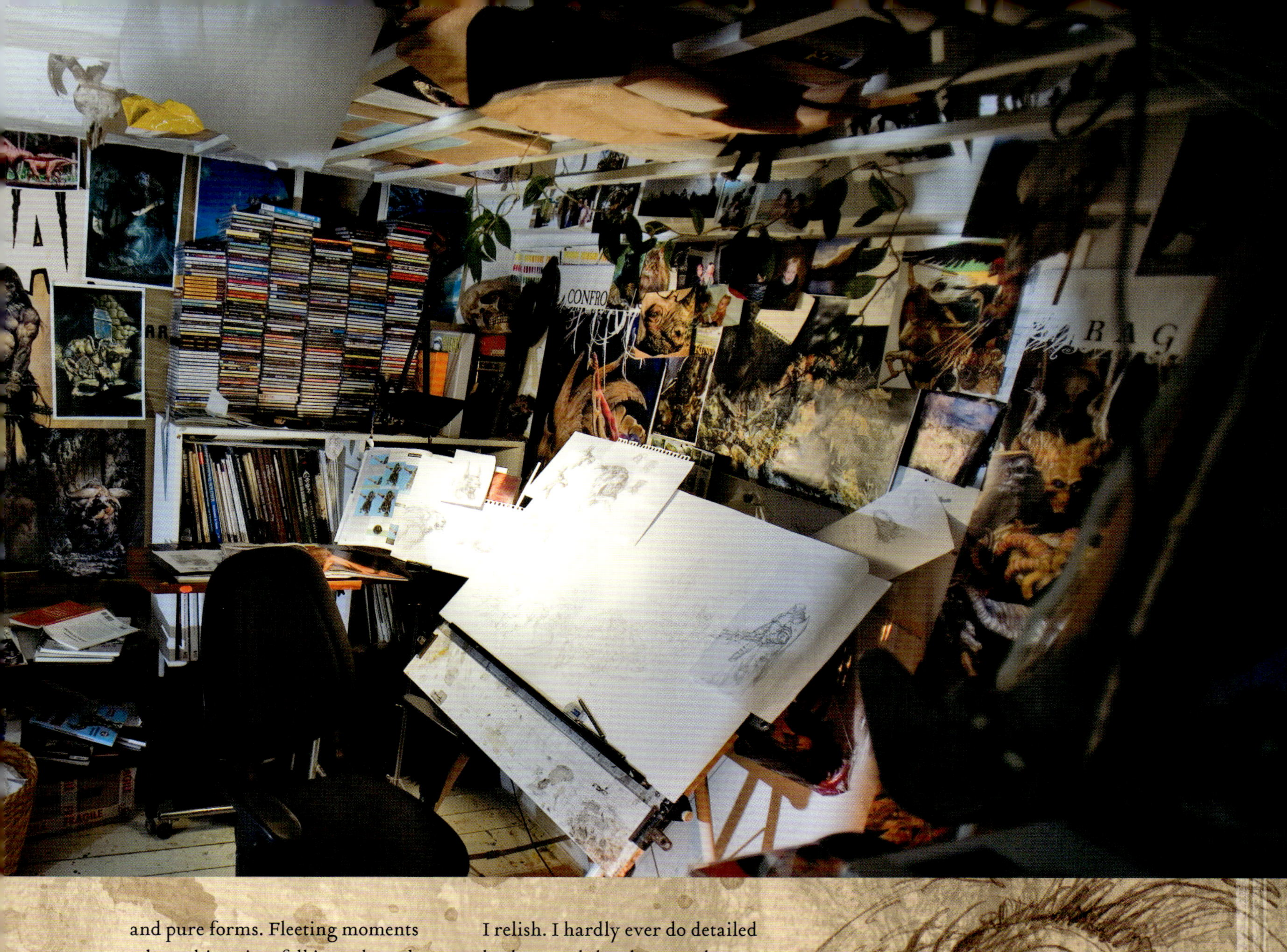

and pure forms. Fleeting moments where things just fall into place almost without the need for thought. That is the constant goal, but it is like adding a single little stone to a cairn on top of a mountain, after which the only way possible is to go down to the bottom. OK, the muted and plaintive strings of Sibelius or the twanging thunder of a Gretsch guitar don't guarantee flawless results every time, but they can lead to the place where I feel achieving flawless results is distinctly possible. Naturally, perfection is unattainable and a hopeless delusion; the trick being to resolutely ignore the years of experience confirming this and naively soldier on.

This musical and often drawn-out process, has, in recent years led to a rather carefree, and sometimes reckless approach to the actual painting that I relish. I hardly ever do detailed background sketches. Maybe an abstract scribble that only I could possibly see anything in. And colour studies are a complete no-go area. Instead, relying on images "paused" in my head, maybe influences from some photos taken on my wanderings, or in a book, I try to make it up as I go along. Paint is squeezed from tubes on to a big plastic dinner plate - and off I go.

Trying to be spontaneous sometimes results in capturing something essential relatively quickly, and having pinned down some kind of two dimensional mood, I can then happily become my own landscape gardener. Planting some trees here, tumbling some lichen covered rocks there, maybe a dark pool with mirrored reflections. Adjusting the mood with some sprawling shadows dappled with pools of sunlight so they illuminate moss on the stones or the glowing bark of the pine trees. Tweaking the atmosphere until the setting feels right for some kind of entrance.

I would not want people thinking I have too much fun, so I must add that, once in a while, it has been necessary to undertake a frantic dash to the cold water tap, under which, upon arrival, the whole board has been unceremoniously thrust. With the assistance of a sponge, many pre-nascent mountain ranges and forests have been sent swirling down the plug hole.

Another, almost constant problem is knowing when to stop and leave it alone. This is often more risky than the birth pains that accompany the initial drawing. This winding down to a point where I can walk away from a painting often holds the potential for disaster. With the drawing, I know what I want and can only go forward - but now there is that feeling of simply having nowhere left to go, but, nevertheless, being haunted by a myriad nagging dissatisfactions. Not being ruthless enough to walk away leads to frantically trying to make everything perfect (an impossibility) and, in doing so, more often than not pushing everything over some kind of edge. Overworking leads to a loss of spontaneity, and colours lose their vibrancy, buried under excessive detail. I think they are quite obvious, but none the less I will keep it to myself which of the paintings here would have benefited from being left alone, instead of having to suffer constant and indecisive fiddling.

Because the visual process is so immediate, I can usually see straight away when something is wrong, looks plain suspicious, or just doesn't match up to the painting I had in my head.

It becomes a necessity to accept that I have done something as well as I could this time, and any of those nagging dissatisfactions will have to be left until the next time. Not accepting this, and resorting to a doomed attempt at perfection, has, though I've never done it, led to several paintings coming perilously close to being hurled out of my third floor studio window.

I just as equally can't have people thinking that, in suffering for my art, it became necessary to remove my ears a long time ago, and rely on a steady intake of absinthe to make the whole thing bearable. Far from it. Without trying to break new ground or attempting fresh victories, no matter how miniscule the area of paint involved, one would not be open to the chance of occasionally exceeding expectations.

At the end of it, each painting has become a kind of mosaic; both a map and journal that consist of often conflicting levels of success. A patchwork that, along with areas best forgotten about, hopefully manages to include some happy accidents, unexpected moments of elation, and bits where, against the odds, everything just happened to go along exactly as you had hoped.

Paul Bonner

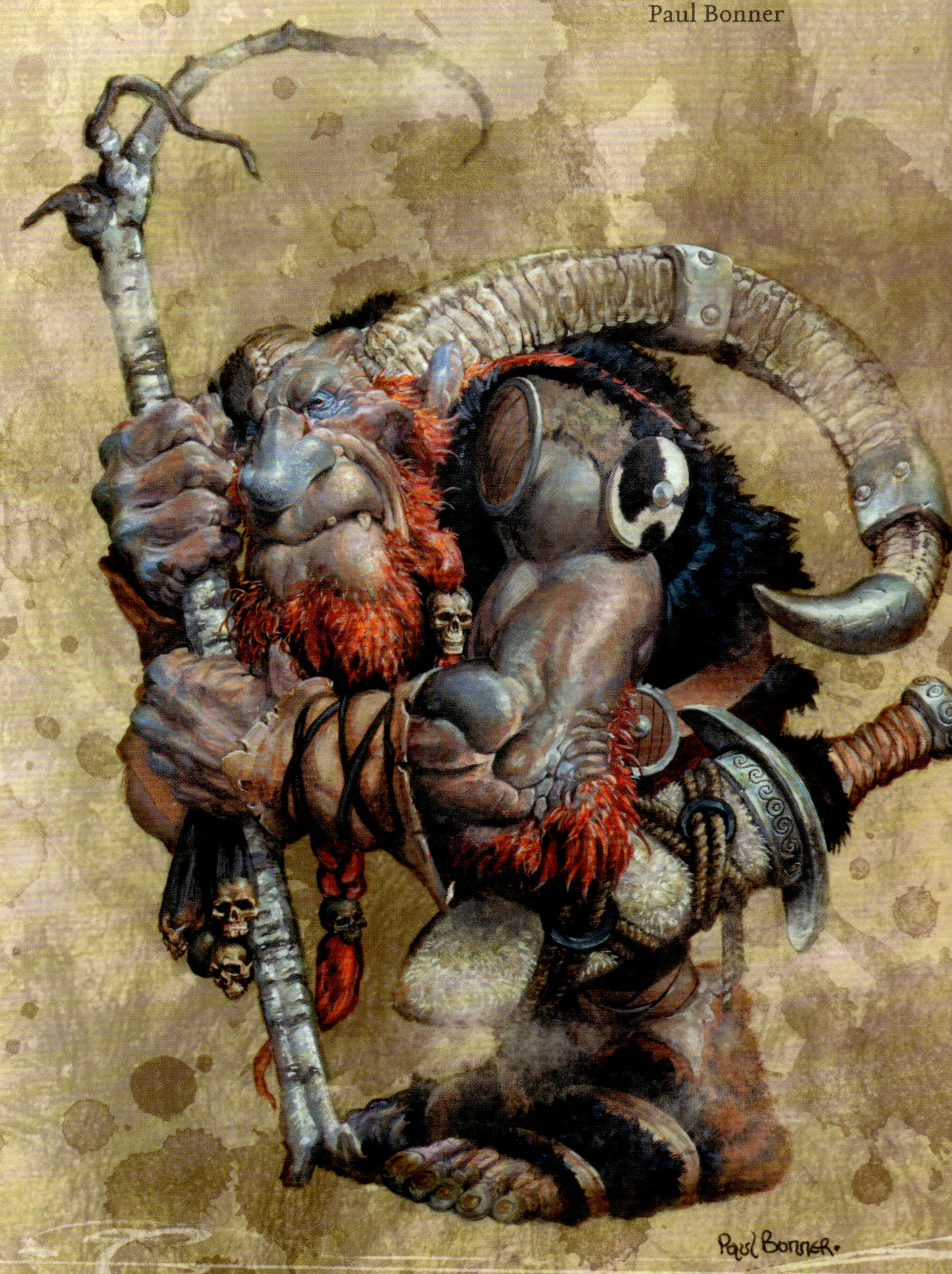

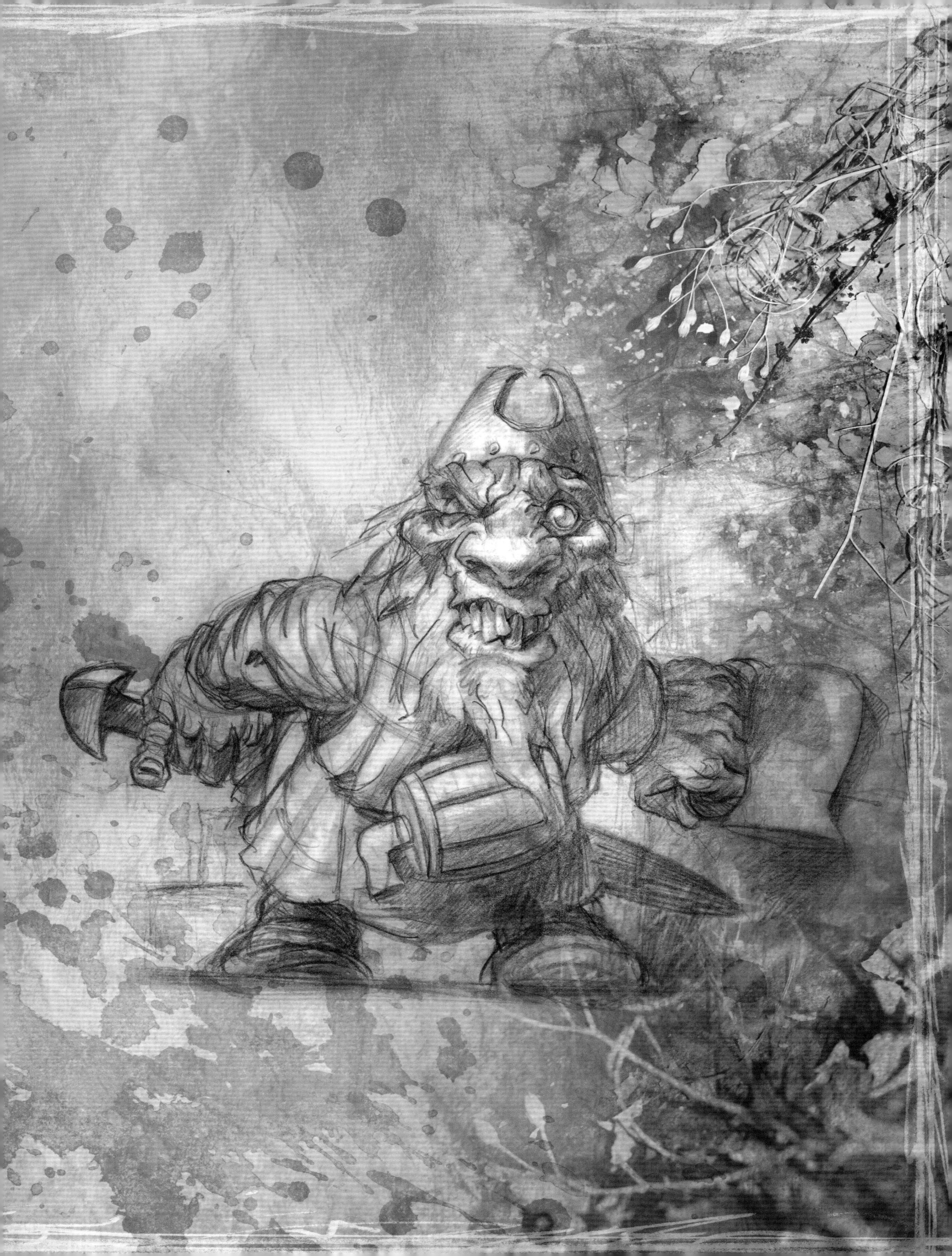

The publisher wishes to thank Games Workshop LTD, Paradox Entertainment, Rackham, RiotMinds, WizKidz Inc. and all the people that made this book possible.

OUT OF THE FORESTS: THE ART OF PAUL BONNER

ISBN: 9781845767051
Published by Titan Books
A division of Titan Publishing Group Ltd
144 Southwark Street London SE1 0UP

First edition November 2007
10 9

EU RP (for authorities only)
eucomply OÜ Pärnu mnt 139b-14 11317
Talinn, Estonia
hello@eucompliancepartner.com
+33756902 41

Visit our website: www.titanbooks.com

Did you enjoy this book? We love to hear from our readers.
Please email us at: readerfeedback@titanemail.com
or write to Reader Feedback at the above address.

To receive advance information, news, competitions, and exclusive offers online,
please sign up for the Titan newsletter on our website: www.titanbooks.com

A CIP catalogue record for this title is available from the British Library.

Printed and bound in China.

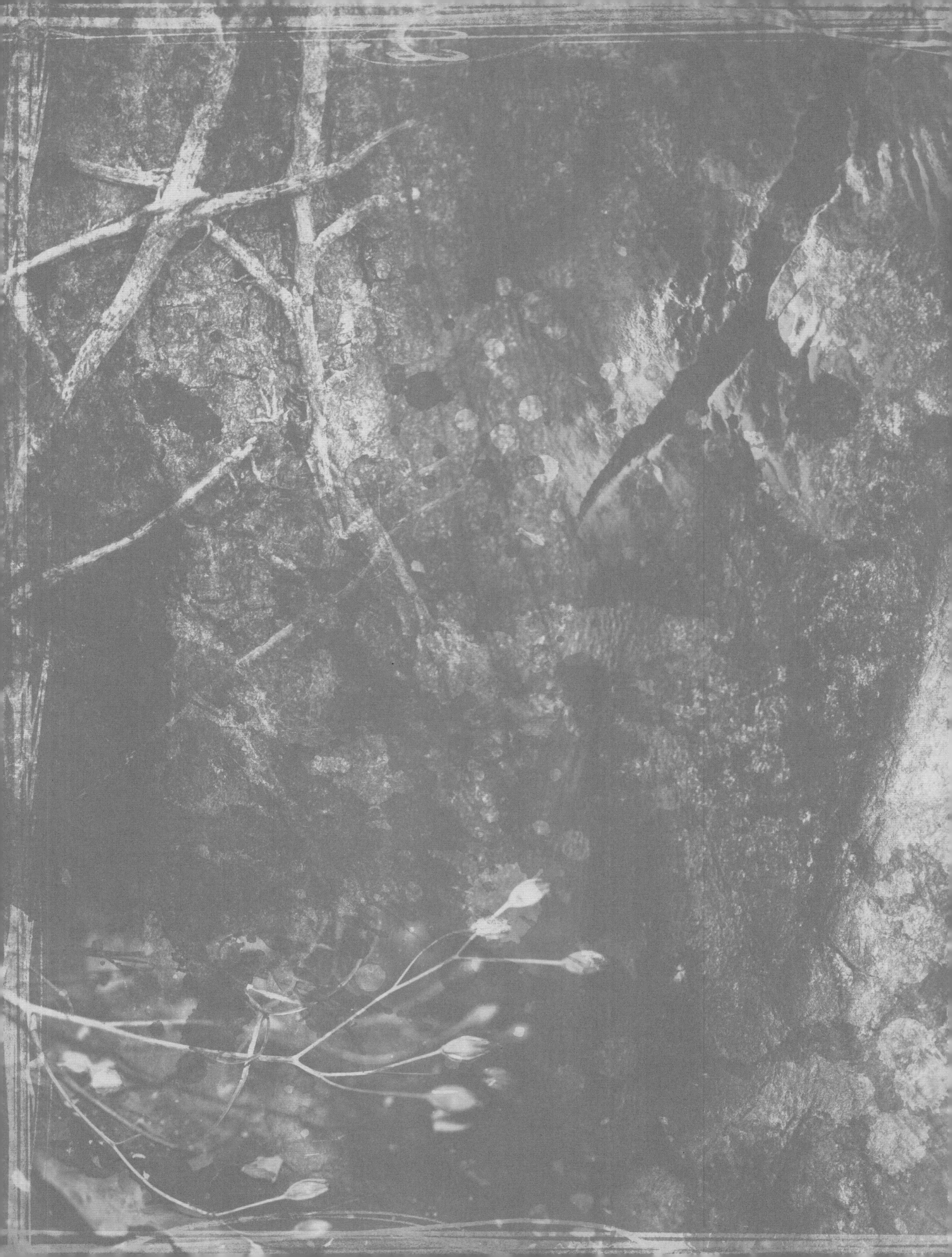